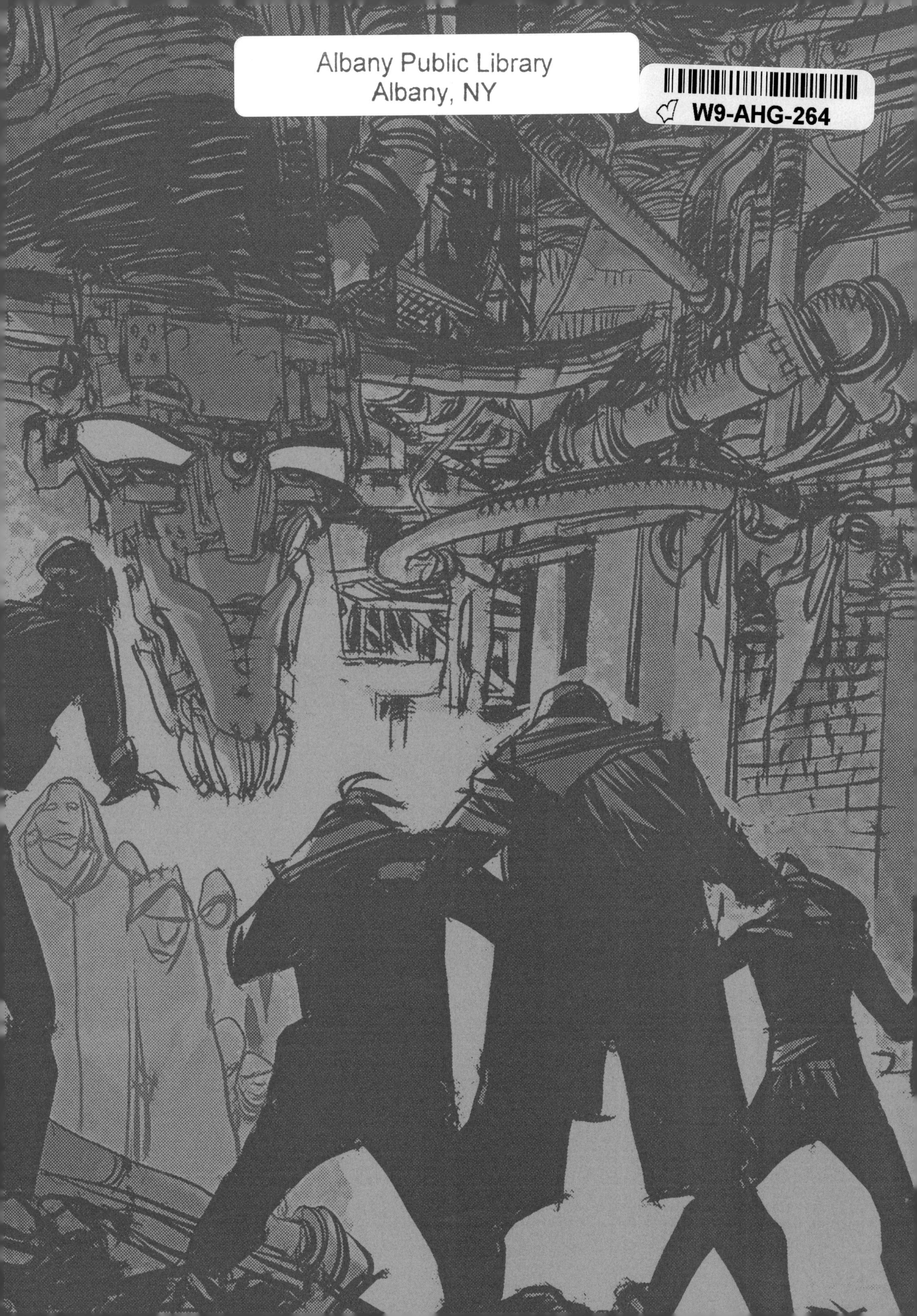

CUTTING EDGE

TITAN®
COMICS

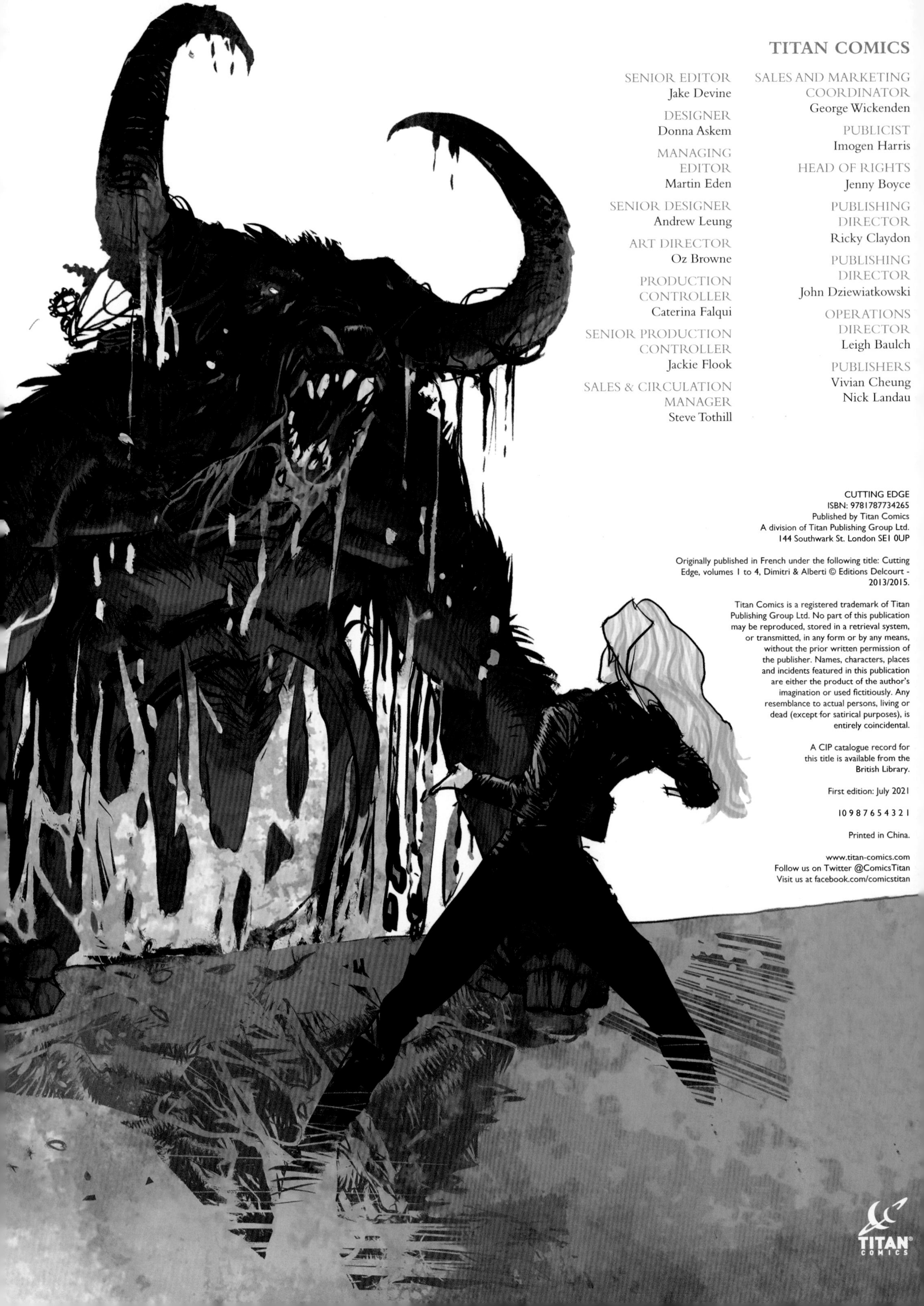

TITAN COMICS

SENIOR EDITOR
Jake Devine

DESIGNER
Donna Askem

MANAGING EDITOR
Martin Eden

SENIOR DESIGNER
Andrew Leung

ART DIRECTOR
Oz Browne

PRODUCTION CONTROLLER
Caterina Falqui

SENIOR PRODUCTION CONTROLLER
Jackie Flook

SALES & CIRCULATION MANAGER
Steve Tothill

SALES AND MARKETING COORDINATOR
George Wickenden

PUBLICIST
Imogen Harris

HEAD OF RIGHTS
Jenny Boyce

PUBLISHING DIRECTOR
Ricky Claydon

PUBLISHING DIRECTOR
John Dziewiatkowski

OPERATIONS DIRECTOR
Leigh Baulch

PUBLISHERS
Vivian Cheung
Nick Landau

CUTTING EDGE
ISBN: 9781787734265
Published by Titan Comics
A division of Titan Publishing Group Ltd.
144 Southwark St. London SE1 0UP

A CIP catalogue record for this title is available from the British Library.

First edition: July 2021

10 9 8 7 6 5 4 3 2 1

Printed in China.

www.titan-comics.com
Follow us on Twitter @ComicsTitan
Visit us at facebook.com/comicstitan

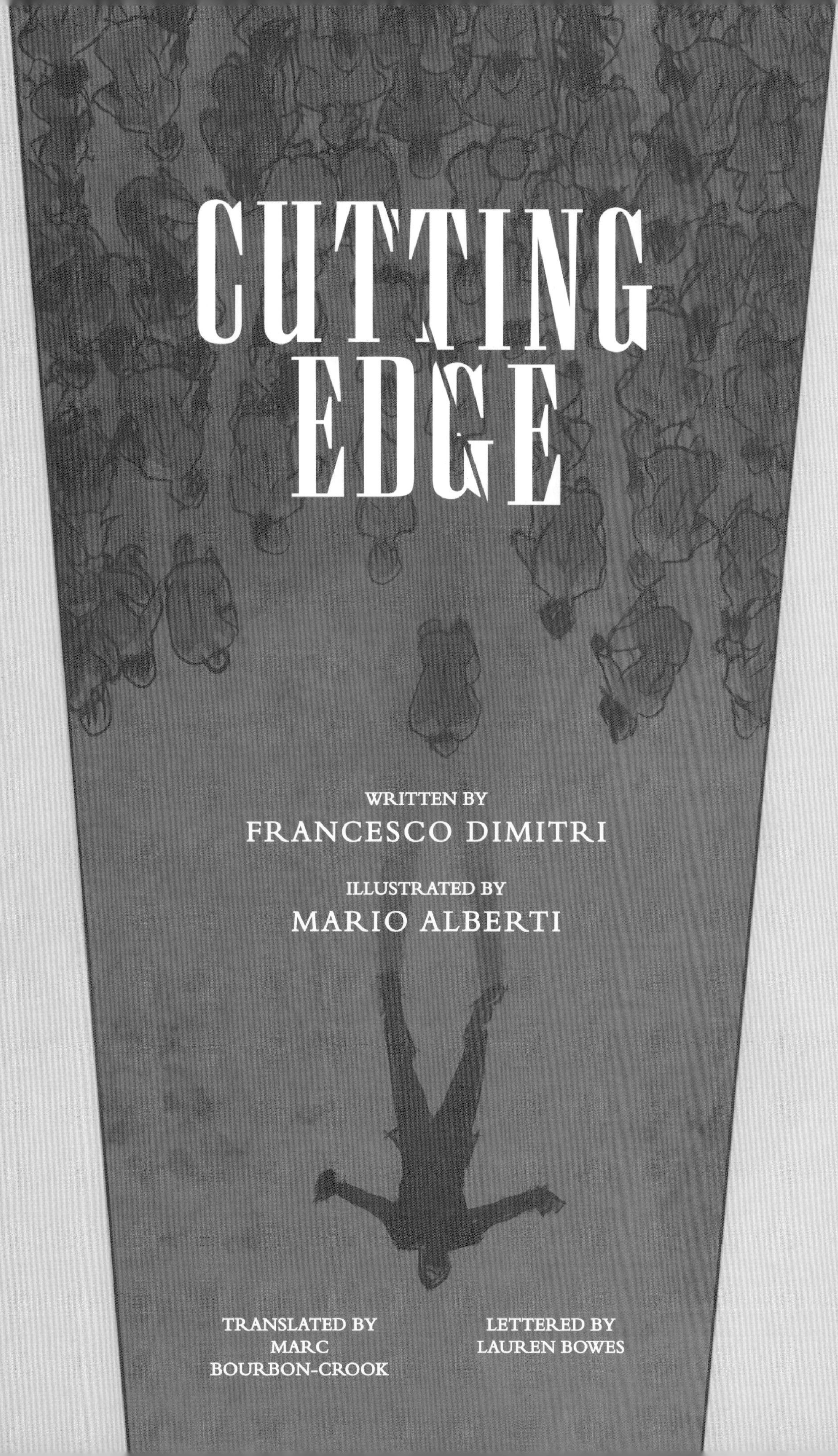

CUTTING EDGE

WRITTEN BY
FRANCESCO DIMITRI

ILLUSTRATED BY
MARIO ALBERTI

TRANSLATED BY
MARC
BOURBON-CROOK

LETTERED BY
LAUREN BOWES

CAST OF CHARACTERS

MARK UNDERWOOD
Mark is an expert in social psychology, and is the only one who understands there's something larger at play. A born sceptic, he takes nothing at face value, willing to put the truth before his own desires. While often frenetic and unsure of himself, he acts as the moral compass of the group.

STELLA ORSINI DEL GIGLIO
If money is power, then there is none more powerful than Stella, heiress to the incredibly wealthy Orsini Del Giglio family enterprise. Both bold and beautiful, Stella is a socialite and 'star' of a scandalous viral video, but it would be a sin to underestimate her intelligence.

HIROSHI ITOU
Hiroshi is a scientist first and foremost, using his intelligence to solve problems and uncover the truth behind what appear to be supernatural mysteries. He is more than happy to lend his expertise, often jumping at the chance to show off his knowledge and prove his worth.

DELROY
The most enigmatic of the group, Delroy's background is as unknown as his emotions. Always wise to the situation, he knows how to handle himself, both physically and mentally. Delroy usually works alone, but his determination to win brings him close to his allies.

JIRAKEE WALKER
At just 24 years old, Jirakee is the youngest and brightest member of the group. Her exceptional talent has earned her 3 Pulitzer prizes for Best Photography, with 18 covers for National Geographic. She motivates the team with her positivity and eagerness.

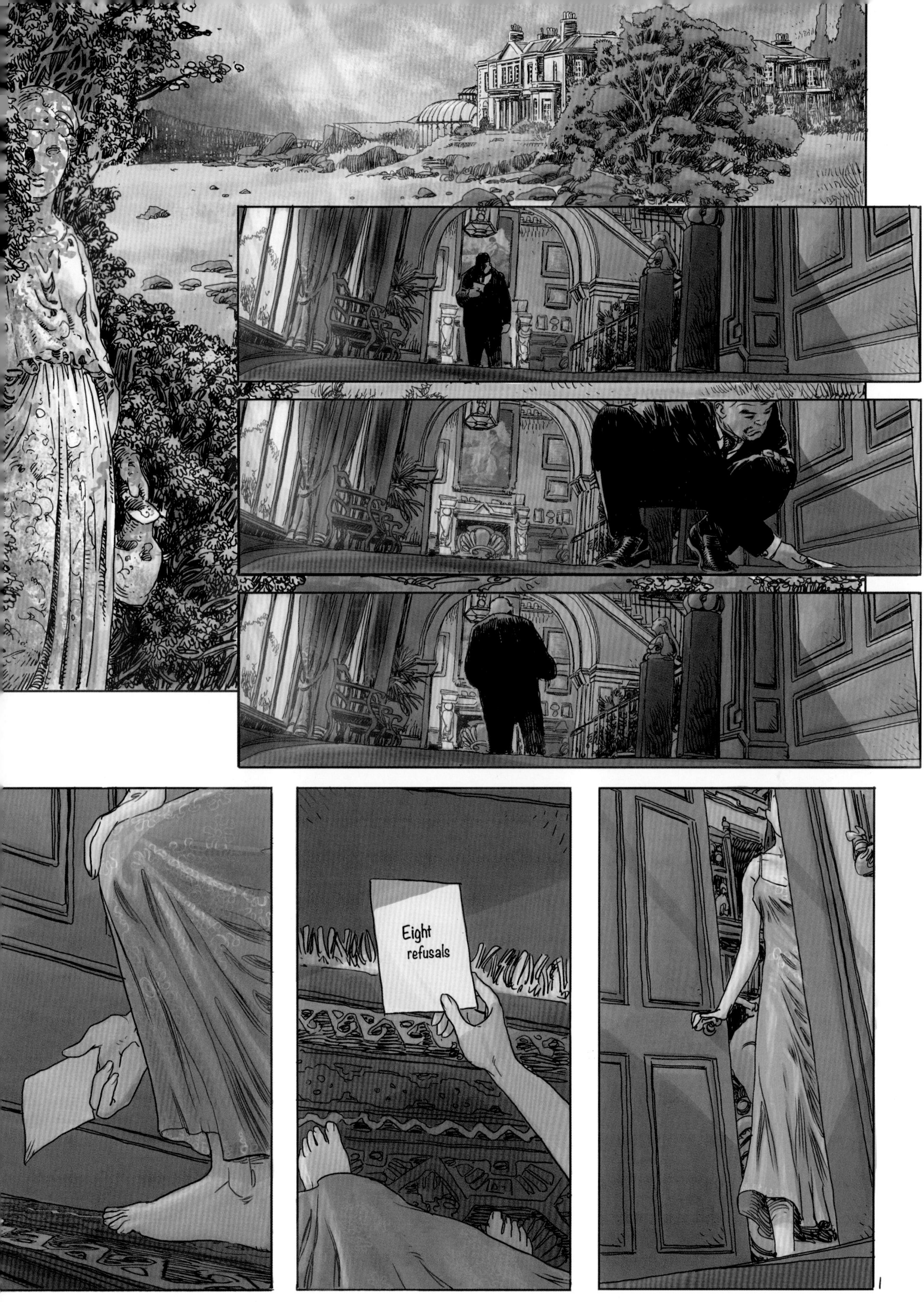
Eight
refusals

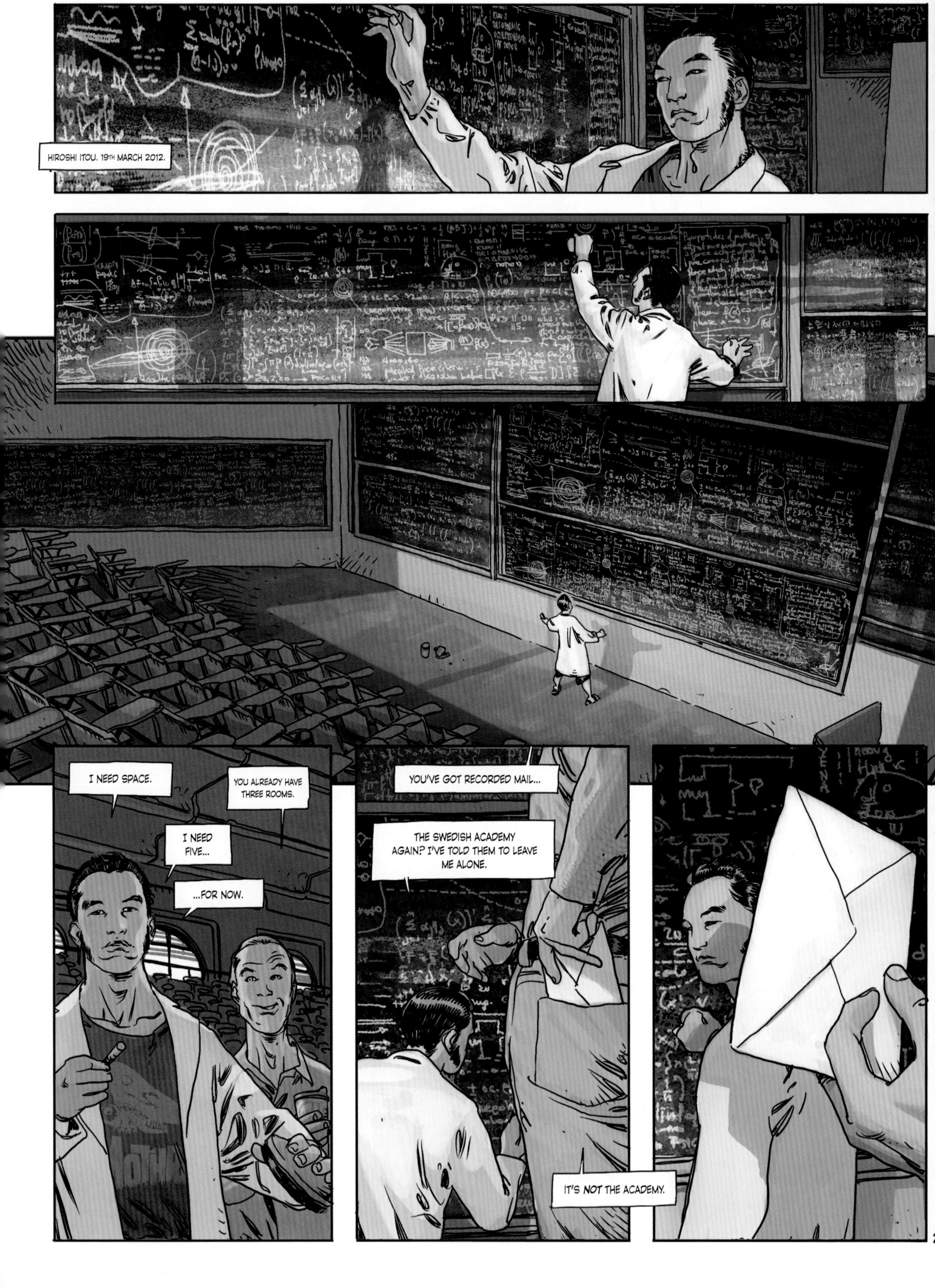
HIROSHI ITOU. 19TH MARCH 2012.
I NEED SPACE.
YOU ALREADY HAVE THREE ROOMS.
I NEED FIVE...
...FOR NOW.
YOU'VE GOT RECORDED MAIL...
THE SWEDISH ACADEMY AGAIN? I'VE TOLD THEM TO LEAVE ME ALONE.
IT'S NOT THE ACADEMY.

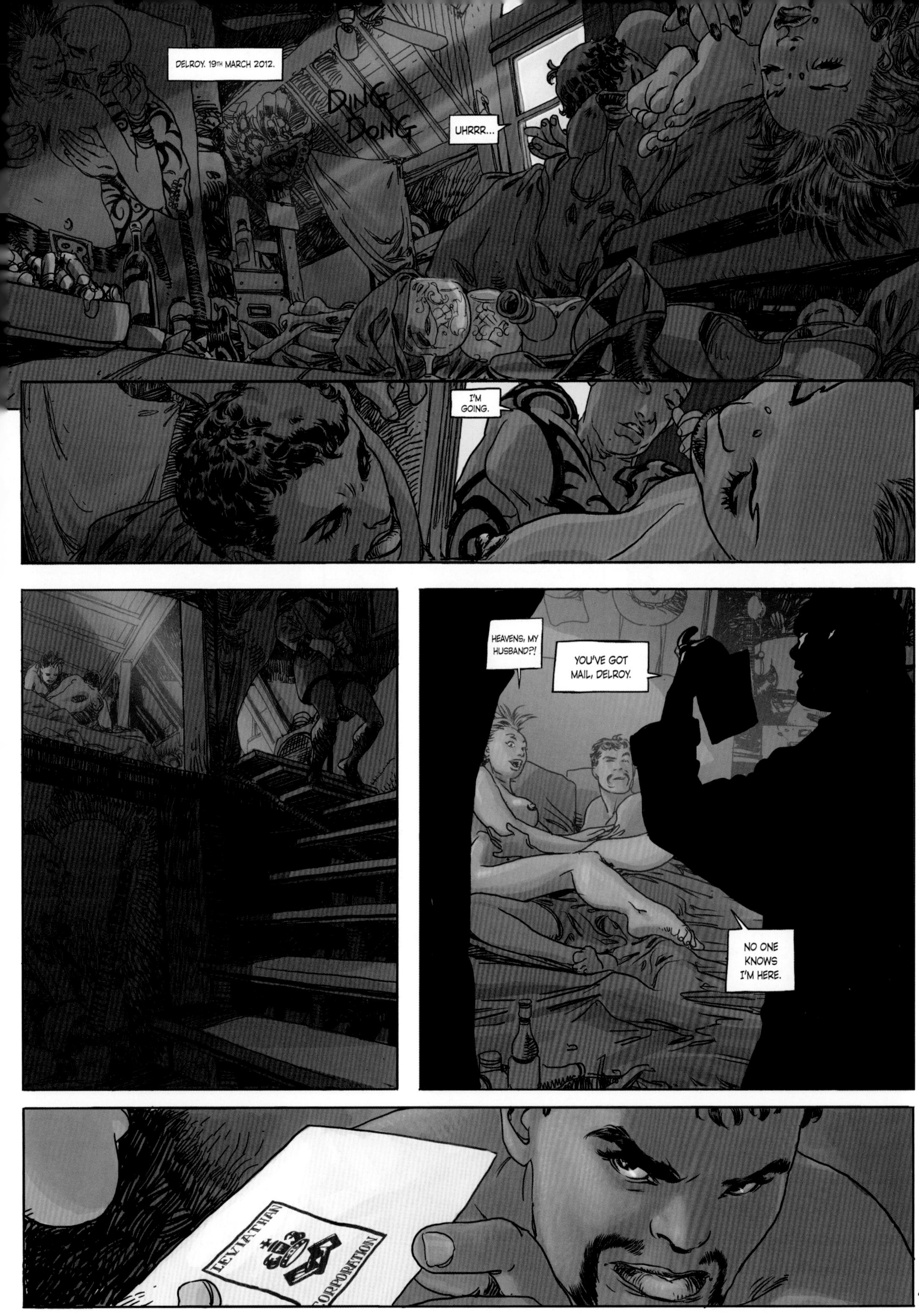
DELROY. 19TH MARCH 2012.
DING DONG
UHRRR...
I'M GOING.
HEAVENS, MY HUSBAND?!
YOU'VE GOT MAIL, DELROY.
NO ONE KNOWS I'M HERE.
LEVIATHAN CORPORATION

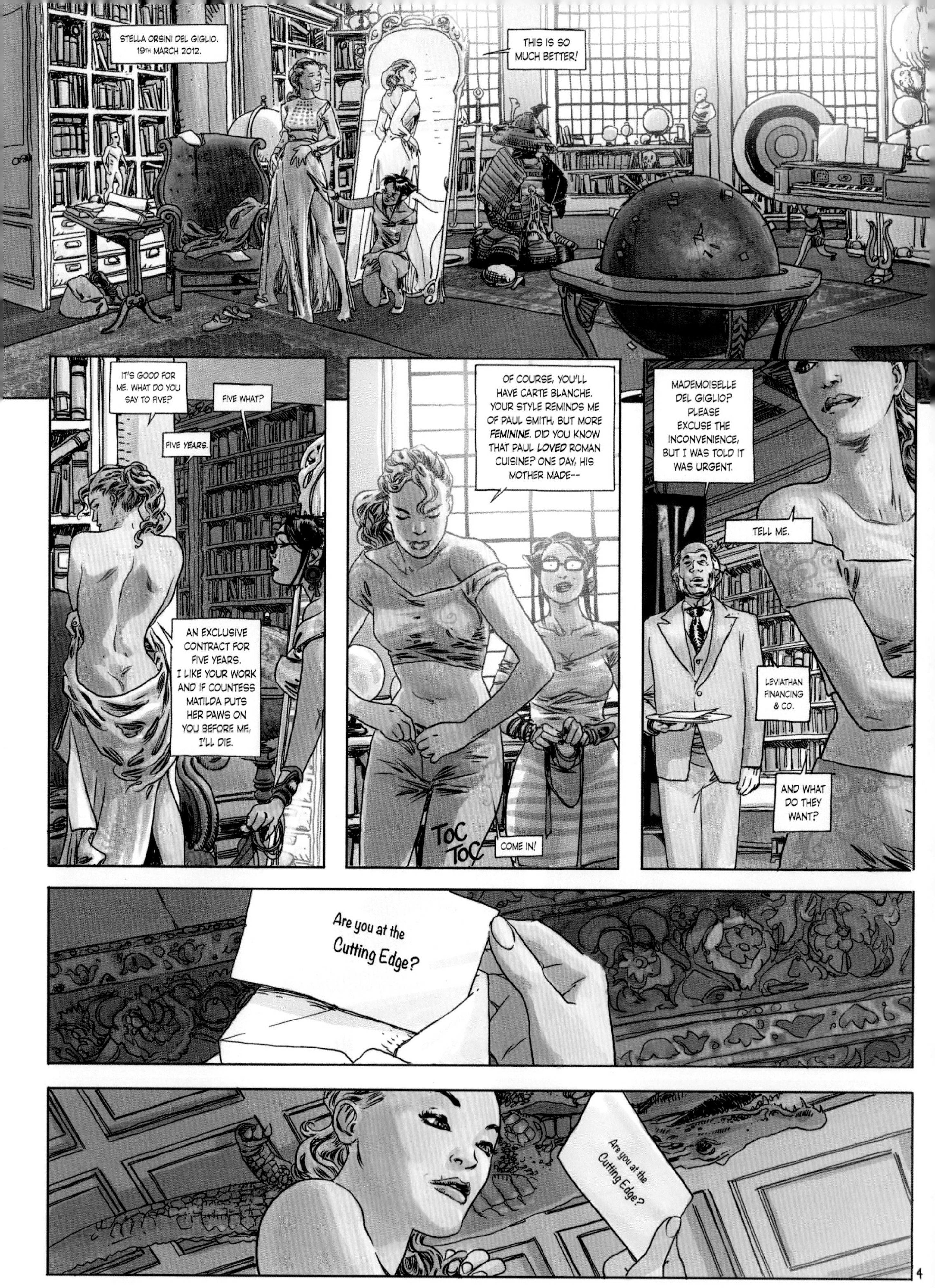

STELLA ORSINI DEL GIGLIO. 19TH MARCH 2012.
THIS IS SO MUCH BETTER!
IT'S GOOD FOR ME. WHAT DO YOU SAY TO FIVE?
FIVE WHAT?
FIVE YEARS.
AN EXCLUSIVE CONTRACT FOR FIVE YEARS. I LIKE YOUR WORK AND IF COUNTESS MATILDA PUTS HER PAWS ON YOU BEFORE ME, I'LL DIE.
OF COURSE, YOU'LL HAVE CARTE BLANCHE. YOUR STYLE REMINDS ME OF PAUL SMITH, BUT MORE FEMININE. DID YOU KNOW THAT PAUL LOVED ROMAN CUISINE? ONE DAY, HIS MOTHER MADE--
TOC TOC
COME IN!
MADEMOISELLE DEL GIGLIO? PLEASE EXCUSE THE INCONVENIENCE, BUT I WAS TOLD IT WAS URGENT.
TELL ME.
LEVIATHAN FINANCING & CO.
AND WHAT DO THEY WANT?
Are you at the Cutting Edge?
Are you at the Cutting Edge?

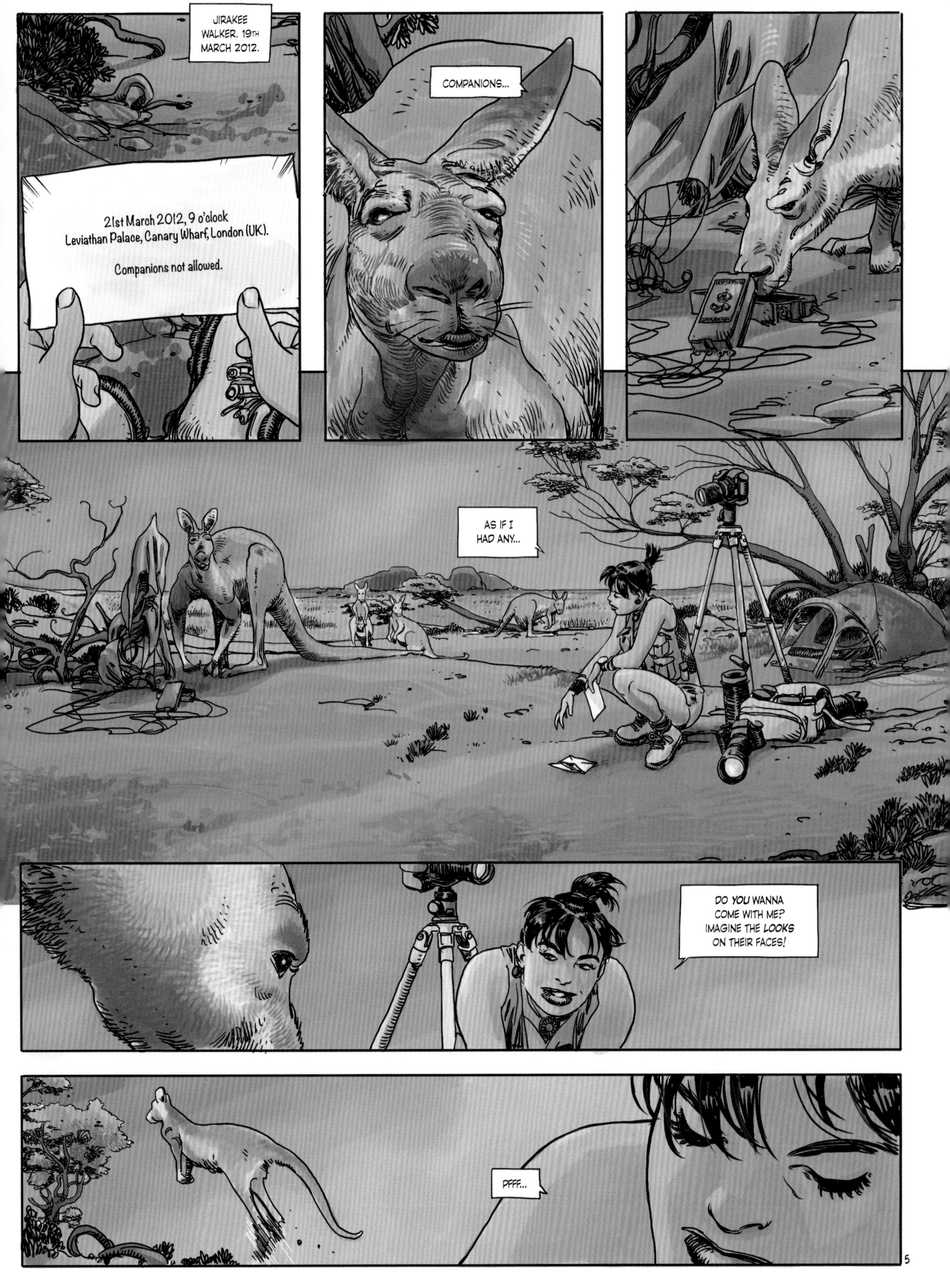

JIRAKEE WALKER. 19TH MARCH 2012.
21st March 2012, 9 o'clock
Leviathan Palace, Canary Wharf, London (UK).
Companions not allowed.
COMPANIONS...
AS IF I HAD ANY...
DO *YOU* WANNA COME WITH ME? IMAGINE THE *LOOKS* ON THEIR FACES!
PFFF...

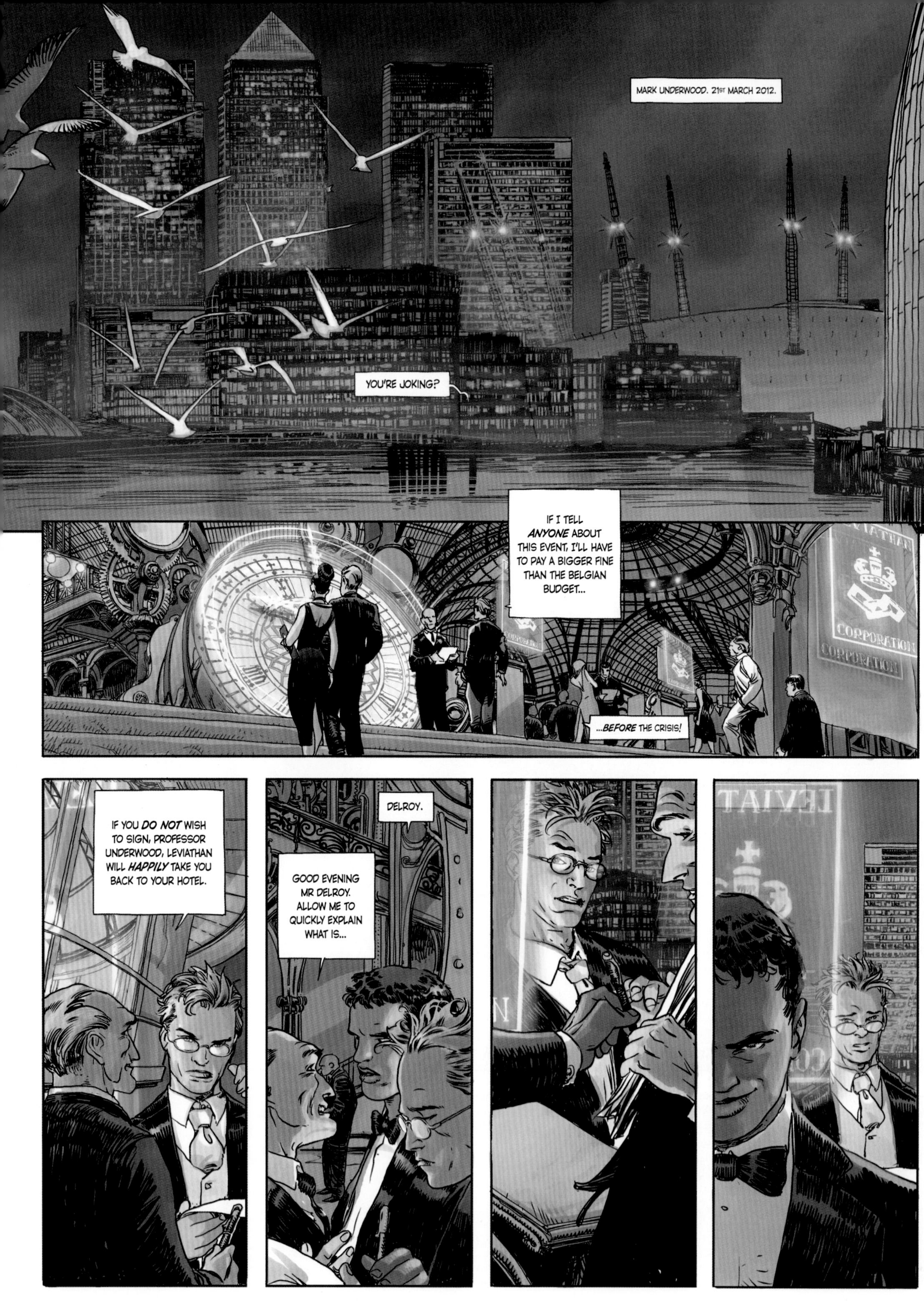
MARK UNDERWOOD. 21ST MARCH 2012.
YOU'RE JOKING?
IF I TELL ANYONE ABOUT THIS EVENT, I'LL HAVE TO PAY A BIGGER FINE THAN THE BELGIAN BUDGET...
...BEFORE THE CRISIS!
IF YOU DO NOT WISH TO SIGN, PROFESSOR UNDERWOOD, LEVIATHAN WILL HAPPILY TAKE YOU BACK TO YOUR HOTEL.
DELROY.
GOOD EVENING MR DELROY. ALLOW ME TO QUICKLY EXPLAIN WHAT IS...

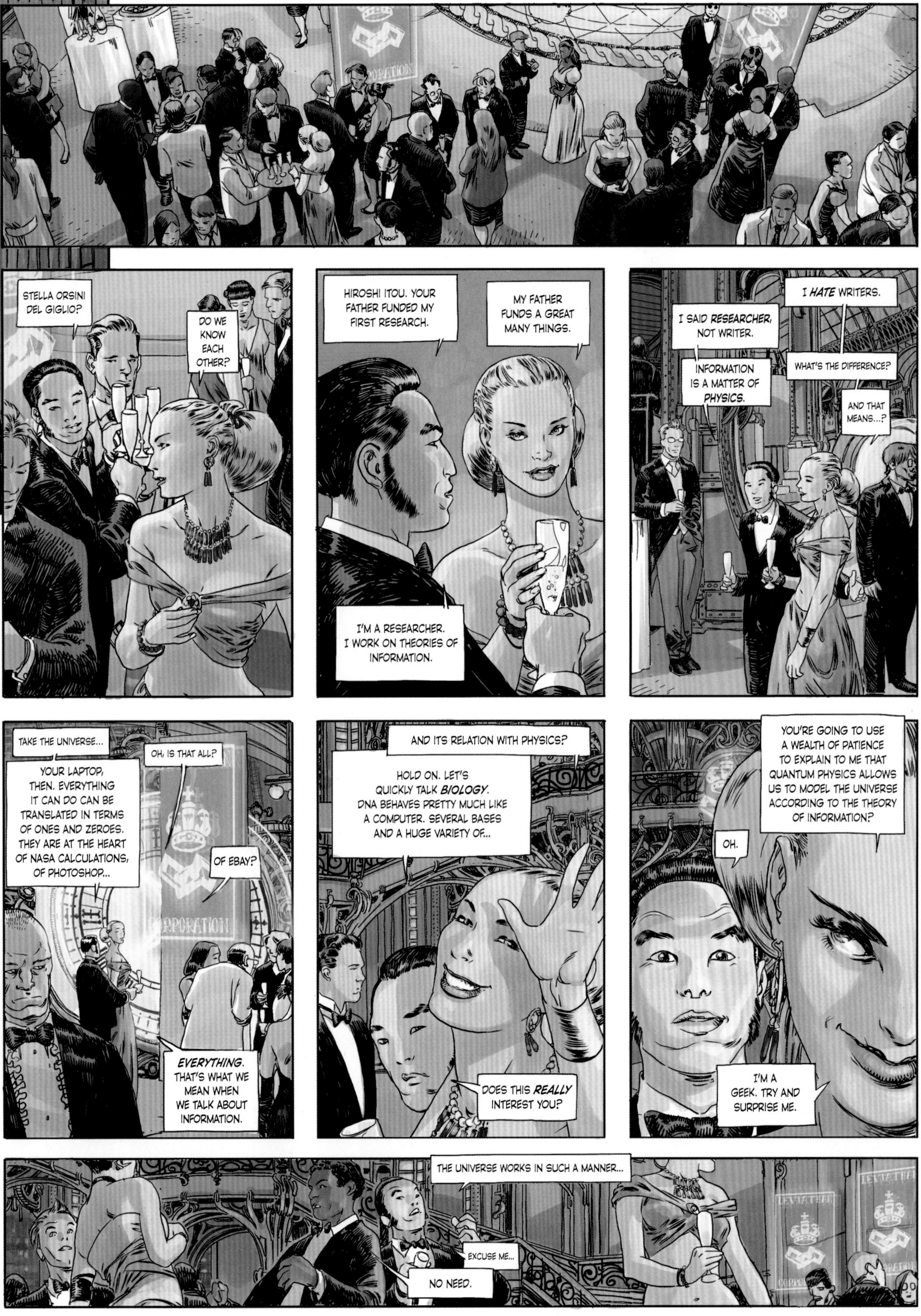

STELLA ORSINI DEL GIGLIO?
DO WE KNOW EACH OTHER?
HIROSHI ITOU. YOUR FATHER FUNDED MY FIRST RESEARCH.
MY FATHER FUNDS A GREAT MANY THINGS.
I'M A RESEARCHER. I WORK ON THEORIES OF INFORMATION.
I HATE WRITERS.
I SAID RESEARCHER, NOT WRITER.
WHAT'S THE DIFFERENCE?
INFORMATION IS A MATTER OF PHYSICS.
AND THAT MEANS...?
TAKE THE UNIVERSE...
OH, IS THAT ALL?
YOUR LAPTOP, THEN. EVERYTHING IT CAN DO CAN BE TRANSLATED IN TERMS OF ONES AND ZEROES. THEY ARE AT THE HEART OF NASA CALCULATIONS, OF PHOTOSHOP...
OF EBAY?
EVERYTHING. THAT'S WHAT WE MEAN WHEN WE TALK ABOUT INFORMATION.
AND ITS RELATION WITH PHYSICS?
HOLD ON. LET'S QUICKLY TALK BIOLOGY. DNA BEHAVES PRETTY MUCH LIKE A COMPUTER. SEVERAL BASES AND A HUGE VARIETY OF...
DOES THIS REALLY INTEREST YOU?
YOU'RE GOING TO USE A WEALTH OF PATIENCE TO EXPLAIN TO ME THAT QUANTUM PHYSICS ALLOWS US TO MODEL THE UNIVERSE ACCORDING TO THE THEORY OF INFORMATION?
OH.
I'M A GEEK. TRY AND SURPRISE ME.
THE UNIVERSE WORKS IN SUCH A MANNER...
EXCUSE ME...
NO NEED.

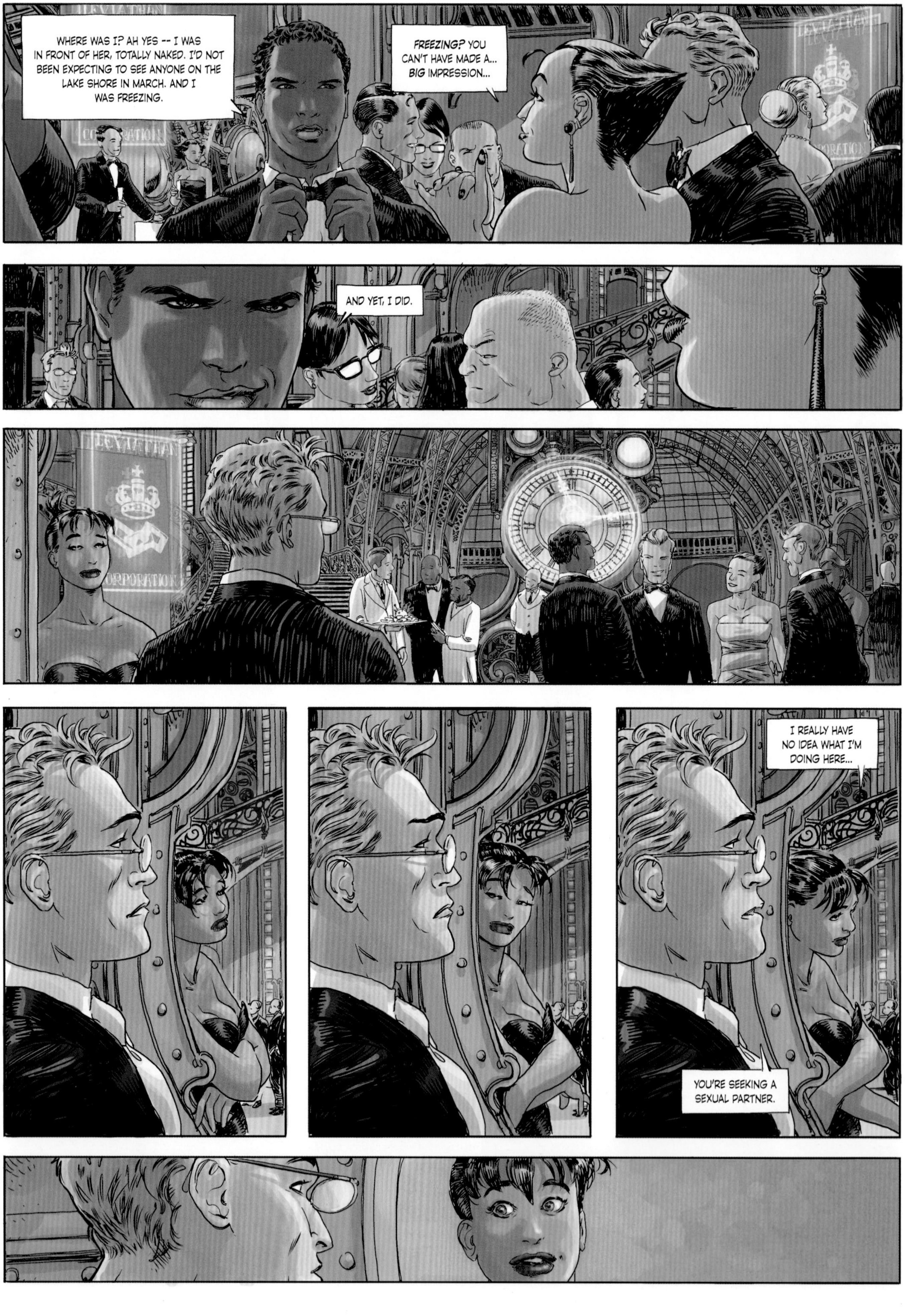
WHERE WAS I? AH YES -- I WAS IN FRONT OF HER, TOTALLY NAKED. I'D NOT BEEN EXPECTING TO SEE ANYONE ON THE LAKE SHORE IN MARCH. AND I WAS FREEZING.
FREEZING? YOU CAN'T HAVE MADE A... *BIG* IMPRESSION...
AND YET, I DID.
I REALLY HAVE NO IDEA WHAT I'M DOING HERE...
YOU'RE SEEKING A SEXUAL PARTNER.

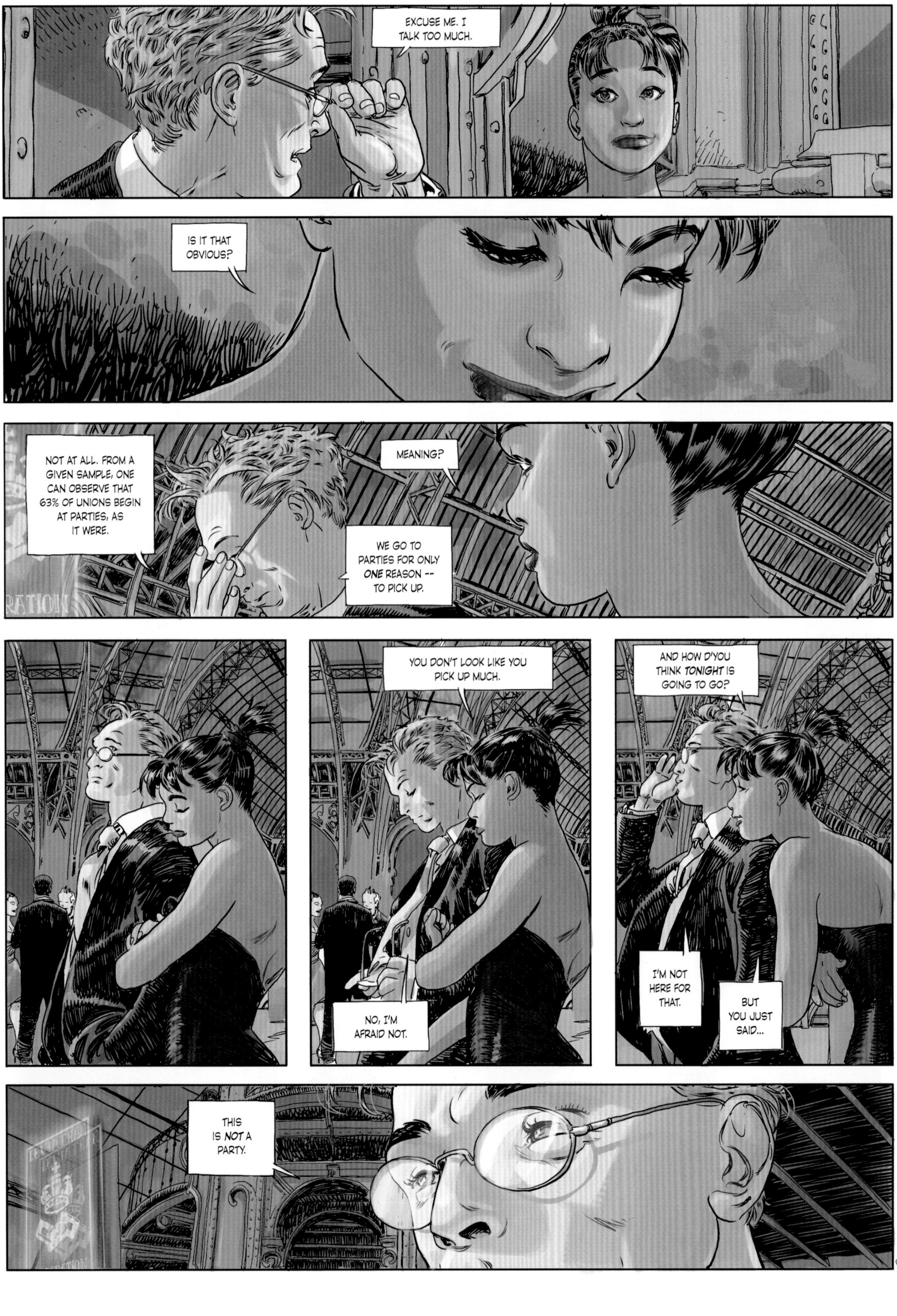
EXCUSE ME. I TALK TOO MUCH.
IS IT THAT OBVIOUS?
NOT AT ALL. FROM A GIVEN SAMPLE, ONE CAN OBSERVE THAT 63% OF UNIONS BEGIN AT PARTIES, AS IT WERE.
MEANING?
WE GO TO PARTIES FOR ONLY *ONE* REASON -- TO PICK UP.
RATION
YOU DON'T LOOK LIKE YOU PICK UP MUCH.
NO, I'M AFRAID NOT.
AND HOW D'YOU THINK *TONIGHT* IS GOING TO GO?
I'M NOT HERE FOR THAT.
BUT YOU JUST SAID...
THIS IS *NOT* A PARTY.

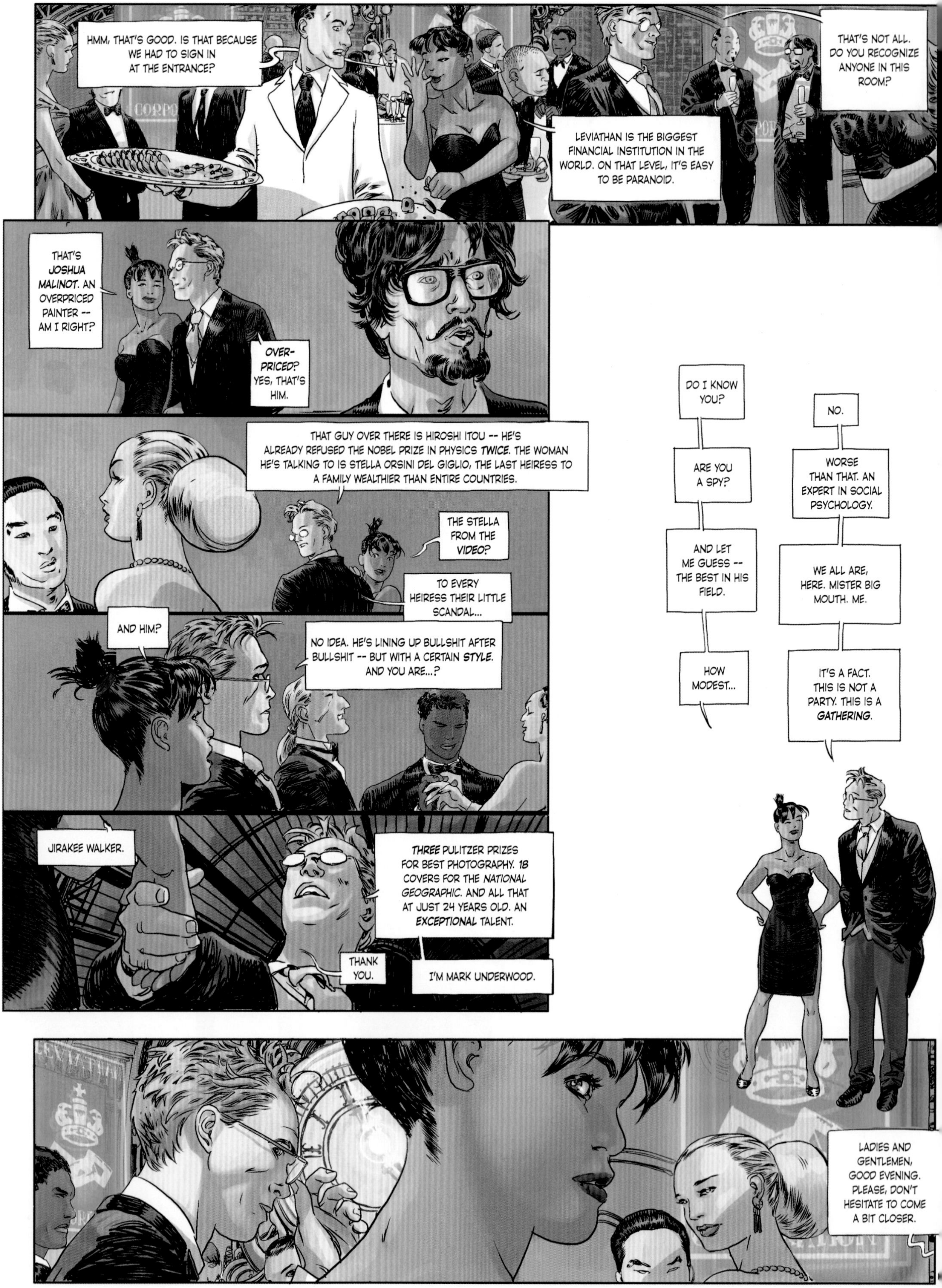
HMM, THAT'S GOOD. IS THAT BECAUSE WE HAD TO SIGN IN AT THE ENTRANCE?
LEVIATHAN IS THE BIGGEST FINANCIAL INSTITUTION IN THE WORLD. ON THAT LEVEL, IT'S EASY TO BE PARANOID.
THAT'S NOT ALL. DO YOU RECOGNIZE ANYONE IN THIS ROOM?
THAT'S *JOSHUA MALINOT*. AN OVERPRICED PAINTER -- AM I RIGHT?
OVER-PRICED? YES, THAT'S HIM.
THAT GUY OVER THERE IS HIROSHI ITOU -- HE'S ALREADY REFUSED THE NOBEL PRIZE IN PHYSICS *TWICE*. THE WOMAN HE'S TALKING TO IS STELLA ORSINI DEL GIGLIO, THE LAST HEIRESS TO A FAMILY WEALTHIER THAN ENTIRE COUNTRIES.
THE STELLA FROM THE *VIDEO?*
TO EVERY HEIRESS THEIR LITTLE SCANDAL...
AND HIM?
NO IDEA. HE'S LINING UP BULLSHIT AFTER BULLSHIT -- BUT WITH A CERTAIN *STYLE*. AND YOU ARE...?
JIRAKEE WALKER.
THREE PULITZER PRIZES FOR BEST PHOTOGRAPHY. *18* COVERS FOR THE *NATIONAL GEOGRAPHIC*. AND ALL THAT AT JUST 24 YEARS OLD. AN *EXCEPTIONAL* TALENT.
THANK YOU.
I'M MARK UNDERWOOD.
DO I KNOW YOU?
NO.
ARE YOU A SPY?
WORSE THAN THAT. AN EXPERT IN SOCIAL PSYCHOLOGY.
AND LET ME GUESS -- THE BEST IN HIS FIELD.
WE ALL ARE, HERE. MISTER BIG MOUTH. ME.
HOW MODEST...
IT'S A FACT. THIS IS NOT A PARTY. THIS IS A *GATHERING*.
LADIES AND GENTLEMEN, GOOD EVENING. PLEASE, DON'T HESITATE TO COME A BIT CLOSER.

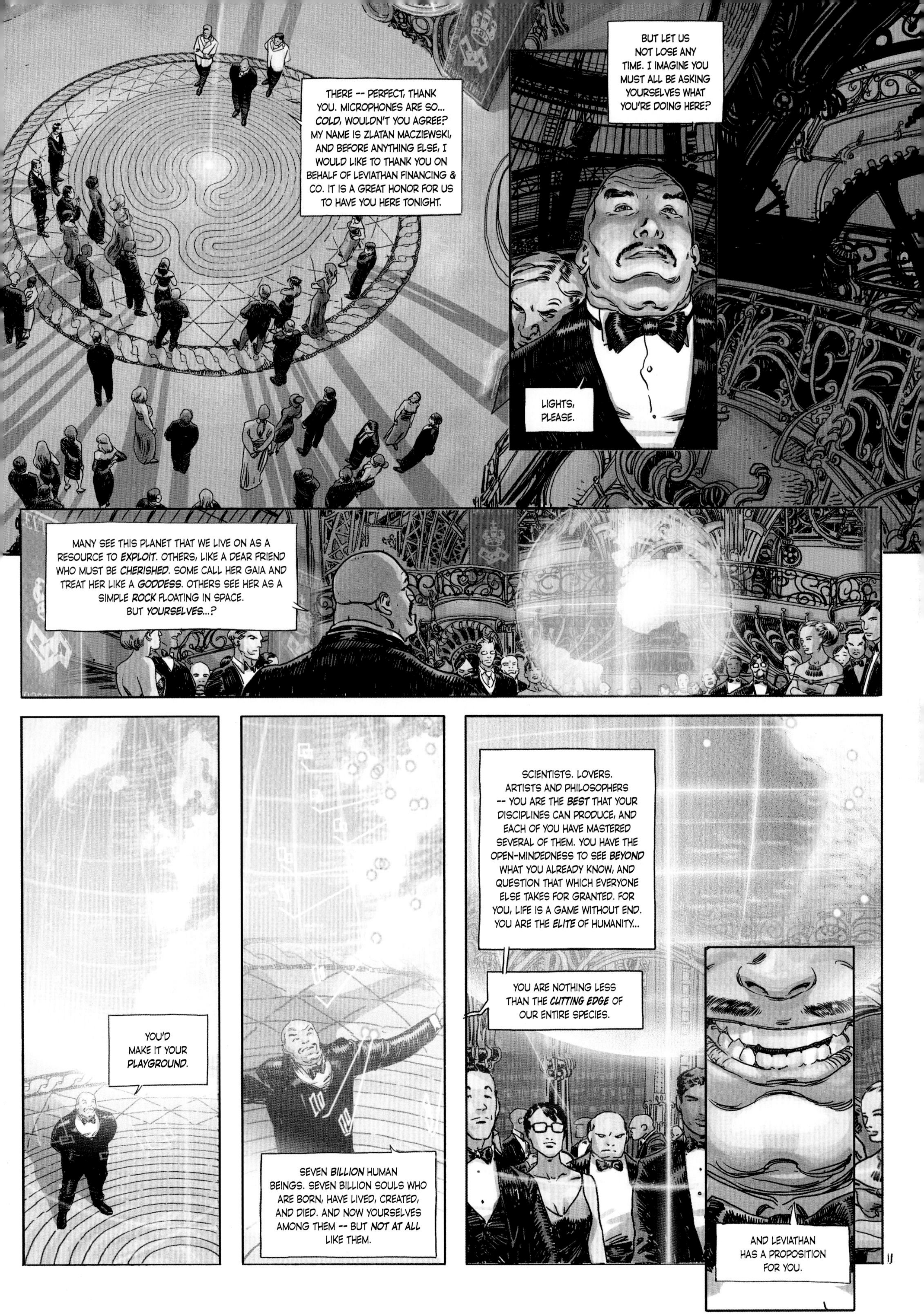
THERE -- PERFECT, THANK YOU. MICROPHONES ARE SO... COLD, WOULDN'T YOU AGREE? MY NAME IS ZLATAN MACZIEWSKI, AND BEFORE ANYTHING ELSE, I WOULD LIKE TO THANK YOU ON BEHALF OF LEVIATHAN FINANCING & CO. IT IS A GREAT HONOR FOR US TO HAVE YOU HERE TONIGHT.
BUT LET US NOT LOSE ANY TIME. I IMAGINE YOU MUST ALL BE ASKING YOURSELVES WHAT YOU'RE DOING HERE?
LIGHTS, PLEASE.
MANY SEE THIS PLANET THAT WE LIVE ON AS A RESOURCE TO EXPLOIT. OTHERS, LIKE A DEAR FRIEND WHO MUST BE CHERISHED. SOME CALL HER GAIA AND TREAT HER LIKE A GODDESS. OTHERS SEE HER AS A SIMPLE ROCK FLOATING IN SPACE. BUT YOURSELVES...?
YOU'D MAKE IT YOUR PLAYGROUND.
SEVEN BILLION HUMAN BEINGS. SEVEN BILLION SOULS WHO ARE BORN, HAVE LIVED, CREATED, AND DIED. AND NOW YOURSELVES AMONG THEM -- BUT NOT AT ALL LIKE THEM.
SCIENTISTS. LOVERS. ARTISTS AND PHILOSOPHERS -- YOU ARE THE BEST THAT YOUR DISCIPLINES CAN PRODUCE, AND EACH OF YOU HAVE MASTERED SEVERAL OF THEM. YOU HAVE THE OPEN-MINDEDNESS TO SEE BEYOND WHAT YOU ALREADY KNOW, AND QUESTION THAT WHICH EVERYONE ELSE TAKES FOR GRANTED. FOR YOU, LIFE IS A GAME WITHOUT END. YOU ARE THE ELITE OF HUMANITY...
YOU ARE NOTHING LESS THAN THE CUTTING EDGE OF OUR ENTIRE SPECIES.
AND LEVIATHAN HAS A PROPOSITION FOR YOU.

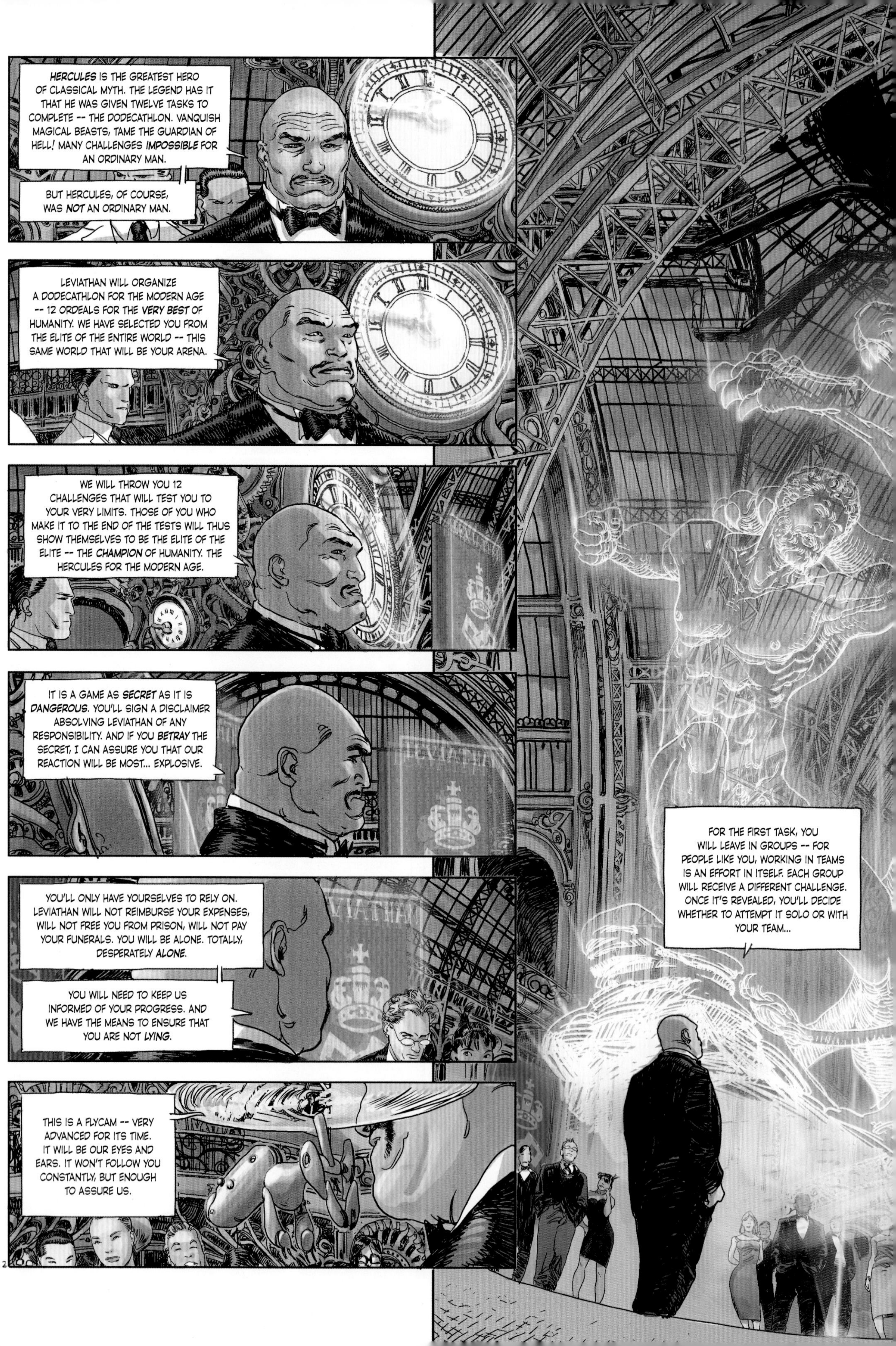
HERCULES IS THE GREATEST HERO OF CLASSICAL MYTH. THE LEGEND HAS IT THAT HE WAS GIVEN TWELVE TASKS TO COMPLETE -- THE DODECATHLON. VANQUISH MAGICAL BEASTS, TAME THE GUARDIAN OF HELL! MANY CHALLENGES IMPOSSIBLE FOR AN ORDINARY MAN.
BUT HERCULES, OF COURSE, WAS NOT AN ORDINARY MAN.
LEVIATHAN WILL ORGANIZE A DODECATHLON FOR THE MODERN AGE -- 12 ORDEALS FOR THE VERY BEST OF HUMANITY. WE HAVE SELECTED YOU FROM THE ELITE OF THE ENTIRE WORLD -- THIS SAME WORLD THAT WILL BE YOUR ARENA.
WE WILL THROW YOU 12 CHALLENGES THAT WILL TEST YOU TO YOUR VERY LIMITS. THOSE OF YOU WHO MAKE IT TO THE END OF THE TESTS WILL THUS SHOW THEMSELVES TO BE THE ELITE OF THE ELITE -- THE CHAMPION OF HUMANITY. THE HERCULES FOR THE MODERN AGE.
LEVIATHAN
IT IS A GAME AS SECRET AS IT IS DANGEROUS. YOU'LL SIGN A DISCLAIMER ABSOLVING LEVIATHAN OF ANY RESPONSIBILITY. AND IF YOU BETRAY THE SECRET, I CAN ASSURE YOU THAT OUR REACTION WILL BE MOST... EXPLOSIVE.
YOU'LL ONLY HAVE YOURSELVES TO RELY ON. LEVIATHAN WILL NOT REIMBURSE YOUR EXPENSES, WILL NOT FREE YOU FROM PRISON, WILL NOT PAY YOUR FUNERALS. YOU WILL BE ALONE. TOTALLY, DESPERATELY ALONE.
YOU WILL NEED TO KEEP US INFORMED OF YOUR PROGRESS. AND WE HAVE THE MEANS TO ENSURE THAT YOU ARE NOT LYING.
THIS IS A FLYCAM -- VERY ADVANCED FOR ITS TIME. IT WILL BE OUR EYES AND EARS. IT WON'T FOLLOW YOU CONSTANTLY, BUT ENOUGH TO ASSURE US.
FOR THE FIRST TASK, YOU WILL LEAVE IN GROUPS -- FOR PEOPLE LIKE YOU, WORKING IN TEAMS IS AN EFFORT IN ITSELF. EACH GROUP WILL RECEIVE A DIFFERENT CHALLENGE. ONCE IT'S REVEALED, YOU'LL DECIDE WHETHER TO ATTEMPT IT SOLO OR WITH YOUR TEAM...

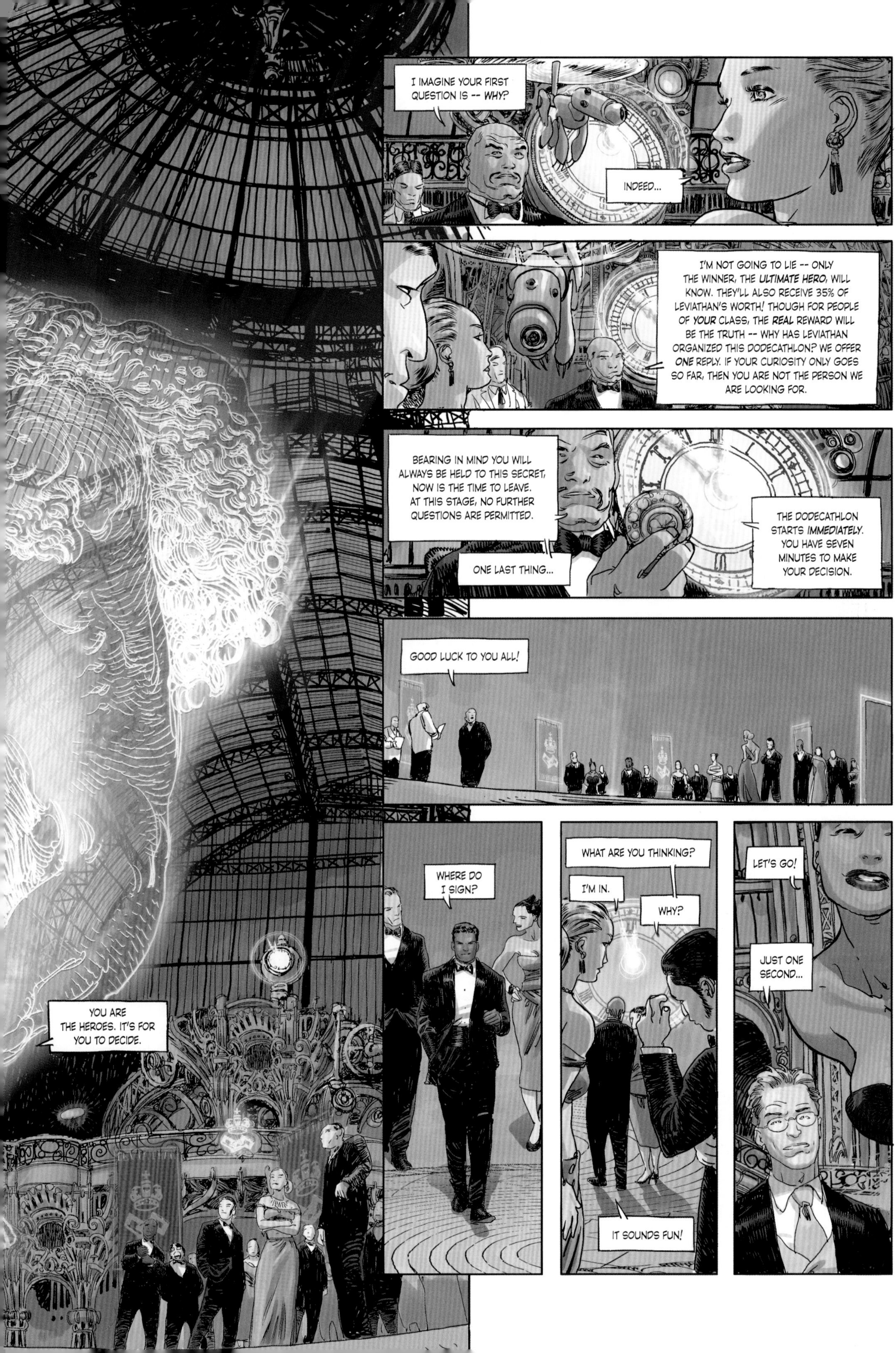
I IMAGINE YOUR FIRST QUESTION IS -- WHY?
INDEED...
I'M NOT GOING TO LIE -- ONLY THE WINNER, THE ULTIMATE HERO, WILL KNOW. THEY'LL ALSO RECEIVE 35% OF LEVIATHAN'S WORTH! THOUGH FOR PEOPLE OF YOUR CLASS, THE REAL REWARD WILL BE THE TRUTH -- WHY HAS LEVIATHAN ORGANIZED THIS DODECATHLON? WE OFFER ONE REPLY. IF YOUR CURIOSITY ONLY GOES SO FAR, THEN YOU ARE NOT THE PERSON WE ARE LOOKING FOR.
BEARING IN MIND YOU WILL ALWAYS BE HELD TO THIS SECRET, NOW IS THE TIME TO LEAVE. AT THIS STAGE, NO FURTHER QUESTIONS ARE PERMITTED.
ONE LAST THING...
THE DODECATHLON STARTS IMMEDIATELY. YOU HAVE SEVEN MINUTES TO MAKE YOUR DECISION.
GOOD LUCK TO YOU ALL!
YOU ARE THE HEROES. IT'S FOR YOU TO DECIDE.
WHERE DO I SIGN?
WHAT ARE YOU THINKING?
I'M IN.
WHY?
IT SOUNDS FUN!
LET'S GO!
JUST ONE SECOND...

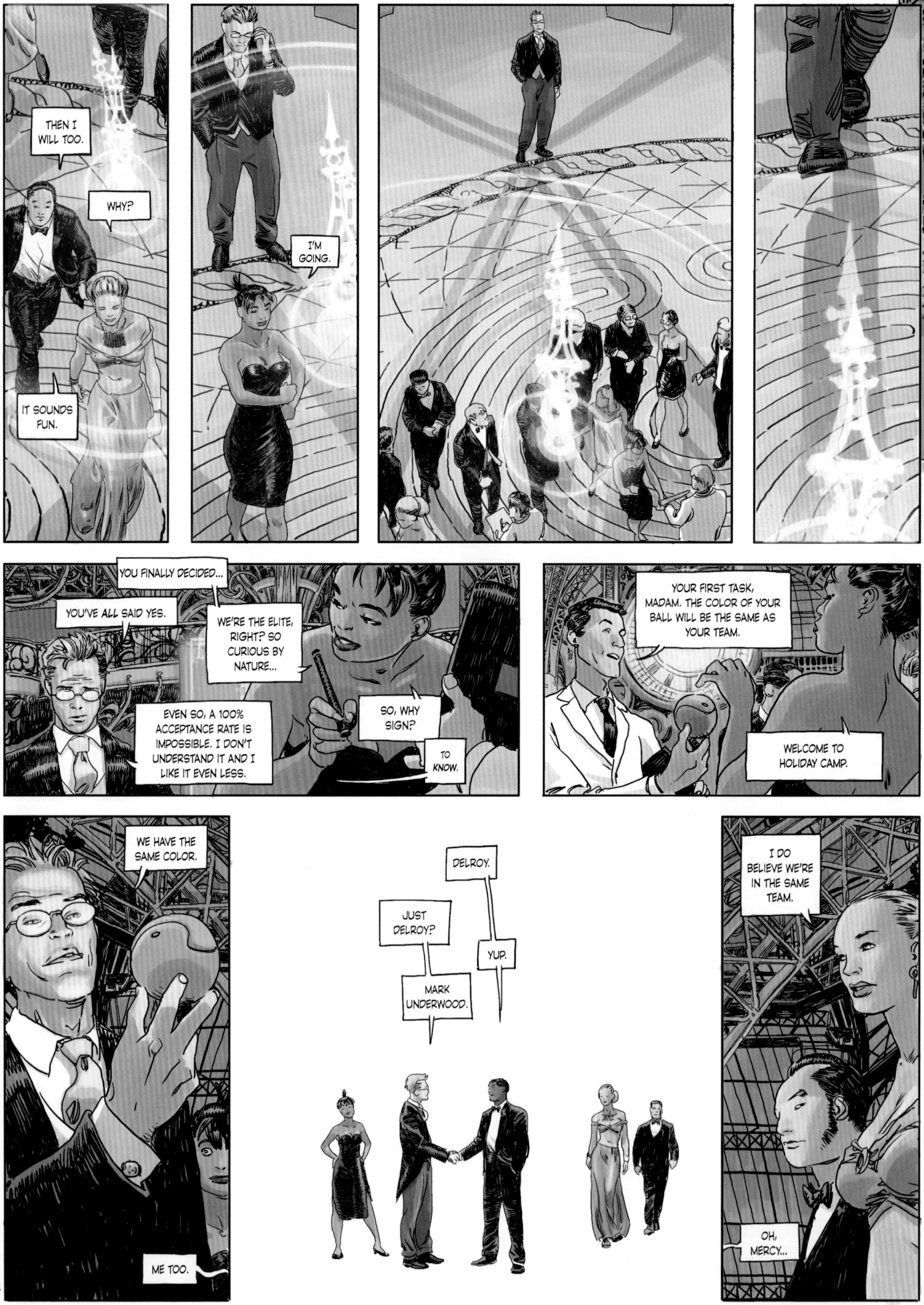
THEN I WILL TOO.
WHY?
IT SOUNDS FUN.
I'M GOING.
YOU FINALLY DECIDED...
YOU'VE ALL SAID YES.
WE'RE THE ELITE, RIGHT? SO CURIOUS BY NATURE...
EVEN SO, A 100% ACCEPTANCE RATE IS IMPOSSIBLE. I DON'T UNDERSTAND IT AND I LIKE IT EVEN LESS.
SO, WHY SIGN?
TO KNOW.
YOUR FIRST TASK, MADAM. THE COLOR OF YOUR BALL WILL BE THE SAME AS YOUR TEAM.
WELCOME TO HOLIDAY CAMP.
WE HAVE THE SAME COLOR.
ME TOO.
DELROY.
JUST DELROY?
YUP.
MARK UNDERWOOD.
I DO BELIEVE WE'RE IN THE SAME TEAM.
OH, MERCY...

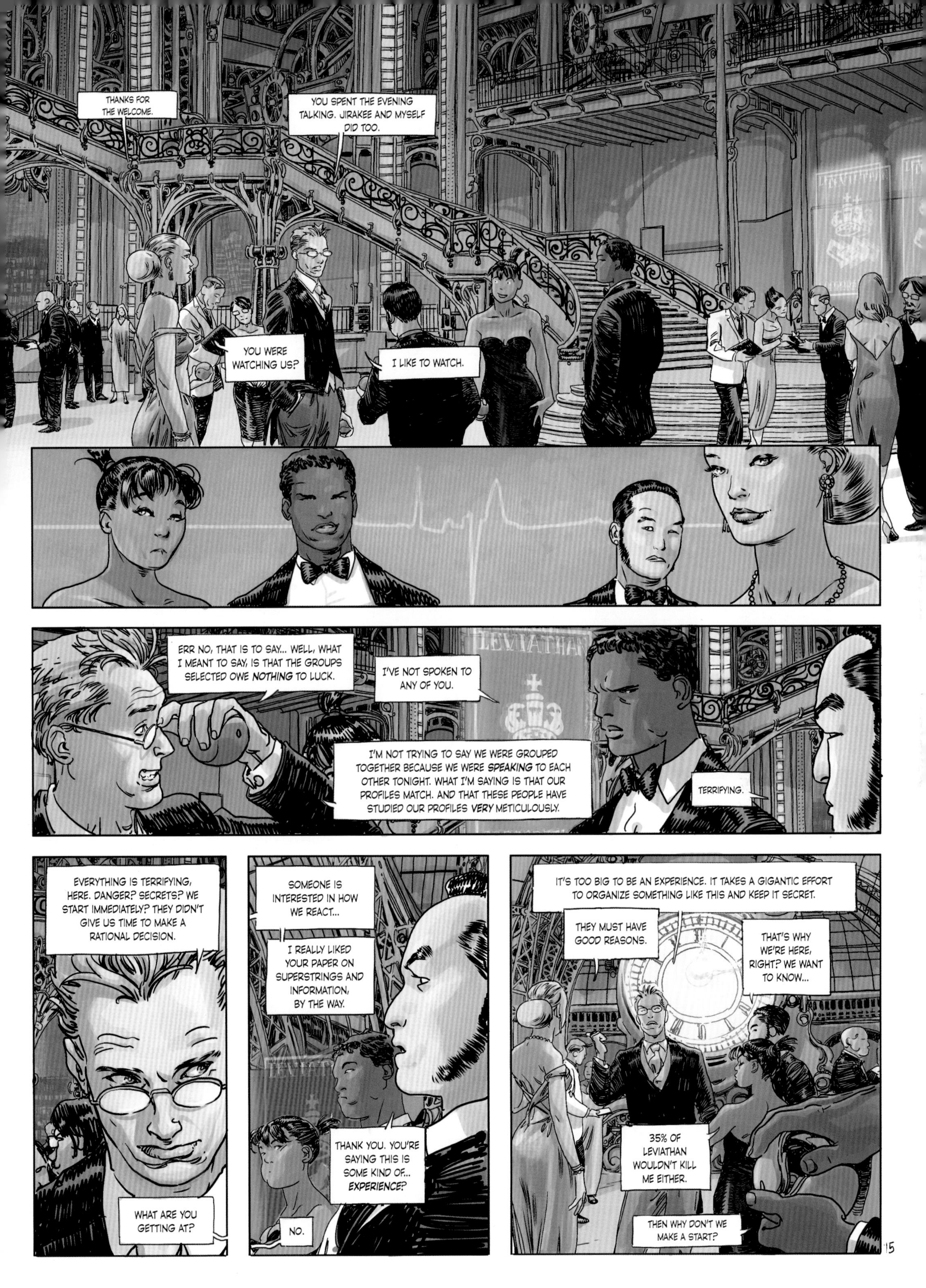
THANKS FOR THE WELCOME.
YOU SPENT THE EVENING TALKING. JIRAKEE AND MYSELF DID TOO.
YOU WERE WATCHING US?
I LIKE TO WATCH.
LEVIATHAN
ERR NO, THAT IS TO SAY... WELL, WHAT I MEANT TO SAY, IS THAT THE GROUPS SELECTED OWE NOTHING TO LUCK.
I'VE NOT SPOKEN TO ANY OF YOU.
I'M NOT TRYING TO SAY WE WERE GROUPED TOGETHER BECAUSE WE WERE SPEAKING TO EACH OTHER TONIGHT. WHAT I'M SAYING IS THAT OUR PROFILES MATCH. AND THAT THESE PEOPLE HAVE STUDIED OUR PROFILES VERY METICULOUSLY.
TERRIFYING.
EVERYTHING IS TERRIFYING, HERE. DANGER? SECRETS? WE START IMMEDIATELY? THEY DIDN'T GIVE US TIME TO MAKE A RATIONAL DECISION.
WHAT ARE YOU GETTING AT?
SOMEONE IS INTERESTED IN HOW WE REACT...
I REALLY LIKED YOUR PAPER ON SUPERSTRINGS AND INFORMATION, BY THE WAY.
THANK YOU. YOU'RE SAYING THIS IS SOME KIND OF... EXPERIENCE?
NO.
IT'S TOO BIG TO BE AN EXPERIENCE. IT TAKES A GIGANTIC EFFORT TO ORGANIZE SOMETHING LIKE THIS AND KEEP IT SECRET.
THEY MUST HAVE GOOD REASONS.
THAT'S WHY WE'RE HERE, RIGHT? WE WANT TO KNOW...
35% OF LEVIATHAN WOULDN'T KILL ME EITHER.
THEN WHY DON'T WE MAKE A START?

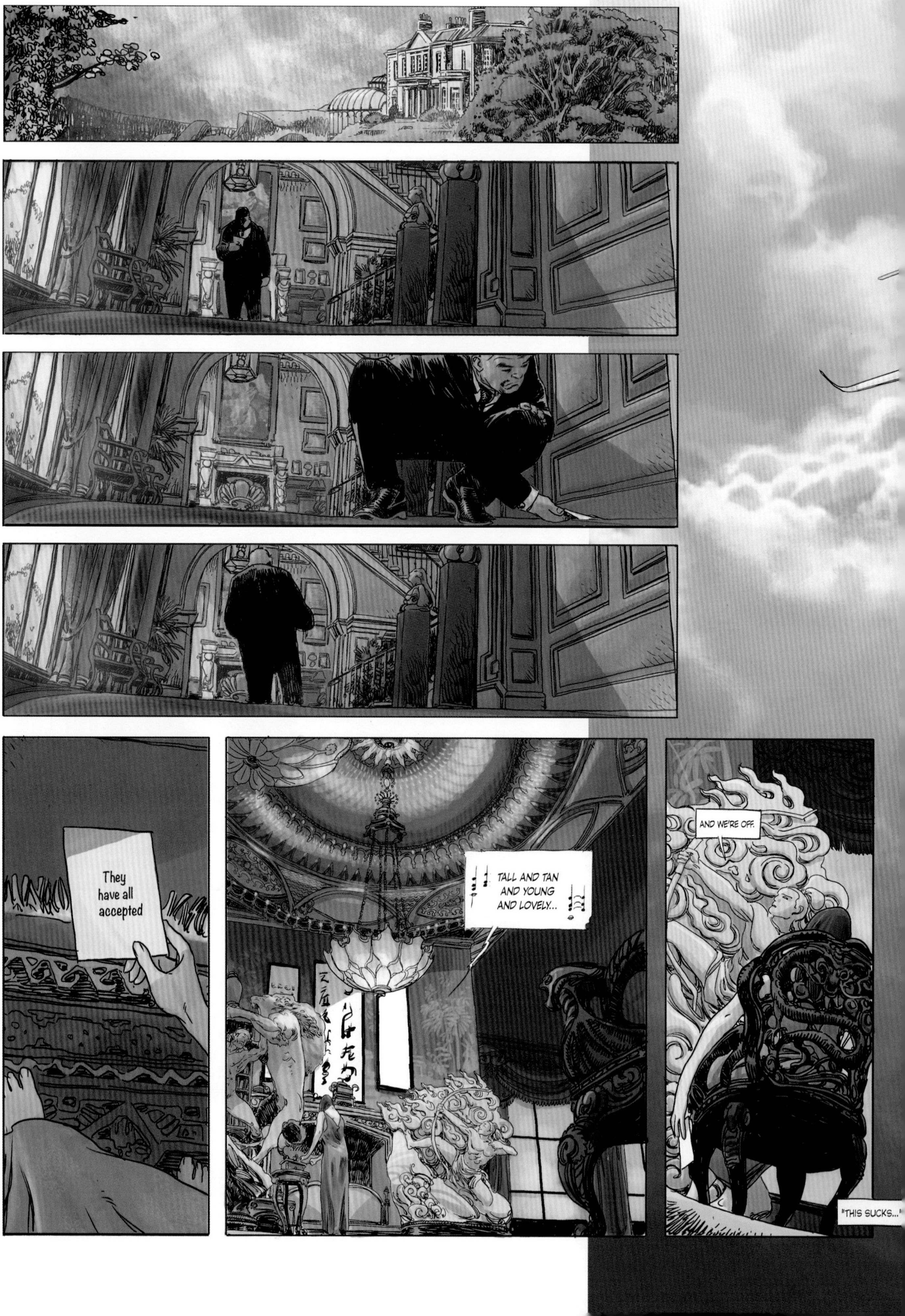
They have all accepted
TALL AND TAN AND YOUNG AND LOVELY...
AND WE'RE OFF.
"THIS SUCKS..."

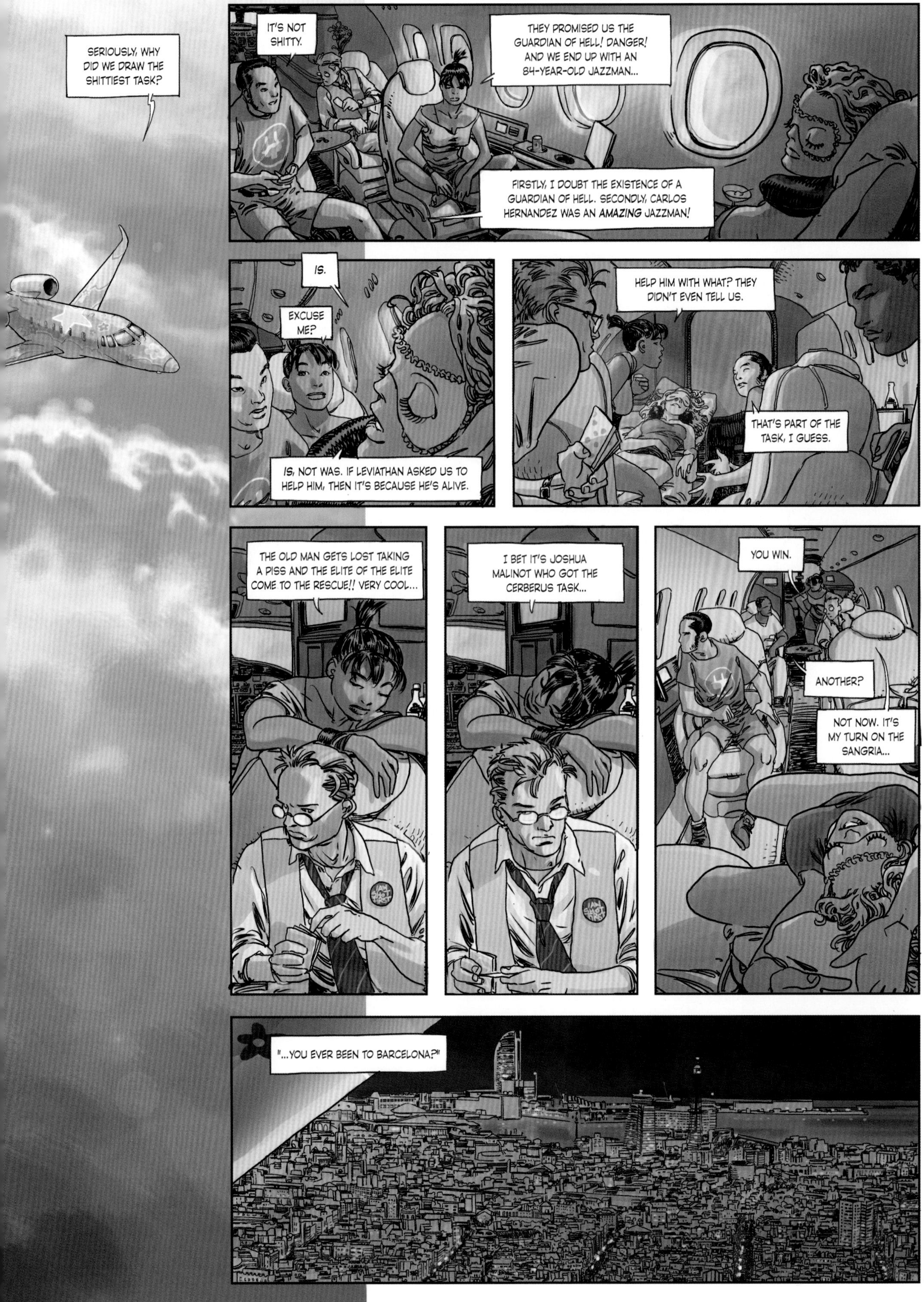
SERIOUSLY, WHY DID WE DRAW THE SHITTIEST TASK?
IT'S NOT SHITTY.
THEY PROMISED US THE GUARDIAN OF HELL! DANGER! AND WE END UP WITH AN 84-YEAR-OLD JAZZMAN...
FIRSTLY, I DOUBT THE EXISTENCE OF A GUARDIAN OF HELL. SECONDLY, CARLOS HERNANDEZ WAS AN AMAZING JAZZMAN!
IS.
EXCUSE ME?
IS, NOT WAS. IF LEVIATHAN ASKED US TO HELP HIM, THEN IT'S BECAUSE HE'S ALIVE.
HELP HIM WITH WHAT? THEY DIDN'T EVEN TELL US.
THAT'S PART OF THE TASK, I GUESS.
THE OLD MAN GETS LOST TAKING A PISS AND THE ELITE OF THE ELITE COME TO THE RESCUE!! VERY COOL...
I BET IT'S JOSHUA MALINOT WHO GOT THE CERBERUS TASK...
YOU WIN.
ANOTHER?
NOT NOW. IT'S MY TURN ON THE SANGRIA...
"...YOU EVER BEEN TO BARCELONA?"

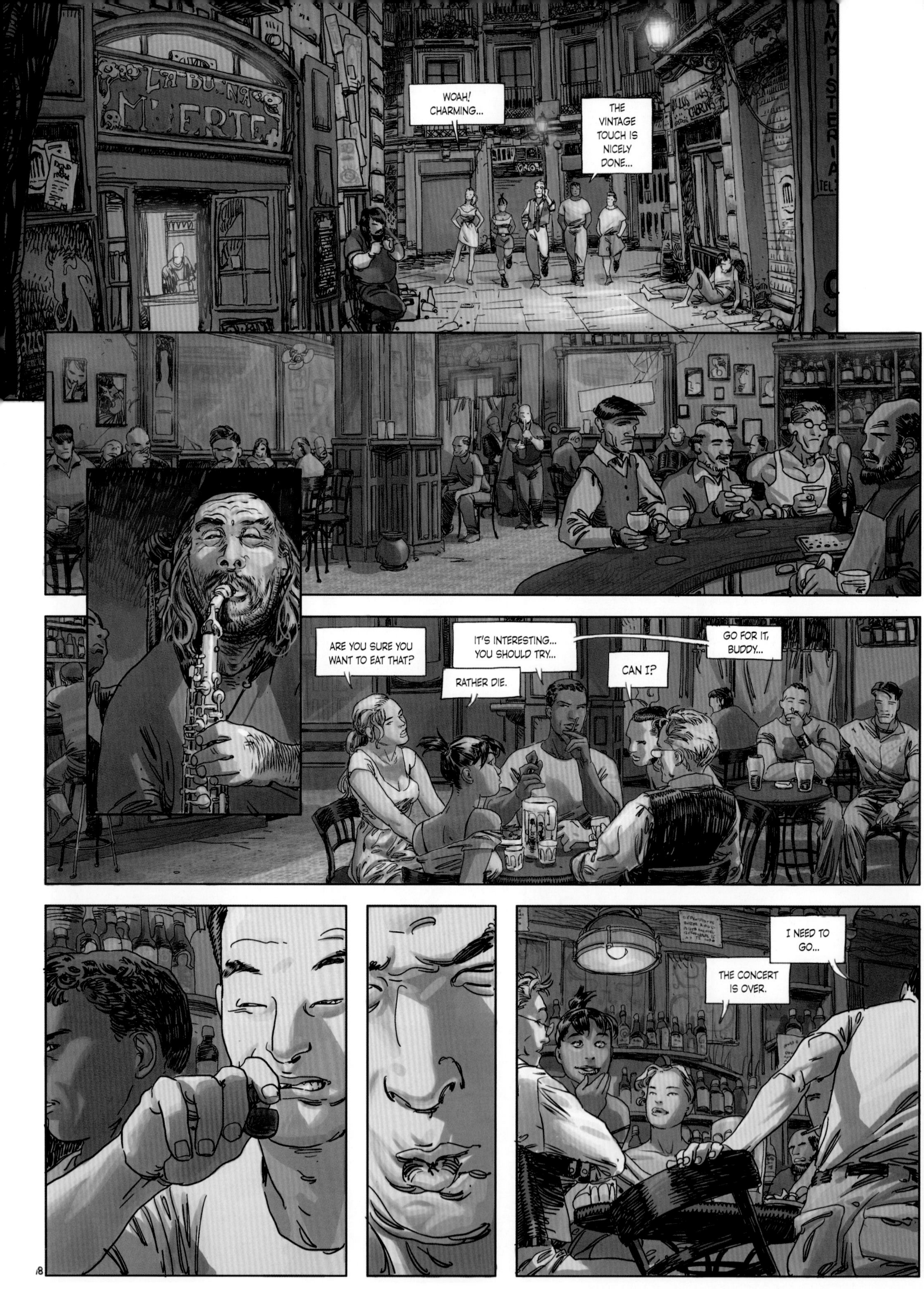

LA BUENA MUERTE
WOAH! CHARMING...
THE VINTAGE TOUCH IS NICELY DONE...
LAMPISTERIA
ARE YOU SURE YOU WANT TO EAT THAT?
RATHER DIE.
IT'S INTERESTING... YOU SHOULD TRY...
CAN I?
GO FOR IT, BUDDY...
I NEED TO GO...
THE CONCERT IS OVER.

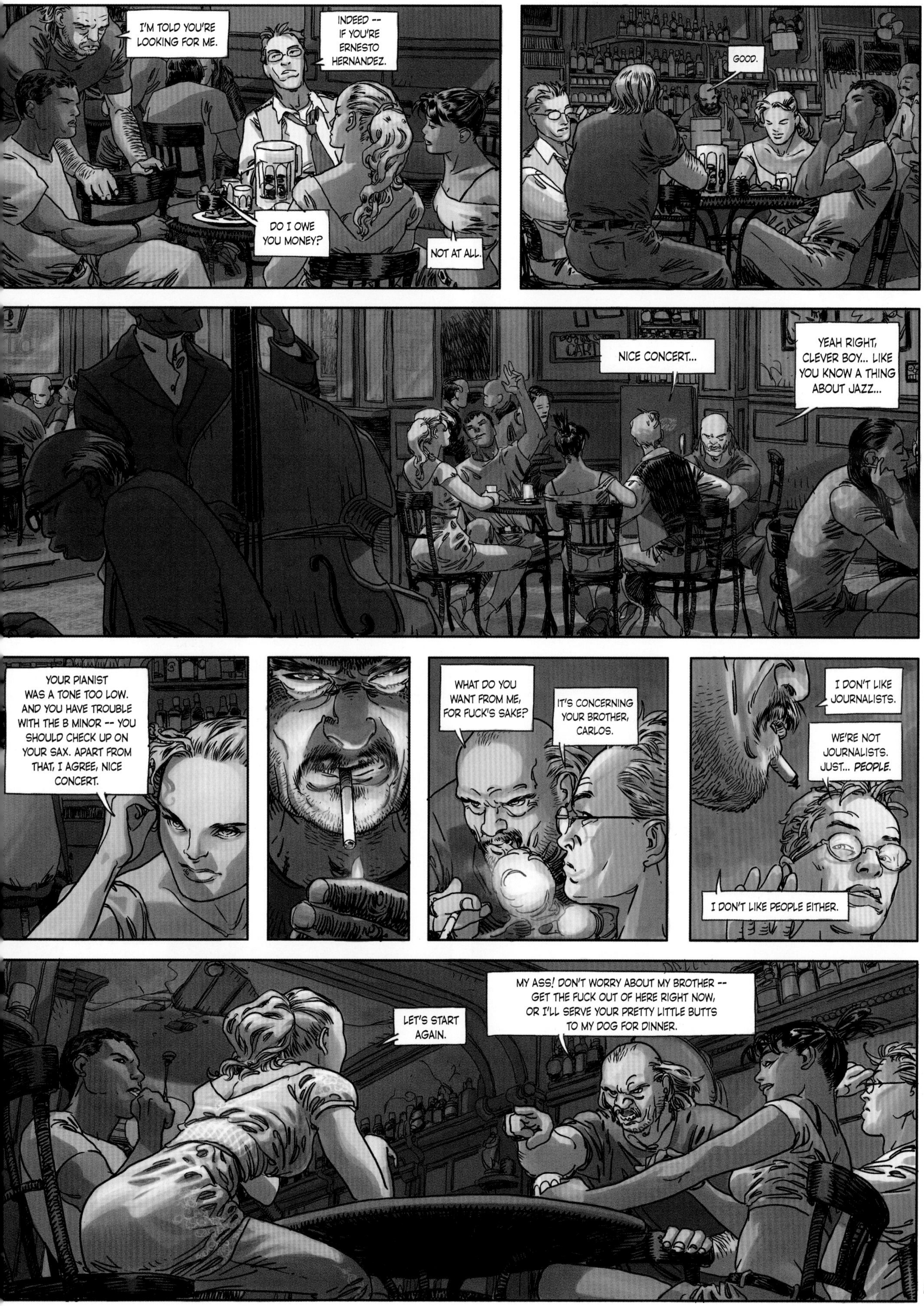
I'M TOLD YOU'RE LOOKING FOR ME.
INDEED -- IF YOU'RE ERNESTO HERNANDEZ.
DO I OWE YOU MONEY?
NOT AT ALL.
GOOD.
NICE CONCERT...
YEAH RIGHT, CLEVER BOY... LIKE YOU KNOW A THING ABOUT JAZZ...
YOUR PIANIST WAS A TONE TOO LOW. AND YOU HAVE TROUBLE WITH THE B MINOR -- YOU SHOULD CHECK UP ON YOUR SAX. APART FROM THAT, I AGREE, NICE CONCERT.
WHAT DO YOU WANT FROM ME, FOR FUCK'S SAKE?
IT'S CONCERNING YOUR BROTHER, CARLOS.
I DON'T LIKE JOURNALISTS.
WE'RE NOT JOURNALISTS. JUST... *PEOPLE*.
I DON'T LIKE PEOPLE EITHER.
LET'S START AGAIN.
MY ASS! DON'T WORRY ABOUT MY BROTHER -- GET THE FUCK OUT OF HERE RIGHT NOW, OR I'LL SERVE YOUR PRETTY LITTLE BUTTS TO MY DOG FOR DINNER.

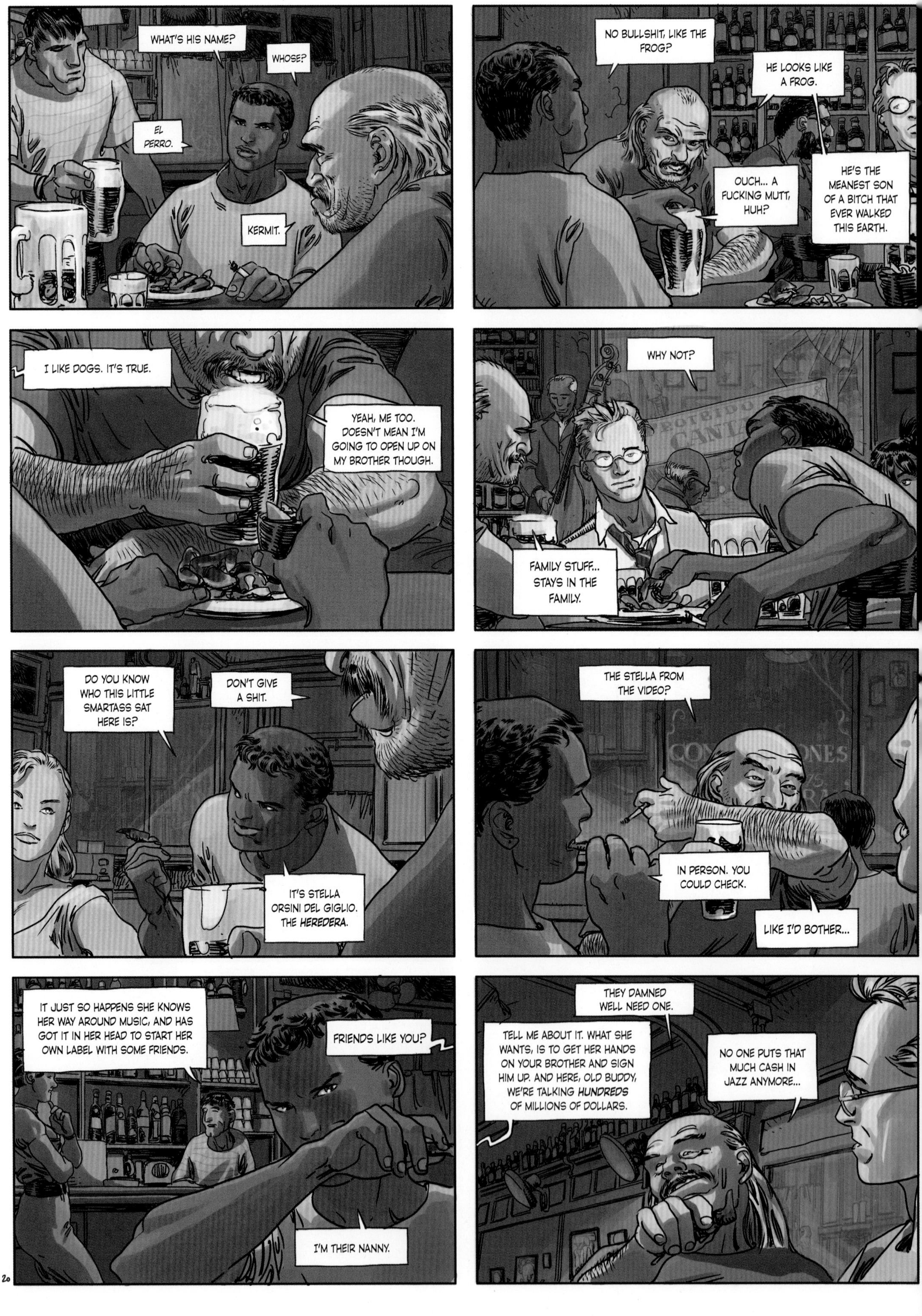
WHAT'S HIS NAME?
WHOSE?
EL PERRO.
KERMIT.
NO BULLSHIT, LIKE THE FROG?
HE LOOKS LIKE A FROG.
OUCH... A FUCKING MUTT, HUH?
HE'S THE MEANEST SON OF A BITCH THAT EVER WALKED THIS EARTH.
I LIKE DOGS. IT'S TRUE.
YEAH, ME TOO. DOESN'T MEAN I'M GOING TO OPEN UP ON MY BROTHER THOUGH.
WHY NOT?
FAMILY STUFF... STAYS IN THE FAMILY.
DO YOU KNOW WHO THIS LITTLE SMARTASS SAT HERE IS?
DON'T GIVE A SHIT.
IT'S STELLA ORSINI DEL GIGLIO. THE *HEREDERA*.
THE STELLA FROM THE VIDEO?
IN PERSON. YOU COULD CHECK.
LIKE I'D BOTHER...
IT JUST SO HAPPENS SHE KNOWS HER WAY AROUND MUSIC, AND HAS GOT IT IN HER HEAD TO START HER OWN LABEL WITH SOME FRIENDS.
FRIENDS LIKE YOU?
I'M THEIR NANNY.
THEY DAMNED WELL NEED ONE.
TELL ME ABOUT IT. WHAT SHE WANTS, IS TO GET HER HANDS ON YOUR BROTHER AND SIGN HIM UP. AND HERE, OLD BUDDY, WE'RE TALKING *HUNDREDS* OF MILLIONS OF DOLLARS.
NO ONE PUTS THAT MUCH CASH IN JAZZ ANYMORE...

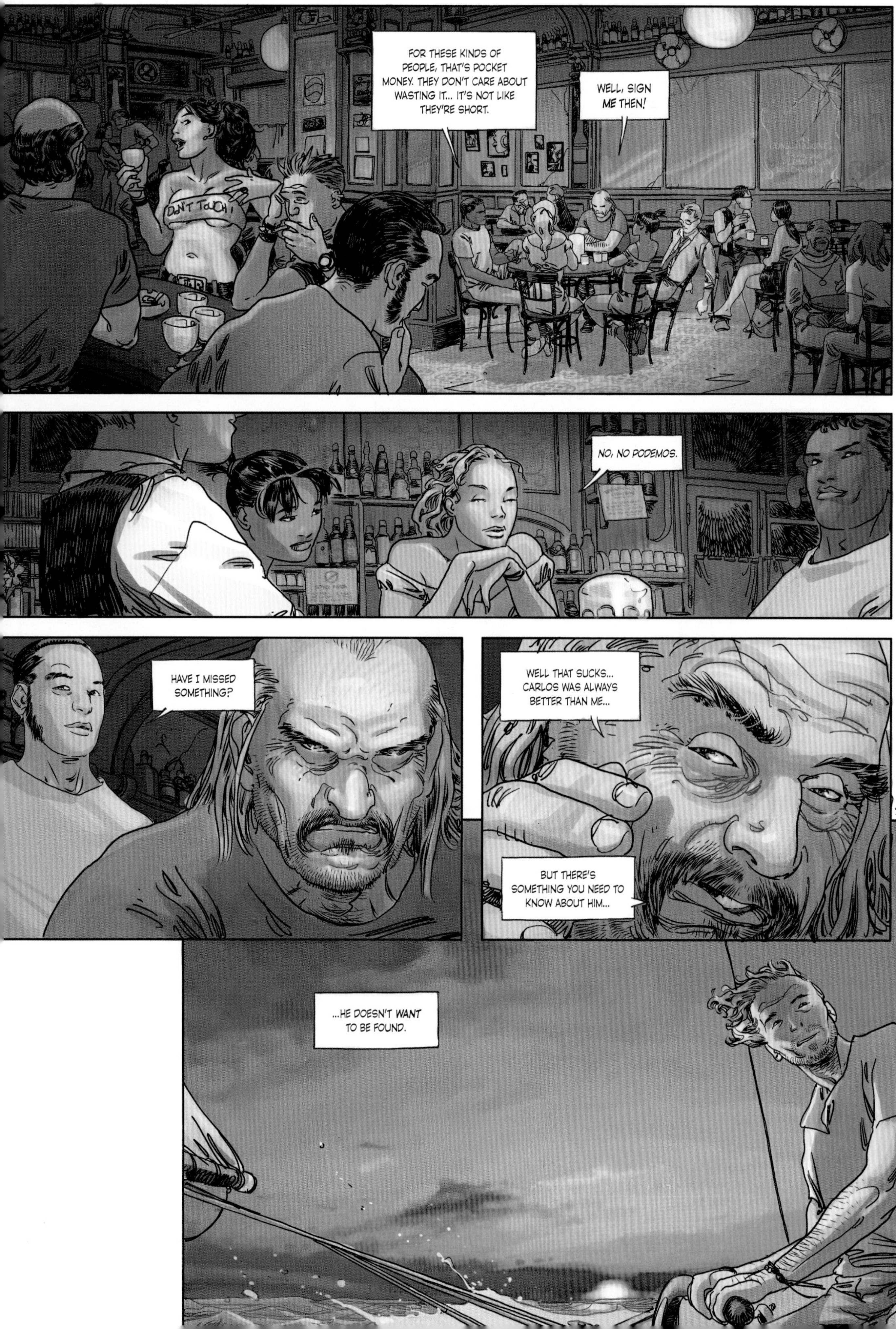

FOR THESE KINDS OF PEOPLE, THAT'S POCKET MONEY. THEY DON'T CARE ABOUT WASTING IT... IT'S NOT LIKE THEY'RE SHORT.
WELL, SIGN *ME* THEN!
DON'T TOUCH!
NO, NO PODEMOS.
HAVE I MISSED SOMETHING?
WELL THAT SUCKS... CARLOS WAS ALWAYS BETTER THAN ME...
BUT THERE'S SOMETHING YOU NEED TO KNOW ABOUT HIM...
...HE DOESN'T *WANT* TO BE FOUND.

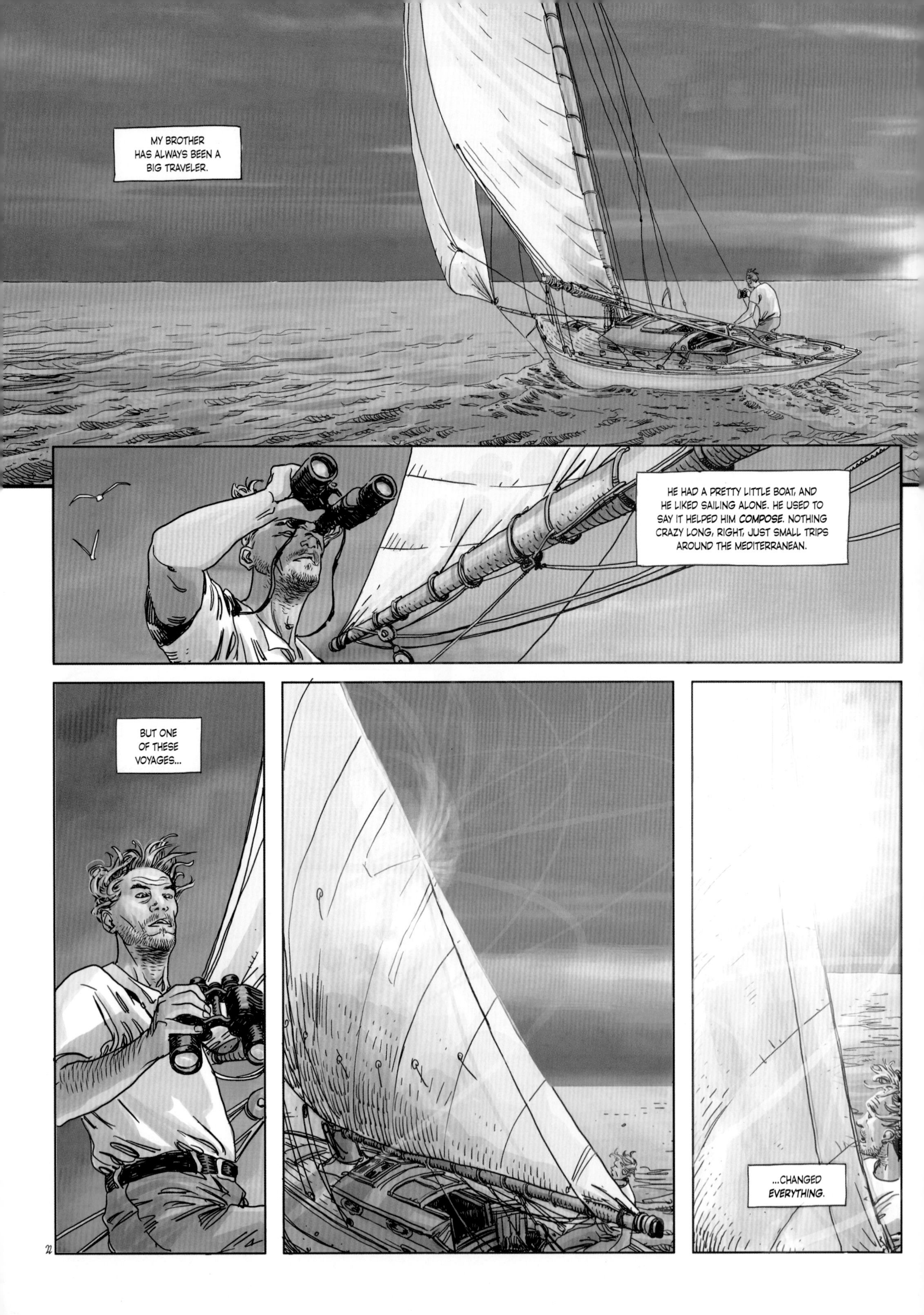
MY BROTHER HAS ALWAYS BEEN A BIG TRAVELER.
HE HAD A PRETTY LITTLE BOAT, AND HE LIKED SAILING ALONE. HE USED TO SAY IT HELPED HIM COMPOSE. NOTHING CRAZY LONG, RIGHT, JUST SMALL TRIPS AROUND THE MEDITERRANEAN.
BUT ONE OF THESE VOYAGES...
...CHANGED EVERYTHING.

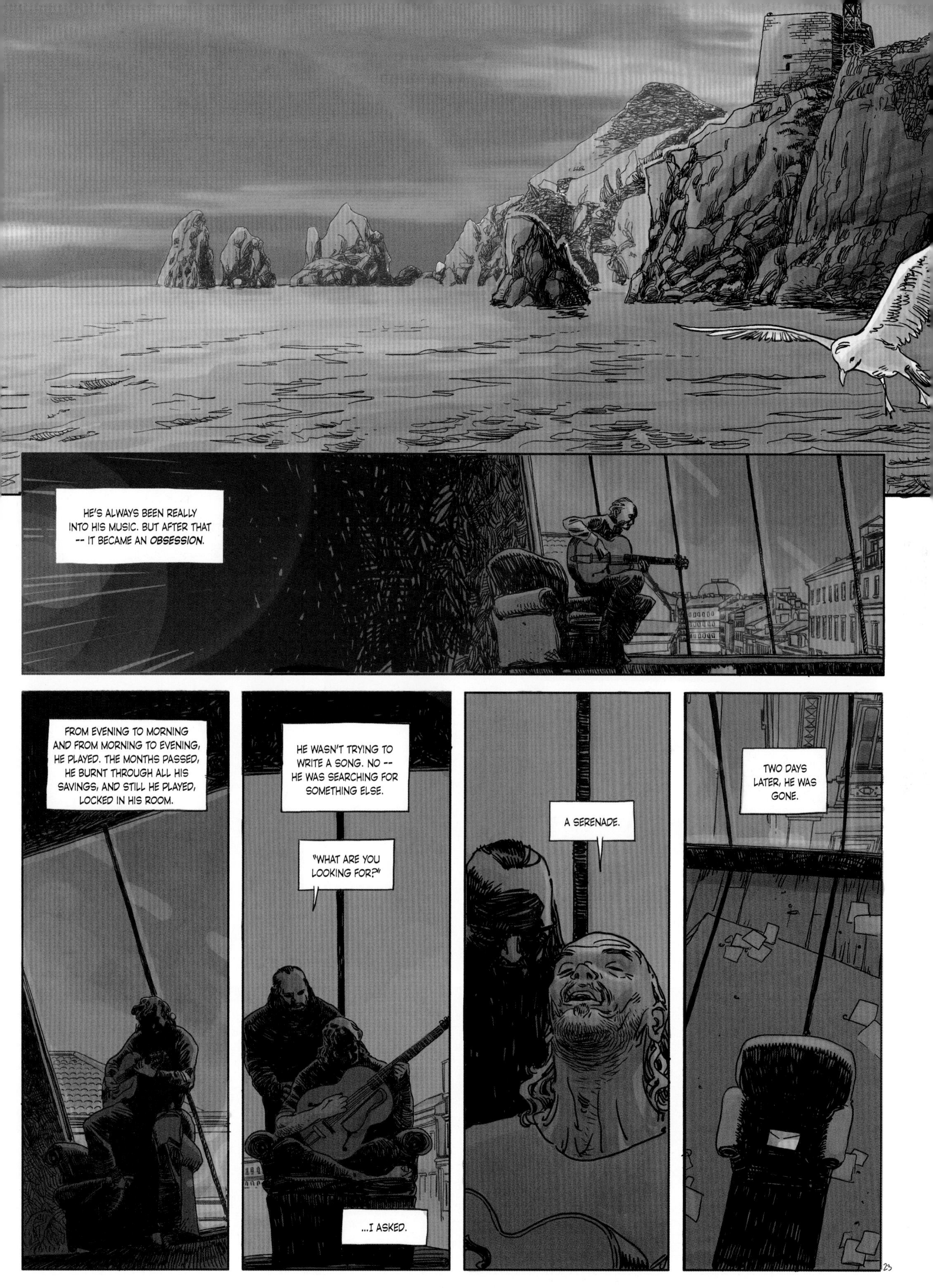
HE'S ALWAYS BEEN REALLY INTO HIS MUSIC. BUT AFTER THAT -- IT BECAME AN *OBSESSION*.
FROM EVENING TO MORNING AND FROM MORNING TO EVENING, HE PLAYED. THE MONTHS PASSED, HE BURNT THROUGH ALL HIS SAVINGS, AND STILL HE PLAYED, LOCKED IN HIS ROOM.
HE WASN'T TRYING TO WRITE A SONG. NO -- HE WAS SEARCHING FOR SOMETHING ELSE.
"WHAT ARE YOU LOOKING FOR?"
...I ASKED.
A SERENADE.
TWO DAYS LATER, HE WAS GONE.

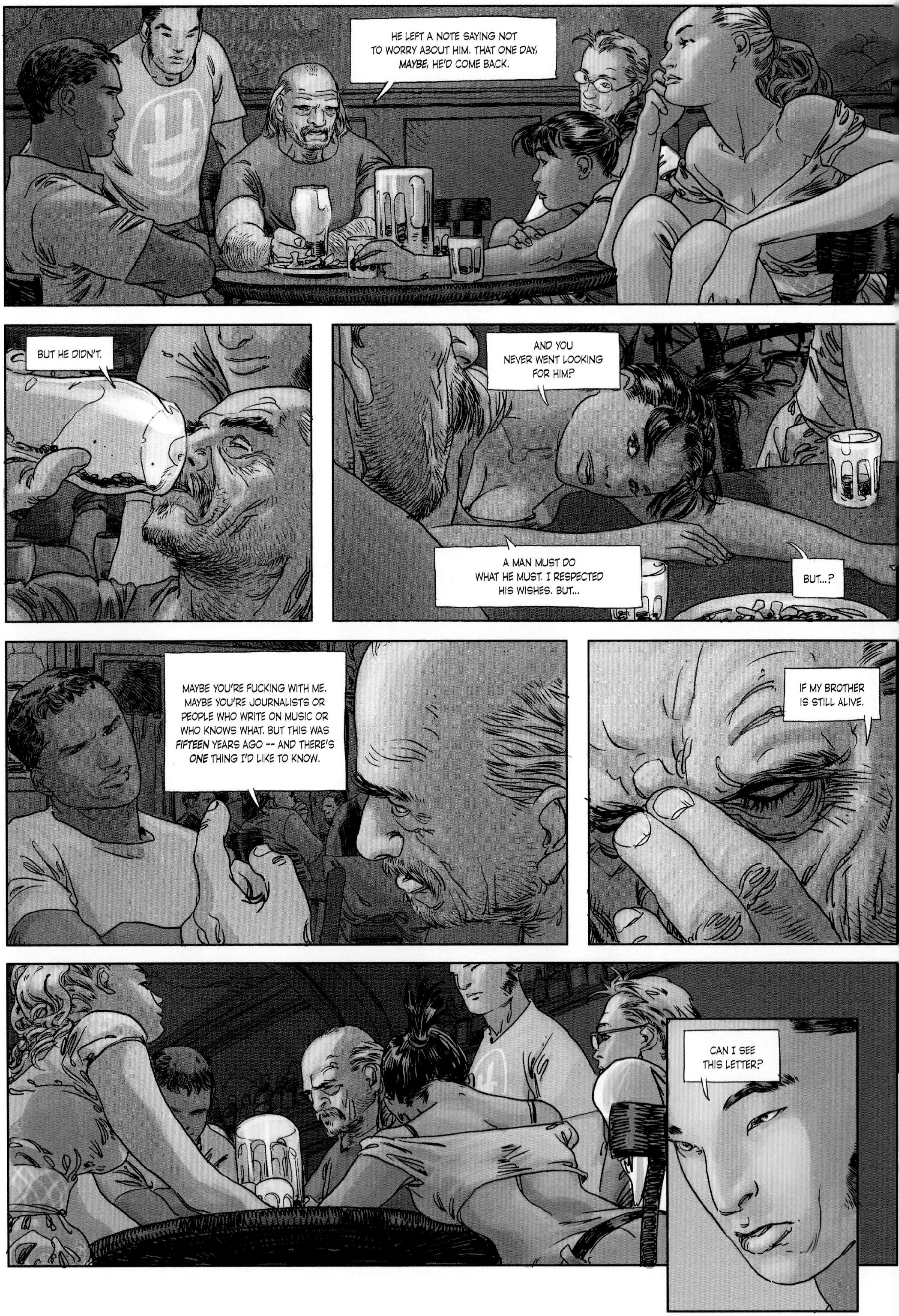
HE LEFT A NOTE SAYING NOT TO WORRY ABOUT HIM. THAT ONE DAY, *MAYBE*, HE'D COME BACK.
BUT HE DIDN'T.
AND YOU NEVER WENT LOOKING FOR HIM?
A MAN MUST DO WHAT HE MUST. I RESPECTED HIS WISHES. BUT...
BUT...?
MAYBE YOU'RE FUCKING WITH ME. MAYBE YOU'RE JOURNALISTS OR PEOPLE WHO WRITE ON MUSIC OR WHO KNOWS WHAT. BUT THIS WAS *FIFTEEN* YEARS AGO -- AND THERE'S *ONE* THING I'D LIKE TO KNOW.
IF MY BROTHER IS STILL ALIVE.
CAN I SEE THIS LETTER?

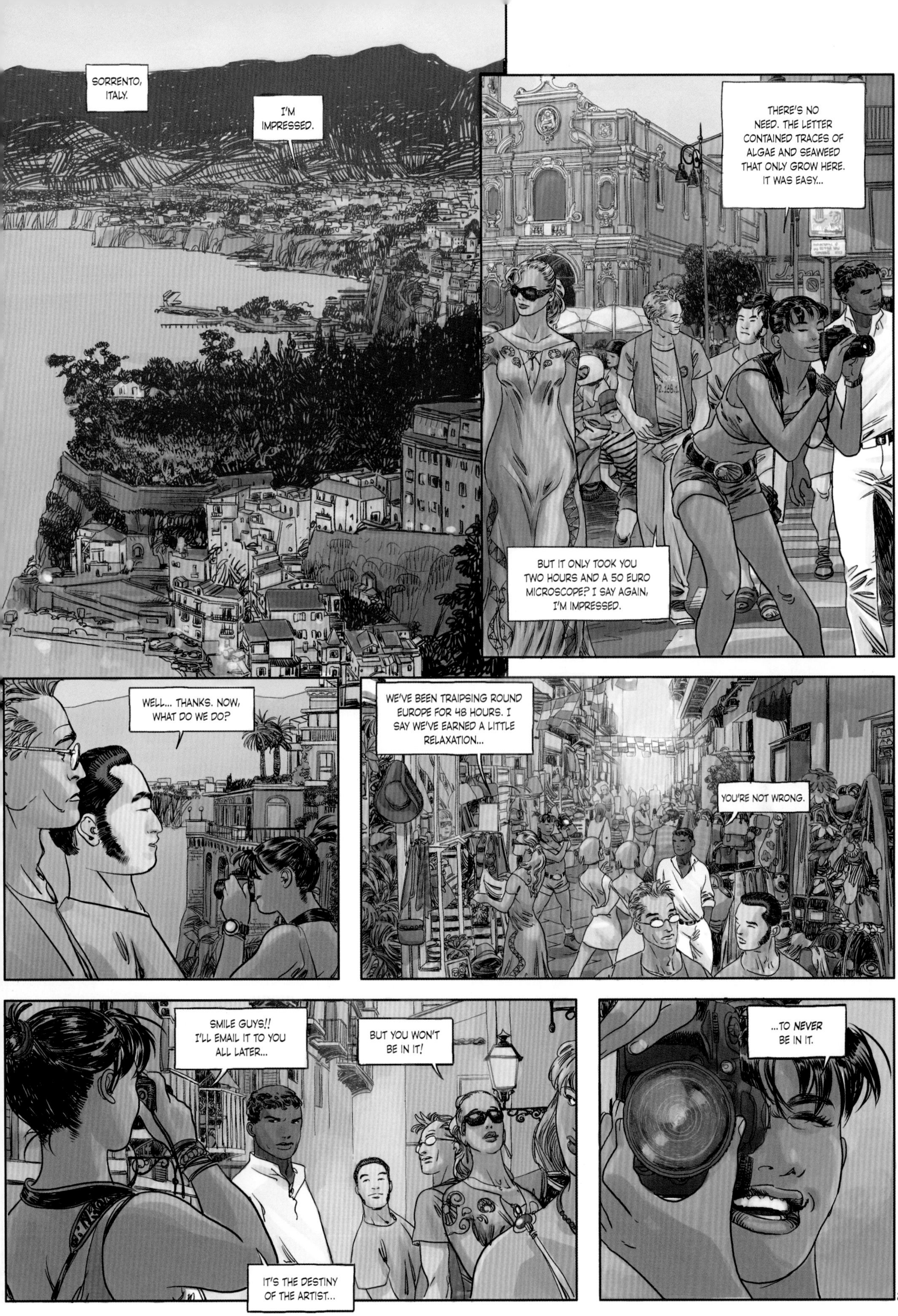
SORRENTO, ITALY.
I'M IMPRESSED.
THERE'S NO NEED. THE LETTER CONTAINED TRACES OF ALGAE AND SEAWEED THAT ONLY GROW HERE. IT WAS EASY...
BUT IT ONLY TOOK YOU TWO HOURS AND A 50 EURO MICROSCOPE? I SAY AGAIN, I'M IMPRESSED.
WELL... THANKS. NOW, WHAT DO WE DO?
WE'VE BEEN TRAIPSING ROUND EUROPE FOR 48 HOURS. I SAY WE'VE EARNED A LITTLE RELAXATION...
YOU'RE NOT WRONG.
SMILE GUYS!! I'LL EMAIL IT TO YOU ALL LATER...
BUT YOU WON'T BE IN IT!
IT'S THE DESTINY OF THE ARTIST...
...TO NEVER BE IN IT.

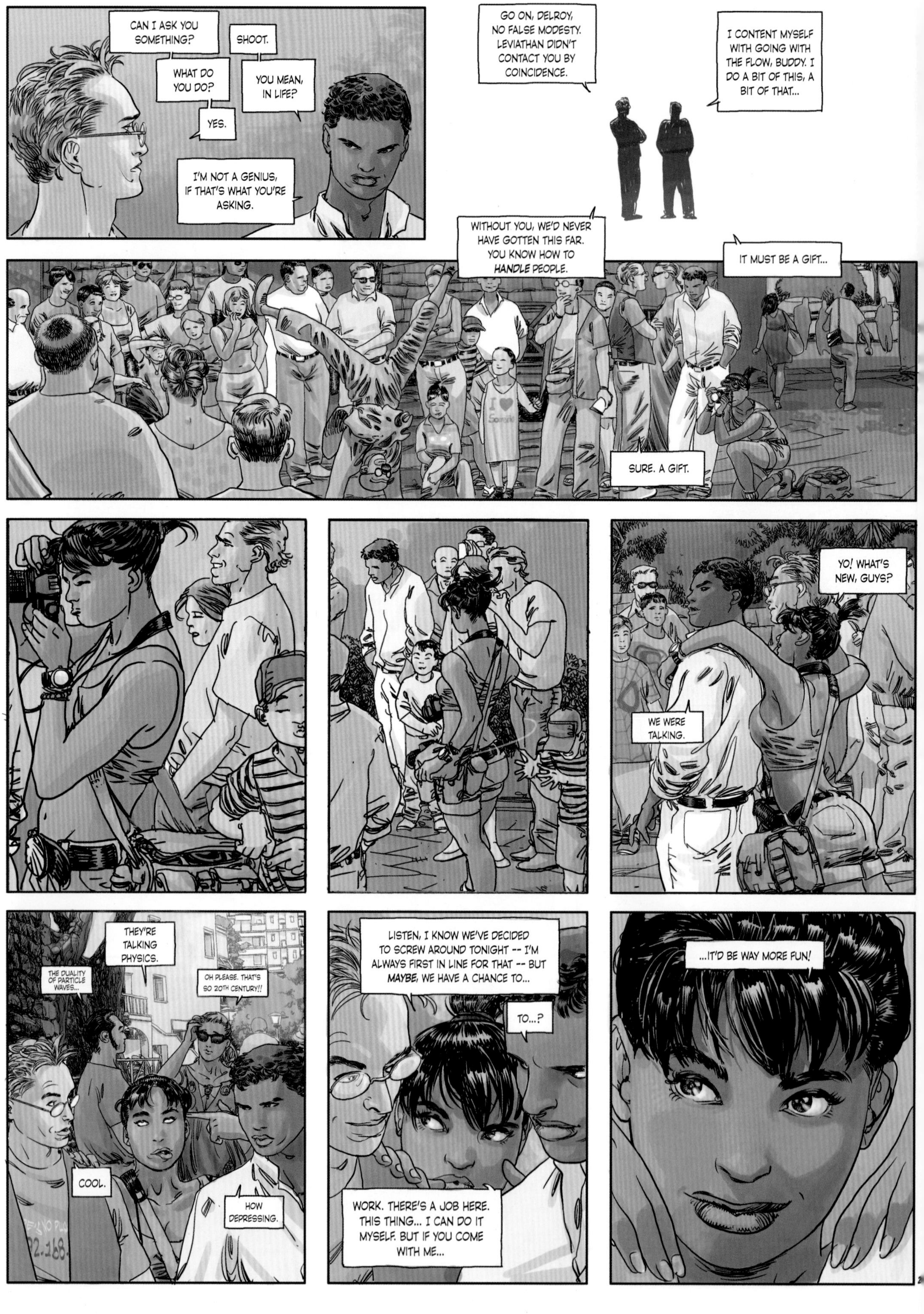
CAN I ASK YOU SOMETHING?
SHOOT.
WHAT DO YOU DO?
YOU MEAN, IN LIFE?
YES.
I'M NOT A GENIUS, IF THAT'S WHAT YOU'RE ASKING.
GO ON, DELROY, NO FALSE MODESTY. LEVIATHAN DIDN'T CONTACT YOU BY COINCIDENCE.
I CONTENT MYSELF WITH GOING WITH THE FLOW, BUDDY. I DO A BIT OF THIS, A BIT OF THAT...
WITHOUT YOU, WE'D NEVER HAVE GOTTEN THIS FAR. YOU KNOW HOW TO *HANDLE* PEOPLE.
IT MUST BE A GIFT...
SURE. A GIFT.
YO! WHAT'S NEW, GUYS?
WE WERE TALKING.
THEY'RE TALKING PHYSICS.
THE DUALITY OF PARTICLE WAVES...
OH PLEASE. THAT'S SO 20TH CENTURY!!
COOL.
HOW DEPRESSING.
LISTEN, I KNOW WE'VE DECIDED TO SCREW AROUND TONIGHT -- I'M ALWAYS FIRST IN LINE FOR THAT -- BUT *MAYBE*, WE HAVE A CHANCE TO...
TO...?
WORK. THERE'S A JOB HERE. THIS THING... I CAN DO IT MYSELF. BUT IF YOU COME WITH ME...
...IT'D BE WAY MORE FUN!

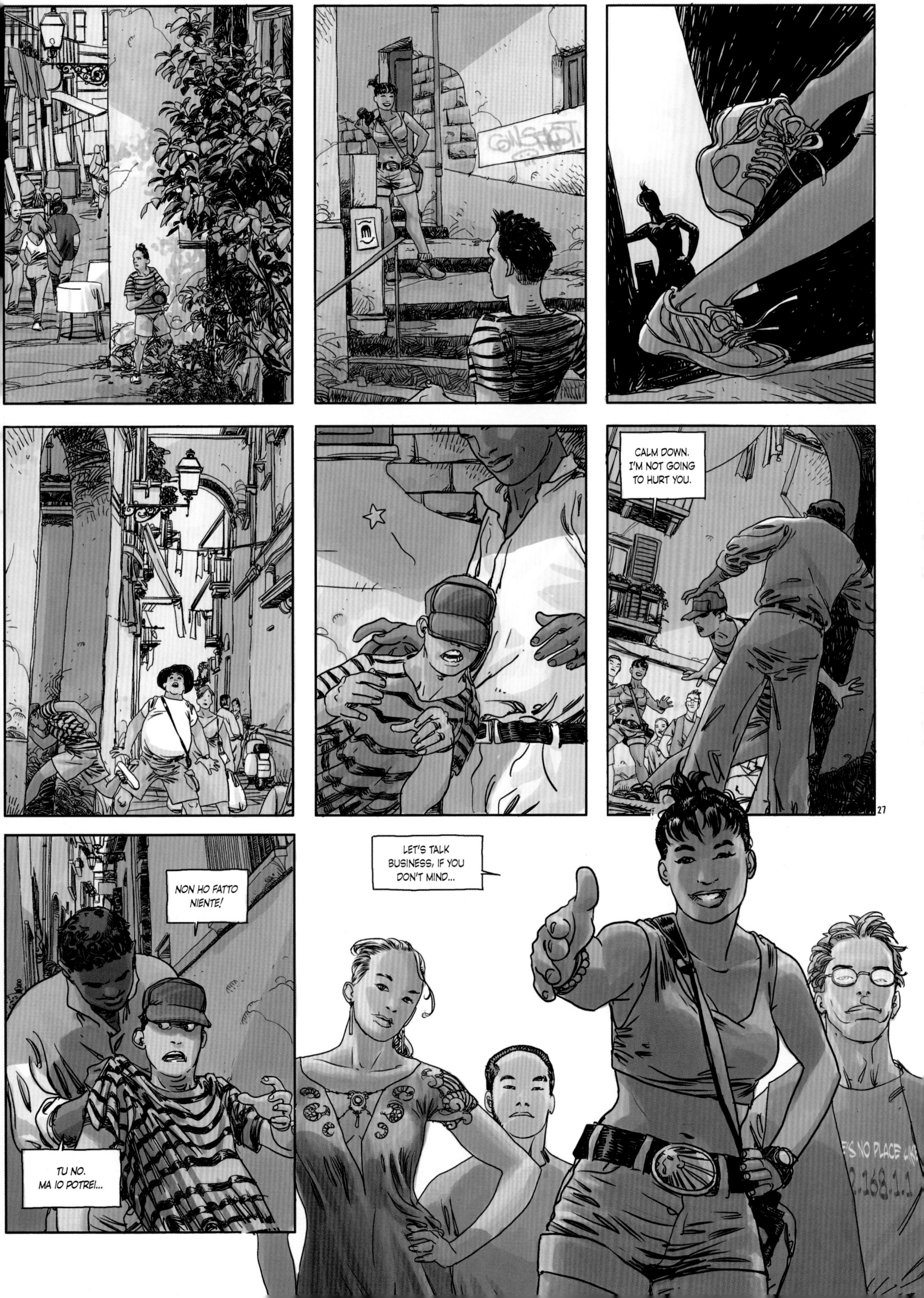
CALM DOWN. I'M NOT GOING TO HURT YOU.
NON HO FATTO NIENTE!
TU NO. MA IO POTREI...
LET'S TALK BUSINESS, IF YOU DON'T MIND...

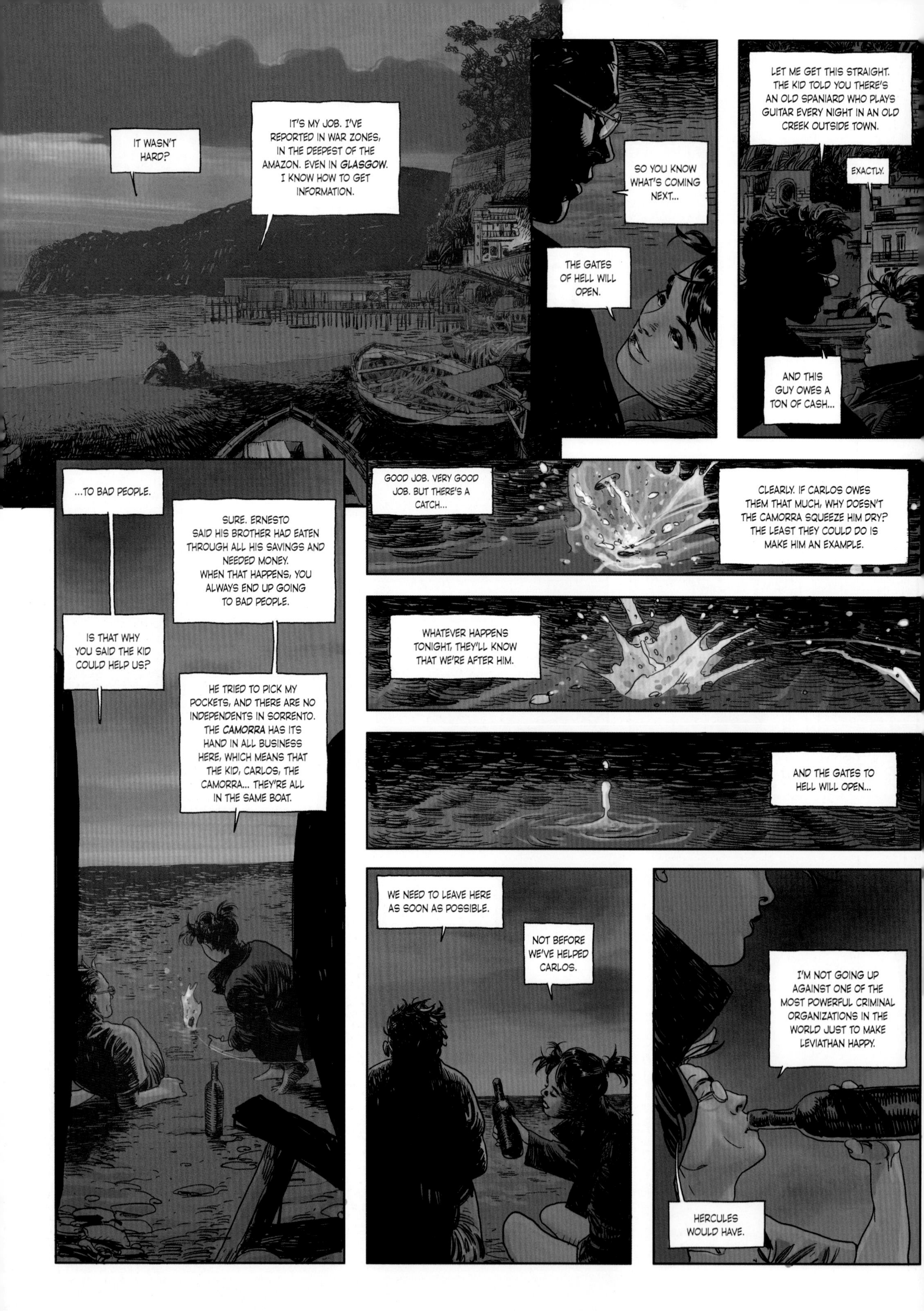
IT WASN'T HARD?
IT'S MY JOB. I'VE REPORTED IN WAR ZONES, IN THE DEEPEST OF THE AMAZON. EVEN IN GLASGOW. I KNOW HOW TO GET INFORMATION.
SO YOU KNOW WHAT'S COMING NEXT...
THE GATES OF HELL WILL OPEN.
LET ME GET THIS STRAIGHT. THE KID TOLD YOU THERE'S AN OLD SPANIARD WHO PLAYS GUITAR EVERY NIGHT IN AN OLD CREEK OUTSIDE TOWN.
EXACTLY.
AND THIS GUY OWES A TON OF CASH...
...TO BAD PEOPLE.
SURE. ERNESTO SAID HIS BROTHER HAD EATEN THROUGH ALL HIS SAVINGS AND NEEDED MONEY. WHEN THAT HAPPENS, YOU ALWAYS END UP GOING TO BAD PEOPLE.
IS THAT WHY YOU SAID THE KID COULD HELP US?
HE TRIED TO PICK MY POCKETS, AND THERE ARE NO INDEPENDENTS IN SORRENTO. THE CAMORRA HAS ITS HAND IN ALL BUSINESS HERE, WHICH MEANS THAT THE KID, CARLOS, THE CAMORRA... THEY'RE ALL IN THE SAME BOAT.
GOOD JOB. VERY GOOD JOB. BUT THERE'S A CATCH...
CLEARLY. IF CARLOS OWES THEM THAT MUCH, WHY DOESN'T THE CAMORRA SQUEEZE HIM DRY? THE LEAST THEY COULD DO IS MAKE HIM AN EXAMPLE.
WHATEVER HAPPENS TONIGHT, THEY'LL KNOW THAT WE'RE AFTER HIM.
AND THE GATES TO HELL WILL OPEN...
WE NEED TO LEAVE HERE AS SOON AS POSSIBLE.
NOT BEFORE WE'VE HELPED CARLOS.
I'M NOT GOING UP AGAINST ONE OF THE MOST POWERFUL CRIMINAL ORGANIZATIONS IN THE WORLD JUST TO MAKE LEVIATHAN HAPPY.
HERCULES WOULD HAVE.

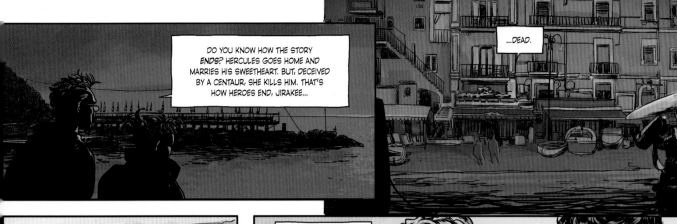

DO YOU KNOW HOW THE STORY *ENDS?* HERCULES GOES HOME AND MARRIES HIS SWEETHEART. BUT, DECEIVED BY A CENTAUR, SHE KILLS HIM. THAT'S HOW HEROES END, JIRAKEE...

...DEAD.

IT'S OUT OF THE QUESTION.

I'M SERIOUS. YOU CAN STAY IF YOU WANT. BUT I'M LEAVING.

YOU CAN'T JUST LEAVE. JIRAKEE, SAY SOMETHING...

I TRIED!

THEN DO SOMETHING.

THIS IS THE *REAL* WORLD, STELLA. AND IN THE REAL WORLD, PEOPLE GET *KILLED.* FOR THOSE FRIENDS OF CARLOS, LIFE HAS THE SAME VALUE AS... I DON'T KNOW... FOR *YOU,* A MASERATI!

WE DON'T KNOW IF THEY'RE HIS FRIENDS.

IT DOESN'T MATTER. HANGING AROUND HIM IS STILL DANGEROUS.

A SCIENTIST NEVER RETREATS.

NO -- MARIE CURIE DIDN'T. AND SHE'S DEAD.

YOU SEE? MORE DEAD. THANKS FOR THE PRESENT.

STAY.

29

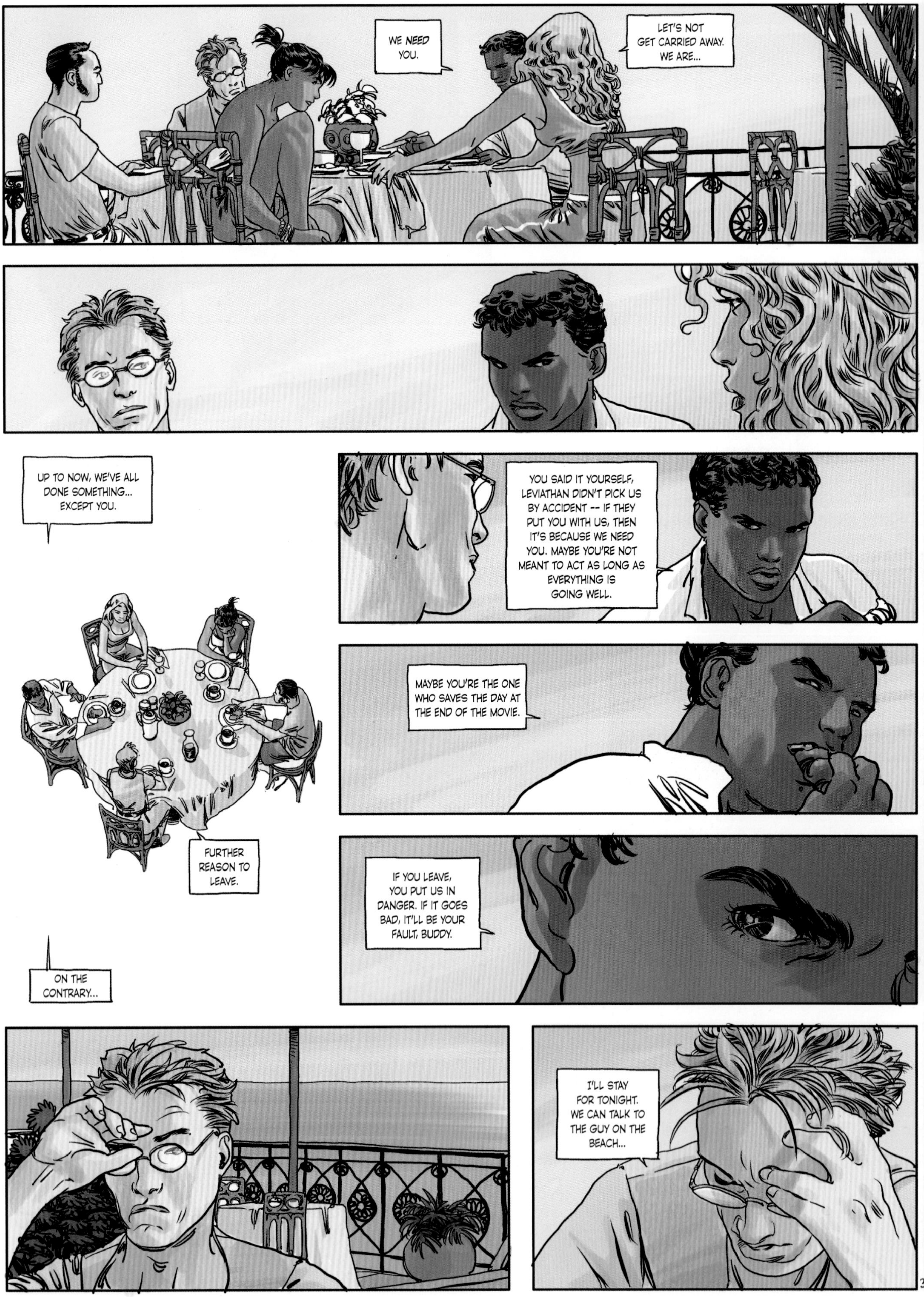
WE NEED YOU.
LET'S NOT GET CARRIED AWAY. WE ARE...
UP TO NOW, WE'VE ALL DONE SOMETHING... EXCEPT YOU.
YOU SAID IT YOURSELF, LEVIATHAN DIDN'T PICK US BY ACCIDENT -- IF THEY PUT YOU WITH US, THEN IT'S BECAUSE WE NEED YOU. MAYBE YOU'RE NOT MEANT TO ACT AS LONG AS EVERYTHING IS GOING WELL.
MAYBE YOU'RE THE ONE WHO SAVES THE DAY AT THE END OF THE MOVIE.
FURTHER REASON TO LEAVE.
IF YOU LEAVE, YOU PUT US IN DANGER. IF IT GOES BAD, IT'LL BE YOUR FAULT, BUDDY.
ON THE CONTRARY...
I'LL STAY FOR TONIGHT. WE CAN TALK TO THE GUY ON THE BEACH...

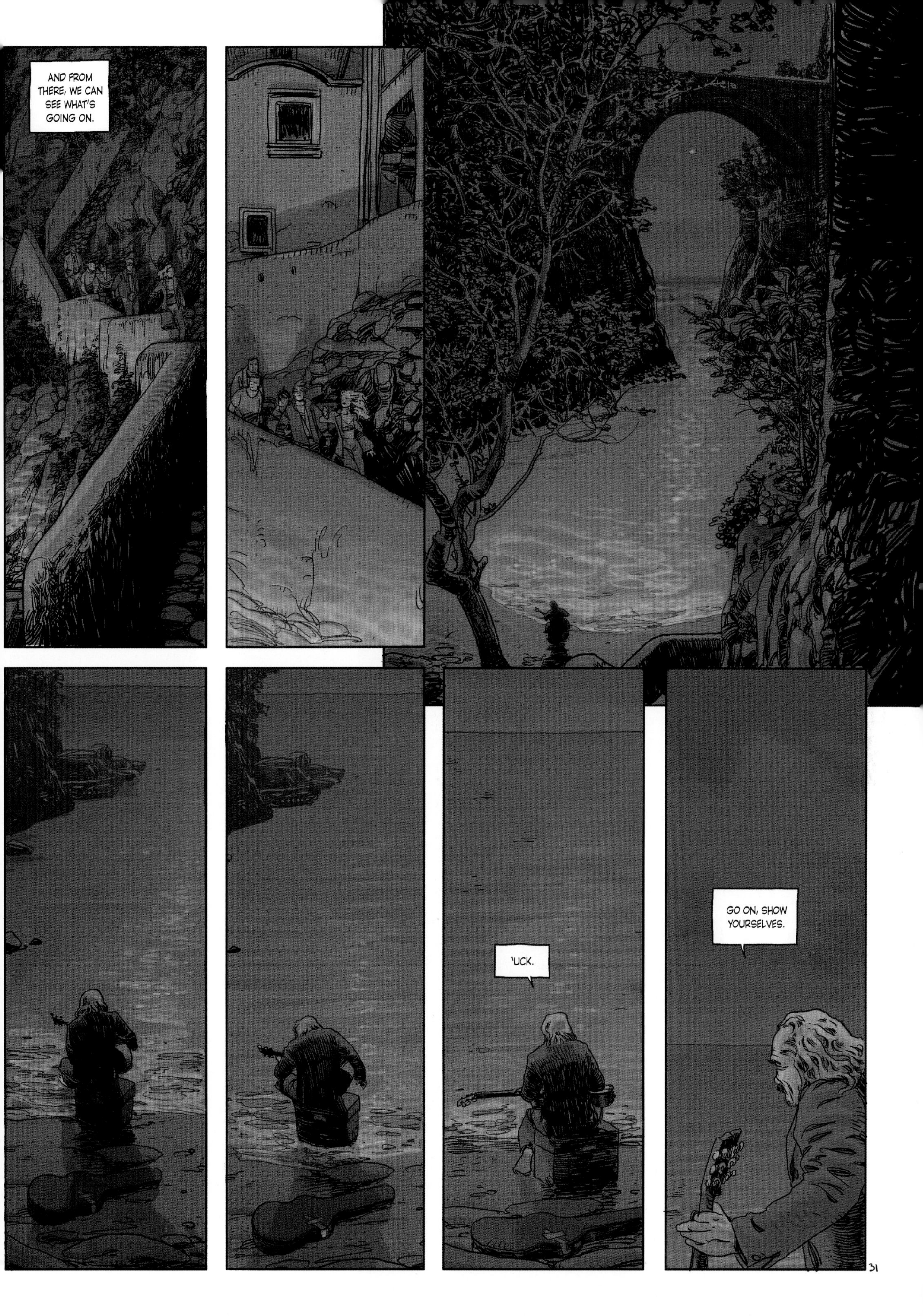
AND FROM THERE, WE CAN SEE WHAT'S GOING ON.
'UCK.
GO ON, SHOW YOURSELVES.

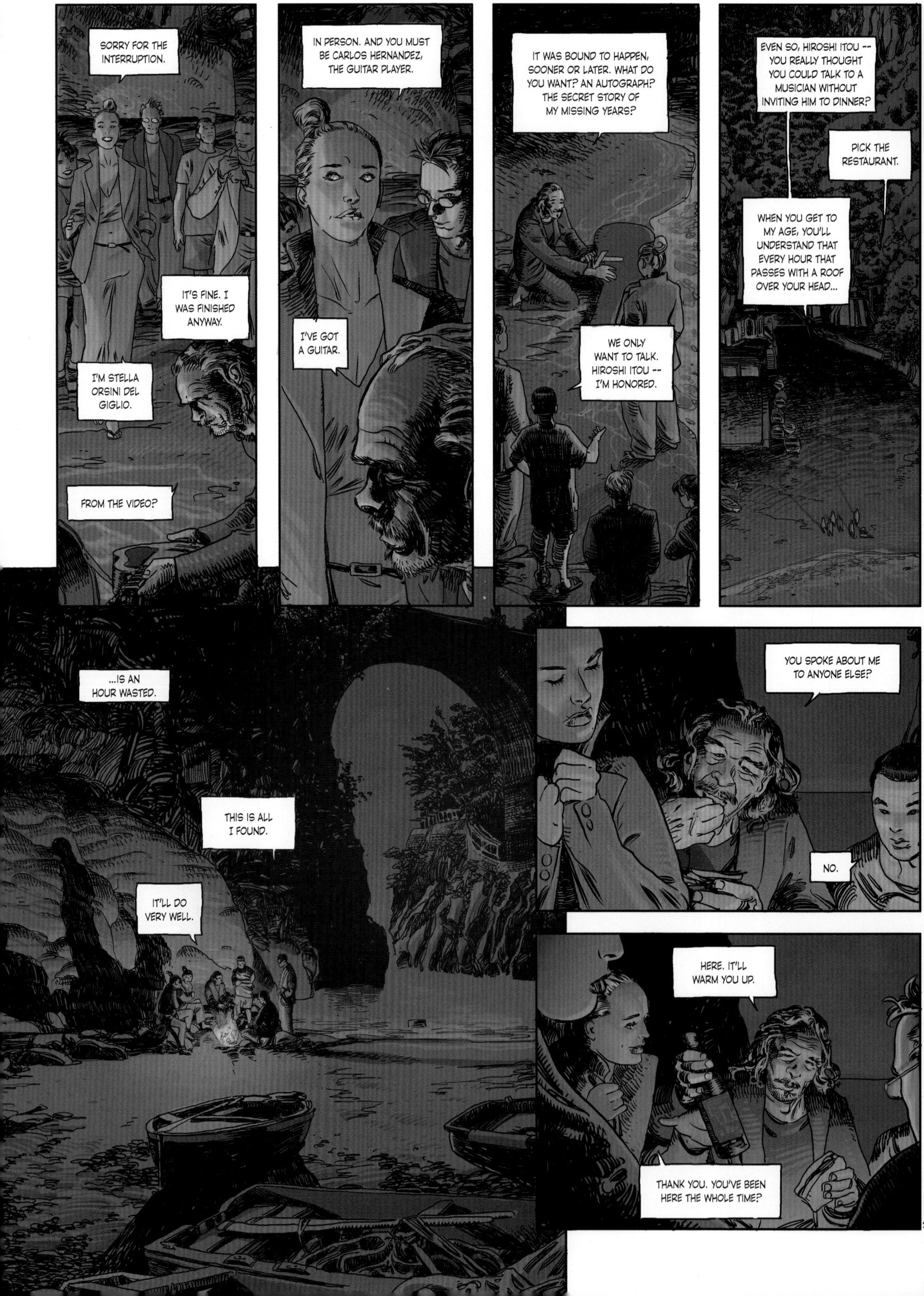
SORRY FOR THE INTERRUPTION.
IT'S FINE. I WAS FINISHED ANYWAY.
I'M STELLA ORSINI DEL GIGLIO.
FROM THE VIDEO?
IN PERSON. AND YOU MUST BE CARLOS HERNANDEZ, THE GUITAR PLAYER.
I'VE GOT A GUITAR.
IT WAS BOUND TO HAPPEN, SOONER OR LATER. WHAT DO YOU WANT? AN AUTOGRAPH? THE SECRET STORY OF MY MISSING YEARS?
WE ONLY WANT TO TALK. HIROSHI ITOU -- I'M HONORED.
EVEN SO, HIROSHI ITOU -- YOU REALLY THOUGHT YOU COULD TALK TO A MUSICIAN WITHOUT INVITING HIM TO DINNER?
PICK THE RESTAURANT.
WHEN YOU GET TO MY AGE, YOU'LL UNDERSTAND THAT EVERY HOUR THAT PASSES WITH A ROOF OVER YOUR HEAD...
...IS AN HOUR WASTED.
THIS IS ALL I FOUND.
IT'LL DO VERY WELL.
YOU SPOKE ABOUT ME TO ANYONE ELSE?
NO.
HERE. IT'LL WARM YOU UP.
THANK YOU. YOU'VE BEEN HERE THE WHOLE TIME?

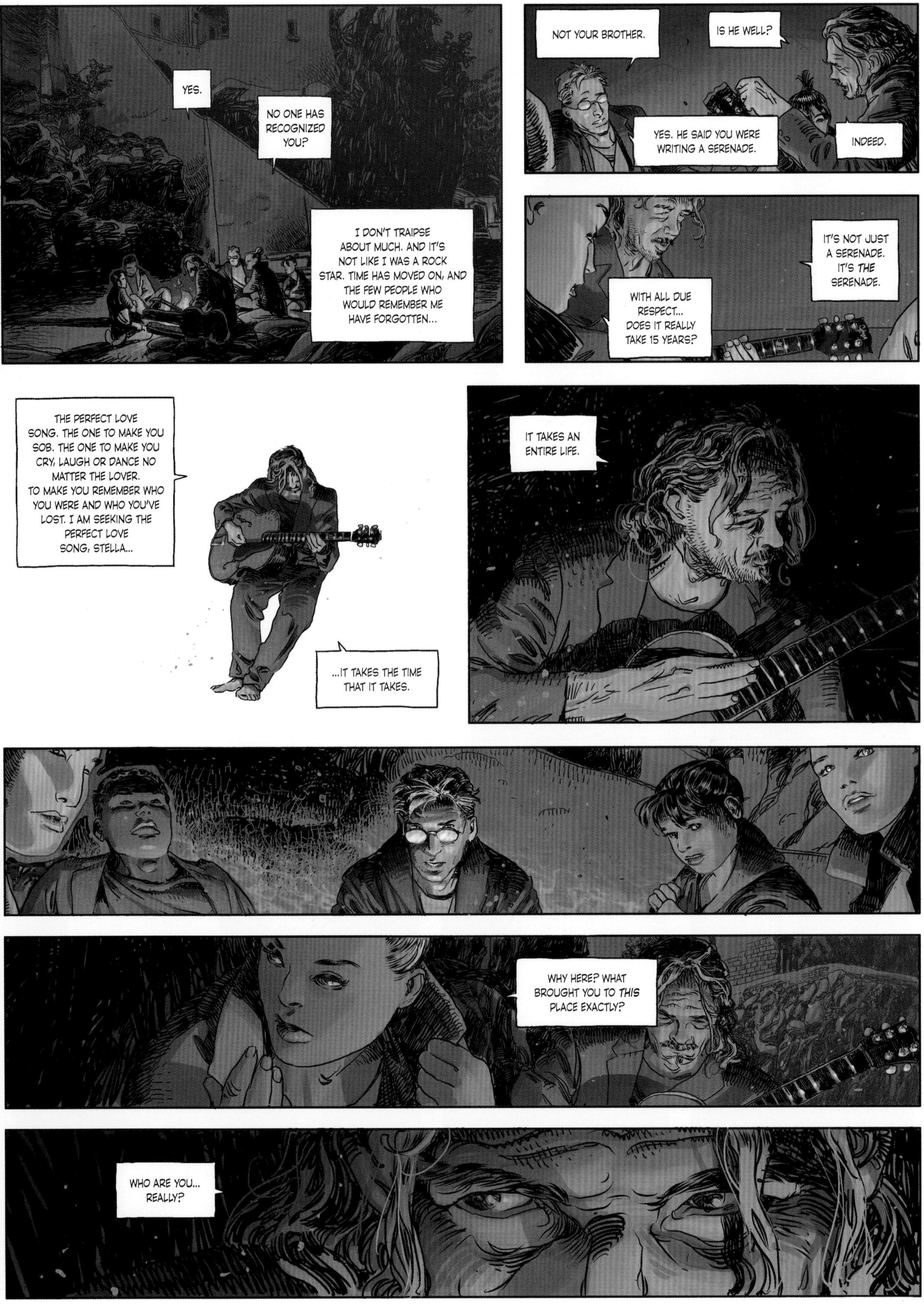
YES.
NO ONE HAS RECOGNIZED YOU?
I DON'T TRAIPSE ABOUT MUCH. AND IT'S NOT LIKE I WAS A ROCK STAR. TIME HAS MOVED ON, AND THE FEW PEOPLE WHO WOULD REMEMBER ME HAVE FORGOTTEN...
NOT YOUR BROTHER.
IS HE WELL?
YES. HE SAID YOU WERE WRITING A SERENADE.
INDEED.
IT'S NOT JUST A SERENADE. IT'S *THE* SERENADE.
WITH ALL DUE RESPECT... DOES IT REALLY TAKE 15 YEARS?
THE PERFECT LOVE SONG. THE ONE TO MAKE YOU SOB. THE ONE TO MAKE YOU CRY, LAUGH OR DANCE NO MATTER THE LOVER. TO MAKE YOU REMEMBER WHO YOU WERE AND WHO YOU'VE LOST. I AM SEEKING THE PERFECT LOVE SONG, STELLA...
IT TAKES AN ENTIRE LIFE.
...IT TAKES THE TIME THAT IT TAKES.
WHY HERE? WHAT BROUGHT YOU TO *THIS* PLACE EXACTLY?
WHO ARE YOU... REALLY?

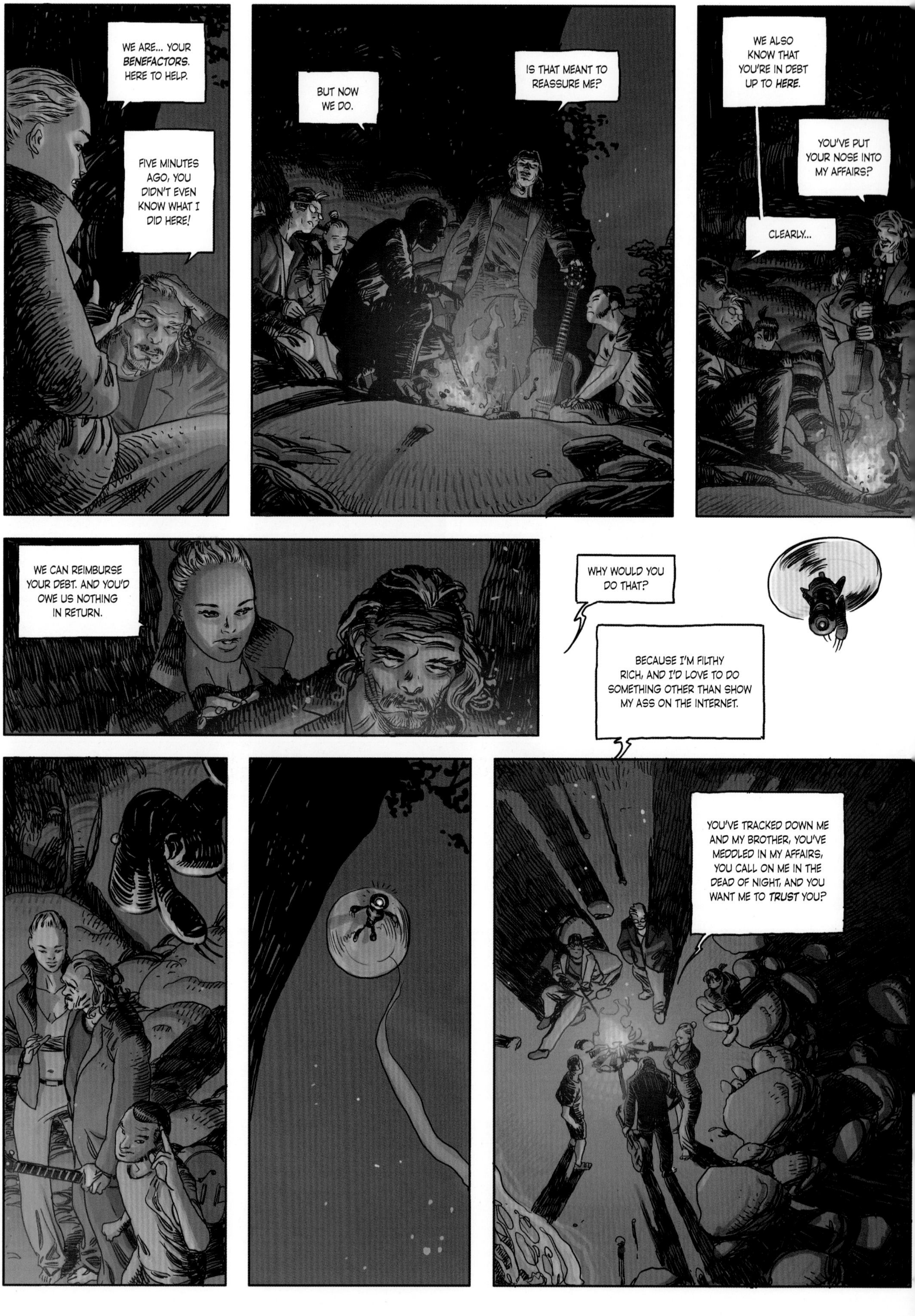
WE ARE... YOUR BENEFACTORS. HERE TO HELP.
FIVE MINUTES AGO, YOU DIDN'T EVEN KNOW WHAT I DID HERE!
BUT NOW WE DO.
IS THAT MEANT TO REASSURE ME?
WE ALSO KNOW THAT YOU'RE IN DEBT UP TO HERE.
YOU'VE PUT YOUR NOSE INTO MY AFFAIRS?
CLEARLY...
WE CAN REIMBURSE YOUR DEBT. AND YOU'D OWE US NOTHING IN RETURN.
WHY WOULD YOU DO THAT?
BECAUSE I'M FILTHY RICH, AND I'D LOVE TO DO SOMETHING OTHER THAN SHOW MY ASS ON THE INTERNET.
YOU'VE TRACKED DOWN ME AND MY BROTHER, YOU'VE MEDDLED IN MY AFFAIRS, YOU CALL ON ME IN THE DEAD OF NIGHT, AND YOU WANT ME TO TRUST YOU?

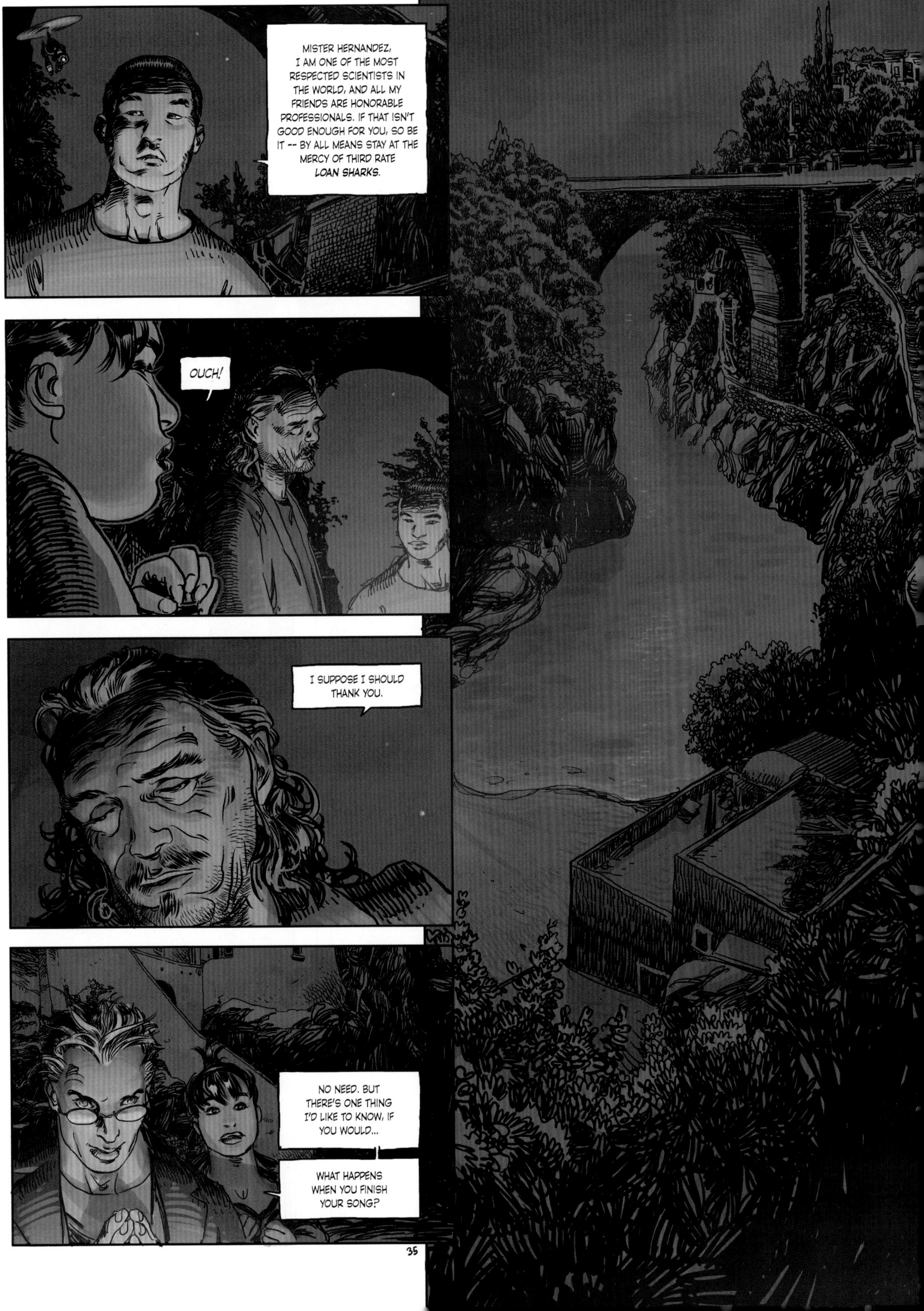
MISTER HERNANDEZ, I AM ONE OF THE MOST RESPECTED SCIENTISTS IN THE WORLD, AND ALL MY FRIENDS ARE HONORABLE PROFESSIONALS. IF THAT ISN'T GOOD ENOUGH FOR YOU, SO BE IT -- BY ALL MEANS STAY AT THE MERCY OF THIRD RATE **LOAN SHARKS**.
OUCH!
I SUPPOSE I SHOULD THANK YOU.
NO NEED. BUT THERE'S ONE THING I'D LIKE TO KNOW, IF YOU WOULD...
WHAT HAPPENS WHEN YOU FINISH YOUR SONG?

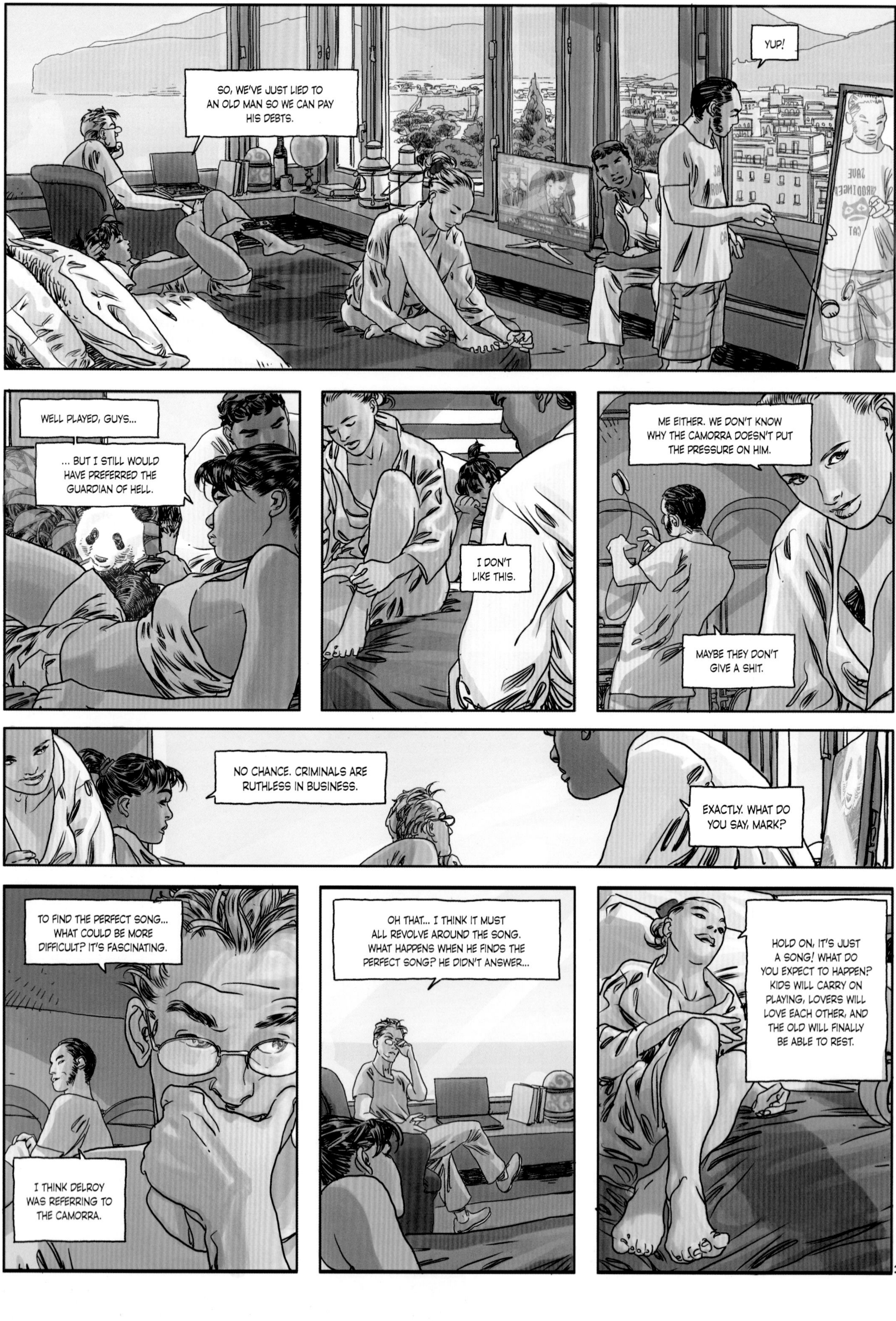
SO, WE'VE JUST LIED TO AN OLD MAN SO WE CAN PAY HIS DEBTS.
YUP!
WELL PLAYED, GUYS...
... BUT I STILL WOULD HAVE PREFERRED THE GUARDIAN OF HELL.
I DON'T LIKE THIS.
ME EITHER. WE DON'T KNOW WHY THE CAMORRA DOESN'T PUT THE PRESSURE ON HIM.
MAYBE THEY DON'T GIVE A SHIT.
NO CHANCE. CRIMINALS ARE RUTHLESS IN BUSINESS.
EXACTLY. WHAT DO YOU SAY, MARK?
TO FIND THE PERFECT SONG... WHAT COULD BE MORE DIFFICULT? IT'S FASCINATING.
I THINK DELROY WAS REFERRING TO THE CAMORRA.
OH THAT... I THINK IT MUST ALL REVOLVE AROUND THE SONG. WHAT HAPPENS WHEN HE FINDS THE PERFECT SONG? HE DIDN'T ANSWER...
HOLD ON, IT'S JUST A SONG! WHAT DO YOU EXPECT TO HAPPEN? KIDS WILL CARRY ON PLAYING, LOVERS WILL LOVE EACH OTHER, AND THE OLD WILL FINALLY BE ABLE TO REST.

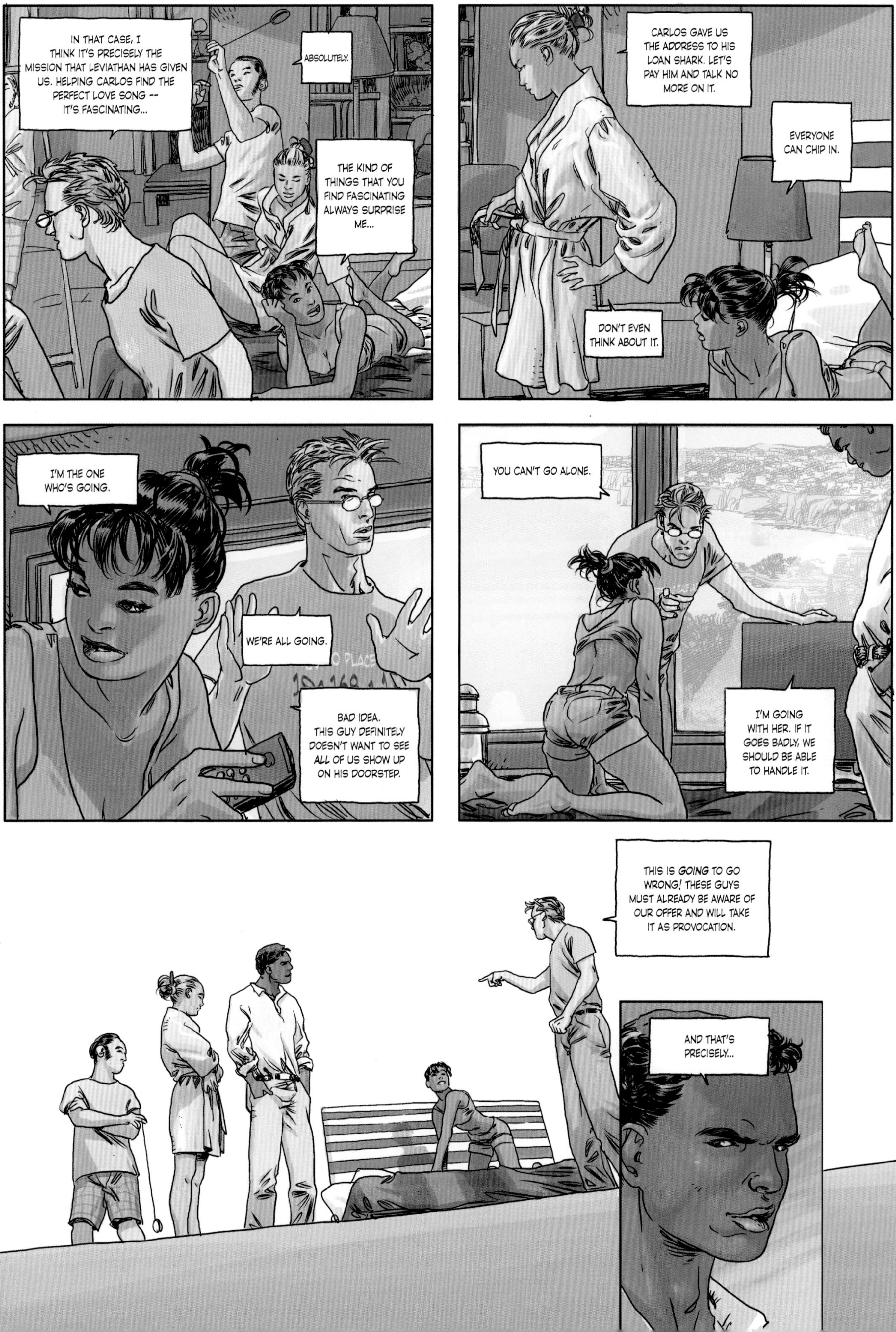
IN THAT CASE, I THINK IT'S PRECISELY THE MISSION THAT LEVIATHAN HAS GIVEN US. HELPING CARLOS FIND THE PERFECT LOVE SONG -- IT'S FASCINATING...
ABSOLUTELY.
THE KIND OF THINGS THAT YOU FIND FASCINATING ALWAYS SURPRISE ME...
CARLOS GAVE US THE ADDRESS TO HIS LOAN SHARK. LET'S PAY HIM AND TALK NO MORE ON IT.
EVERYONE CAN CHIP IN.
DON'T EVEN THINK ABOUT IT.
I'M THE ONE WHO'S GOING.
WE'RE ALL GOING.
BAD IDEA. THIS GUY DEFINITELY DOESN'T WANT TO SEE ALL OF US SHOW UP ON HIS DOORSTEP.
YOU CAN'T GO ALONE.
I'M GOING WITH HER. IF IT GOES BADLY, WE SHOULD BE ABLE TO HANDLE IT.
THIS IS GOING TO GO WRONG! THESE GUYS MUST ALREADY BE AWARE OF OUR OFFER AND WILL TAKE IT AS PROVOCATION.
AND THAT'S PRECISELY...

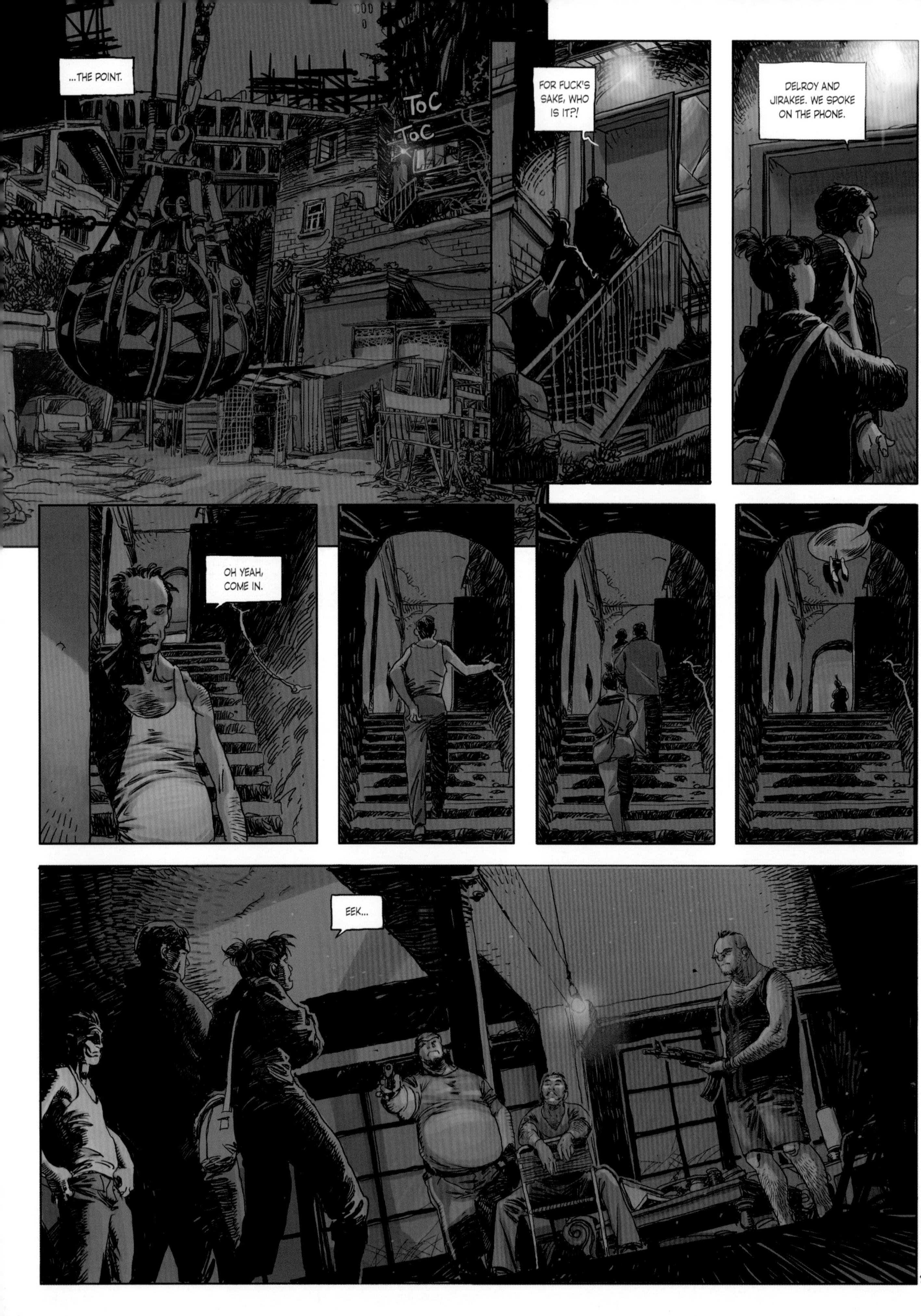
...THE POINT.
ToC
ToC
FOR FUCK'S SAKE, WHO IS IT?!
DELROY AND JIRAKEE. WE SPOKE ON THE PHONE.
OH YEAH, COME IN.
EEK...

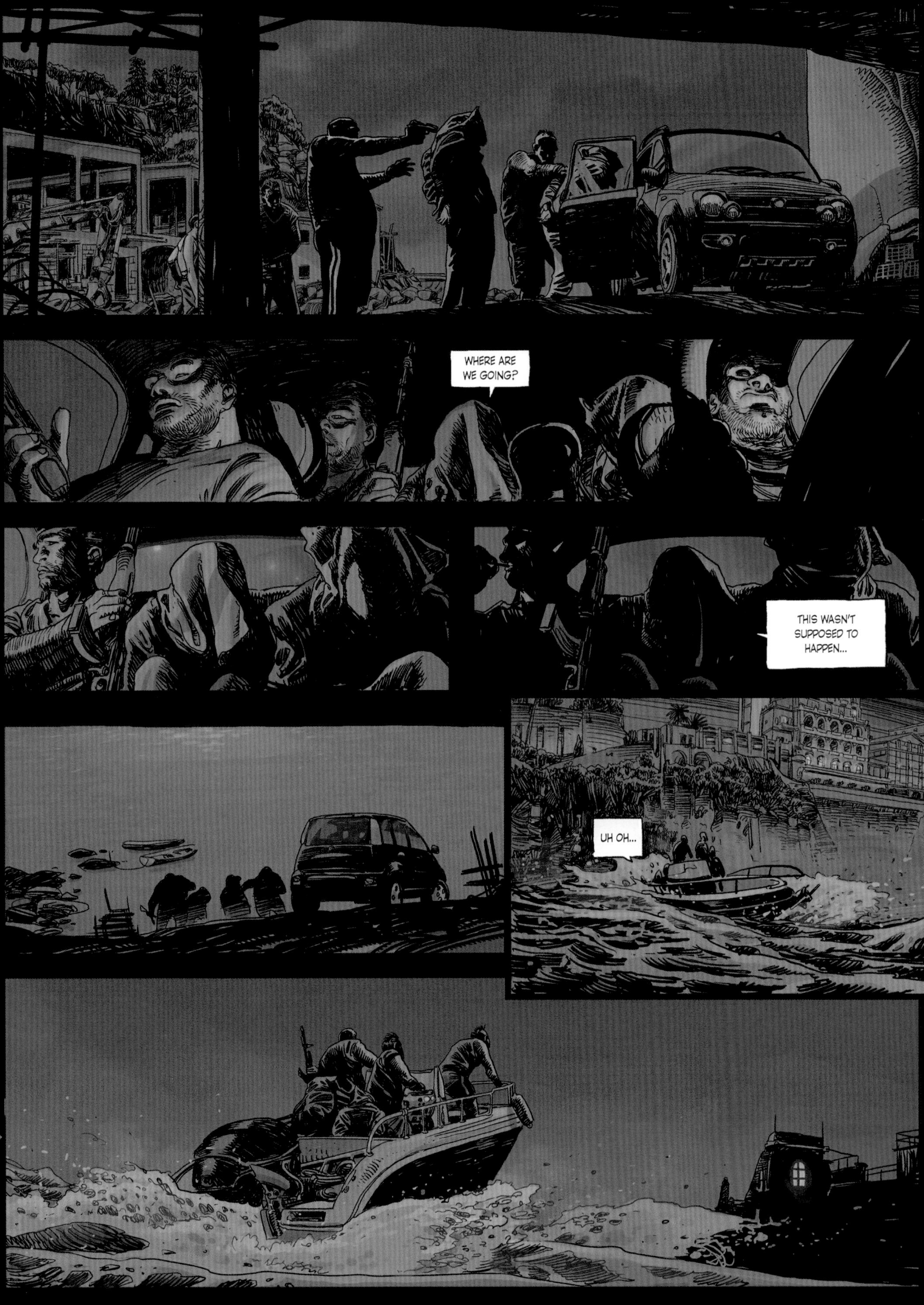
WHERE ARE WE GOING?
THIS WASN'T SUPPOSED TO HAPPEN...
UH OH...

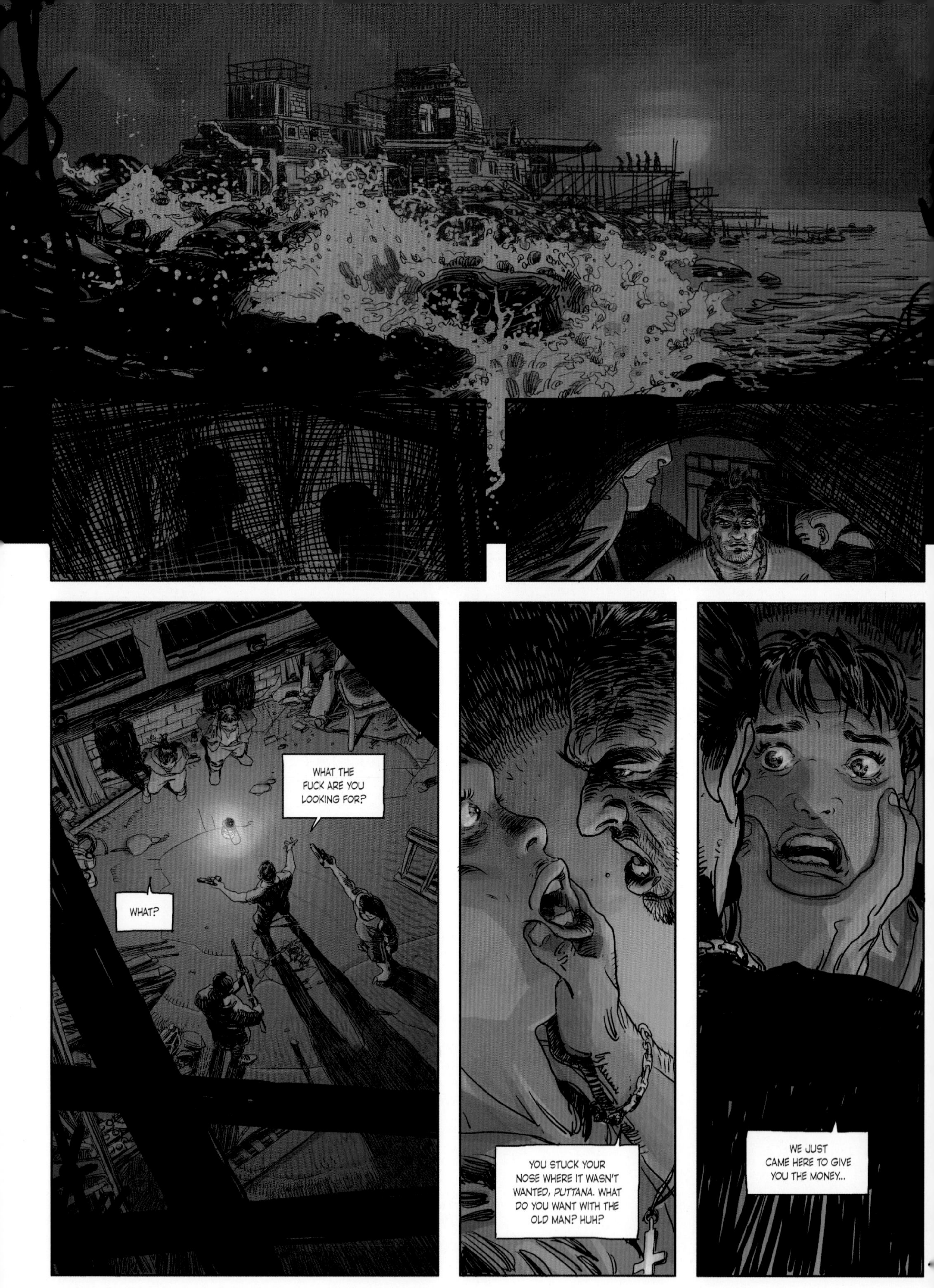
WHAT THE FUCK ARE YOU LOOKING FOR?
WHAT?
YOU STUCK YOUR NOSE WHERE IT WASN'T WANTED, *PUTTANA*. WHAT DO YOU WANT WITH THE OLD MAN? HUH?
WE JUST CAME HERE TO GIVE YOU THE MONEY...

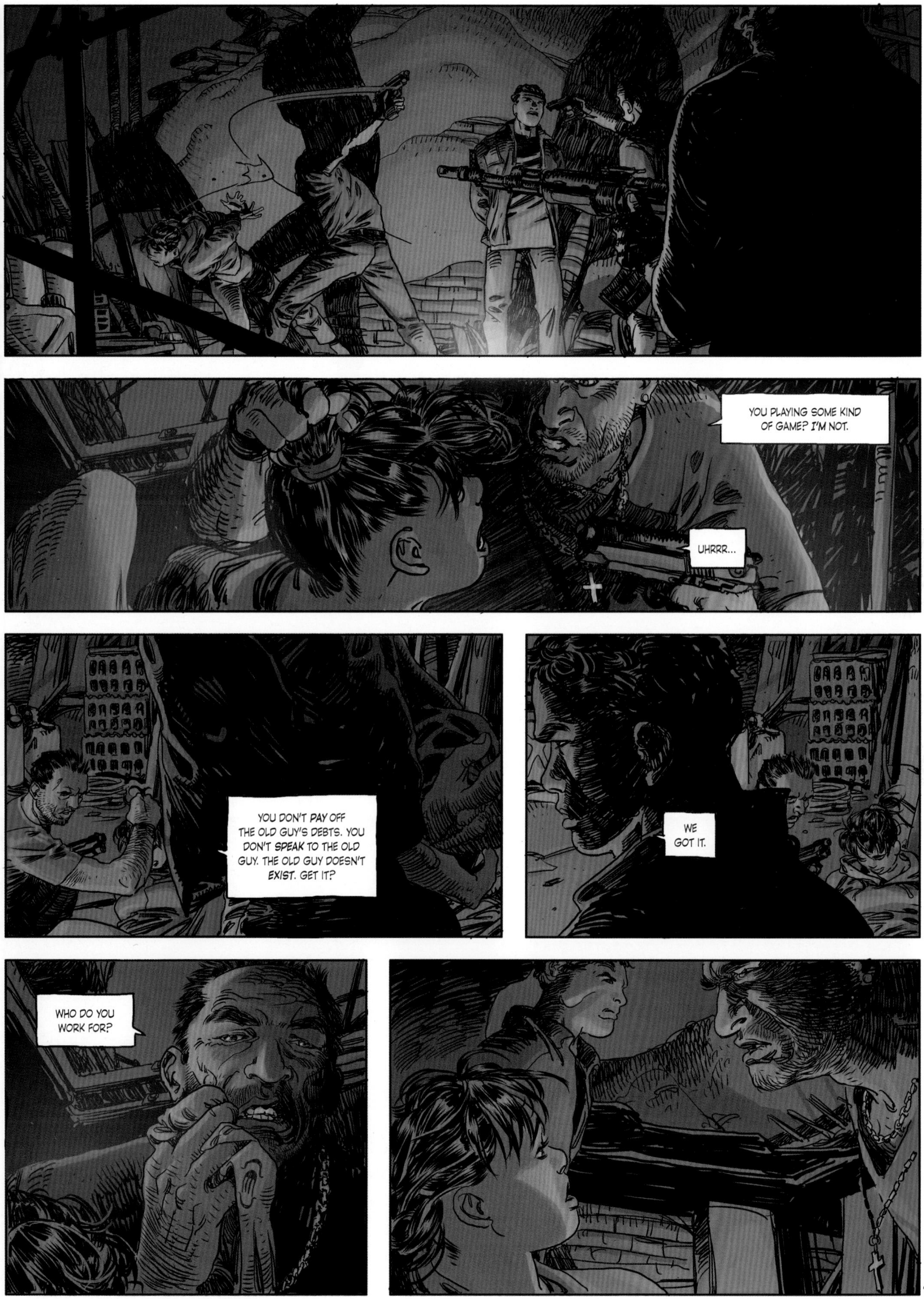
YOU PLAYING SOME KIND OF GAME? I'M NOT.
UHRRR...
YOU DON'T PAY OFF THE OLD GUY'S DEBTS. YOU DON'T SPEAK TO THE OLD GUY. THE OLD GUY DOESN'T EXIST. GET IT?
WE GOT IT.
WHO DO YOU WORK FOR?

I WAS TOLD TO KILL ONE OF YOU TO MAKE AN *EXAMPLE*. BUT I'M GOING TO KILL *BOTH* OF YOU IF YOU DON'T SPEAK UP...

LE- LEVIATHAN FINANCING.

GOOD. ONLY ONE THEN...

PLEASE... NO...

NO...

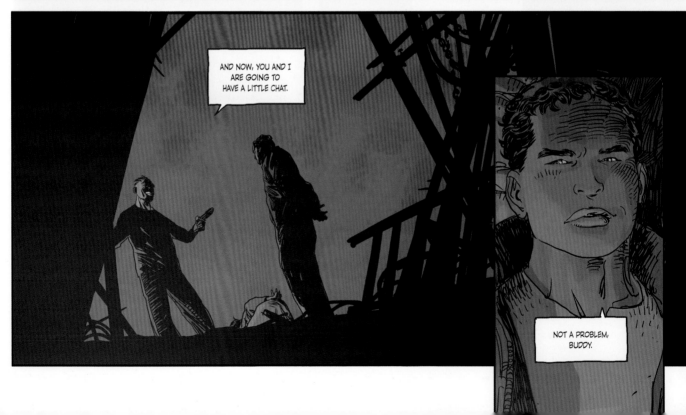

AND NOW, YOU AND I ARE GOING TO HAVE A LITTLE CHAT.

NOT A PROBLEM, BUDDY.

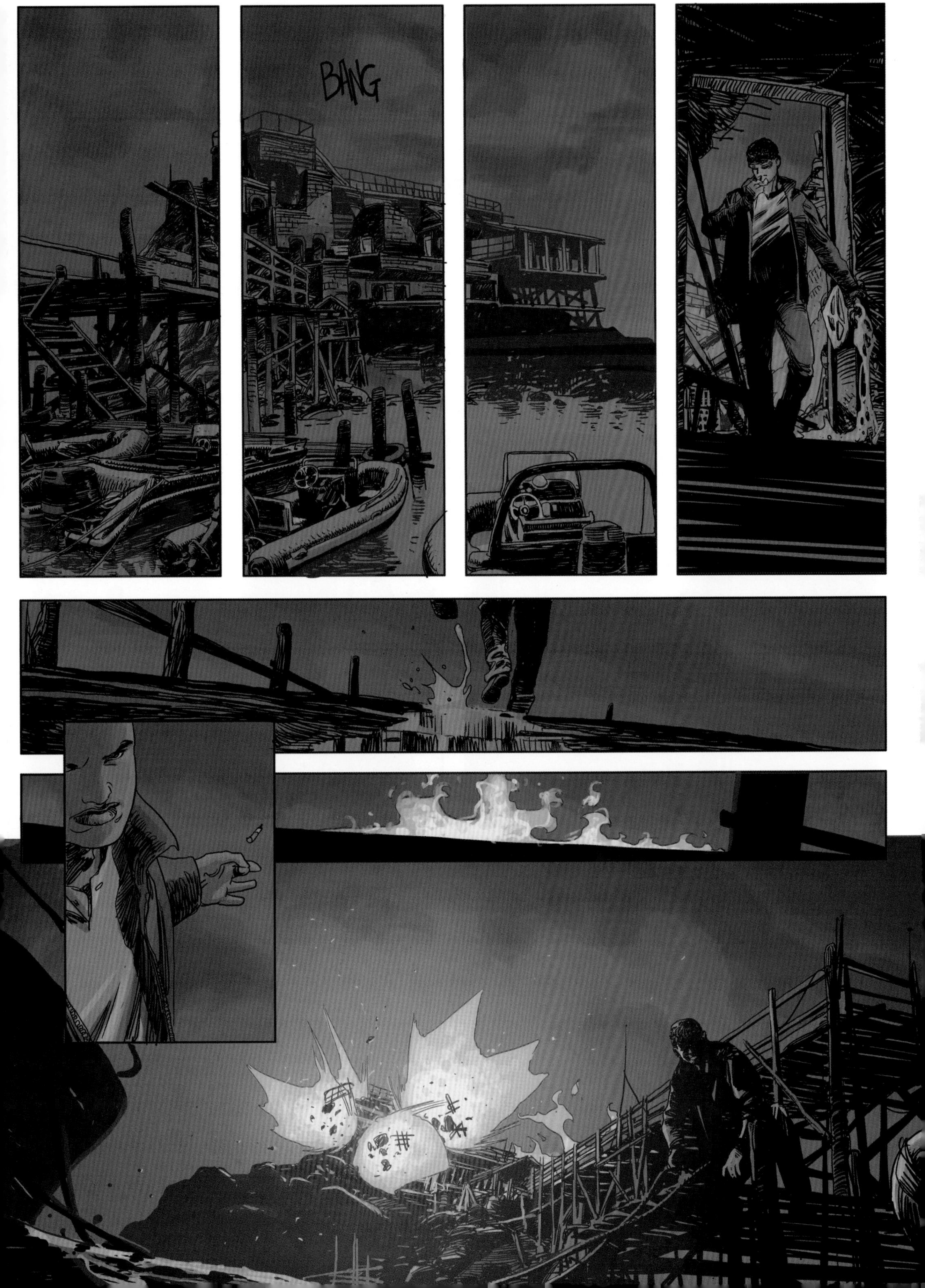
BANG

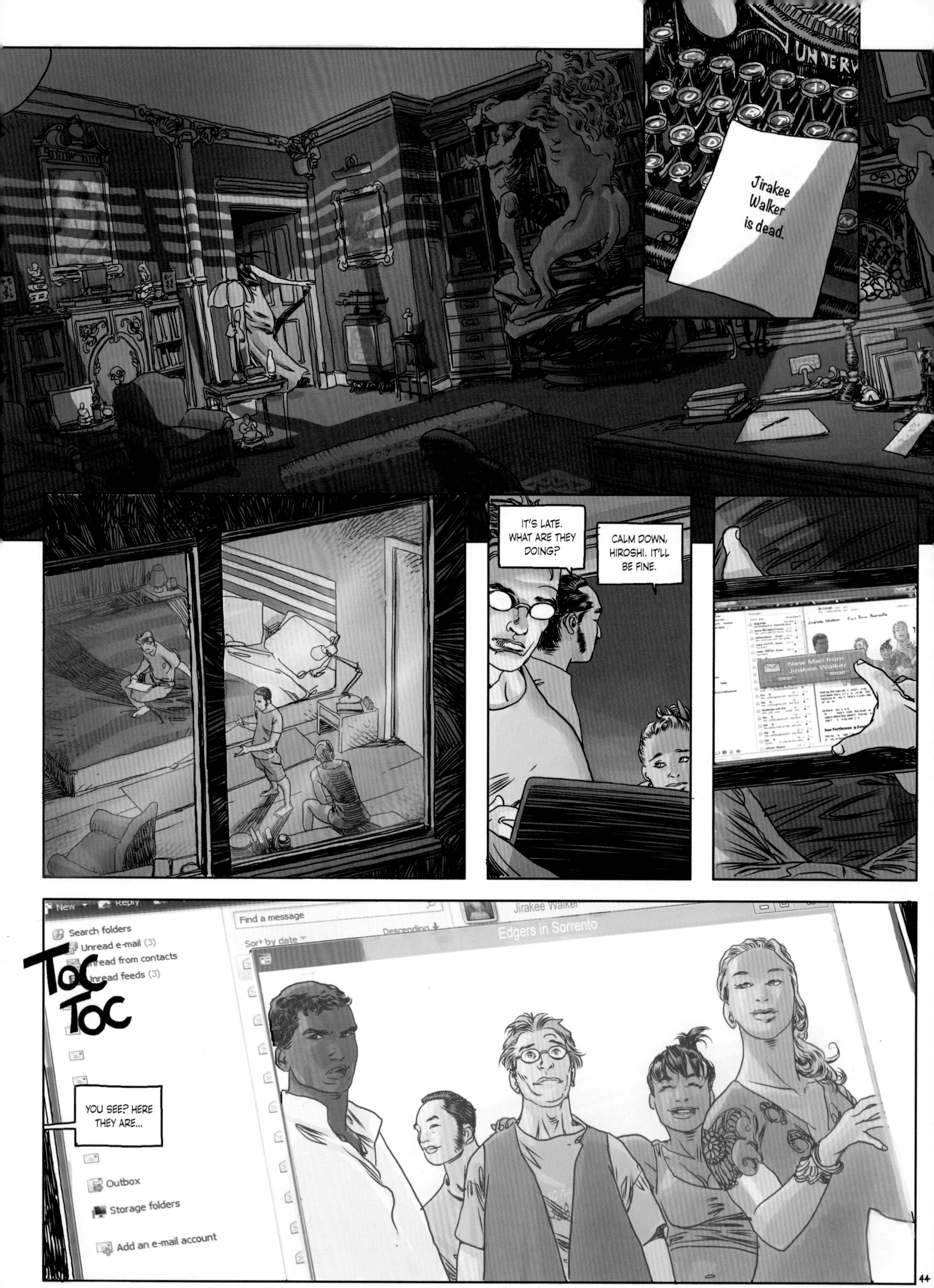
Jirakee Walker is dead.
IT'S LATE. WHAT ARE THEY DOING?
CALM DOWN, HIROSHI. IT'LL BE FINE.
New Mail from Jirakee Walker
Skip
Read
New
Reply
Search folders
Unread e-mail (3)
Unread from contacts
Unread feeds (3)
Find a message
Sort by date
Descending
Jirakee Walker
Edgers in Sorrento
TOC TOC
YOU SEE? HERE THEY ARE...
Outbox
Storage folders
Add an e-mail account

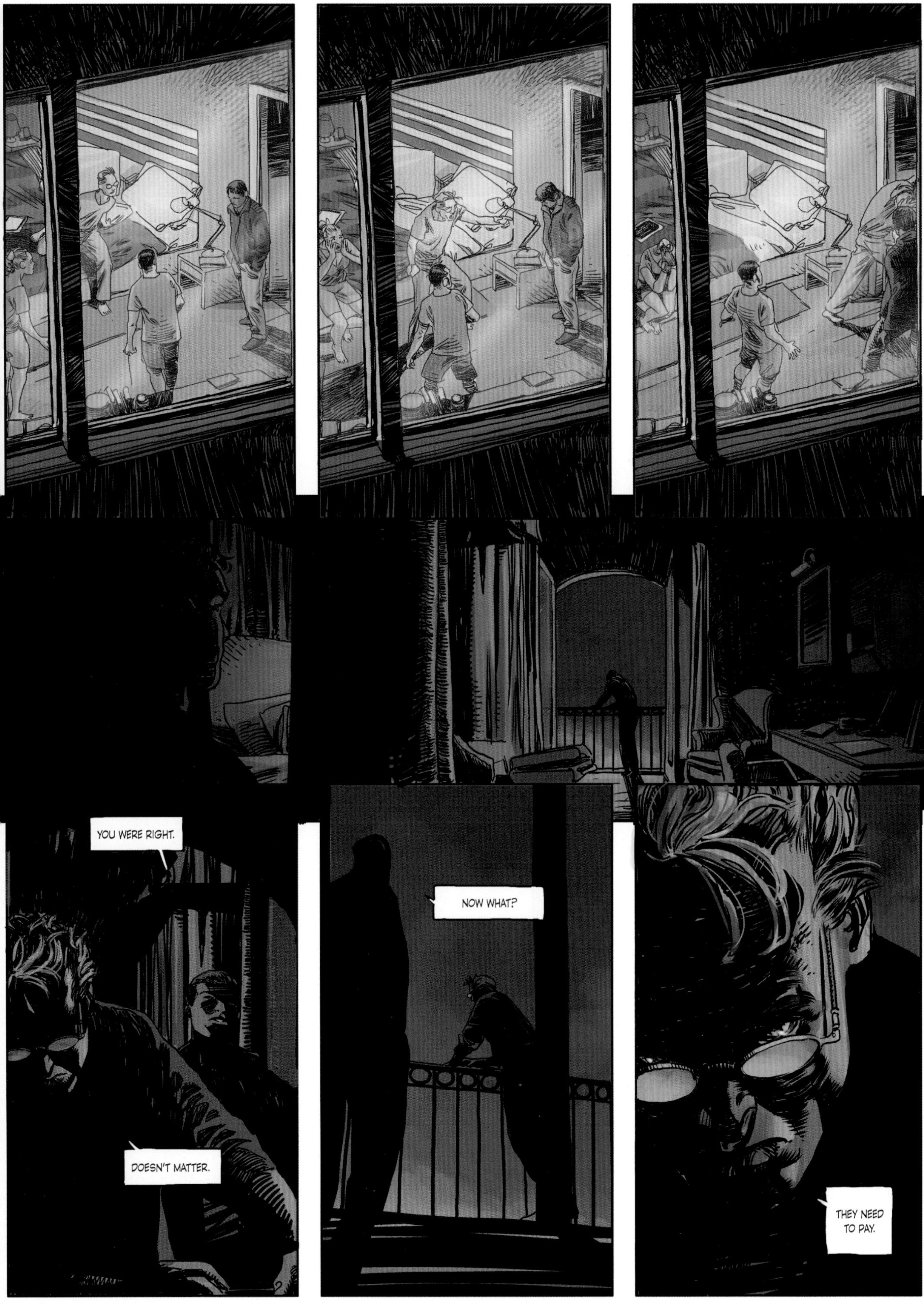
YOU WERE RIGHT.
DOESN'T MATTER.
NOW WHAT?
THEY NEED TO PAY.

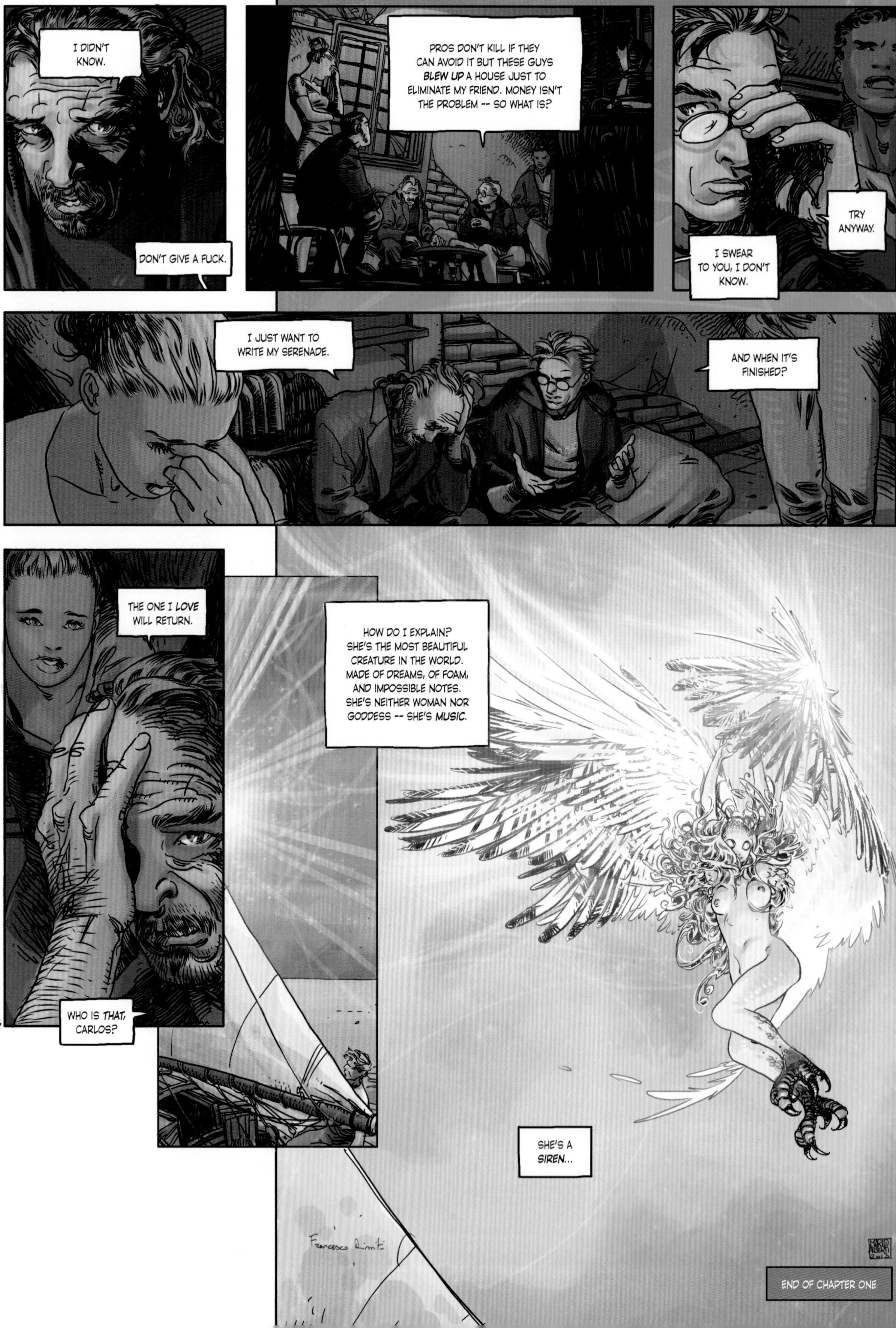
I DIDN'T KNOW.
DON'T GIVE A FUCK.
PROS DON'T KILL IF THEY CAN AVOID IT BUT THESE GUYS BLEW UP A HOUSE JUST TO ELIMINATE MY FRIEND. MONEY ISN'T THE PROBLEM -- SO WHAT IS?
I SWEAR TO YOU, I DON'T KNOW.
TRY ANYWAY.
I JUST WANT TO WRITE MY SERENADE.
AND WHEN IT'S FINISHED?
THE ONE I LOVE WILL RETURN.
WHO IS THAT, CARLOS?
HOW DO I EXPLAIN? SHE'S THE MOST BEAUTIFUL CREATURE IN THE WORLD. MADE OF DREAMS, OF FOAM, AND IMPOSSIBLE NOTES. SHE'S NEITHER WOMAN NOR GODDESS -- SHE'S MUSIC.
SHE'S A SIREN...
Francesco Rimiti
END OF CHAPTER ONE

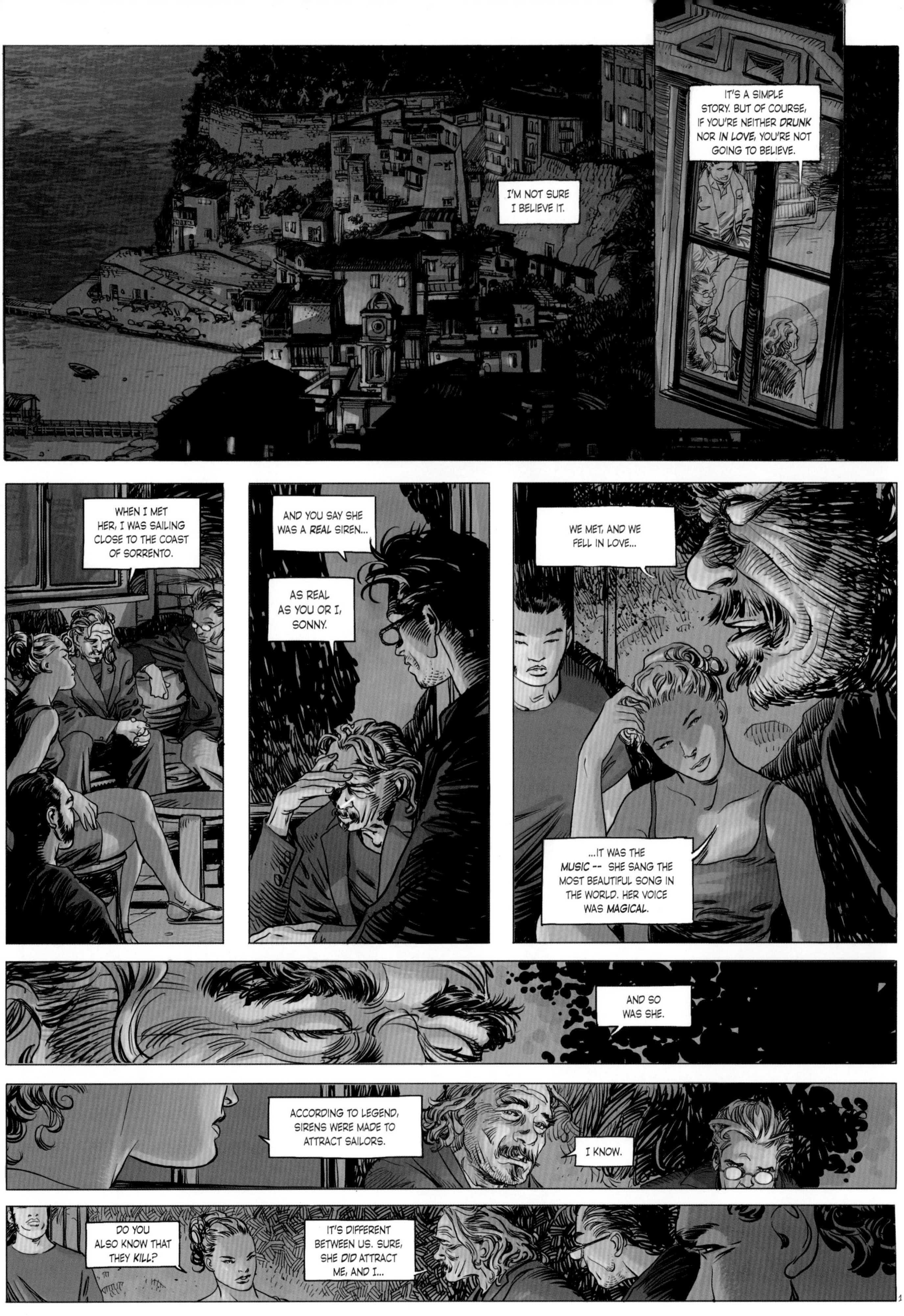
IT'S A SIMPLE STORY. BUT OF COURSE, IF YOU'RE NEITHER DRUNK NOR IN LOVE, YOU'RE NOT GOING TO BELIEVE.
I'M NOT SURE I BELIEVE IT.
WHEN I MET HER, I WAS SAILING CLOSE TO THE COAST OF SORRENTO.
AND YOU SAY SHE WAS A REAL SIREN...
AS REAL AS YOU OR I, SONNY.
WE MET, AND WE FELL IN LOVE...
...IT WAS THE MUSIC -- SHE SANG THE MOST BEAUTIFUL SONG IN THE WORLD. HER VOICE WAS MAGICAL.
AND SO WAS SHE.
ACCORDING TO LEGEND, SIRENS WERE MADE TO ATTRACT SAILORS.
I KNOW.
DO YOU ALSO KNOW THAT THEY KILL?
IT'S DIFFERENT BETWEEN US. SURE, SHE DID ATTRACT ME, AND I...

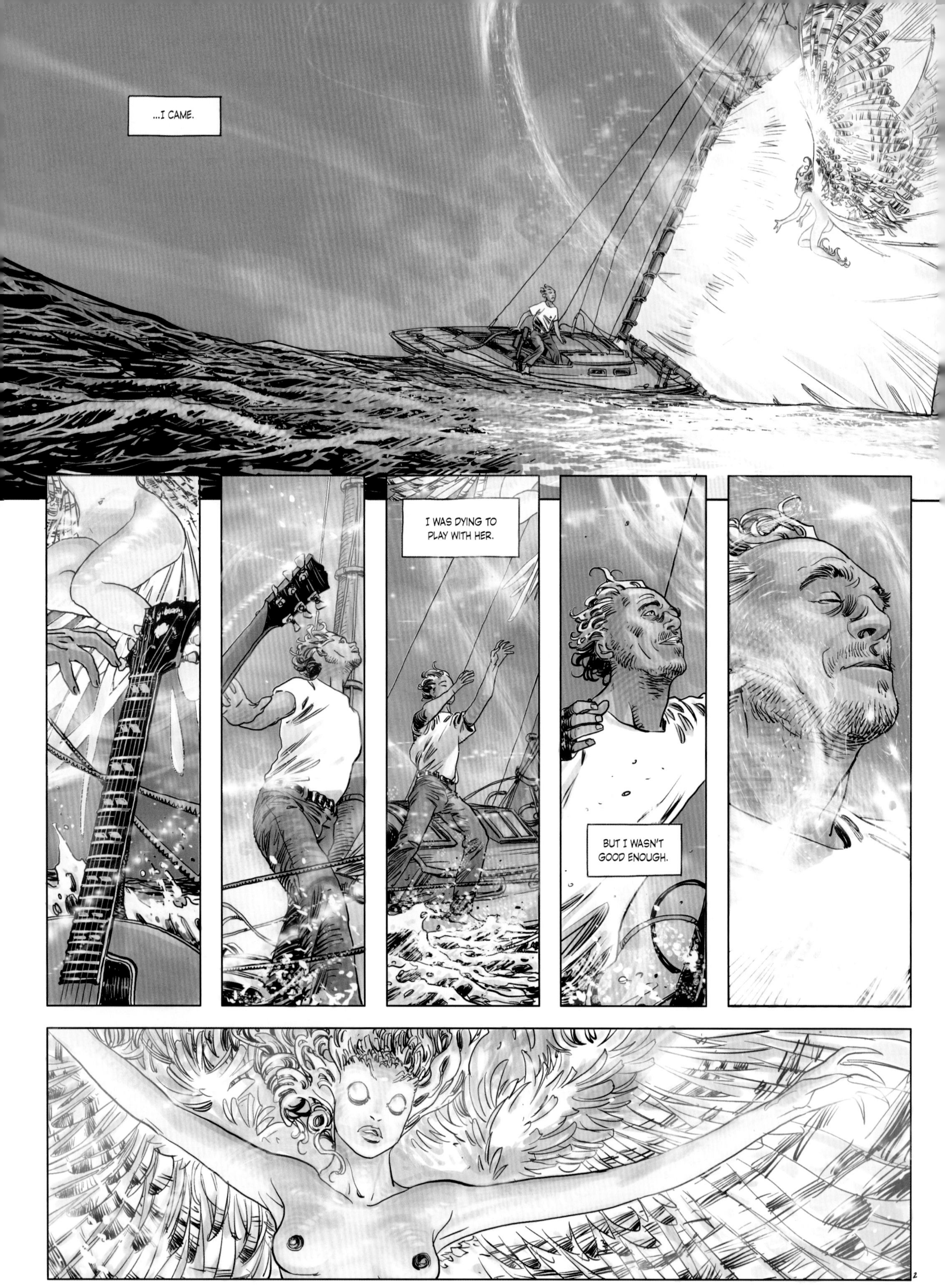
...I CAME.
I WAS DYING TO PLAY WITH HER.
BUT I WASN'T GOOD ENOUGH.

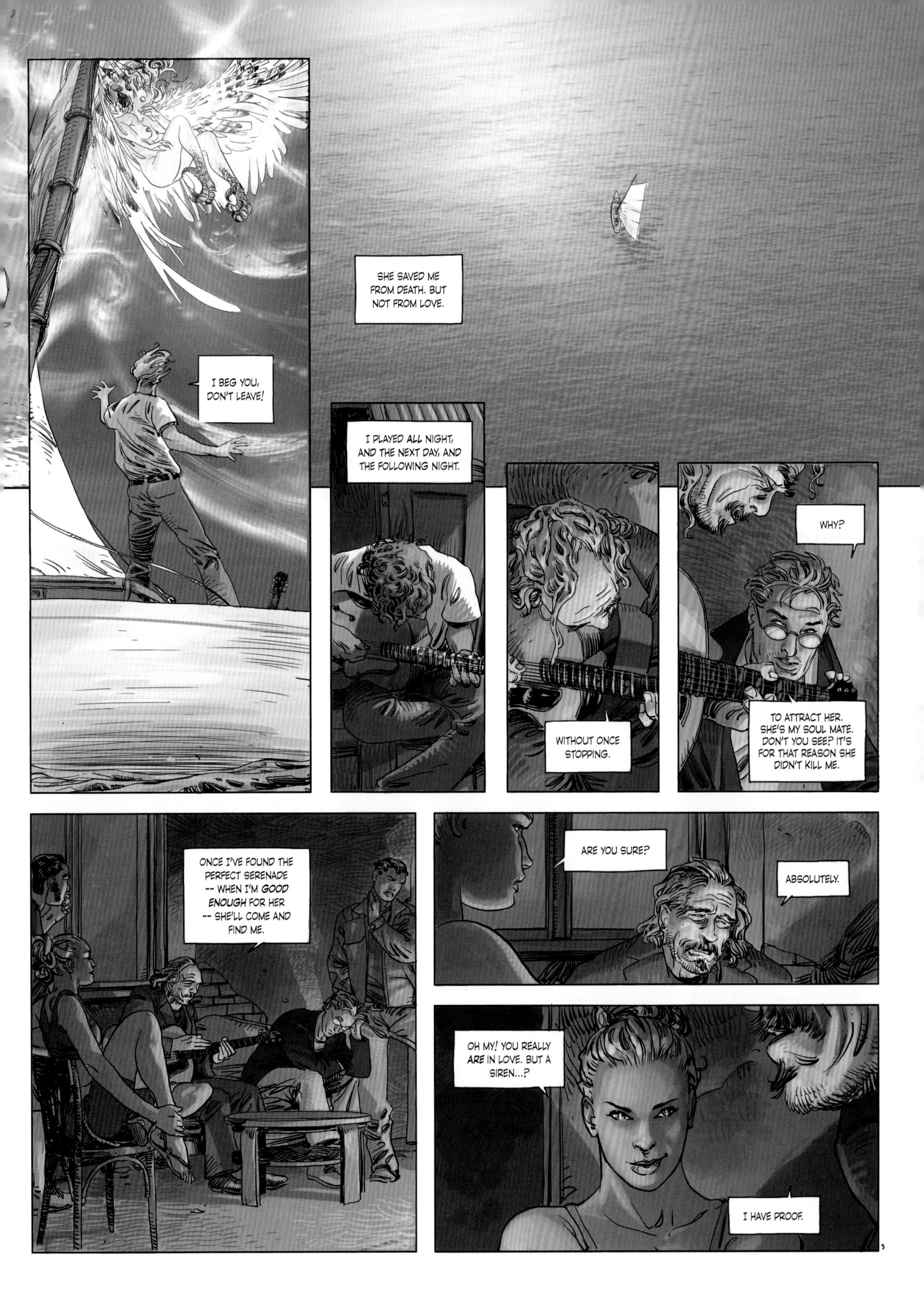
SHE SAVED ME FROM DEATH. BUT NOT FROM LOVE.
I BEG YOU, DON'T LEAVE!
I PLAYED ALL NIGHT, AND THE NEXT DAY, AND THE FOLLOWING NIGHT.
WITHOUT ONCE STOPPING.
WHY?
TO ATTRACT HER. SHE'S MY SOUL MATE. DON'T YOU SEE? IT'S FOR THAT REASON SHE DIDN'T KILL ME.
ONCE I'VE FOUND THE PERFECT SERENADE -- WHEN I'M GOOD ENOUGH FOR HER -- SHE'LL COME AND FIND ME.
ARE YOU SURE?
ABSOLUTELY.
OH MY! YOU REALLY ARE IN LOVE. BUT A SIREN...?
I HAVE PROOF.

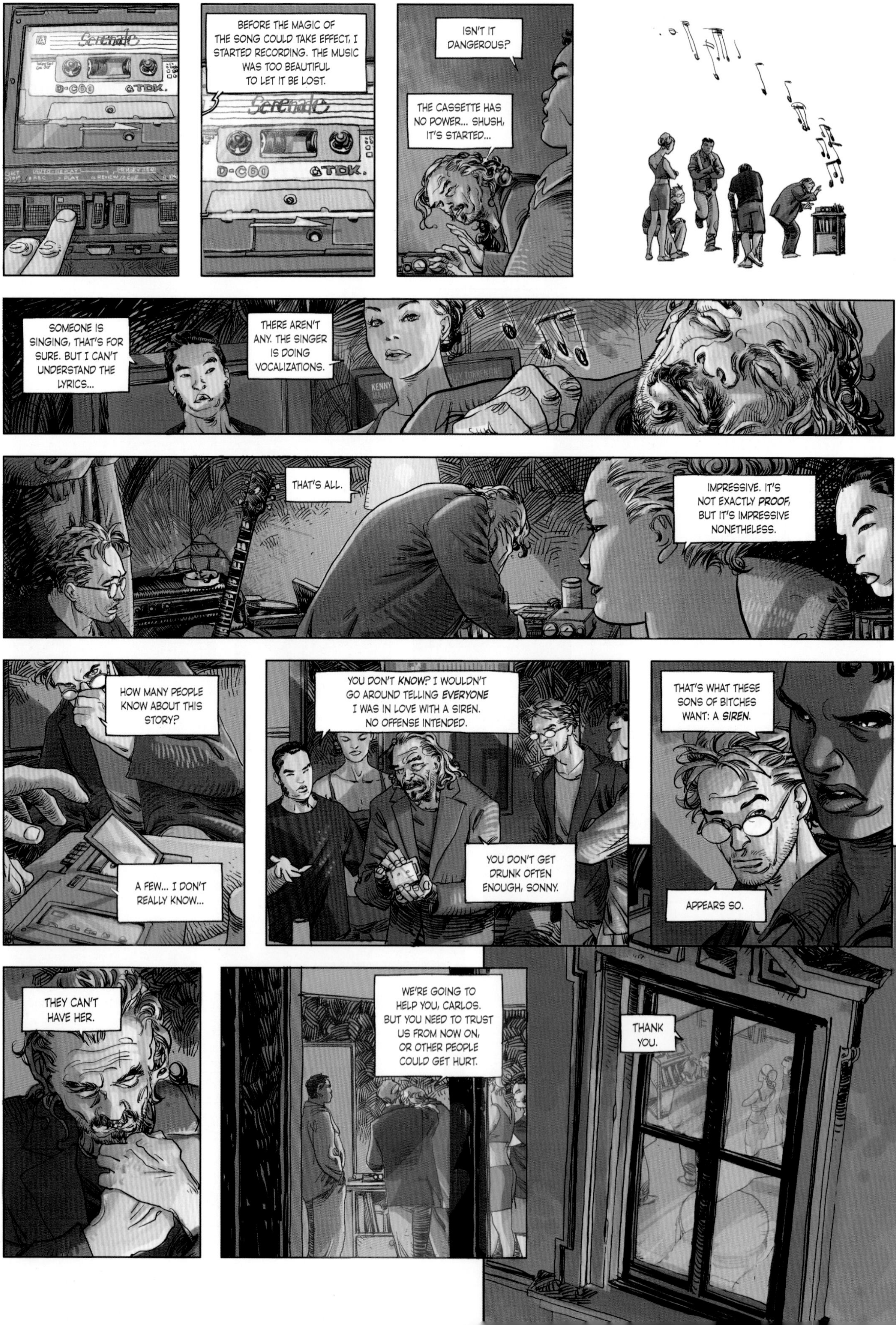

BEFORE THE MAGIC OF THE SONG COULD TAKE EFFECT, I STARTED RECORDING. THE MUSIC WAS TOO BEAUTIFUL TO LET IT BE LOST.
ISN'T IT DANGEROUS?
THE CASSETTE HAS NO POWER... SHUSH, IT'S STARTED...
SOMEONE IS SINGING, THAT'S FOR SURE. BUT I CAN'T UNDERSTAND THE LYRICS...
THERE AREN'T ANY. THE SINGER IS DOING VOCALIZATIONS.
THAT'S ALL.
IMPRESSIVE. IT'S NOT EXACTLY PROOF, BUT IT'S IMPRESSIVE NONETHELESS.
HOW MANY PEOPLE KNOW ABOUT THIS STORY?
A FEW... I DON'T REALLY KNOW...
YOU DON'T KNOW? I WOULDN'T GO AROUND TELLING EVERYONE I WAS IN LOVE WITH A SIREN. NO OFFENSE INTENDED.
YOU DON'T GET DRUNK OFTEN ENOUGH, SONNY.
THAT'S WHAT THESE SONS OF BITCHES WANT: A SIREN.
APPEARS SO.
THEY CAN'T HAVE HER.
WE'RE GOING TO HELP YOU, CARLOS. BUT YOU NEED TO TRUST US FROM NOW ON, OR OTHER PEOPLE COULD GET HURT.
THANK YOU.

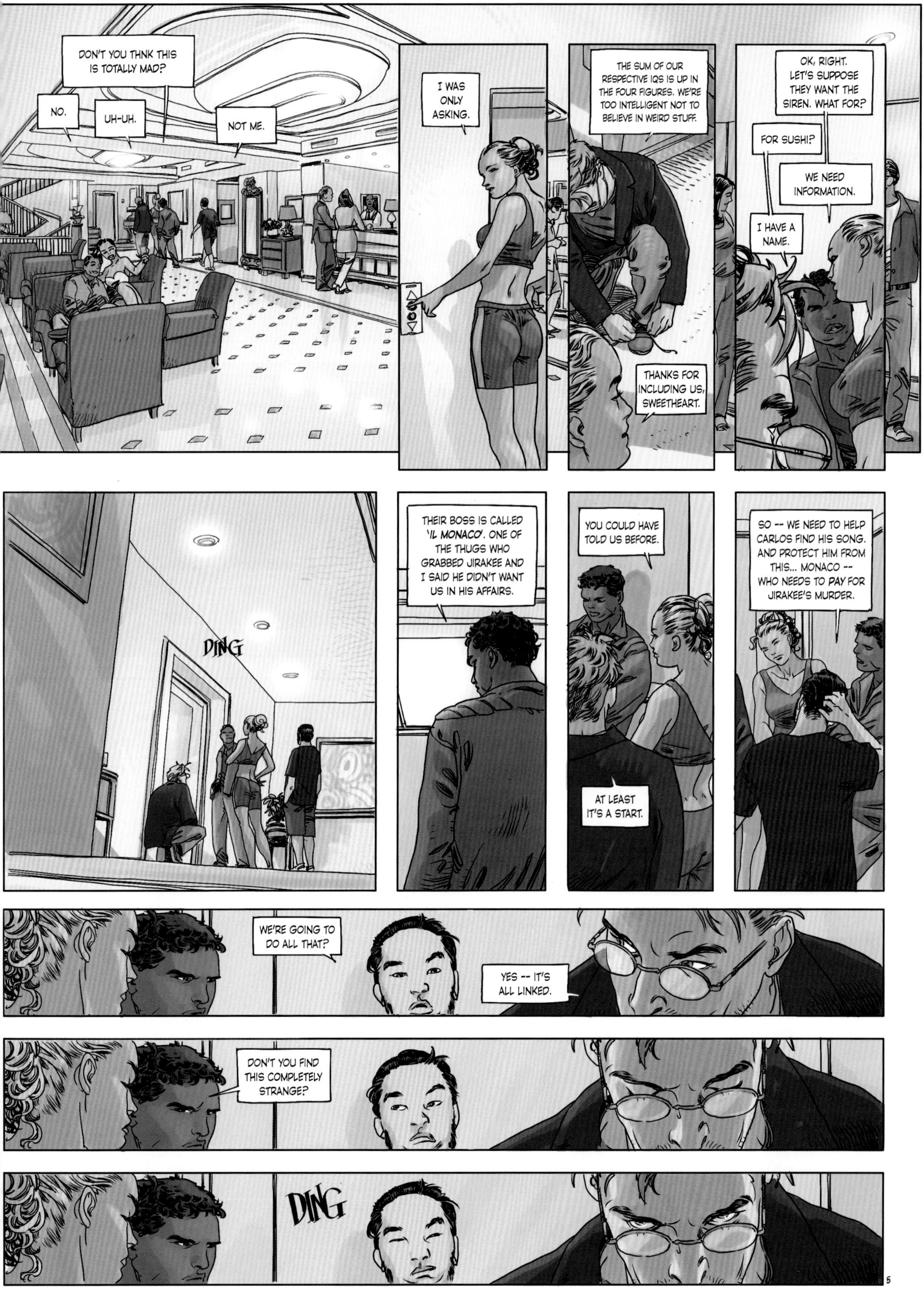
DON'T YOU THNK THIS IS TOTALLY MAD?
NO.
UH-UH.
NOT ME.
I WAS ONLY ASKING.
THE SUM OF OUR RESPECTIVE IQS IS UP IN THE FOUR FIGURES. WE'RE TOO INTELLIGENT NOT TO BELIEVE IN WEIRD STUFF.
THANKS FOR INCLUDING US, SWEETHEART.
OK, RIGHT. LET'S SUPPOSE THEY WANT THE SIREN. WHAT FOR?
FOR SUSHI?
WE NEED INFORMATION.
I HAVE A NAME.
DING
THEIR BOSS IS CALLED 'IL MONACO'. ONE OF THE THUGS WHO GRABBED JIRAKEE AND I SAID HE DIDN'T WANT US IN HIS AFFAIRS.
YOU COULD HAVE TOLD US BEFORE.
AT LEAST IT'S A START.
SO -- WE NEED TO HELP CARLOS FIND HIS SONG. AND PROTECT HIM FROM THIS... MONACO -- WHO NEEDS TO PAY FOR JIRAKEE'S MURDER.
WE'RE GOING TO DO ALL THAT?
YES -- IT'S ALL LINKED.
DON'T YOU FIND THIS COMPLETELY STRANGE?
DING

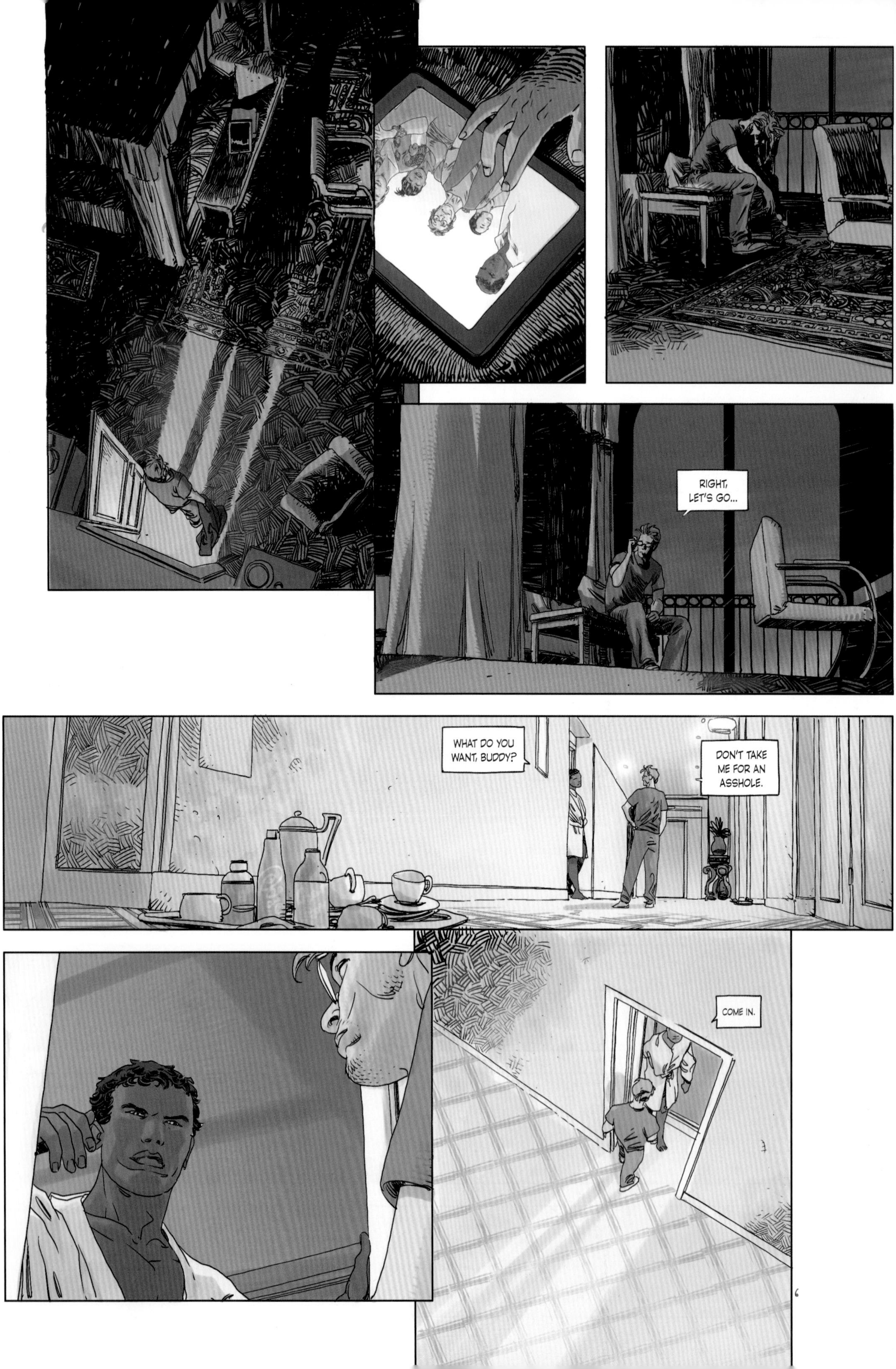
RIGHT, LET'S GO...
WHAT DO YOU WANT, BUDDY?
DON'T TAKE ME FOR AN ASSHOLE.
COME IN.

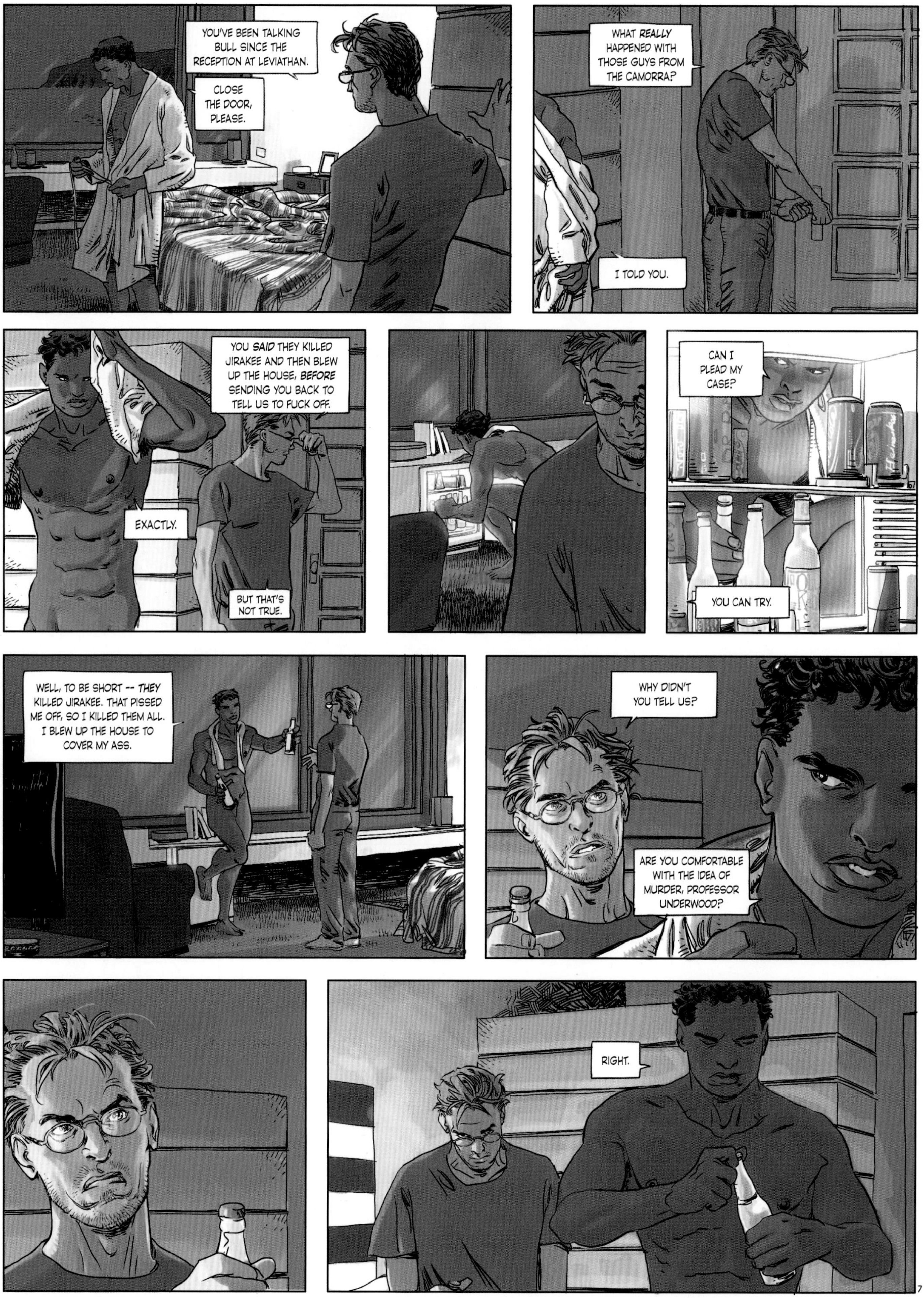
YOU'VE BEEN TALKING BULL SINCE THE RECEPTION AT LEVIATHAN.
CLOSE THE DOOR, PLEASE.
WHAT REALLY HAPPENED WITH THOSE GUYS FROM THE CAMORRA?
I TOLD YOU.
YOU SAID THEY KILLED JIRAKEE AND THEN BLEW UP THE HOUSE, BEFORE SENDING YOU BACK TO TELL US TO FUCK OFF.
EXACTLY.
BUT THAT'S NOT TRUE.
CAN I PLEAD MY CASE?
YOU CAN TRY.
WELL, TO BE SHORT -- THEY KILLED JIRAKEE. THAT PISSED ME OFF, SO I KILLED THEM ALL. I BLEW UP THE HOUSE TO COVER MY ASS.
WHY DIDN'T YOU TELL US?
ARE YOU COMFORTABLE WITH THE IDEA OF MURDER, PROFESSOR UNDERWOOD?
RIGHT.

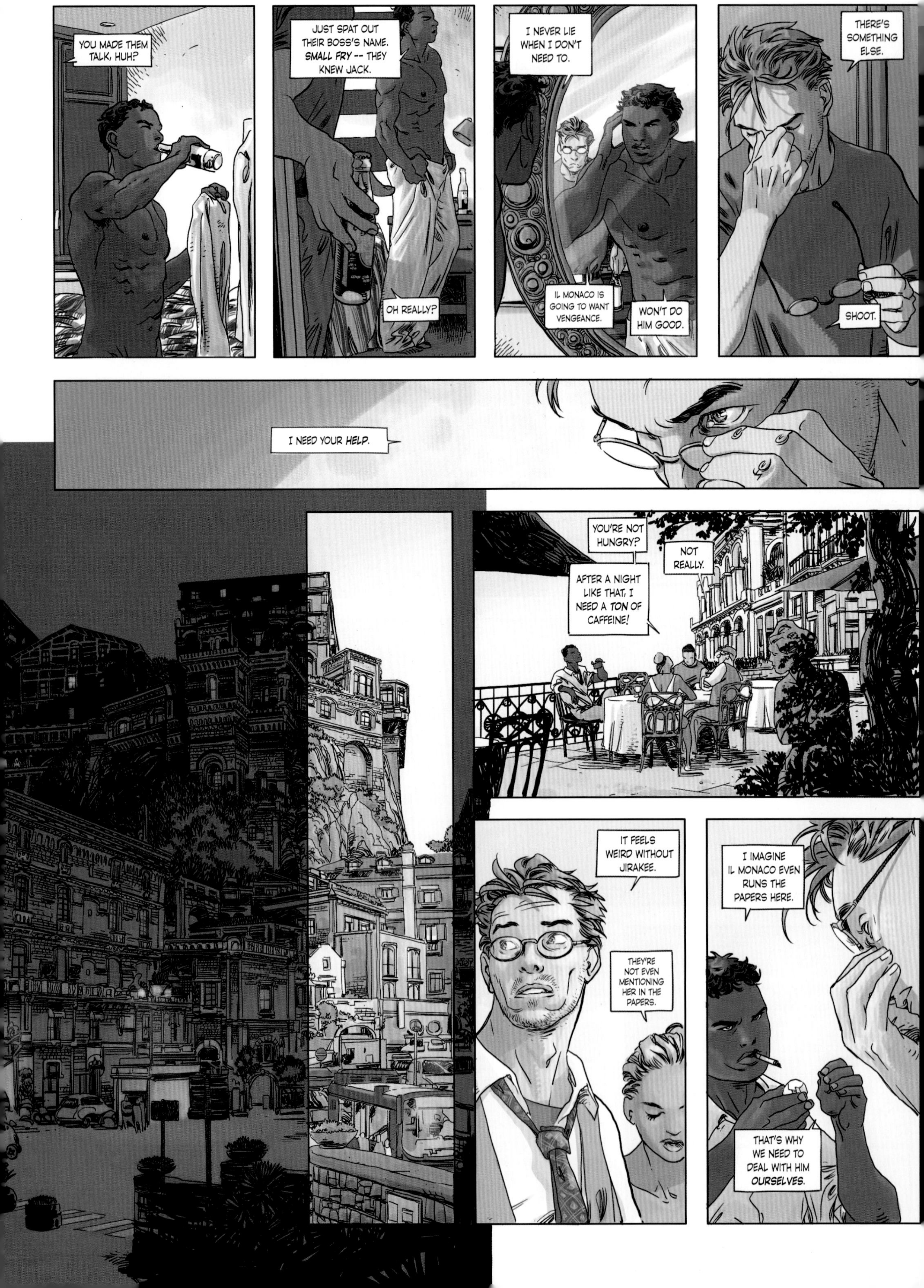
YOU MADE THEM TALK, HUH?
JUST SPAT OUT THEIR BOSS'S NAME. SMALL FRY -- THEY KNEW JACK.
OH REALLY?
I NEVER LIE WHEN I DON'T NEED TO.
IL MONACO IS GOING TO WANT VENGEANCE.
WON'T DO HIM GOOD.
THERE'S SOMETHING ELSE.
SHOOT.
I NEED YOUR HELP.
YOU'RE NOT HUNGRY?
AFTER A NIGHT LIKE THAT, I NEED A TON OF CAFFEINE!
NOT REALLY.
IT FEELS WEIRD WITHOUT JIRAKEE.
THEY'RE NOT EVEN MENTIONING HER IN THE PAPERS.
I IMAGINE IL MONACO EVEN RUNS THE PAPERS HERE.
THAT'S WHY WE NEED TO DEAL WITH HIM OURSELVES.

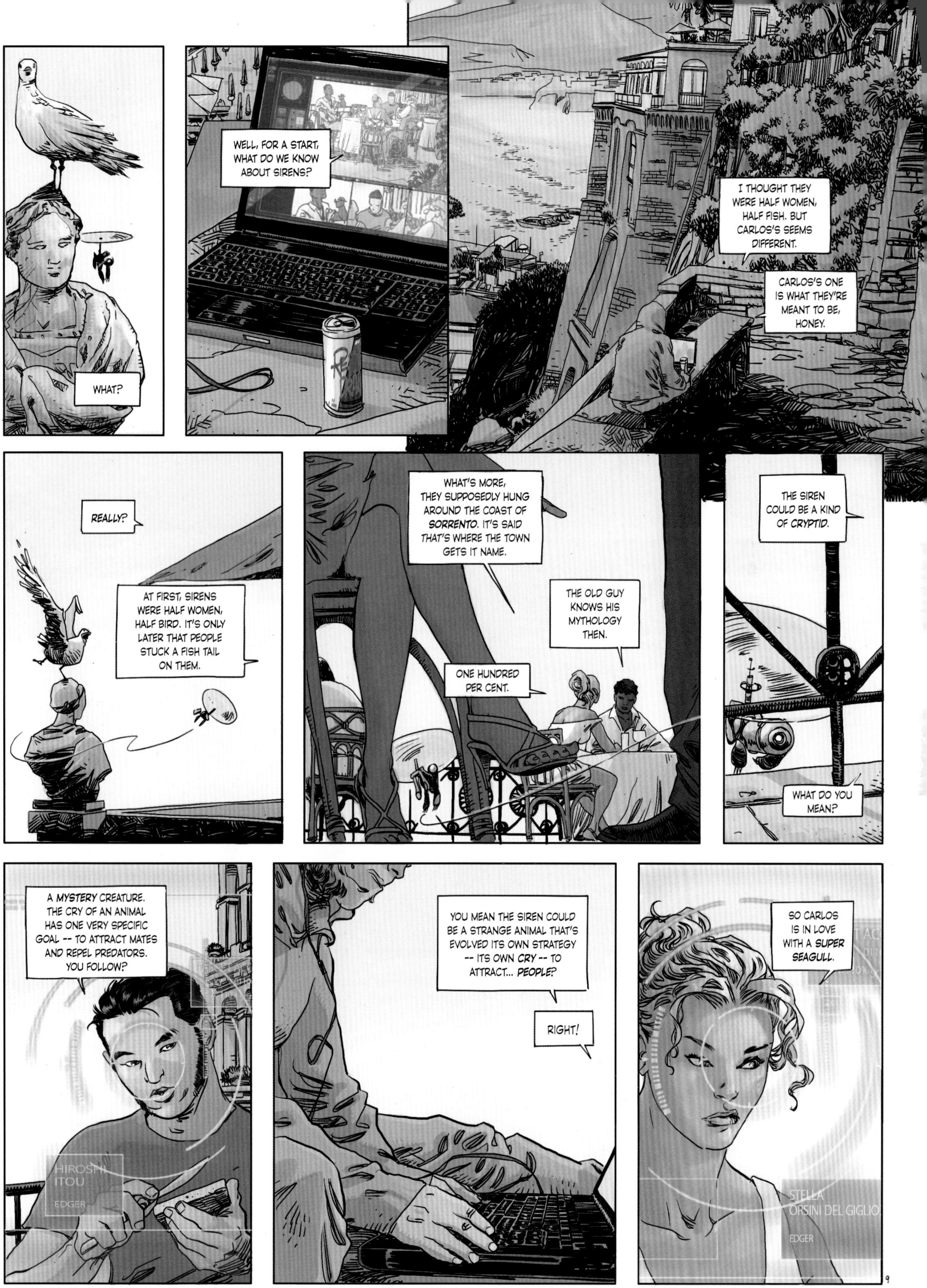
WHAT?
WELL, FOR A START, WHAT DO WE KNOW ABOUT SIRENS?
I THOUGHT THEY WERE HALF WOMEN, HALF FISH. BUT CARLOS'S SEEMS DIFFERENT.
CARLOS'S ONE IS WHAT THEY'RE MEANT TO BE, HONEY.
REALLY?
AT FIRST, SIRENS WERE HALF WOMEN, HALF BIRD. IT'S ONLY LATER THAT PEOPLE STUCK A FISH TAIL ON THEM.
WHAT'S MORE, THEY SUPPOSEDLY HUNG AROUND THE COAST OF ***SORRENTO***. IT'S SAID *THAT'S* WHERE THE TOWN GETS IT NAME.
THE OLD GUY KNOWS HIS MYTHOLOGY THEN.
ONE HUNDRED PER CENT.
THE SIREN COULD BE A KIND OF ***CRYPTID***.
WHAT DO YOU MEAN?
A ***MYSTERY*** CREATURE. THE CRY OF AN ANIMAL HAS ONE VERY SPECIFIC GOAL -- TO ATTRACT MATES AND REPEL PREDATORS. YOU FOLLOW?
HIROSHI ITOU
EDGER
YOU MEAN THE SIREN COULD BE A STRANGE ANIMAL THAT'S EVOLVED ITS OWN STRATEGY -- ITS OWN ***CRY*** -- TO ATTRACT... ***PEOPLE?***
RIGHT!
SO CARLOS IS IN LOVE WITH A ***SUPER SEAGULL***.
STELLA ORSINI DEL GIGLIO
EDGER

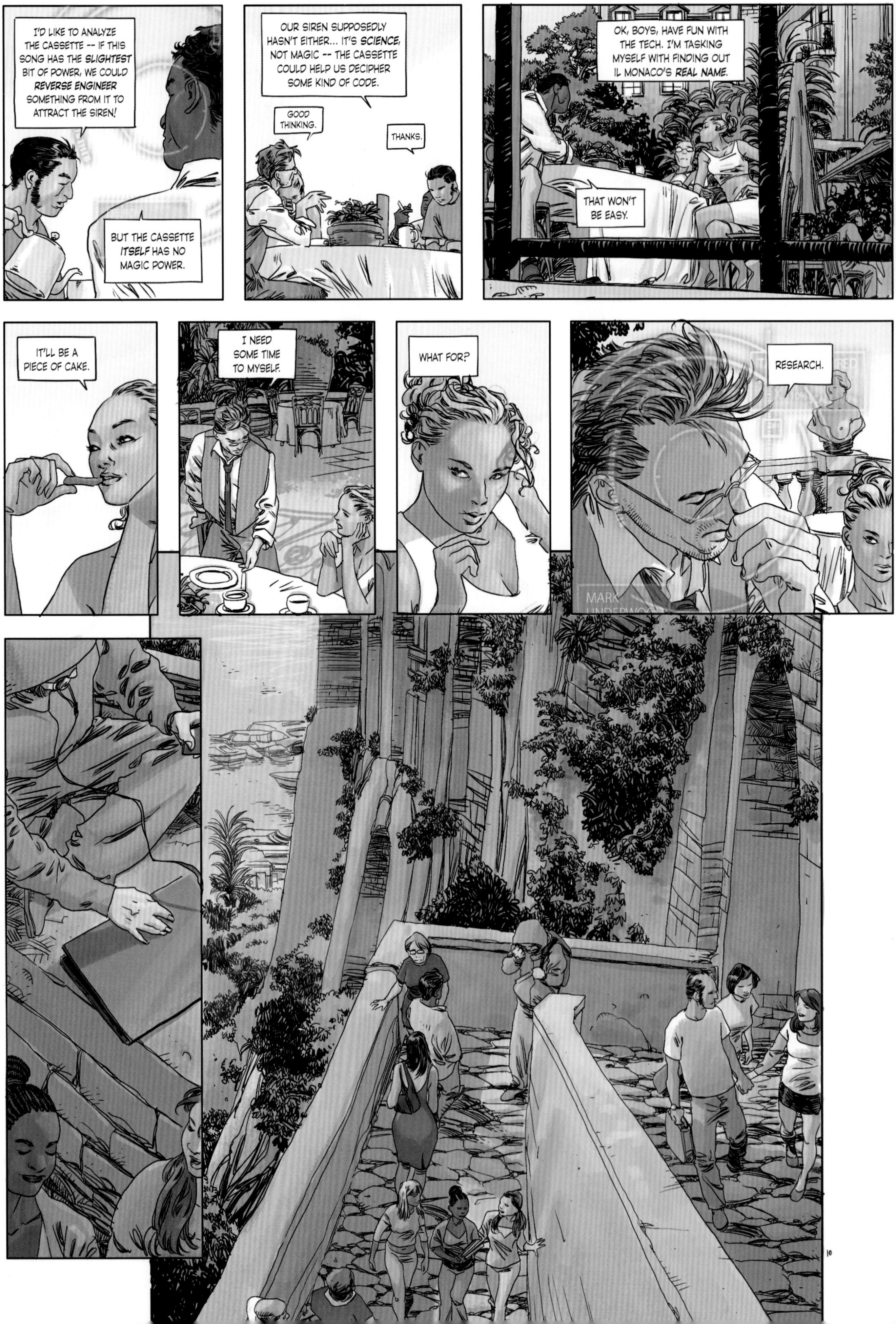
I'D LIKE TO ANALYZE THE CASSETTE -- IF THIS SONG HAS THE SLIGHTEST BIT OF POWER, WE COULD REVERSE ENGINEER SOMETHING FROM IT TO ATTRACT THE SIREN!
BUT THE CASSETTE ITSELF HAS NO MAGIC POWER.
OUR SIREN SUPPOSEDLY HASN'T EITHER... IT'S SCIENCE, NOT MAGIC -- THE CASSETTE COULD HELP US DECIPHER SOME KIND OF CODE.
GOOD THINKING.
THANKS.
OK, BOYS, HAVE FUN WITH THE TECH. I'M TASKING MYSELF WITH FINDING OUT IL MONACO'S REAL NAME.
THAT WON'T BE EASY.
IT'LL BE A PIECE OF CAKE.
I NEED SOME TIME TO MYSELF.
WHAT FOR?
RESEARCH.

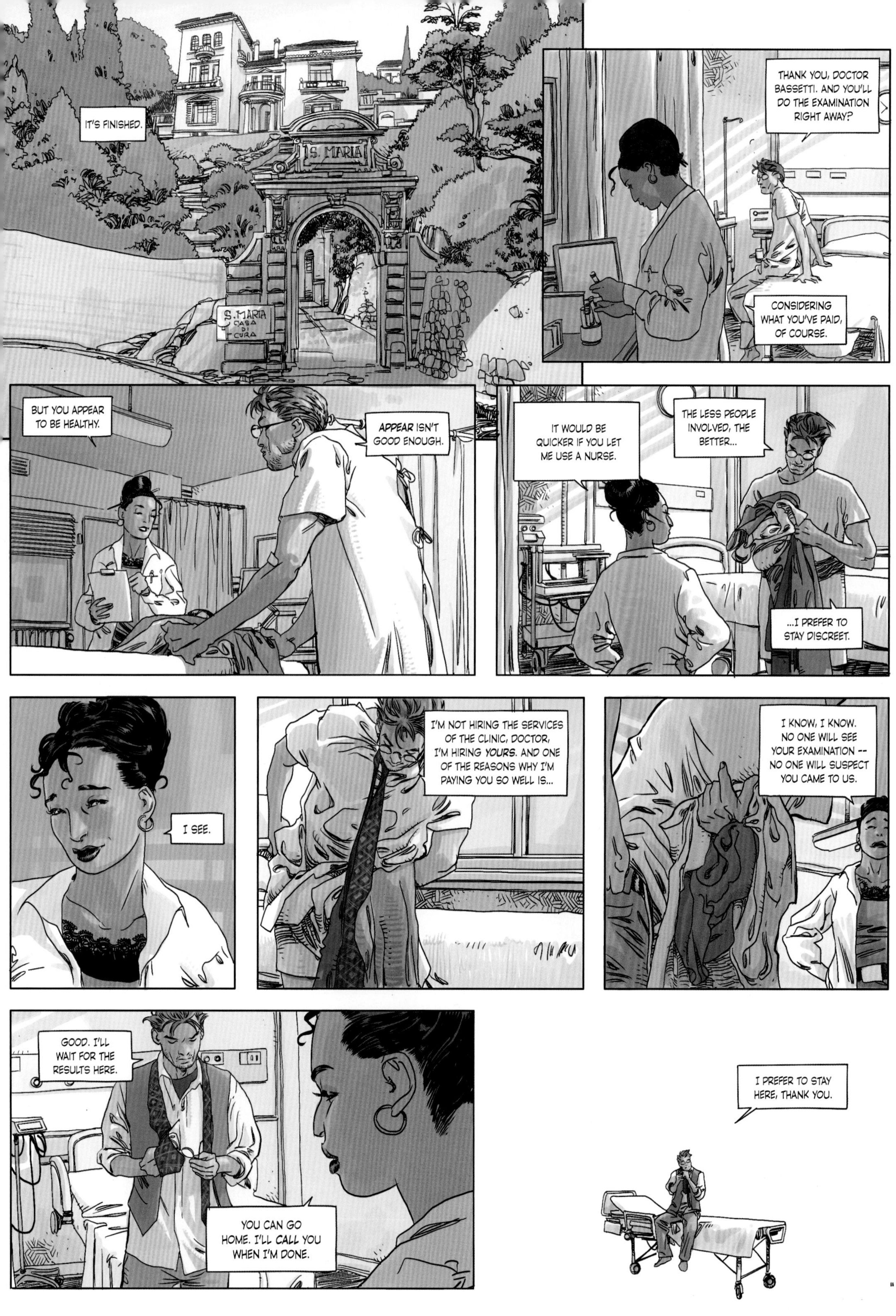
IT'S FINISHED.
THANK YOU, DOCTOR BASSETTI. AND YOU'LL DO THE EXAMINATION RIGHT AWAY?
CONSIDERING WHAT YOU'VE PAID, OF COURSE.
BUT YOU APPEAR TO BE HEALTHY.
APPEAR ISN'T GOOD ENOUGH.
IT WOULD BE QUICKER IF YOU LET ME USE A NURSE.
THE LESS PEOPLE INVOLVED, THE BETTER...
...I PREFER TO STAY DISCREET.
I SEE.
I'M NOT HIRING THE SERVICES OF THE CLINIC, DOCTOR, I'M HIRING YOURS. AND ONE OF THE REASONS WHY I'M PAYING YOU SO WELL IS...
I KNOW, I KNOW. NO ONE WILL SEE YOUR EXAMINATION -- NO ONE WILL SUSPECT YOU CAME TO US.
GOOD. I'LL WAIT FOR THE RESULTS HERE.
YOU CAN GO HOME. I'LL CALL YOU WHEN I'M DONE.
I PREFER TO STAY HERE, THANK YOU.

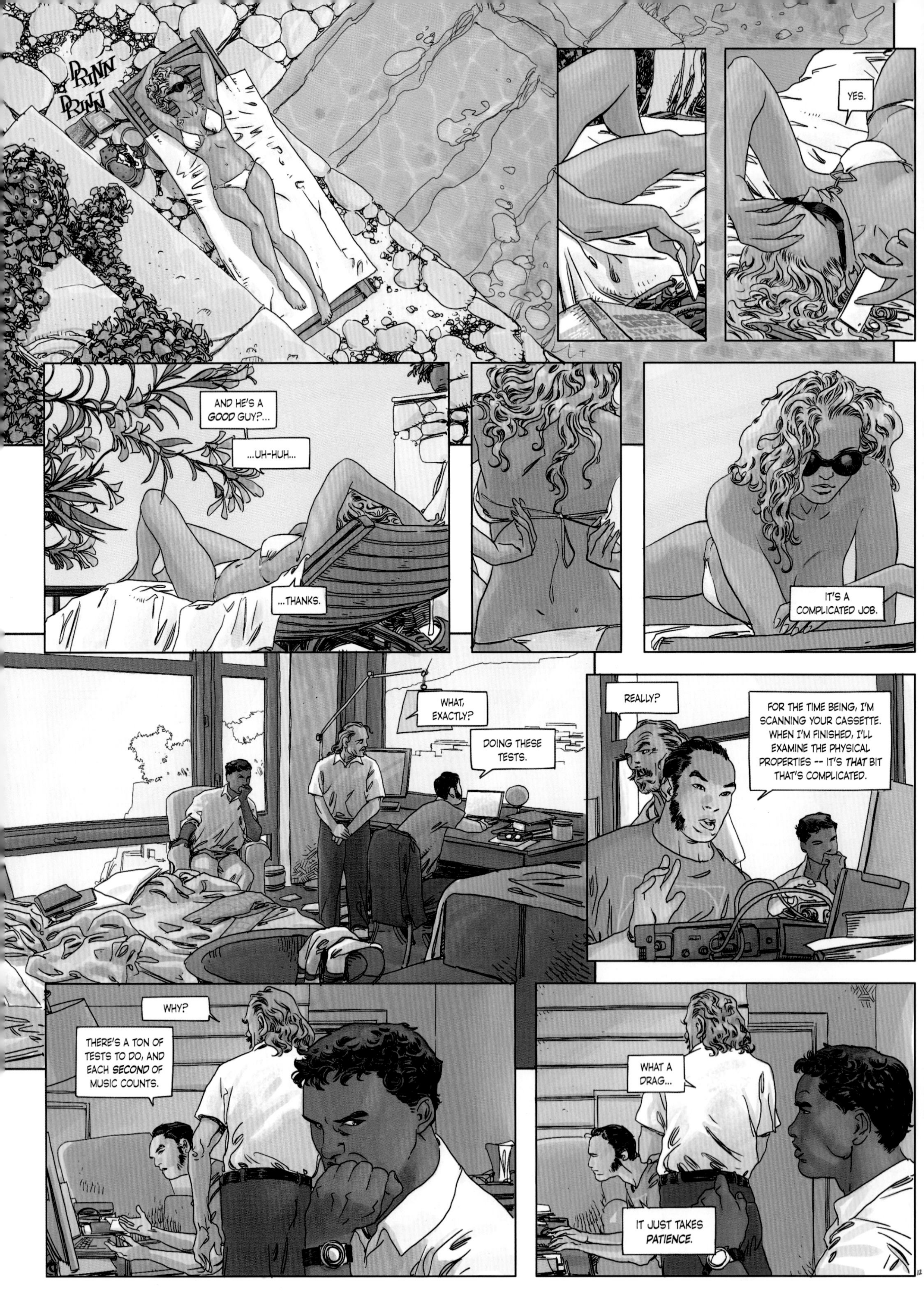
PRINN
PRINN
YES.
AND HE'S A GOOD GUY?...
...UH-HUH...
...THANKS.
IT'S A COMPLICATED JOB.
WHAT, EXACTLY?
DOING THESE TESTS.
REALLY?
FOR THE TIME BEING, I'M SCANNING YOUR CASSETTE. WHEN I'M FINISHED, I'LL EXAMINE THE PHYSICAL PROPERTIES -- IT'S THAT BIT THAT'S COMPLICATED.
WHY?
THERE'S A TON OF TESTS TO DO, AND EACH SECOND OF MUSIC COUNTS.
WHAT A DRAG...
IT JUST TAKES PATIENCE.

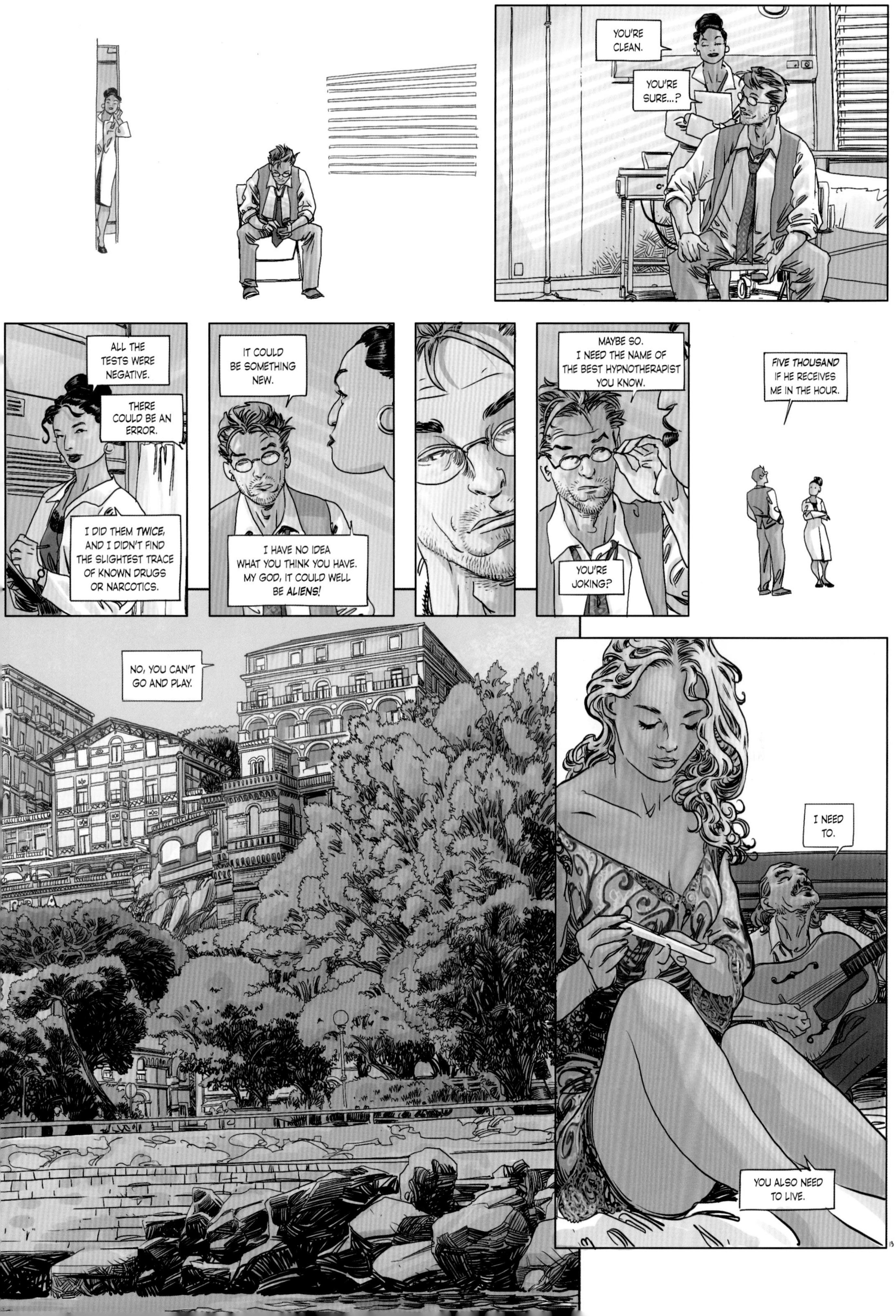
YOU'RE CLEAN.
YOU'RE SURE...?
ALL THE TESTS WERE NEGATIVE.
THERE COULD BE AN ERROR.
I DID THEM *TWICE*, AND I DIDN'T FIND THE SLIGHTEST TRACE OF KNOWN DRUGS OR NARCOTICS.
IT COULD BE SOMETHING NEW.
I HAVE NO IDEA WHAT YOU THINK YOU HAVE. MY GOD, IT COULD WELL BE *ALIENS!*
MAYBE SO. I NEED THE NAME OF THE BEST HYPNOTHERAPIST YOU KNOW.
YOU'RE JOKING?
FIVE THOUSAND IF HE RECEIVES ME IN THE HOUR.
NO, YOU CAN'T GO AND PLAY.
I NEED TO.
YOU ALSO NEED TO LIVE.

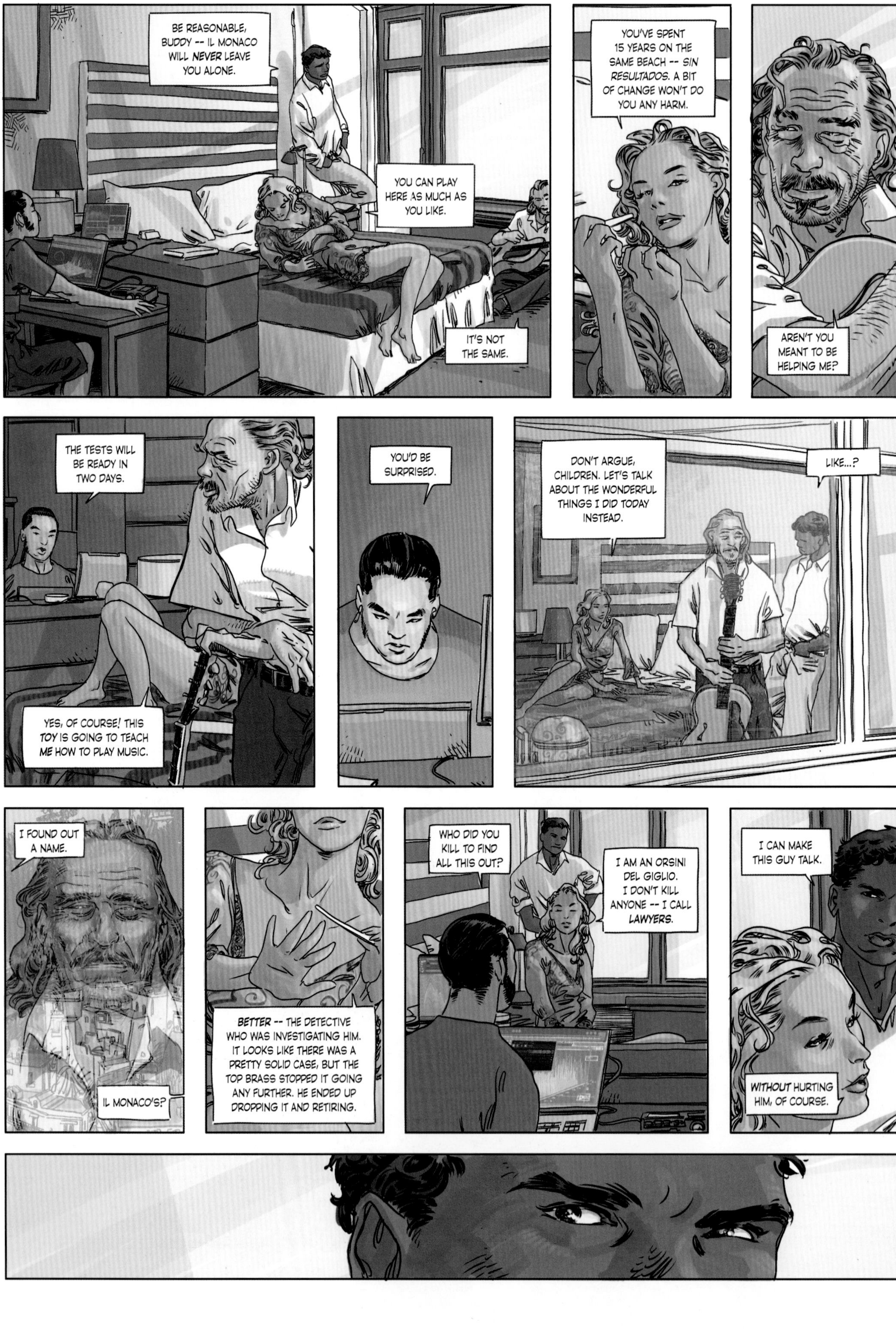
BE REASONABLE, BUDDY -- IL MONACO WILL NEVER LEAVE YOU ALONE.
YOU CAN PLAY HERE AS MUCH AS YOU LIKE.
IT'S NOT THE SAME.
YOU'VE SPENT 15 YEARS ON THE SAME BEACH -- SIN RESULTADOS. A BIT OF CHANGE WON'T DO YOU ANY HARM.
AREN'T YOU MEANT TO BE HELPING ME?
THE TESTS WILL BE READY IN TWO DAYS.
YES, OF COURSE! THIS TOY IS GOING TO TEACH ME HOW TO PLAY MUSIC.
YOU'D BE SURPRISED.
DON'T ARGUE, CHILDREN. LET'S TALK ABOUT THE WONDERFUL THINGS I DID TODAY INSTEAD.
LIKE...?
I FOUND OUT A NAME.
IL MONACO'S?
BETTER -- THE DETECTIVE WHO WAS INVESTIGATING HIM. IT LOOKS LIKE THERE WAS A PRETTY SOLID CASE, BUT THE TOP BRASS STOPPED IT GOING ANY FURTHER. HE ENDED UP DROPPING IT AND RETIRING.
WHO DID YOU KILL TO FIND ALL THIS OUT?
I AM AN ORSINI DEL GIGLIO. I DON'T KILL ANYONE -- I CALL LAWYERS.
I CAN MAKE THIS GUY TALK.
WITHOUT HURTING HIM, OF COURSE.

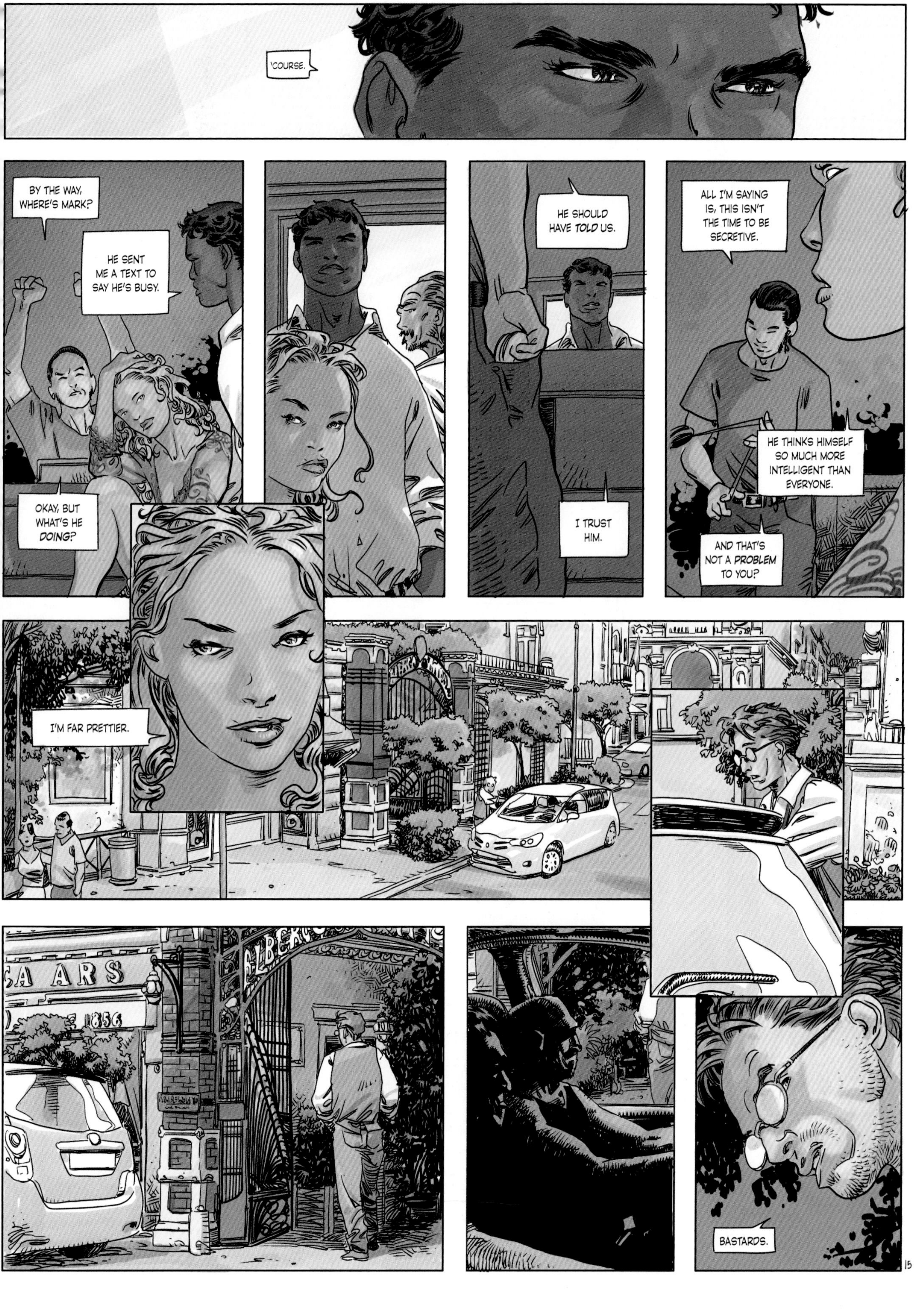
'COURSE.
BY THE WAY, WHERE'S MARK?
HE SENT ME A TEXT TO SAY HE'S BUSY.
OKAY, BUT WHAT'S HE *DOING*?
HE SHOULD HAVE *TOLD* US.
I TRUST HIM.
ALL I'M SAYING IS, THIS ISN'T THE TIME TO BE SECRETIVE.
HE THINKS HIMSELF SO MUCH MORE INTELLIGENT THAN EVERYONE.
AND THAT'S NOT A *PROBLEM* TO YOU?
I'M FAR PRETTIER.
BASTARDS.

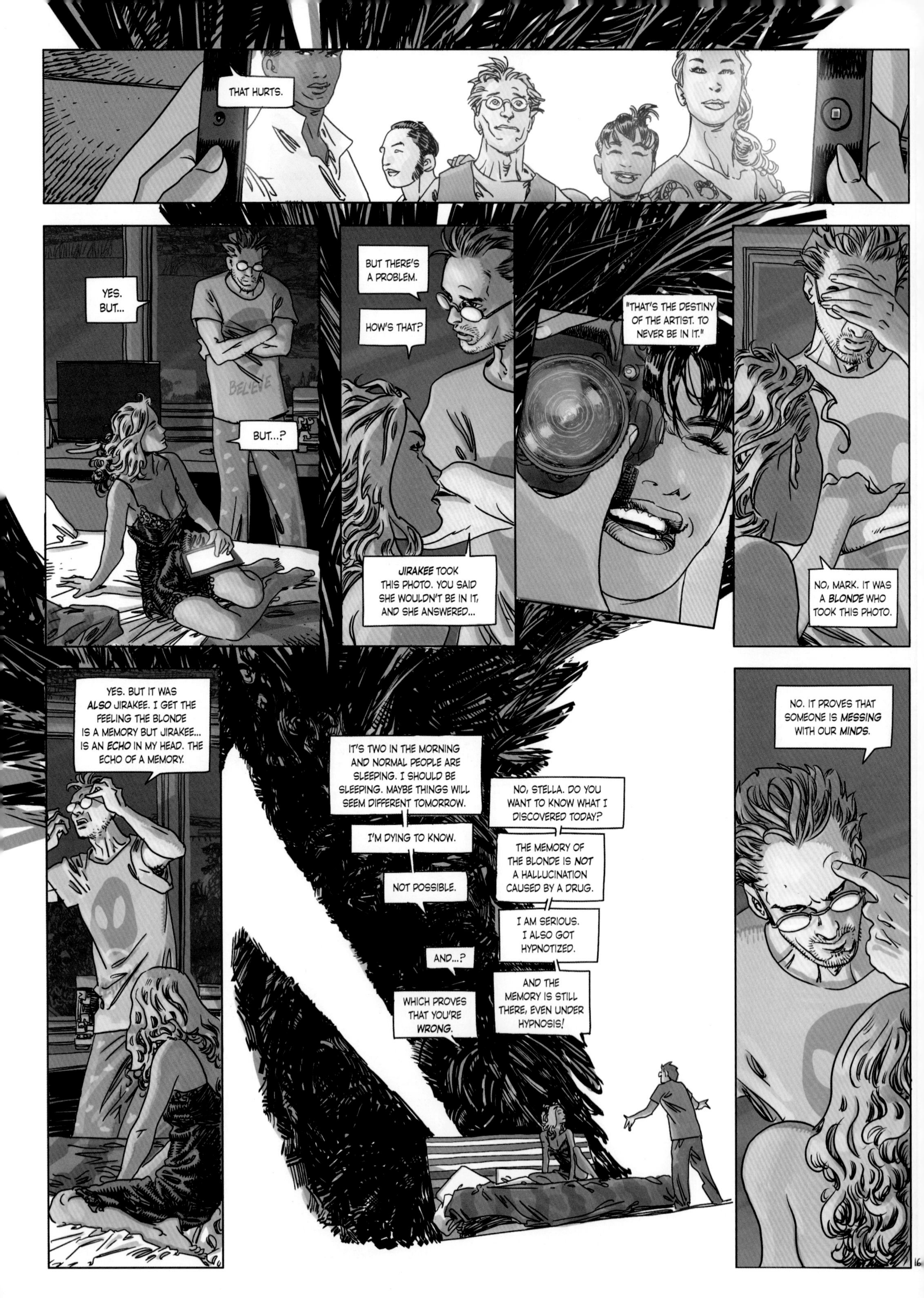

THAT HURTS.
YES. BUT...
BUT...?
BUT THERE'S A PROBLEM.
HOW'S THAT?
JIRAKEE TOOK THIS PHOTO. YOU SAID SHE WOULDN'T BE IN IT, AND SHE ANSWERED...
"THAT'S THE DESTINY OF THE ARTIST. TO NEVER BE IN IT."
NO, MARK. IT WAS A BLONDE WHO TOOK THIS PHOTO.
YES. BUT IT WAS ALSO JIRAKEE. I GET THE FEELING THE BLONDE IS A MEMORY BUT JIRAKEE... IS AN ECHO IN MY HEAD. THE ECHO OF A MEMORY.
IT'S TWO IN THE MORNING AND NORMAL PEOPLE ARE SLEEPING. I SHOULD BE SLEEPING. MAYBE THINGS WILL SEEM DIFFERENT TOMORROW.
NO, STELLA. DO YOU WANT TO KNOW WHAT I DISCOVERED TODAY?
I'M DYING TO KNOW.
THE MEMORY OF THE BLONDE IS NOT A HALLUCINATION CAUSED BY A DRUG.
NOT POSSIBLE.
I AM SERIOUS. I ALSO GOT HYPNOTIZED.
AND...?
AND THE MEMORY IS STILL THERE, EVEN UNDER HYPNOSIS!
WHICH PROVES THAT YOU'RE WRONG.
NO. IT PROVES THAT SOMEONE IS MESSING WITH OUR MINDS.

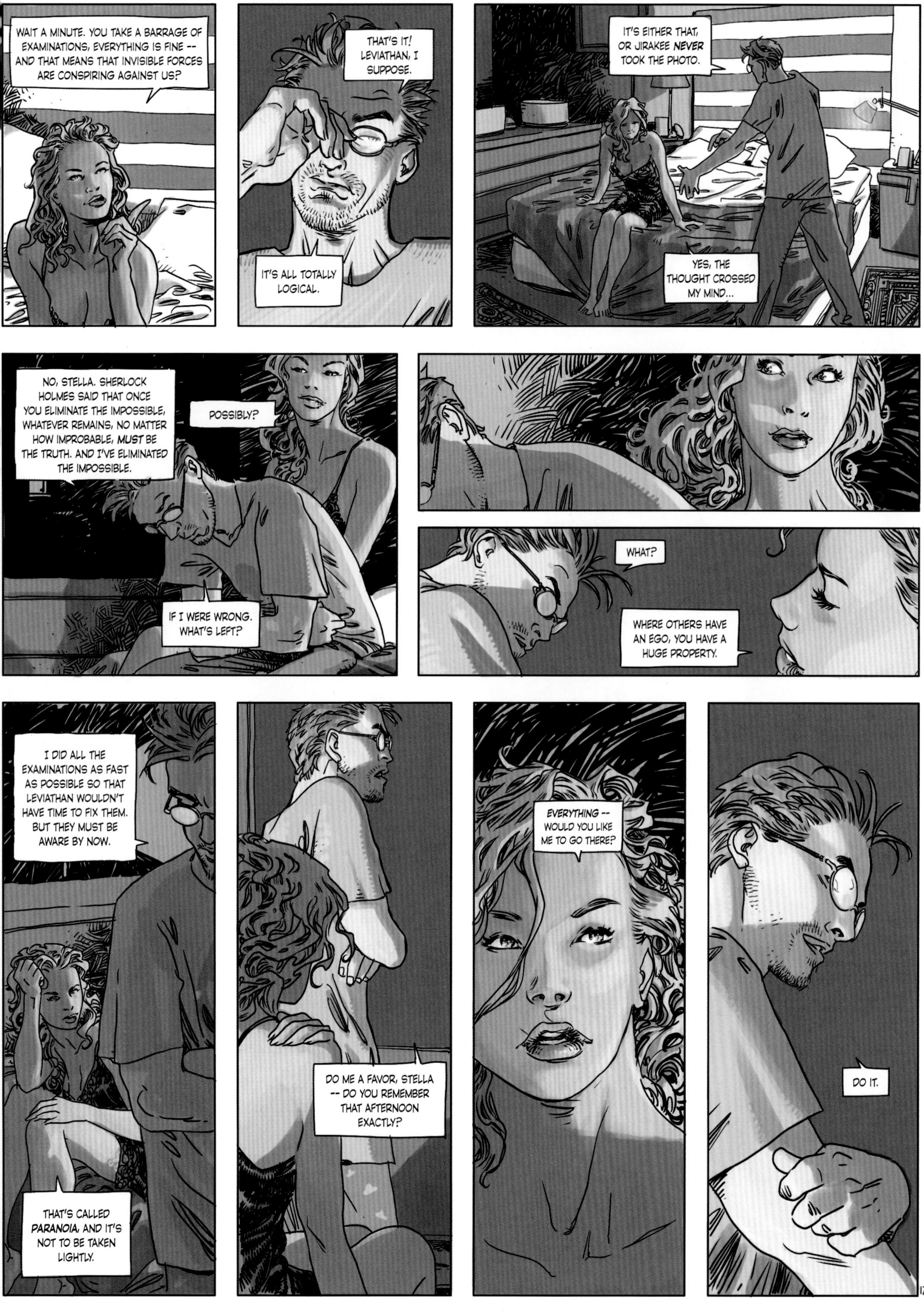
WAIT A MINUTE. YOU TAKE A BARRAGE OF EXAMINATIONS, EVERYTHING IS FINE -- AND THAT MEANS THAT INVISIBLE FORCES ARE CONSPIRING AGAINST US?
THAT'S IT! LEVIATHAN, I SUPPOSE.
IT'S ALL TOTALLY LOGICAL.
IT'S EITHER THAT, OR JIRAKEE **NEVER** TOOK THE PHOTO.
YES, THE THOUGHT CROSSED MY MIND...
NO, STELLA. SHERLOCK HOLMES SAID THAT ONCE YOU ELIMINATE THE IMPOSSIBLE, WHATEVER REMAINS, NO MATTER HOW IMPROBABLE, **MUST** BE THE TRUTH. AND I'VE ELIMINATED THE IMPOSSIBLE.
POSSIBLY?
IF I WERE WRONG. WHAT'S LEFT?
WHAT?
WHERE OTHERS HAVE AN EGO, YOU HAVE A HUGE PROPERTY.
I DID ALL THE EXAMINATIONS AS FAST AS POSSIBLE SO THAT LEVIATHAN WOULDN'T HAVE TIME TO FIX THEM. BUT THEY MUST BE AWARE BY NOW.
THAT'S CALLED **PARANOIA**, AND IT'S NOT TO BE TAKEN LIGHTLY.
DO ME A FAVOR, STELLA -- DO YOU REMEMBER THAT AFTERNOON EXACTLY?
EVERYTHING -- WOULD YOU LIKE ME TO GO THERE?
DO IT.

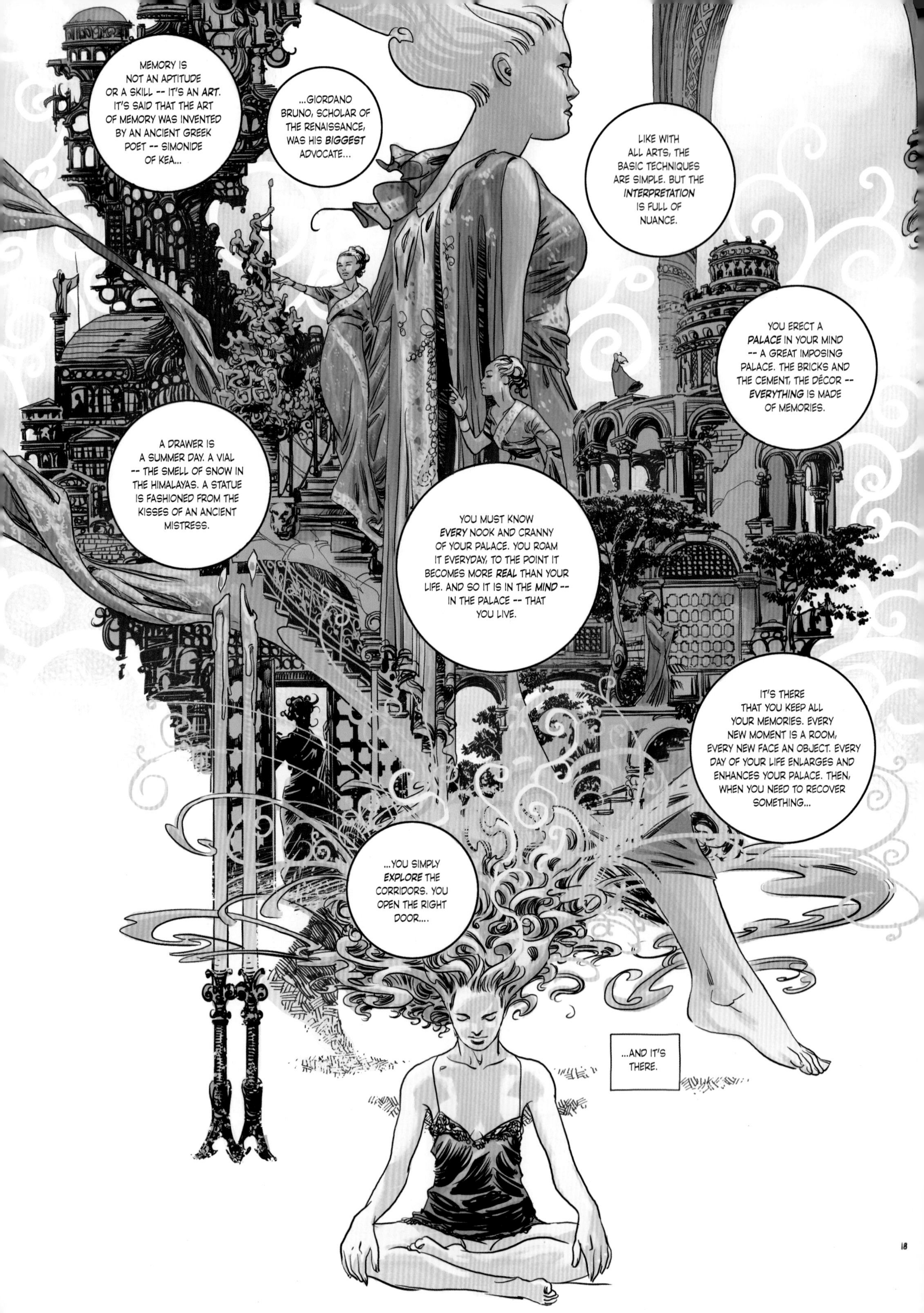
MEMORY IS NOT AN APTITUDE OR A SKILL -- IT'S AN ART. IT'S SAID THAT THE ART OF MEMORY WAS INVENTED BY AN ANCIENT GREEK POET -- SIMONIDE OF KEA...
...GIORDANO BRUNO, SCHOLAR OF THE RENAISSANCE, WAS HIS BIGGEST ADVOCATE...
LIKE WITH ALL ARTS, THE BASIC TECHNIQUES ARE SIMPLE. BUT THE INTERPRETATION IS FULL OF NUANCE.
YOU ERECT A PALACE IN YOUR MIND -- A GREAT IMPOSING PALACE. THE BRICKS AND THE CEMENT, THE DÉCOR -- EVERYTHING IS MADE OF MEMORIES.
A DRAWER IS A SUMMER DAY. A VIAL -- THE SMELL OF SNOW IN THE HIMALAYAS. A STATUE IS FASHIONED FROM THE KISSES OF AN ANCIENT MISTRESS.
YOU MUST KNOW EVERY NOOK AND CRANNY OF YOUR PALACE. YOU ROAM IT EVERYDAY, TO THE POINT IT BECOMES MORE REAL THAN YOUR LIFE. AND SO IT IS IN THE MIND -- IN THE PALACE -- THAT YOU LIVE.
IT'S THERE THAT YOU KEEP ALL YOUR MEMORIES. EVERY NEW MOMENT IS A ROOM, EVERY NEW FACE AN OBJECT. EVERY DAY OF YOUR LIFE ENLARGES AND ENHANCES YOUR PALACE. THEN, WHEN YOU NEED TO RECOVER SOMETHING...
...YOU SIMPLY EXPLORE THE CORRIDORS. YOU OPEN THE RIGHT DOOR....
...AND IT'S THERE.

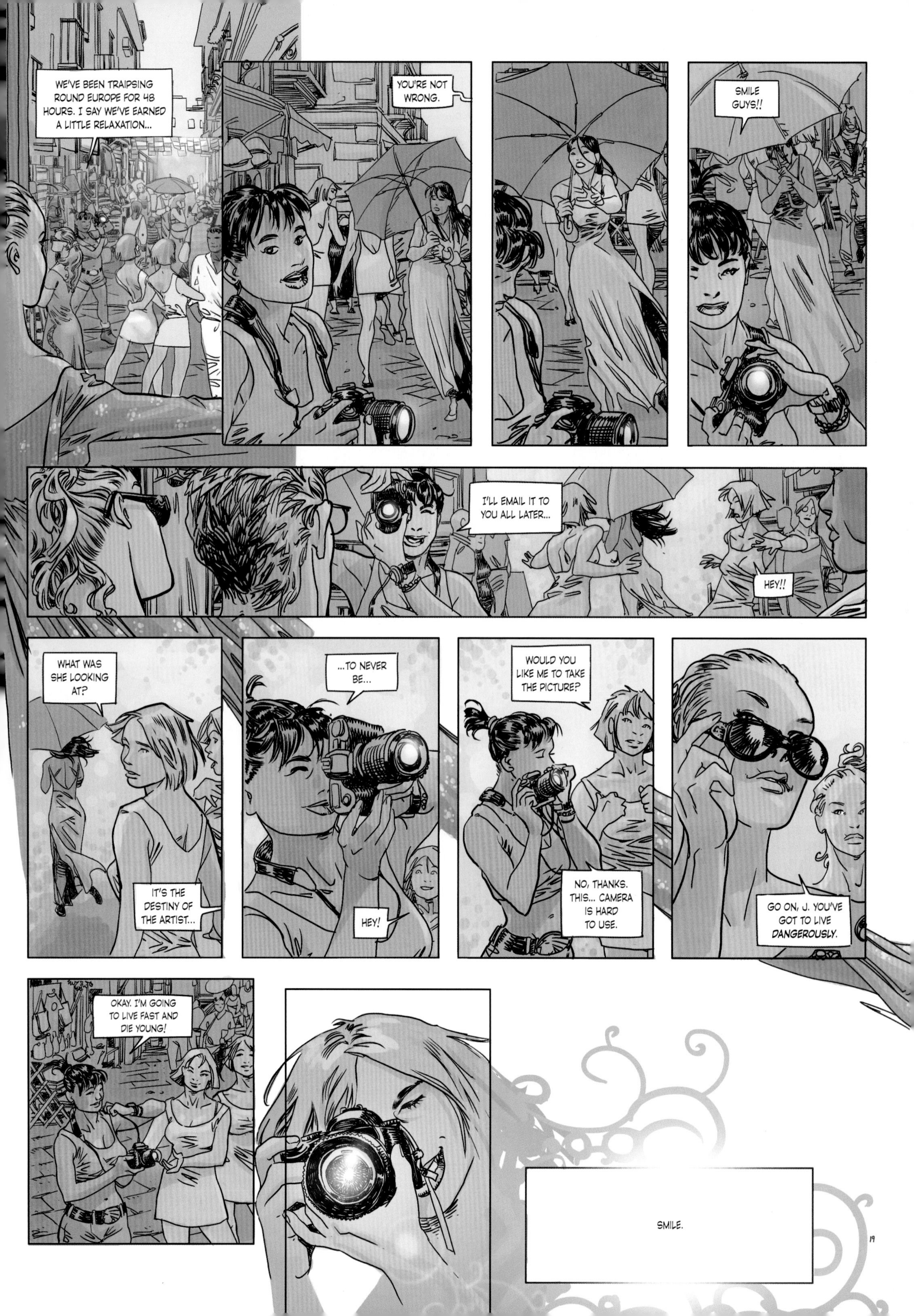
WE'VE BEEN TRAIPSING ROUND EUROPE FOR 48 HOURS. I SAY WE'VE EARNED A LITTLE RELAXATION...
YOU'RE NOT WRONG.
SMILE GUYS!!
I'LL EMAIL IT TO YOU ALL LATER...
HEY!!
WHAT WAS SHE LOOKING AT?
IT'S THE DESTINY OF THE ARTIST...
...TO NEVER BE...
HEY!
WOULD YOU LIKE ME TO TAKE THE PICTURE?
NO, THANKS. THIS... CAMERA IS HARD TO USE.
GO ON, J. YOU'VE GOT TO LIVE *DANGEROUSLY*.
OKAY. I'M GOING TO LIVE FAST AND DIE YOUNG!
SMILE.

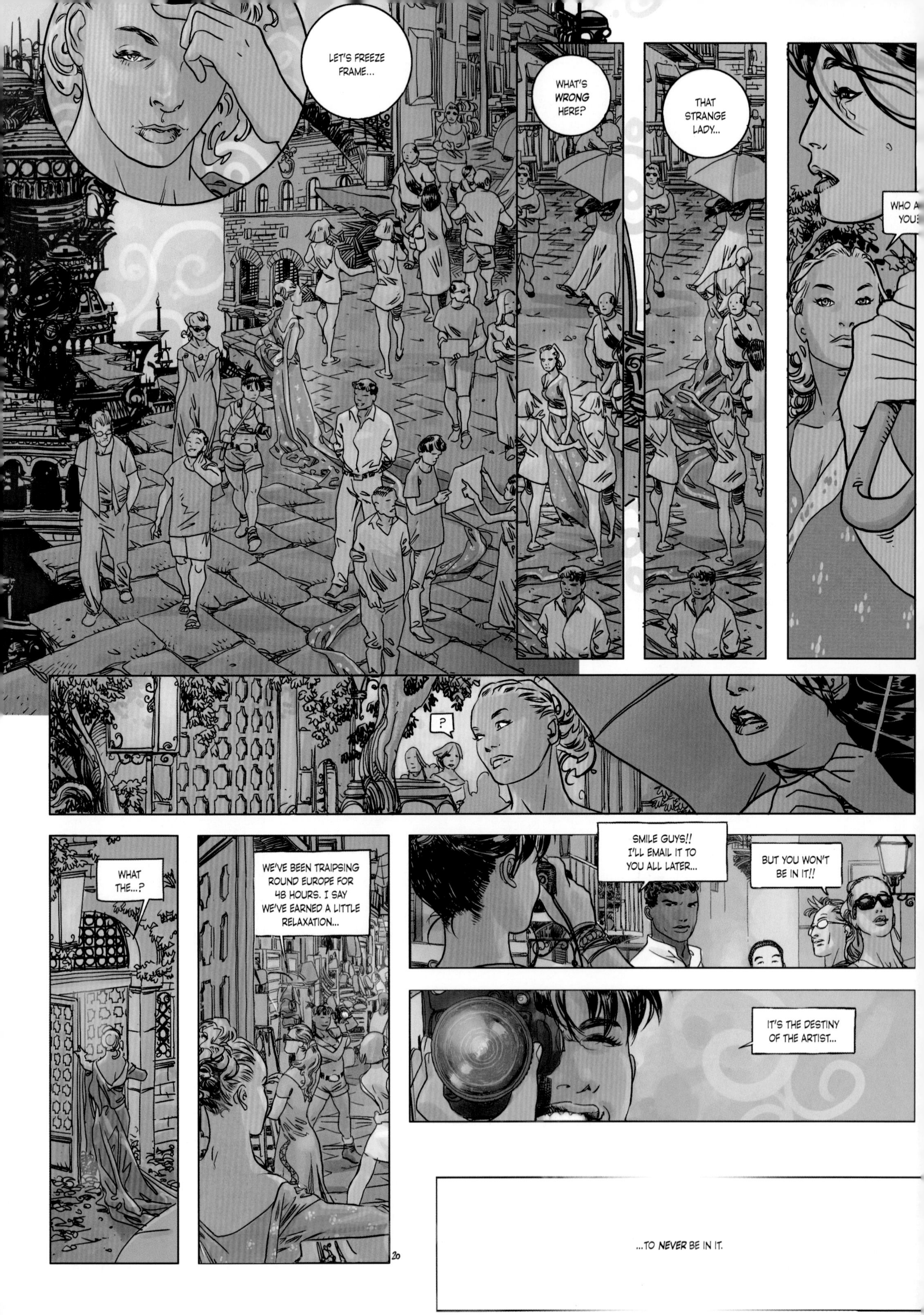
LET'S FREEZE FRAME...
WHAT'S WRONG HERE?
THAT STRANGE LADY...
WHO A YOU
?
WHAT THE...?
WE'VE BEEN TRAIPSING ROUND EUROPE FOR 48 HOURS. I SAY WE'VE EARNED A LITTLE RELAXATION...
SMILE GUYS!! I'LL EMAIL IT TO YOU ALL LATER...
BUT YOU WON'T BE IN IT!!
IT'S THE DESTINY OF THE ARTIST...
...TO NEVER BE IN IT.

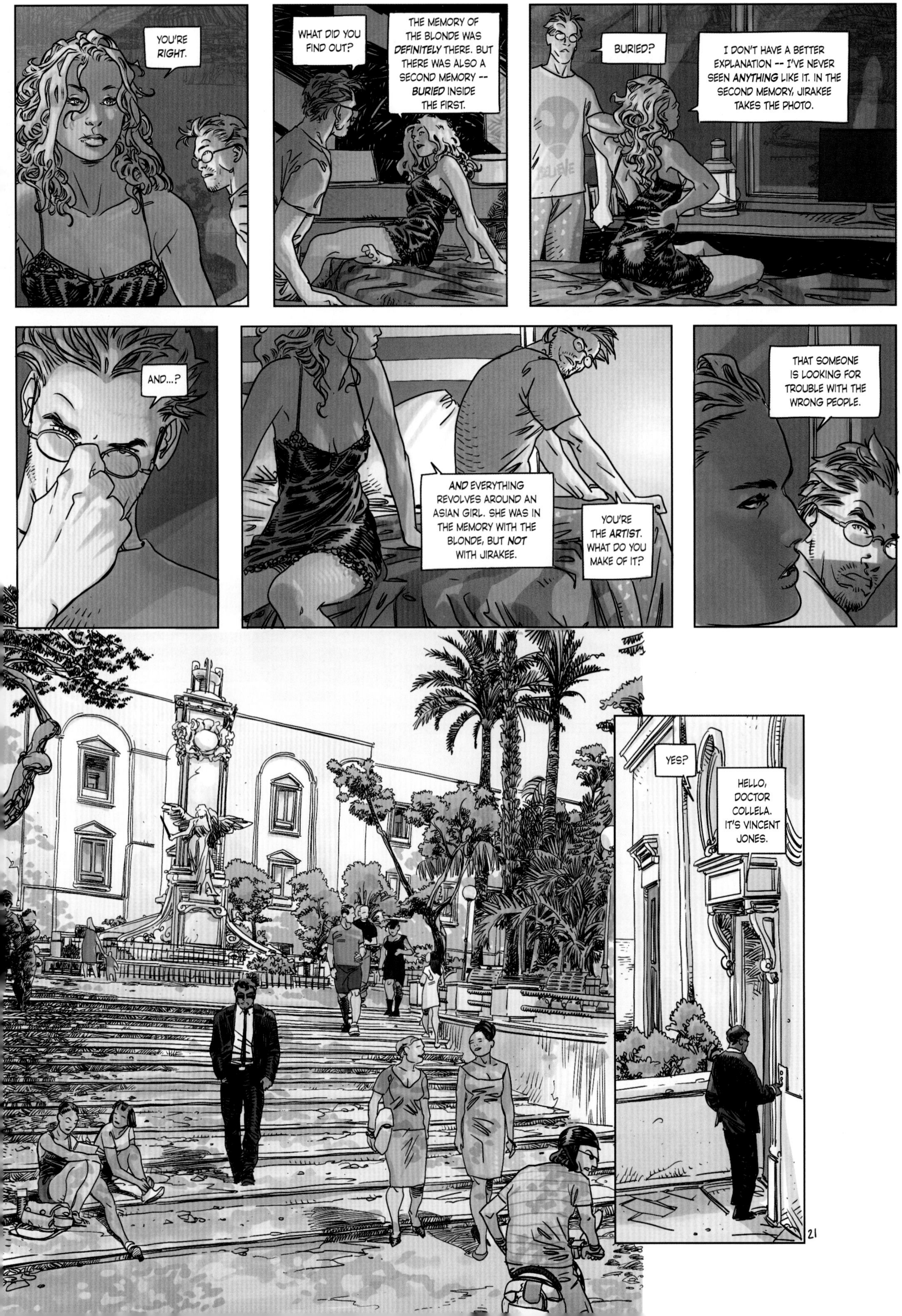
YOU'RE RIGHT.
WHAT DID YOU FIND OUT?
THE MEMORY OF THE BLONDE WAS DEFINITELY THERE. BUT THERE WAS ALSO A SECOND MEMORY -- BURIED INSIDE THE FIRST.
BURIED?
I DON'T HAVE A BETTER EXPLANATION -- I'VE NEVER SEEN ANYTHING LIKE IT. IN THE SECOND MEMORY, JIRAKEE TAKES THE PHOTO.
AND...?
AND EVERYTHING REVOLVES AROUND AN ASIAN GIRL. SHE WAS IN THE MEMORY WITH THE BLONDE, BUT NOT WITH JIRAKEE.
YOU'RE THE ARTIST. WHAT DO YOU MAKE OF IT?
THAT SOMEONE IS LOOKING FOR TROUBLE WITH THE WRONG PEOPLE.
YES?
HELLO, DOCTOR COLLELA. IT'S VINCENT JONES.

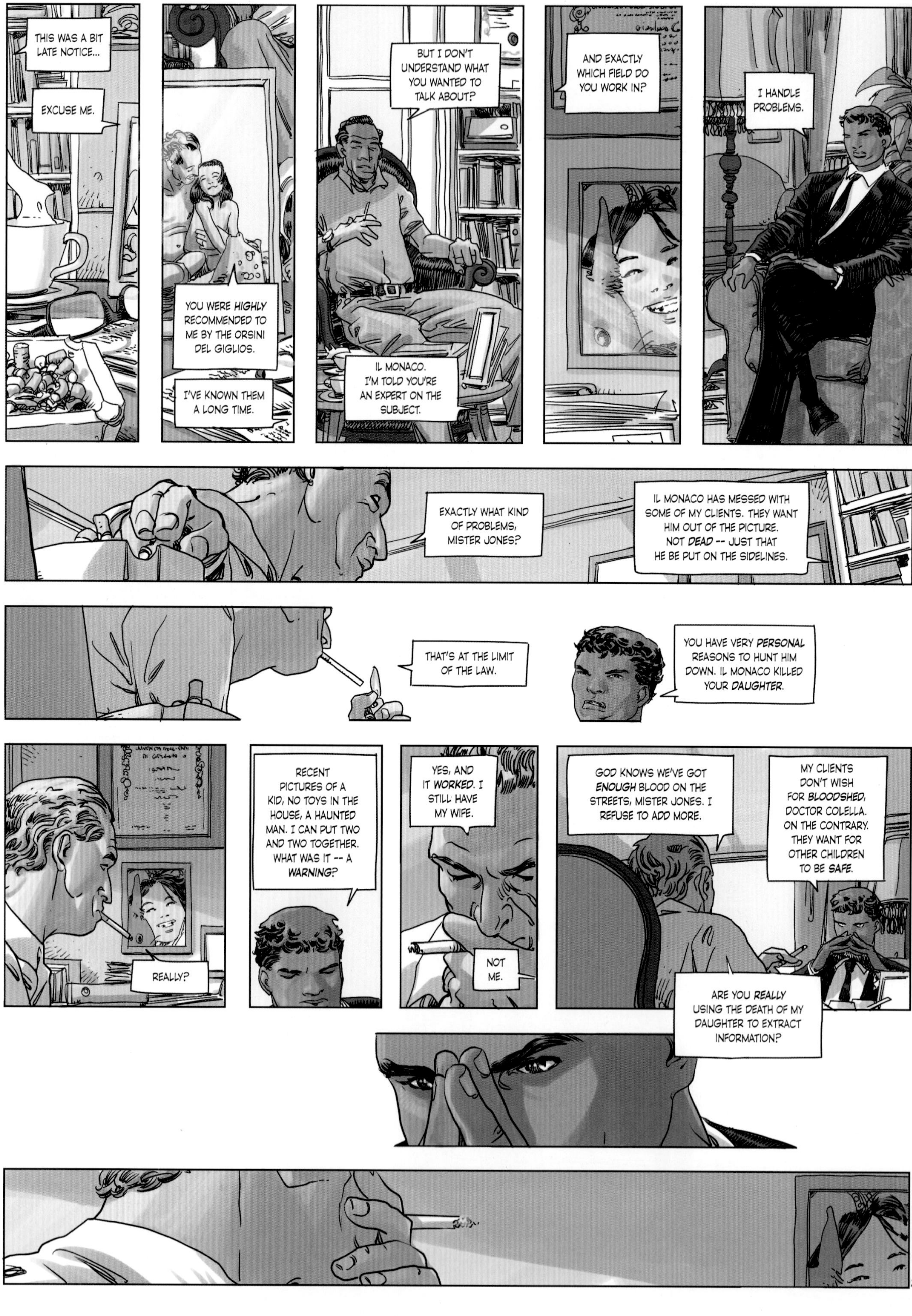
THIS WAS A BIT LATE NOTICE...
EXCUSE ME.
YOU WERE HIGHLY RECOMMENDED TO ME BY THE ORSINI DEL GIGLIOS.
I'VE KNOWN THEM A LONG TIME.
BUT I DON'T UNDERSTAND WHAT YOU WANTED TO TALK ABOUT?
IL MONACO. I'M TOLD YOU'RE AN EXPERT ON THE SUBJECT.
AND EXACTLY WHICH FIELD DO YOU WORK IN?
I HANDLE PROBLEMS.
EXACTLY WHAT KIND OF PROBLEMS, MISTER JONES?
IL MONACO HAS MESSED WITH SOME OF MY CLIENTS. THEY WANT HIM OUT OF THE PICTURE. NOT DEAD -- JUST THAT HE BE PUT ON THE SIDELINES.
THAT'S AT THE LIMIT OF THE LAW.
YOU HAVE VERY PERSONAL REASONS TO HUNT HIM DOWN. IL MONACO KILLED YOUR DAUGHTER.
REALLY?
RECENT PICTURES OF A KID, NO TOYS IN THE HOUSE, A HAUNTED MAN. I CAN PUT TWO AND TWO TOGETHER. WHAT WAS IT -- A WARNING?
YES, AND IT WORKED. I STILL HAVE MY WIFE.
NOT ME.
GOD KNOWS WE'VE GOT ENOUGH BLOOD ON THE STREETS, MISTER JONES. I REFUSE TO ADD MORE.
MY CLIENTS DON'T WISH FOR BLOODSHED, DOCTOR COLELLA. ON THE CONTRARY. THEY WANT FOR OTHER CHILDREN TO BE SAFE.
ARE YOU REALLY USING THE DEATH OF MY DAUGHTER TO EXTRACT INFORMATION?

HIS REAL NAME IS PIERO GAROFALO. HE'S *NOT* DESCENDED FROM ONE THE ANCIENT CAMORRA FAMILIES. IN FACT, HE'S AN *UPSTART*.

HARD TO BELIEVE, RIGHT?

HE IS EVERYTHING A CRIMINAL *SHOULDN'T* BE -- RESPECTED, RICH, AND DAMNED LUCKY.

HE LAUNDERS THE MONEY THROUGH *THREE* DIFFERENT LEGAL FIRMS. YOU COULD SAY THAT HE'S THE *FINANCIAL CONSULTANT* FOR THE CAMORRA.

GAROFALO IS INTO MONEY LAUNDERING, AND HE *EXCELS* AT IT. IT'S FOR THAT REASON THAT THE ANCIENT FAMILIES LEAVE HIM ALONE -- HE PROVIDES THEM WITH A *CRUCIAL* SERVICE.

I HAVE THE NAME OF THOSE ORGANIZATIONS.

HE HAS A CERTAIN AUTHORITY -- INDIRECT BUT *VERY* POWERFUL. HIS TALENTS MAKE HIM AN *ASSET* FOR MANY DANGEROUS PEOPLE. HE IS A SPIDER -- INVISIBLE, SQUATTING IN A GIANT WEB.

NO-ONE KNOWS WHAT HE DOES IN REALITY -- PEOPLE TAKE HIM FOR A *PHILANTHROPIST*. THE FEW WHO ARE INFORMED WORK FOR HIM...

...OR ARE SIMPLY TOO *SCARED* TO MOVE.

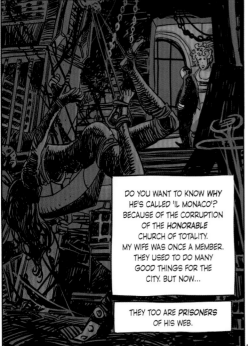

DO YOU WANT TO KNOW *WHY* HE'S CALLED 'IL MONACO'? BECAUSE OF THE CORRUPTION OF THE *HONORABLE* CHURCH OF TOTALITY. MY WIFE WAS ONCE A MEMBER. THEY USED TO DO MANY GOOD THINGS FOR THE CITY. BUT NOW...

THEY TOO ARE *PRISONERS* OF HIS WEB.

I AM NOT A *HERO*, MISTER JONES.

23

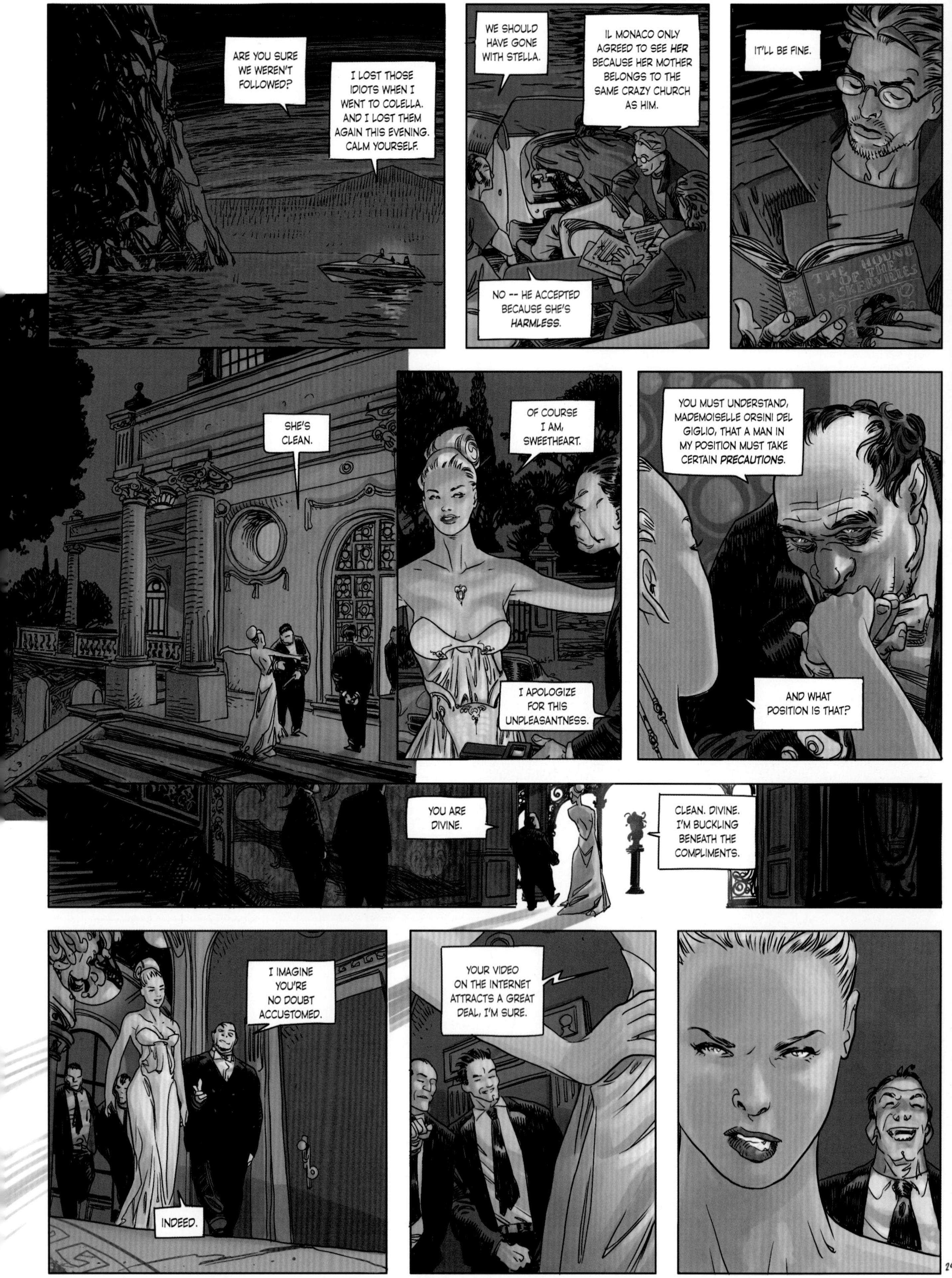
ARE YOU SURE WE WEREN'T FOLLOWED?
I LOST THOSE IDIOTS WHEN I WENT TO COLELLA. AND I LOST THEM AGAIN THIS EVENING. CALM YOURSELF.
WE SHOULD HAVE GONE WITH STELLA.
IL MONACO ONLY AGREED TO SEE *HER* BECAUSE HER MOTHER BELONGS TO THE SAME CRAZY CHURCH AS HIM.
NO -- HE ACCEPTED BECAUSE SHE'S *HARMLESS*.
IT'LL BE FINE.
THE HOUND OF THE BASKERVILLES
SHE'S CLEAN.
OF COURSE I AM, SWEETHEART.
I APOLOGIZE FOR THIS UNPLEASANTNESS.
YOU MUST UNDERSTAND, MADEMOISELLE ORSINI DEL GIGLIO, THAT A MAN IN MY POSITION MUST TAKE CERTAIN *PRECAUTIONS*.
AND WHAT POSITION IS THAT?
YOU ARE DIVINE.
CLEAN. DIVINE. I'M BUCKLING BENEATH THE COMPLIMENTS.
I IMAGINE YOU'RE NO DOUBT ACCUSTOMED.
INDEED.
YOUR VIDEO ON THE INTERNET ATTRACTS A GREAT DEAL, I'M SURE.

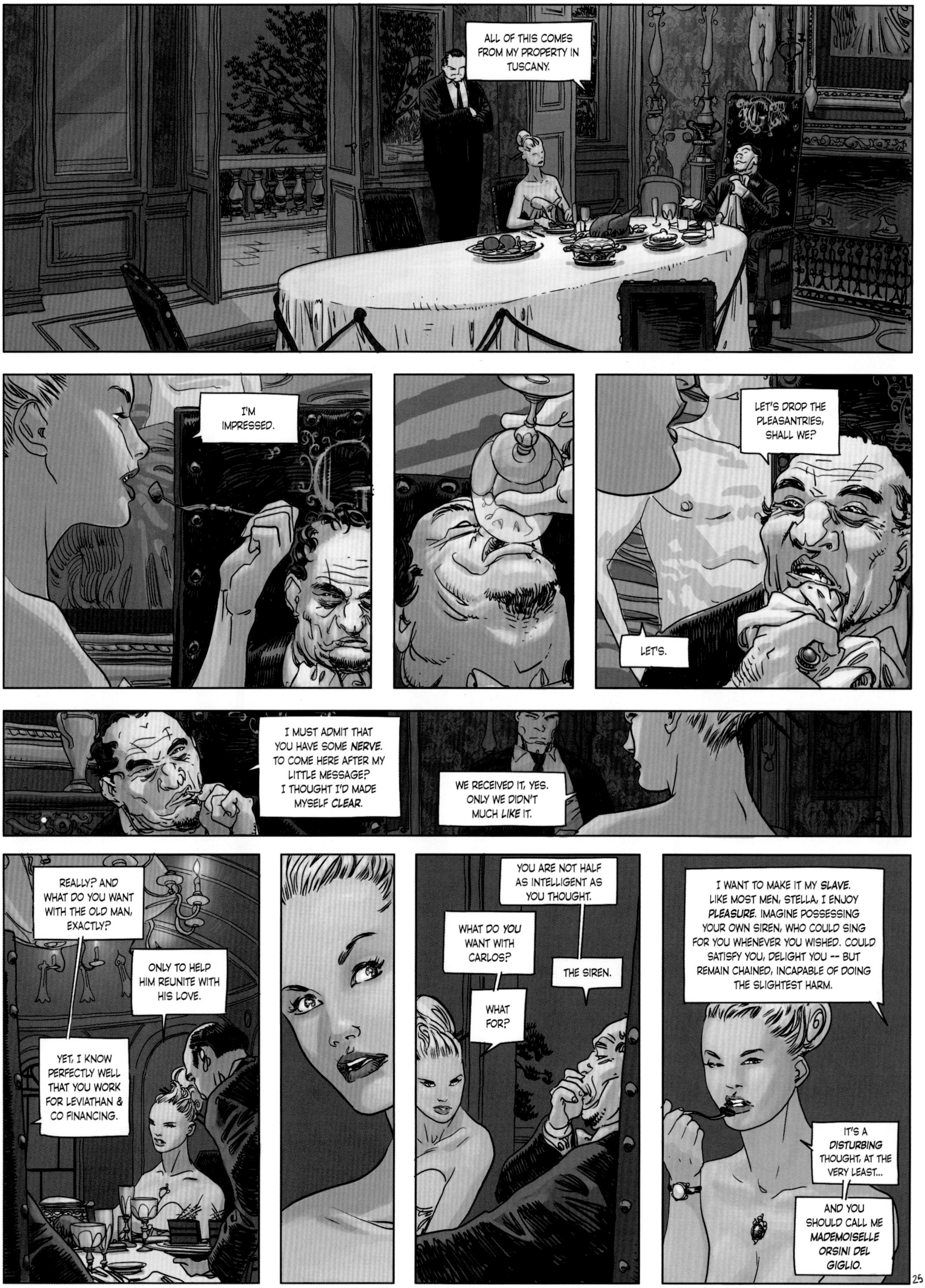
ALL OF THIS COMES FROM MY PROPERTY IN TUSCANY.
I'M IMPRESSED.
LET'S DROP THE PLEASANTRIES, SHALL WE?
LET'S.
I MUST ADMIT THAT YOU HAVE SOME NERVE. TO COME HERE AFTER MY LITTLE MESSAGE? I THOUGHT I'D MADE MYSELF CLEAR.
WE RECEIVED IT, YES. ONLY WE DIDN'T MUCH LIKE IT.
REALLY? AND WHAT DO YOU WANT WITH THE OLD MAN, EXACTLY?
ONLY TO HELP HIM REUNITE WITH HIS LOVE.
YET, I KNOW PERFECTLY WELL THAT YOU WORK FOR LEVIATHAN & CO FINANCING.
YOU ARE NOT HALF AS INTELLIGENT AS YOU THOUGHT.
WHAT DO YOU WANT WITH CARLOS?
THE SIREN.
WHAT FOR?
I WANT TO MAKE IT MY SLAVE. LIKE MOST MEN, STELLA, I ENJOY PLEASURE. IMAGINE POSSESSING YOUR OWN SIREN, WHO COULD SING FOR YOU WHENEVER YOU WISHED. COULD SATISFY YOU, DELIGHT YOU -- BUT REMAIN CHAINED, INCAPABLE OF DOING THE SLIGHTEST HARM.
IT'S A DISTURBING THOUGHT, AT THE VERY LEAST...
AND YOU SHOULD CALL ME MADEMOISELLE ORSINI DEL GIGLIO.

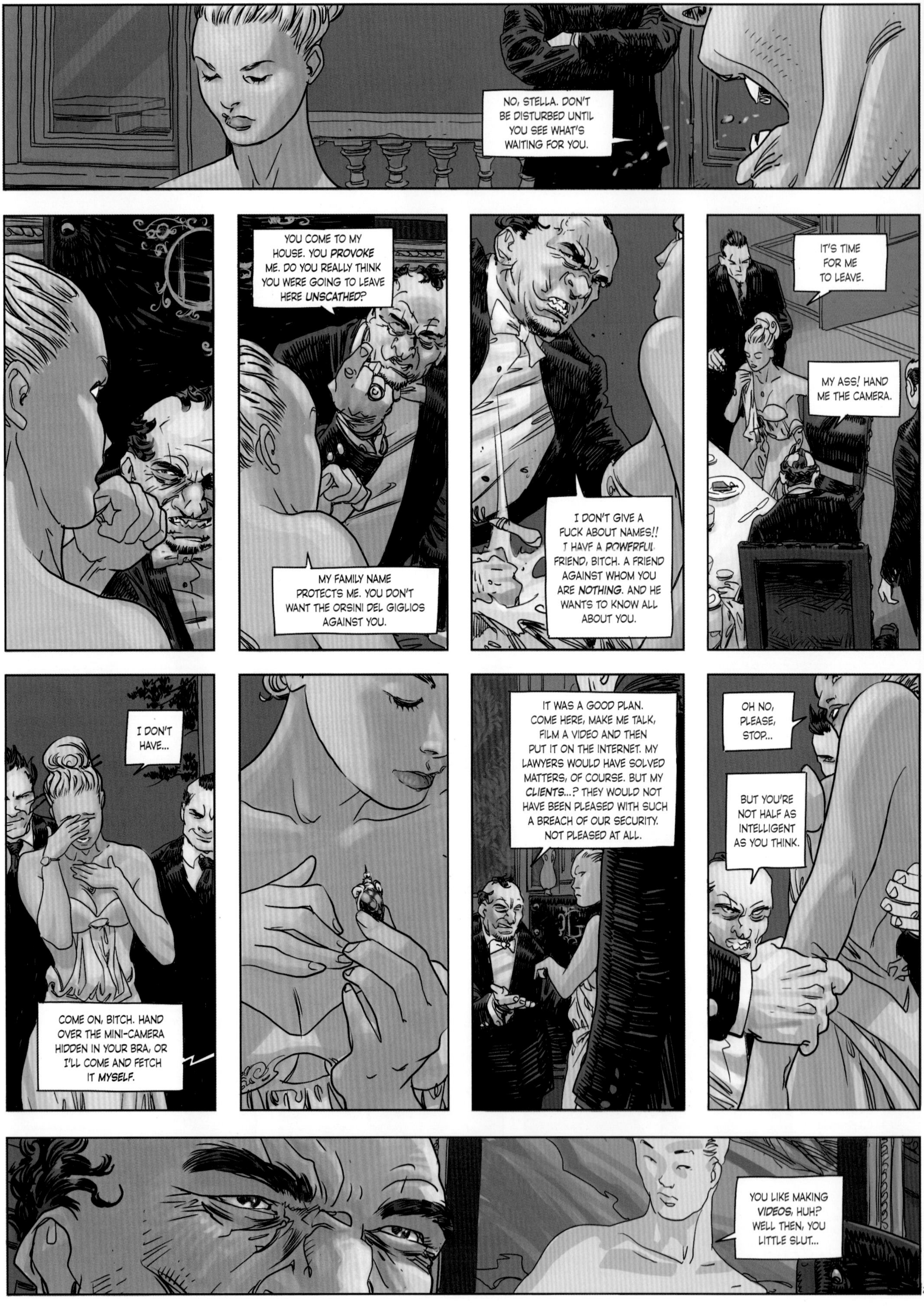
NO, STELLA. DON'T BE DISTURBED UNTIL YOU SEE WHAT'S WAITING FOR YOU.
YOU COME TO MY HOUSE. YOU PROVOKE ME. DO YOU REALLY THINK YOU WERE GOING TO LEAVE HERE UNSCATHED?
MY FAMILY NAME PROTECTS ME. YOU DON'T WANT THE ORSINI DEL GIGLIOS AGAINST YOU.
I DON'T GIVE A FUCK ABOUT NAMES!! I HAVE A POWERFUL FRIEND, BITCH. A FRIEND AGAINST WHOM YOU ARE NOTHING. AND HE WANTS TO KNOW ALL ABOUT YOU.
IT'S TIME FOR ME TO LEAVE.
MY ASS! HAND ME THE CAMERA.
I DON'T HAVE...
COME ON, BITCH. HAND OVER THE MINI-CAMERA HIDDEN IN YOUR BRA, OR I'LL COME AND FETCH IT MYSELF.
IT WAS A GOOD PLAN. COME HERE, MAKE ME TALK, FILM A VIDEO AND THEN PUT IT ON THE INTERNET. MY LAWYERS WOULD HAVE SOLVED MATTERS, OF COURSE. BUT MY CLIENTS...? THEY WOULD NOT HAVE BEEN PLEASED WITH SUCH A BREACH OF OUR SECURITY. NOT PLEASED AT ALL.
OH NO, PLEASE, STOP...
BUT YOU'RE NOT HALF AS INTELLIGENT AS YOU THINK.
YOU LIKE MAKING VIDEOS, HUH? WELL THEN, YOU LITTLE SLUT...

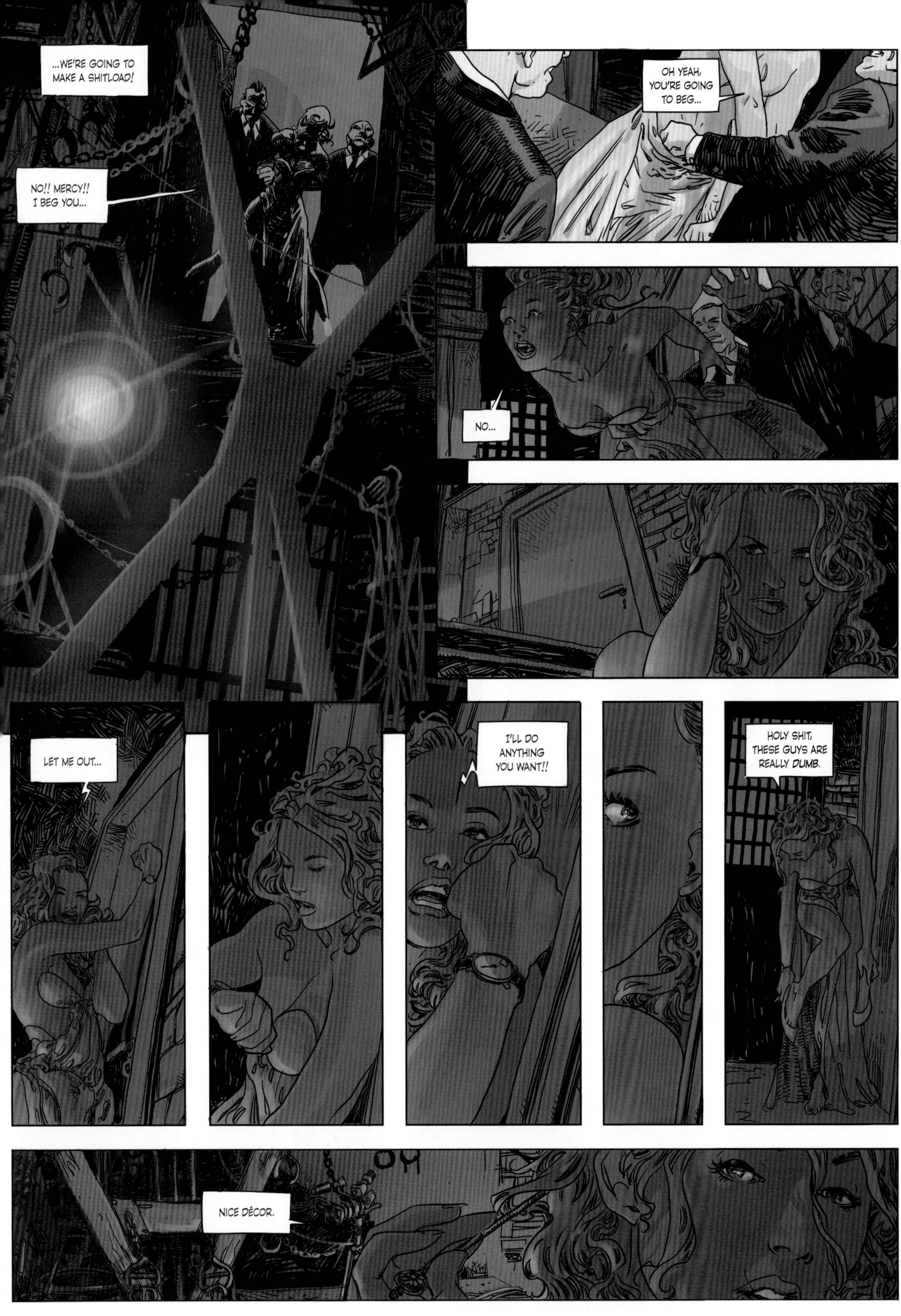
...WE'RE GOING TO MAKE A SHITLOAD!
NO!! MERCY!! I BEG YOU...
OH YEAH, YOU'RE GOING TO BEG...
NO...
LET ME OUT...
I'LL DO ANYTHING YOU WANT!!
HOLY SHIT, THESE GUYS ARE REALLY *DUMB*.
NICE DÉCOR.

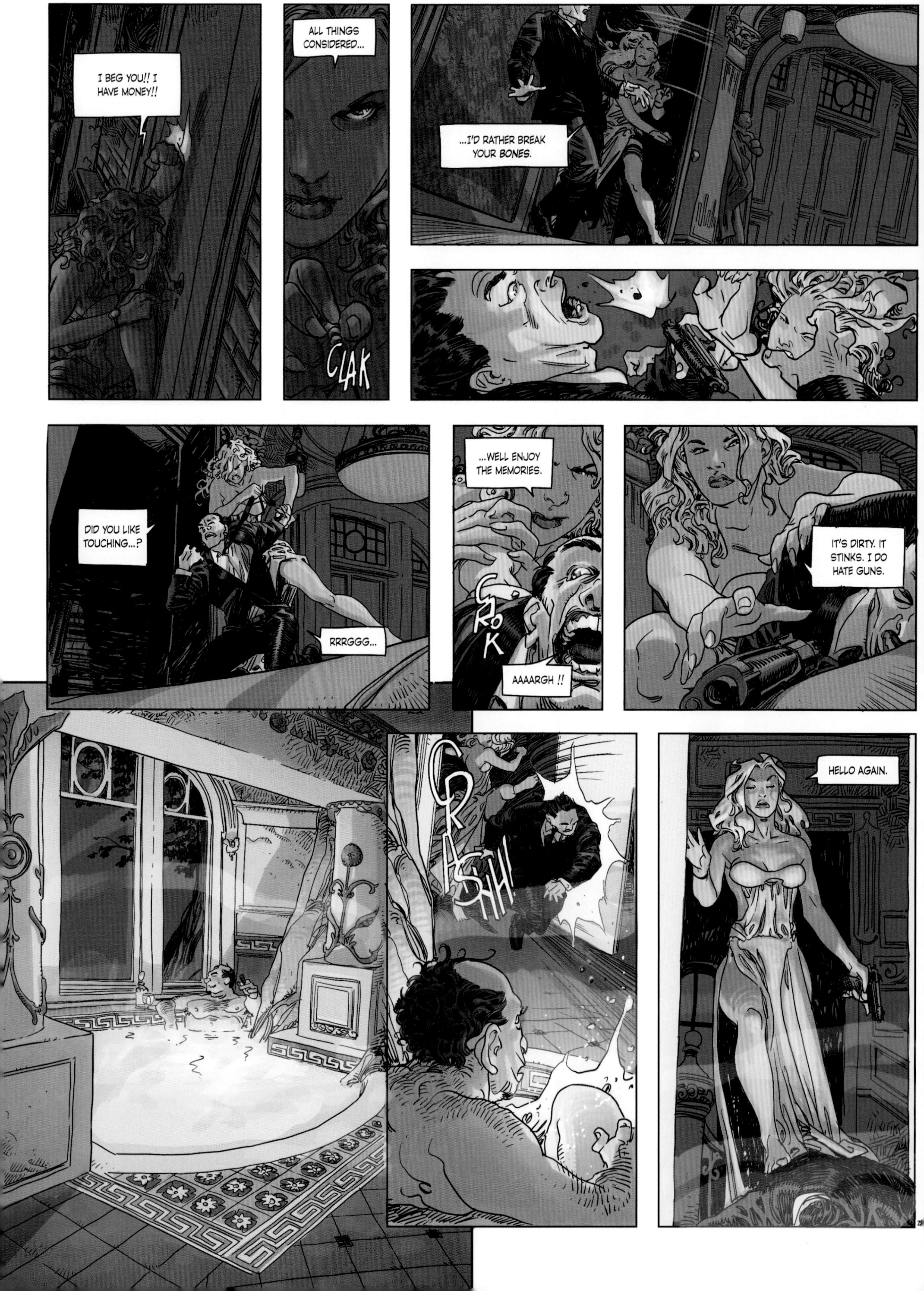
I BEG YOU!! I HAVE MONEY!!
ALL THINGS CONSIDERED...
CLAK
...I'D RATHER BREAK YOUR BONES.
DID YOU LIKE TOUCHING...?
RRRGGG...
...WELL ENJOY THE MEMORIES.
CROK
AAAARGH !!
IT'S DIRTY. IT STINKS. I DO HATE GUNS.
CRASHH!
HELLO AGAIN.

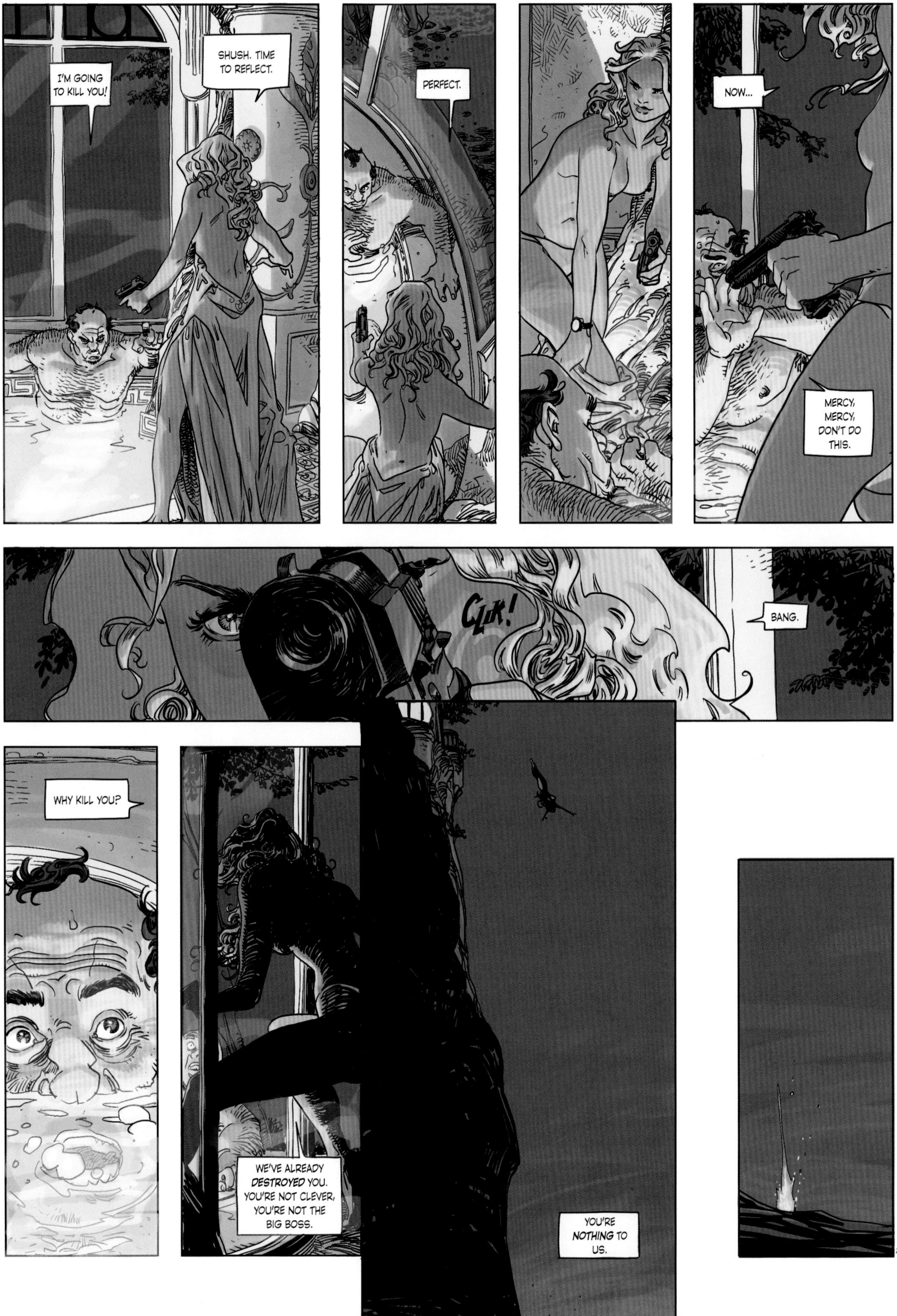
I'M GOING TO KILL YOU!
SHUSH. TIME TO REFLECT.
PERFECT.
NOW...
MERCY, MERCY, DON'T DO THIS.
CLIK!
BANG.
WHY KILL YOU?
WE'VE ALREADY DESTROYED YOU. YOU'RE NOT CLEVER, YOU'RE NOT THE BIG BOSS.
YOU'RE NOTHING TO US.

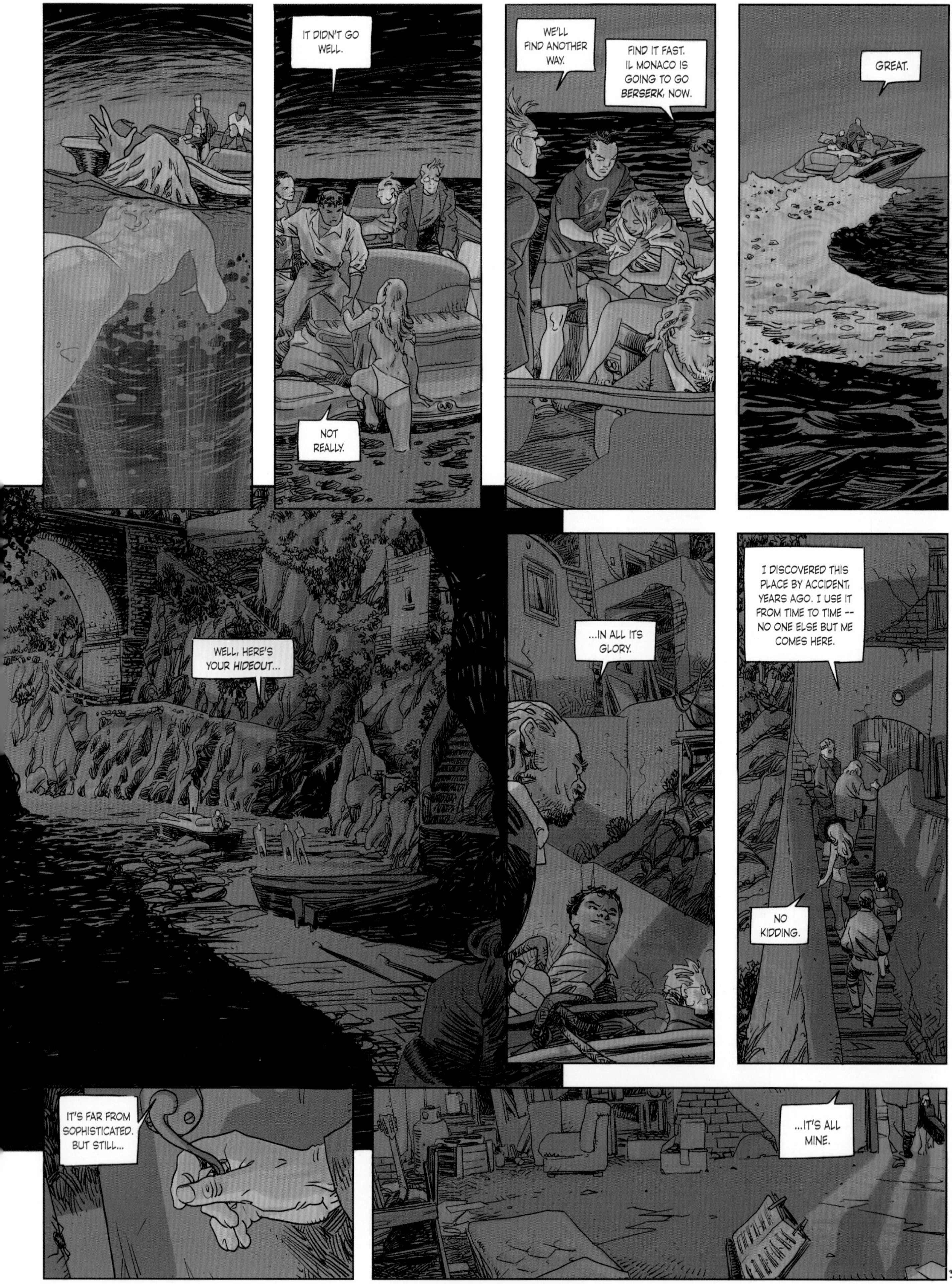
IT DIDN'T GO WELL.
NOT REALLY.
WE'LL FIND ANOTHER WAY.
FIND IT FAST. IL MONACO IS GOING TO GO BERSERK, NOW.
GREAT.
WELL, HERE'S YOUR HIDEOUT...
...IN ALL ITS GLORY.
I DISCOVERED THIS PLACE BY ACCIDENT, YEARS AGO. I USE IT FROM TIME TO TIME -- NO ONE ELSE BUT ME COMES HERE.
NO KIDDING.
IT'S FAR FROM SOPHISTICATED. BUT STILL...
...IT'S ALL MINE.

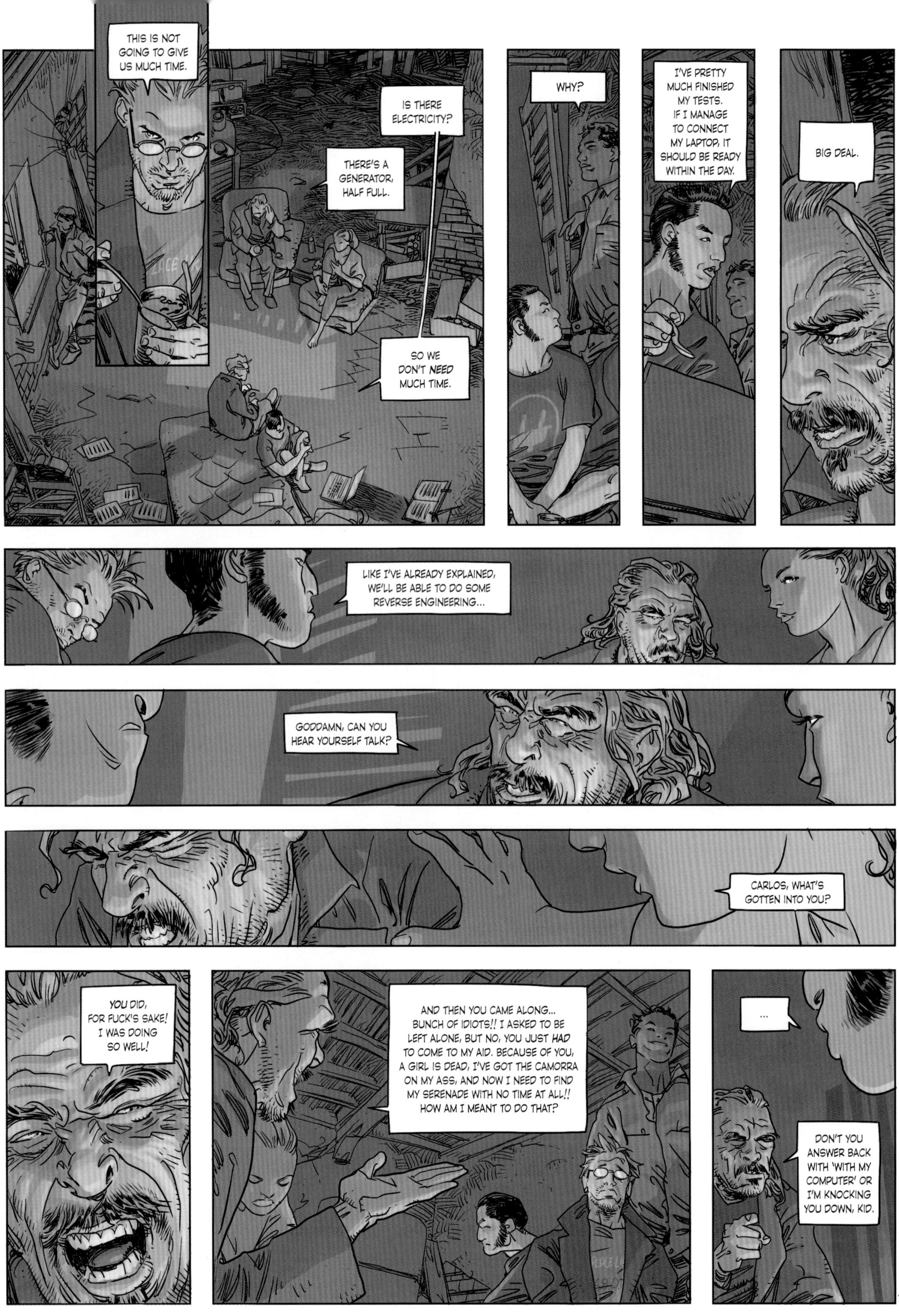
THIS IS NOT GOING TO GIVE US MUCH TIME.
IS THERE ELECTRICITY?
THERE'S A GENERATOR, HALF FULL.
SO WE DON'T NEED MUCH TIME.
WHY?
I'VE PRETTY MUCH FINISHED MY TESTS. IF I MANAGE TO CONNECT MY LAPTOP, IT SHOULD BE READY WITHIN THE DAY.
BIG DEAL.
LIKE I'VE ALREADY EXPLAINED, WE'LL BE ABLE TO DO SOME REVERSE ENGINEERING...
GODDAMN, CAN YOU HEAR YOURSELF TALK?
CARLOS, WHAT'S GOTTEN INTO YOU?
YOU DID, FOR FUCK'S SAKE! I WAS DOING SO WELL!
AND THEN YOU CAME ALONG... BUNCH OF IDIOTS!! I ASKED TO BE LEFT ALONE, BUT NO, YOU JUST HAD TO COME TO MY AID. BECAUSE OF YOU, A GIRL IS DEAD, I'VE GOT THE CAMORRA ON MY ASS, AND NOW I NEED TO FIND MY SERENADE WITH NO TIME AT ALL!! HOW AM I MEANT TO DO THAT?
...
DON'T YOU ANSWER BACK WITH 'WITH MY COMPUTER' OR I'M KNOCKING YOU DOWN, KID.

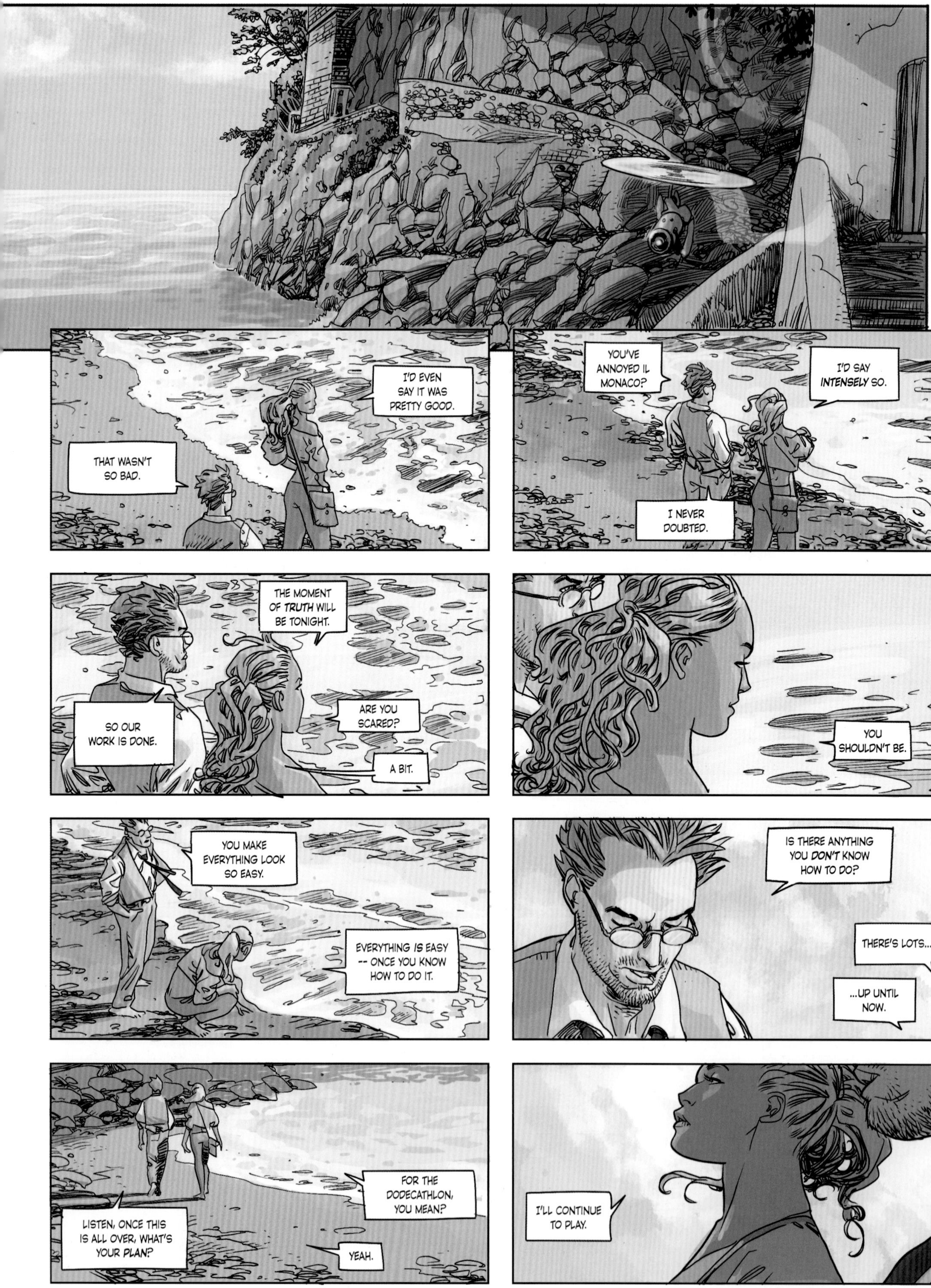
I'D EVEN SAY IT WAS PRETTY GOOD.
THAT WASN'T SO BAD.
YOU'VE ANNOYED IL MONACO?
I'D SAY INTENSELY SO.
I NEVER DOUBTED.
THE MOMENT OF TRUTH WILL BE TONIGHT.
SO OUR WORK IS DONE.
ARE YOU SCARED?
A BIT.
YOU SHOULDN'T BE.
YOU MAKE EVERYTHING LOOK SO EASY.
EVERYTHING IS EASY -- ONCE YOU KNOW HOW TO DO IT.
IS THERE ANYTHING YOU DON'T KNOW HOW TO DO?
THERE'S LOTS...
...UP UNTIL NOW.
LISTEN, ONCE THIS IS ALL OVER, WHAT'S YOUR PLAN?
FOR THE DODECATHLON, YOU MEAN?
YEAH.
I'LL CONTINUE TO PLAY.

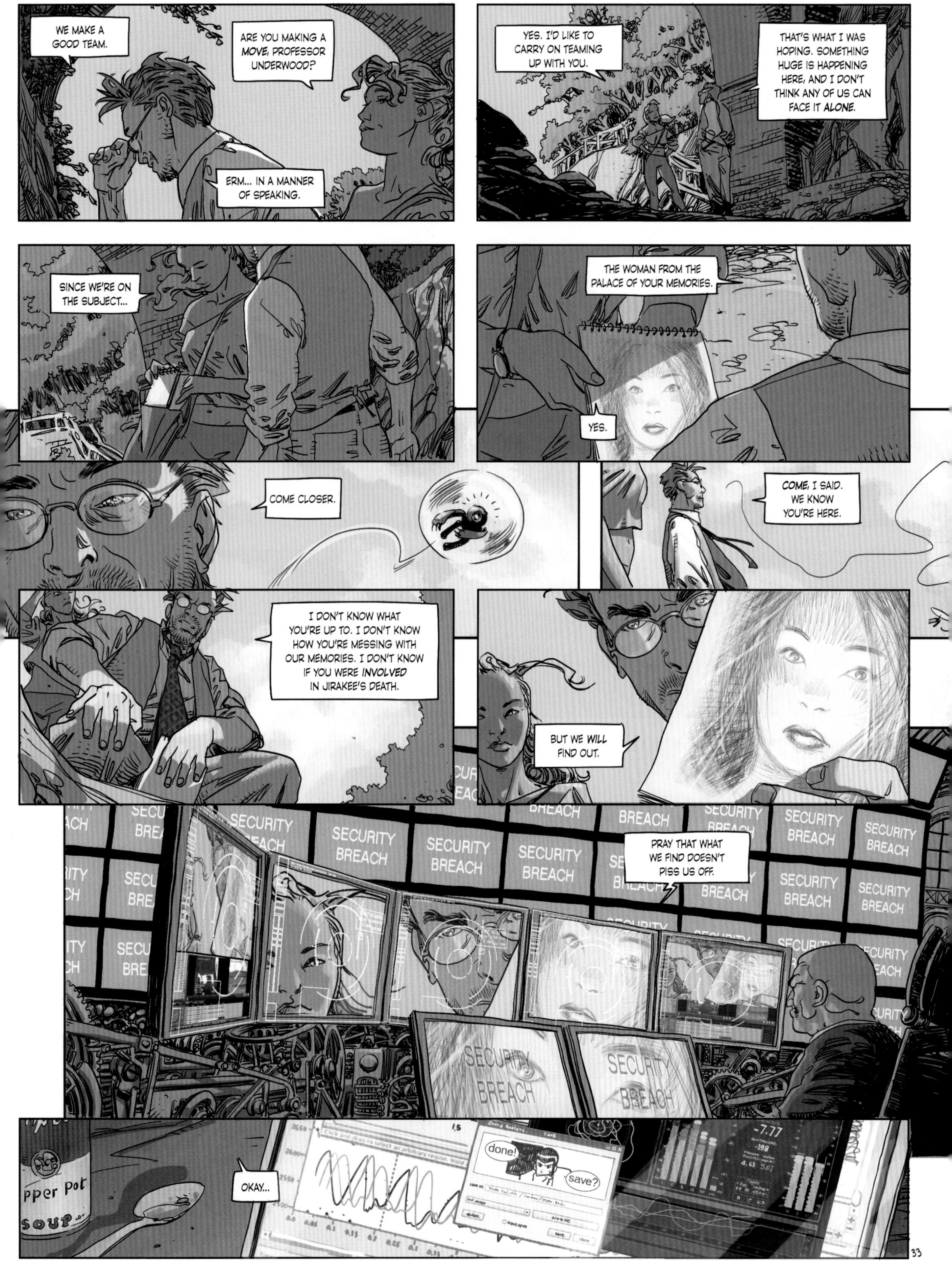
WE MAKE A GOOD TEAM.
ARE YOU MAKING A *MOVE*, PROFESSOR UNDERWOOD?
ERM... IN A MANNER OF SPEAKING.
YES. I'D LIKE TO CARRY ON TEAMING UP WITH YOU.
THAT'S WHAT I WAS HOPING. SOMETHING HUGE IS HAPPENING HERE, AND I DON'T THINK ANY OF US CAN FACE IT *ALONE*.
SINCE WE'RE ON THE SUBJECT...
THE WOMAN FROM THE PALACE OF YOUR MEMORIES.
YES.
COME CLOSER.
COME, I SAID. WE KNOW YOU'RE HERE.
I DON'T KNOW WHAT YOU'RE UP TO. I DON'T KNOW HOW YOU'RE MESSING WITH OUR MEMORIES. I DON'T KNOW IF YOU WERE *INVOLVED* IN JIRAKEE'S DEATH.
BUT WE *WILL* FIND OUT.
SECURITY BREACH
PRAY THAT WHAT WE FIND DOESN'T PISS US OFF.
pper Pot
SOUP
OKAY...
done!
save?
-7.77

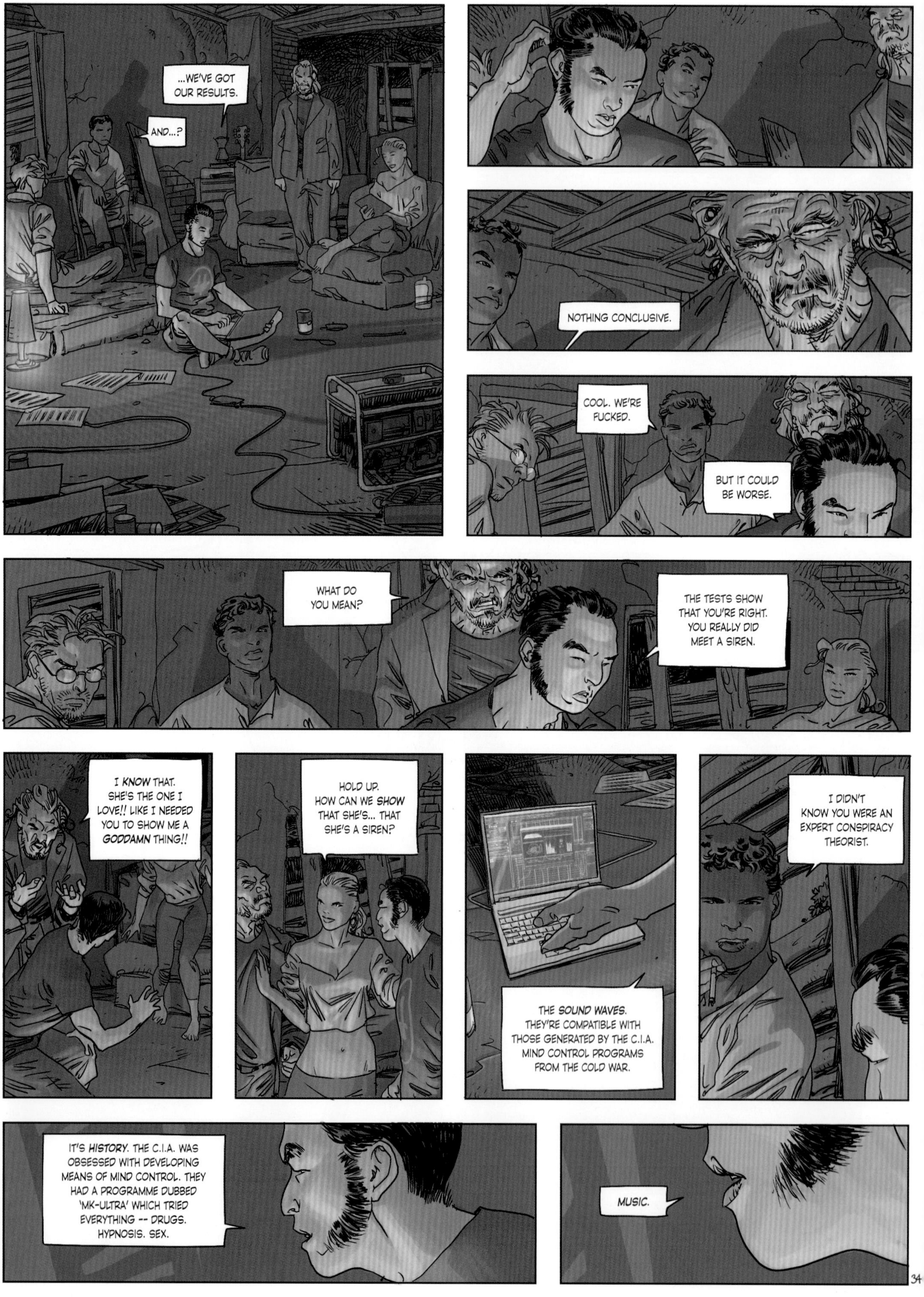
...WE'VE GOT OUR RESULTS.
AND...?
NOTHING CONCLUSIVE.
COOL. WE'RE FUCKED.
BUT IT COULD BE WORSE.
WHAT DO YOU MEAN?
THE TESTS SHOW THAT YOU'RE RIGHT. YOU REALLY DID MEET A SIREN.
I *KNOW* THAT. SHE'S THE ONE I LOVE!! LIKE I NEEDED YOU TO SHOW ME A *GODDAMN* THING!!
HOLD UP. HOW CAN WE *SHOW* THAT SHE'S... THAT SHE'S A SIREN?
THE *SOUND WAVES*. THEY'RE COMPATIBLE WITH THOSE GENERATED BY THE C.I.A. MIND CONTROL PROGRAMS FROM THE COLD WAR.
I DIDN'T KNOW YOU WERE AN EXPERT CONSPIRACY THEORIST.
IT'S *HISTORY*. THE C.I.A. WAS OBSESSED WITH DEVELOPING MEANS OF MIND CONTROL. THEY HAD A PROGRAMME DUBBED 'MK-ULTRA' WHICH TRIED EVERYTHING -- DRUGS. HYPNOSIS. SEX.
MUSIC.

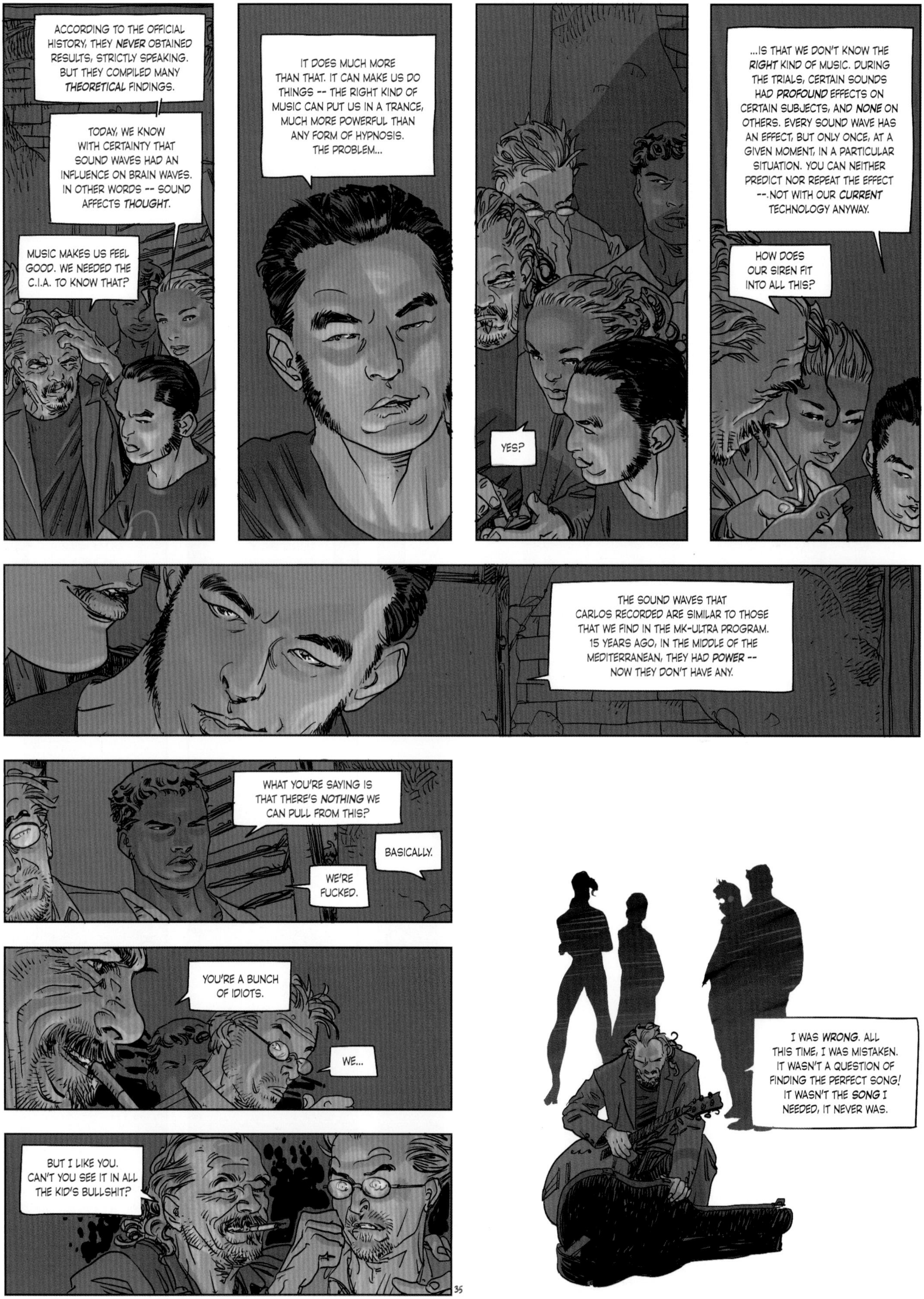

ACCORDING TO THE OFFICIAL HISTORY, THEY *NEVER* OBTAINED RESULTS, STRICTLY SPEAKING. BUT THEY COMPILED MANY *THEORETICAL* FINDINGS.
TODAY, WE KNOW WITH CERTAINTY THAT SOUND WAVES HAD AN INFLUENCE ON BRAIN WAVES. IN OTHER WORDS -- SOUND AFFECTS *THOUGHT*.
MUSIC MAKES US FEEL GOOD. WE NEEDED THE C.I.A. TO KNOW THAT?
IT DOES MUCH MORE THAN THAT. IT CAN MAKE US DO THINGS -- THE RIGHT KIND OF MUSIC CAN PUT US IN A TRANCE, MUCH MORE POWERFUL THAN ANY FORM OF HYPNOSIS. THE PROBLEM...
YES?
...IS THAT WE DON'T KNOW THE *RIGHT* KIND OF MUSIC. DURING THE TRIALS, CERTAIN SOUNDS HAD *PROFOUND* EFFECTS ON CERTAIN SUBJECTS, AND *NONE* ON OTHERS. EVERY SOUND WAVE HAS AN EFFECT, BUT ONLY ONCE, AT A GIVEN MOMENT, IN A PARTICULAR SITUATION. YOU CAN NEITHER PREDICT NOR REPEAT THE EFFECT --.NOT WITH OUR *CURRENT* TECHNOLOGY ANYWAY.
HOW DOES OUR SIREN FIT INTO ALL THIS?
THE SOUND WAVES THAT CARLOS RECORDED ARE SIMILAR TO THOSE THAT WE FIND IN THE MK-ULTRA PROGRAM. 15 YEARS AGO, IN THE MIDDLE OF THE MEDITERRANEAN, THEY HAD *POWER* -- NOW THEY DON'T HAVE ANY.
WHAT YOU'RE SAYING IS THAT THERE'S *NOTHING* WE CAN PULL FROM THIS?
BASICALLY.
WE'RE FUCKED.
YOU'RE A BUNCH OF IDIOTS.
WE...
BUT I LIKE YOU. CAN'T YOU SEE IT IN ALL THE KID'S BULLSHIT?
I WAS *WRONG*. ALL THIS TIME, I WAS MISTAKEN. IT WASN'T A QUESTION OF FINDING THE PERFECT SONG! IT WASN'T THE *SONG* I NEEDED, IT NEVER WAS.

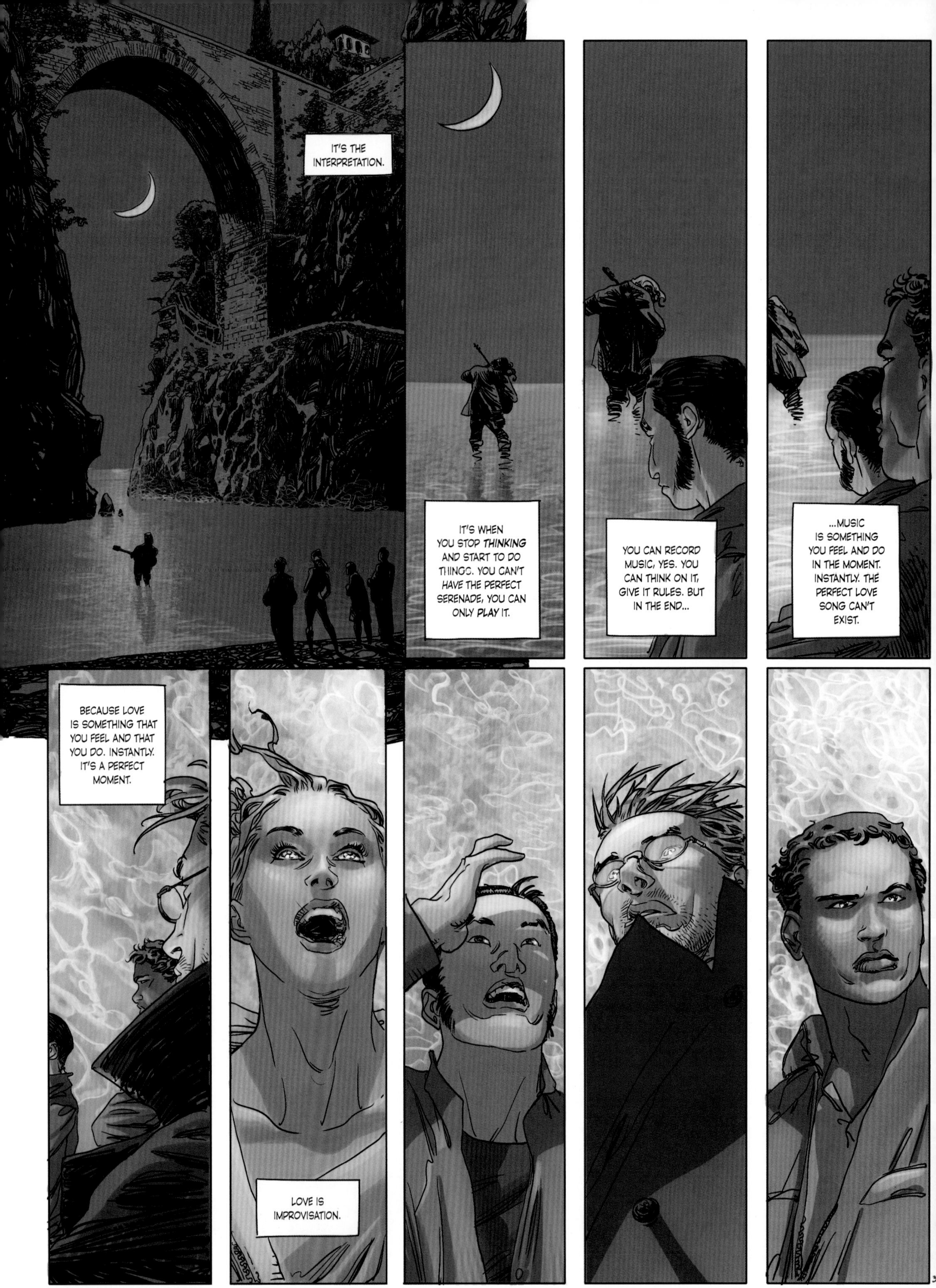
IT'S THE INTERPRETATION.
IT'S WHEN YOU STOP THINKING AND START TO DO THINGS. YOU CAN'T HAVE THE PERFECT SERENADE, YOU CAN ONLY PLAY IT.
YOU CAN RECORD MUSIC, YES. YOU CAN THINK ON IT, GIVE IT RULES. BUT IN THE END...
...MUSIC IS SOMETHING YOU FEEL AND DO IN THE MOMENT. INSTANTLY. THE PERFECT LOVE SONG CAN'T EXIST.
BECAUSE LOVE IS SOMETHING THAT YOU FEEL AND THAT YOU DO. INSTANTLY. IT'S A PERFECT MOMENT.
LOVE IS IMPROVISATION.

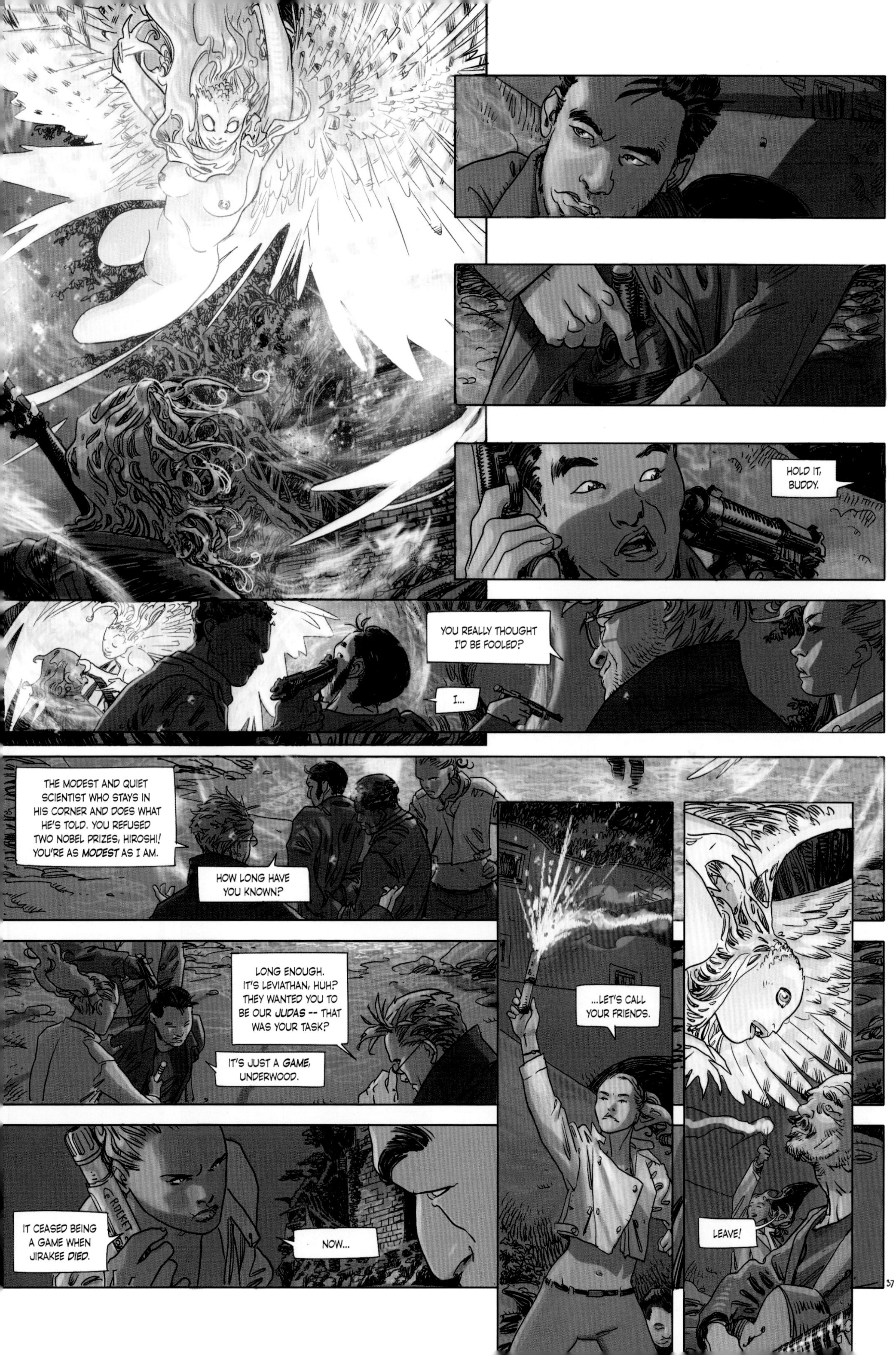
HOLD IT, BUDDY.
YOU REALLY THOUGHT I'D BE FOOLED?
I...
THE MODEST AND QUIET SCIENTIST WHO STAYS IN HIS CORNER AND DOES WHAT HE'S TOLD. YOU REFUSED TWO NOBEL PRIZES, HIROSHI! YOU'RE AS *MODEST* AS I AM.
HOW LONG HAVE YOU KNOWN?
LONG ENOUGH. IT'S LEVIATHAN, HUH? THEY WANTED YOU TO BE OUR *JUDAS* -- THAT WAS YOUR TASK?
IT'S JUST A *GAME*, UNDERWOOD.
IT CEASED BEING A GAME WHEN JIRAKEE *DIED*.
NOW...
...LET'S CALL YOUR FRIENDS.
LEAVE!

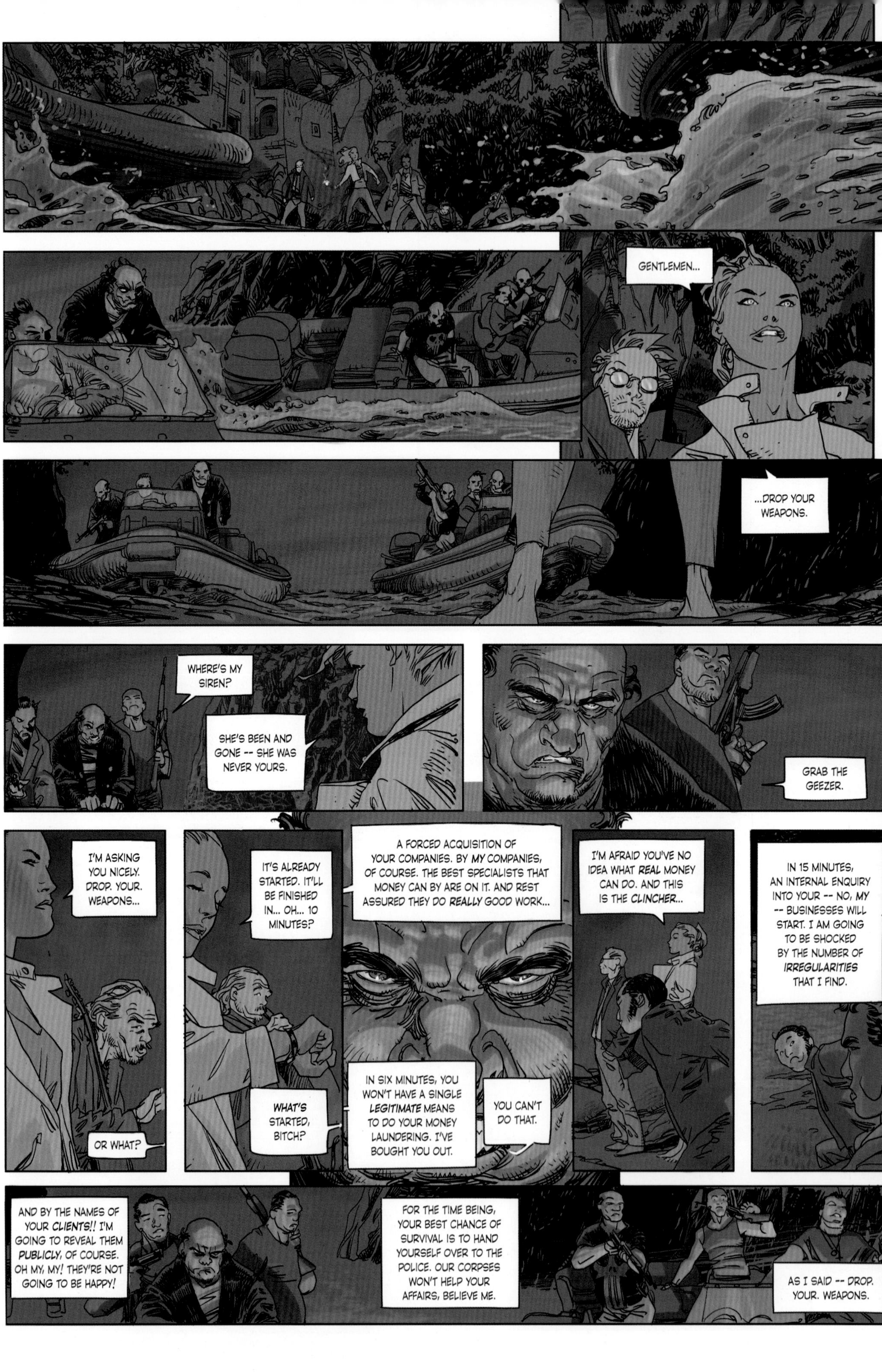
GENTLEMEN...
...DROP YOUR WEAPONS.
WHERE'S MY SIREN?
SHE'S BEEN AND GONE -- SHE WAS NEVER YOURS.
GRAB THE GEEZER.
I'M ASKING YOU NICELY. DROP. YOUR. WEAPONS...
OR WHAT?
IT'S ALREADY STARTED. IT'LL BE FINISHED IN... OH... 10 MINUTES?
WHAT'S STARTED, BITCH?
A FORCED ACQUISITION OF YOUR COMPANIES. BY MY COMPANIES, OF COURSE. THE BEST SPECIALISTS THAT MONEY CAN BY ARE ON IT. AND REST ASSURED THEY DO REALLY GOOD WORK...
IN SIX MINUTES, YOU WON'T HAVE A SINGLE LEGITIMATE MEANS TO DO YOUR MONEY LAUNDERING. I'VE BOUGHT YOU OUT.
YOU CAN'T DO THAT.
I'M AFRAID YOU'VE NO IDEA WHAT REAL MONEY CAN DO. AND THIS IS THE CLINCHER...
IN 15 MINUTES, AN INTERNAL ENQUIRY INTO YOUR -- NO, MY -- BUSINESSES WILL START. I AM GOING TO BE SHOCKED BY THE NUMBER OF IRREGULARITIES THAT I FIND.
AND BY THE NAMES OF YOUR CLIENTS!! I'M GOING TO REVEAL THEM PUBLICLY, OF COURSE. OH MY, MY! THEY'RE NOT GOING TO BE HAPPY!
FOR THE TIME BEING, YOUR BEST CHANCE OF SURVIVAL IS TO HAND YOURSELF OVER TO THE POLICE. OUR CORPSES WON'T HELP YOUR AFFAIRS, BELIEVE ME.
AS I SAID -- DROP. YOUR. WEAPONS.

STOP!

YOU THINK YOU *FRIGHTEN* ME? I'M GOING TO TAKE THE SIREN TO MY *FRIEND* -- HE'LL SORT EVERYTHING OUT!

FIRE.

OKAY. EVERYONE...

...HIT THE DIRT.

300

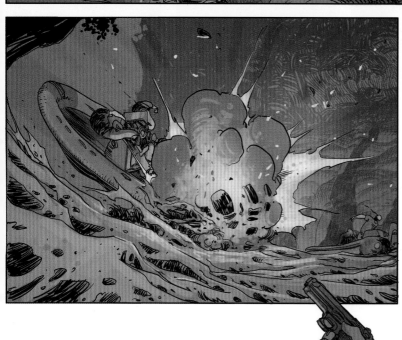

DONE.

39

YOU HAVE NO IDEA WHO YOU'RE ATTACKING.

WHO'S YOUR FAMOUS FRIEND? TELL US.

NEVER!! HIS MIGHT, HIS GRACE, HIS MAGNIFICENCE...

'KAY.

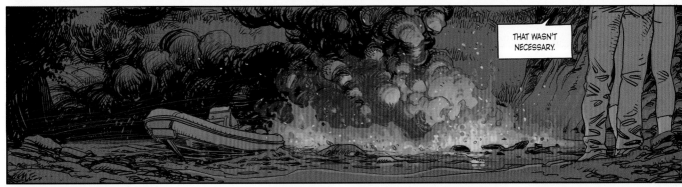

THAT WASN'T NECESSARY.

WHAT?

THIS... THIS CARNAGE.

YOU DON'T POINT A GUN AT A GUY LIKE ME IF YOU DON'T WANT TO USE IT.

NOW...

SPARE HIM!

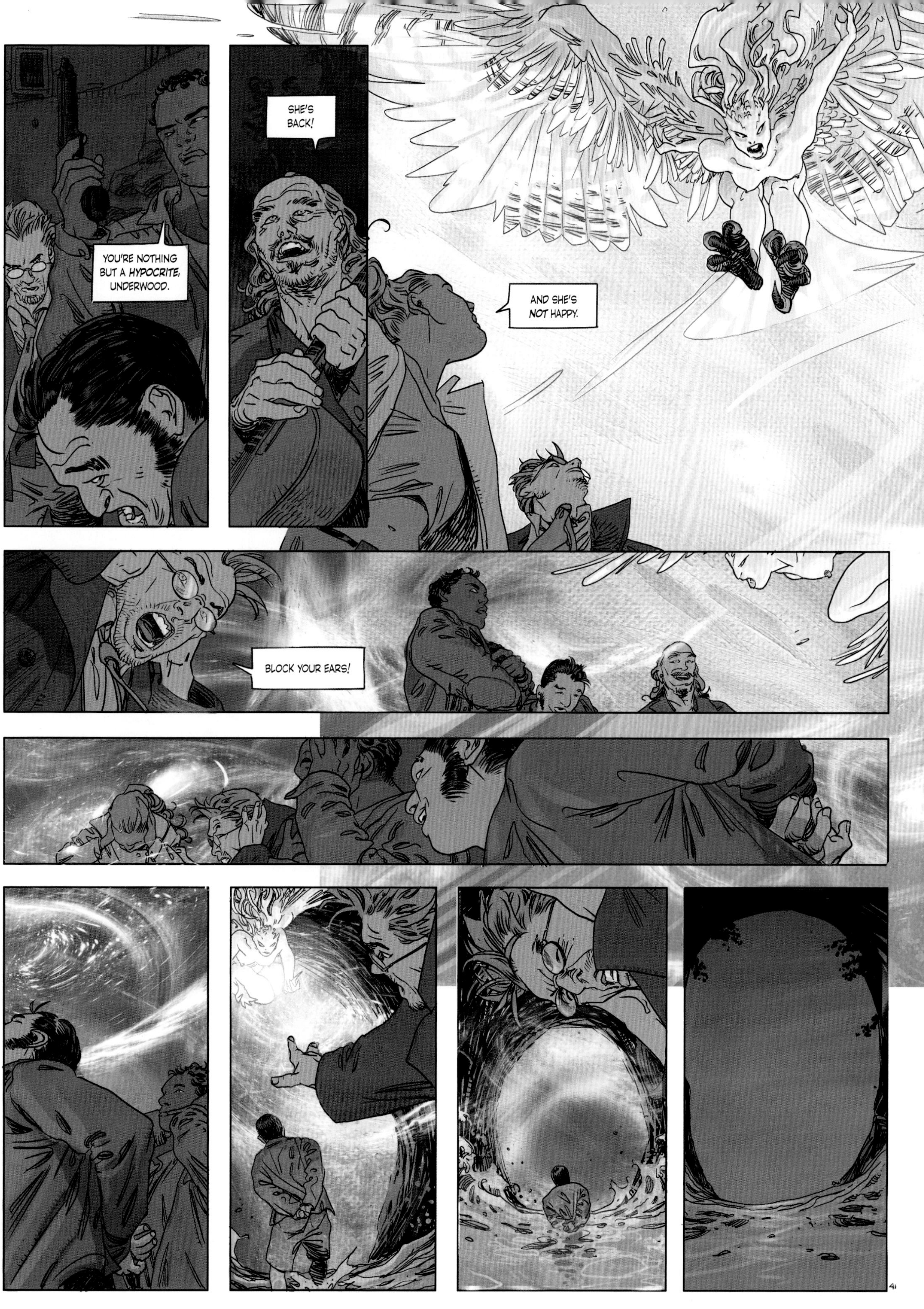
YOU'RE NOTHING BUT A HYPOCRITE, UNDERWOOD.
SHE'S BACK!
AND SHE'S NOT HAPPY.
BLOCK YOUR EARS!

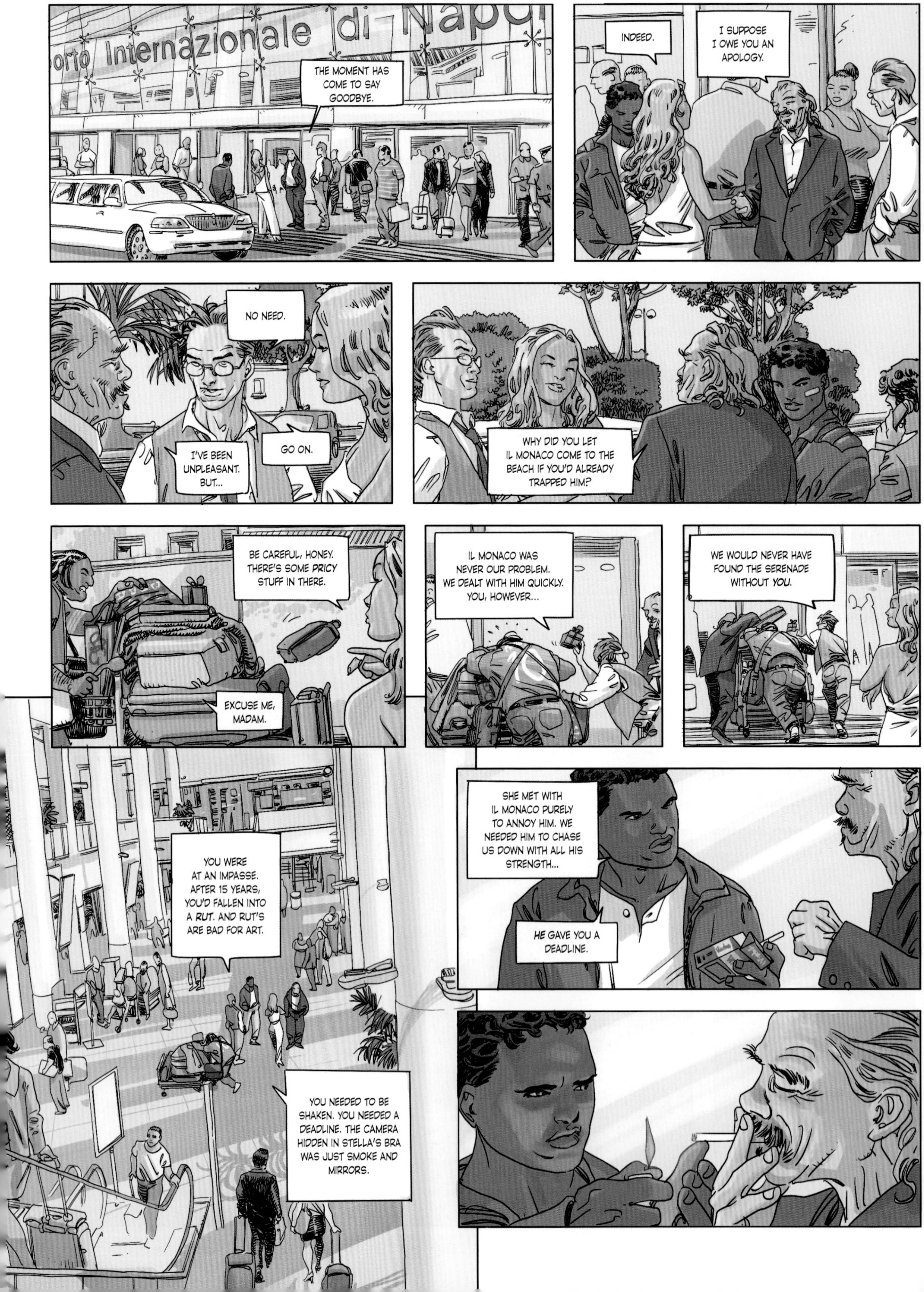
orto Internazionale di Napo
THE MOMENT HAS COME TO SAY GOODBYE.
INDEED.
I SUPPOSE I OWE YOU AN APOLOGY.
NO NEED.
I'VE BEEN UNPLEASANT. BUT...
GO ON.
WHY DID YOU LET IL MONACO COME TO THE BEACH IF YOU'D ALREADY TRAPPED HIM?
BE CAREFUL, HONEY. THERE'S SOME PRICY STUFF IN THERE.
EXCUSE ME, MADAM.
IL MONACO WAS NEVER OUR PROBLEM. WE DEALT WITH HIM QUICKLY. YOU, HOWEVER...
WE WOULD NEVER HAVE FOUND THE SERENADE WITHOUT YOU.
YOU WERE AT AN IMPASSE. AFTER 15 YEARS, YOU'D FALLEN INTO A RUT. AND RUT'S ARE BAD FOR ART.
YOU NEEDED TO BE SHAKEN. YOU NEEDED A DEADLINE. THE CAMERA HIDDEN IN STELLA'S BRA WAS JUST SMOKE AND MIRRORS.
SHE MET WITH IL MONACO PURELY TO ANNOY HIM. WE NEEDED HIM TO CHASE US DOWN WITH ALL HIS STRENGTH...
HE GAVE YOU A DEADLINE.

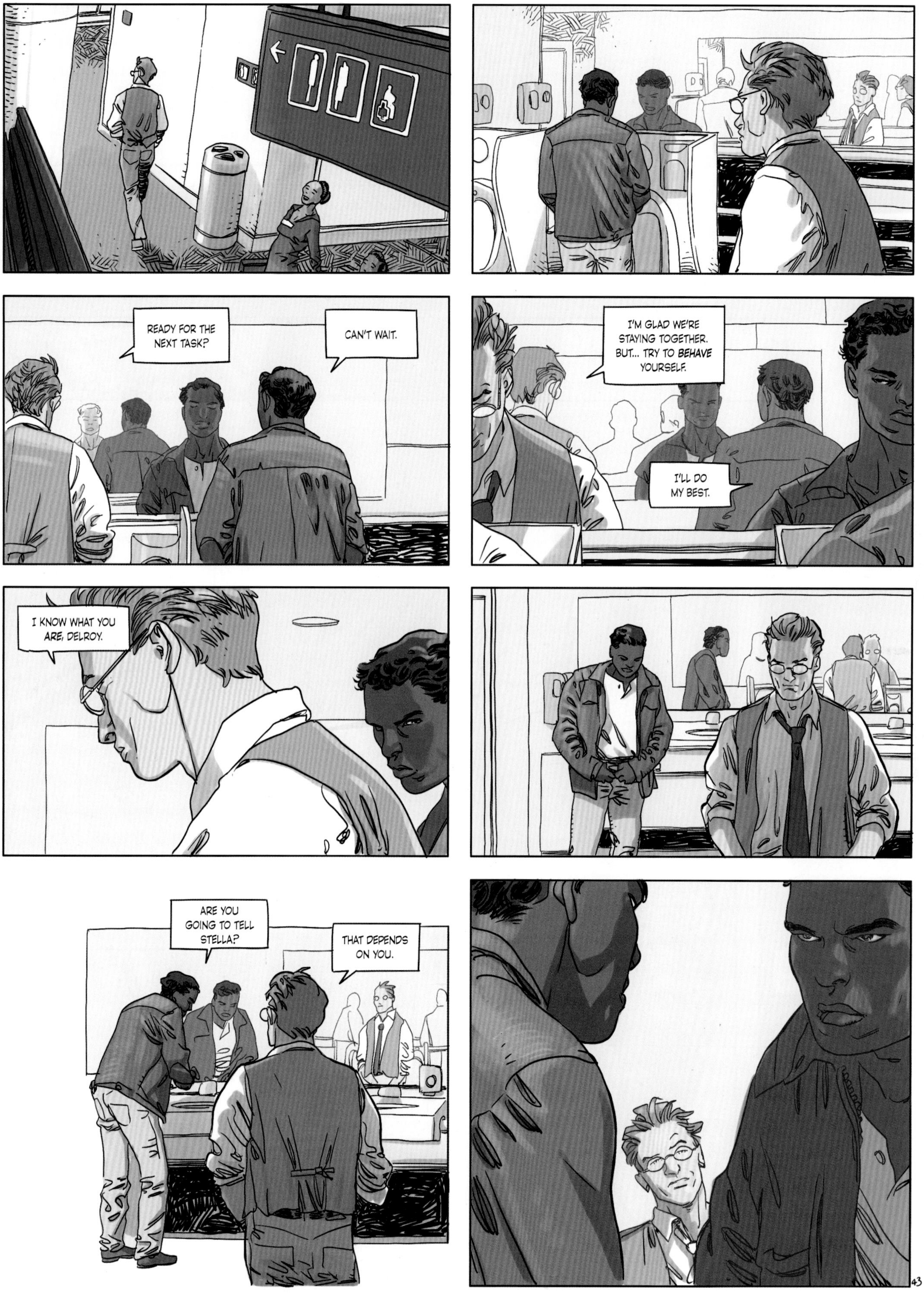
READY FOR THE NEXT TASK?
CAN'T WAIT.
I'M GLAD WE'RE STAYING TOGETHER. BUT... TRY TO BEHAVE YOURSELF.
I'LL DO MY BEST.
I KNOW WHAT YOU ARE, DELROY.
ARE YOU GOING TO TELL STELLA?
THAT DEPENDS ON YOU.

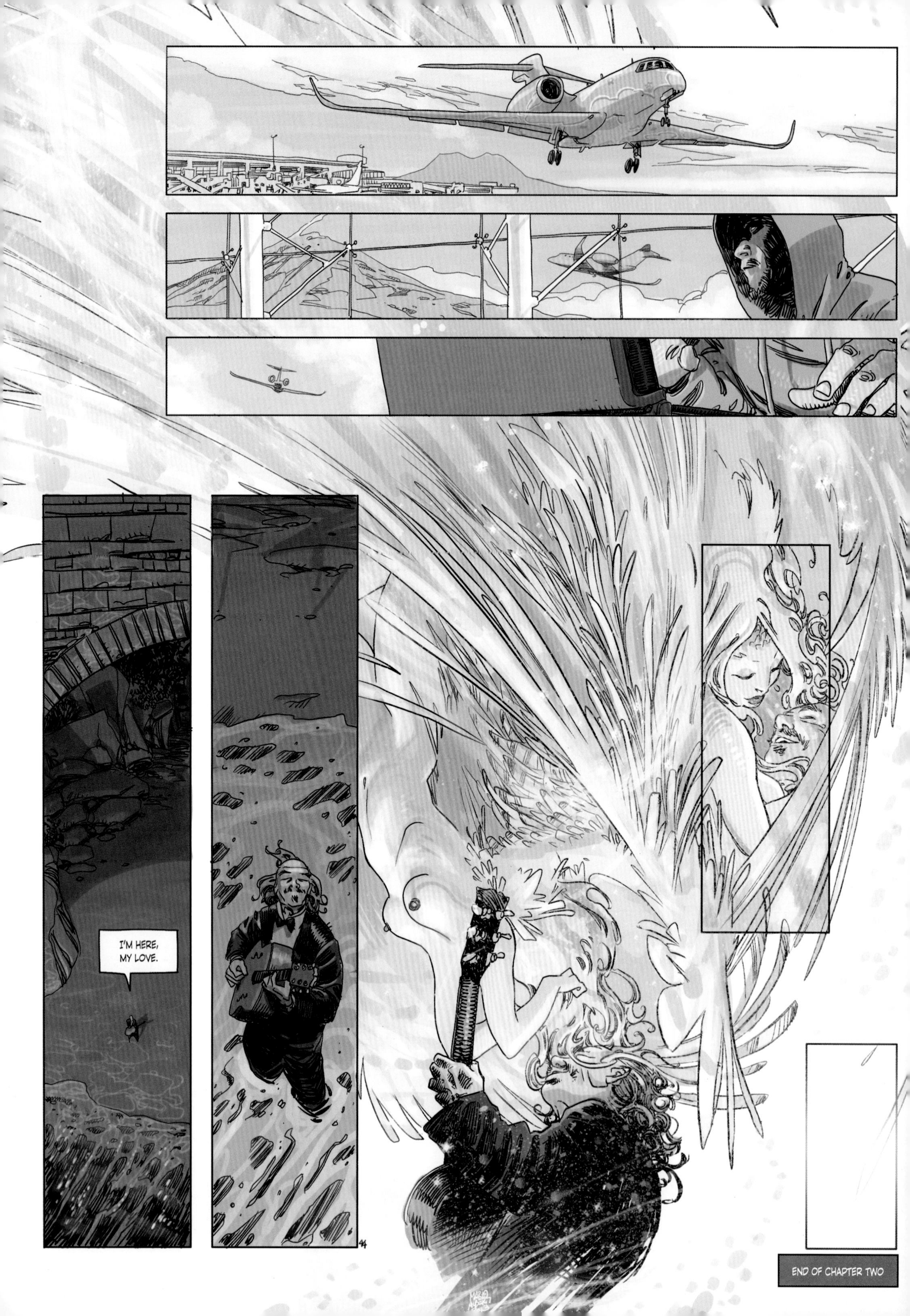

I'M HERE, MY LOVE.
44
END OF CHAPTER TWO

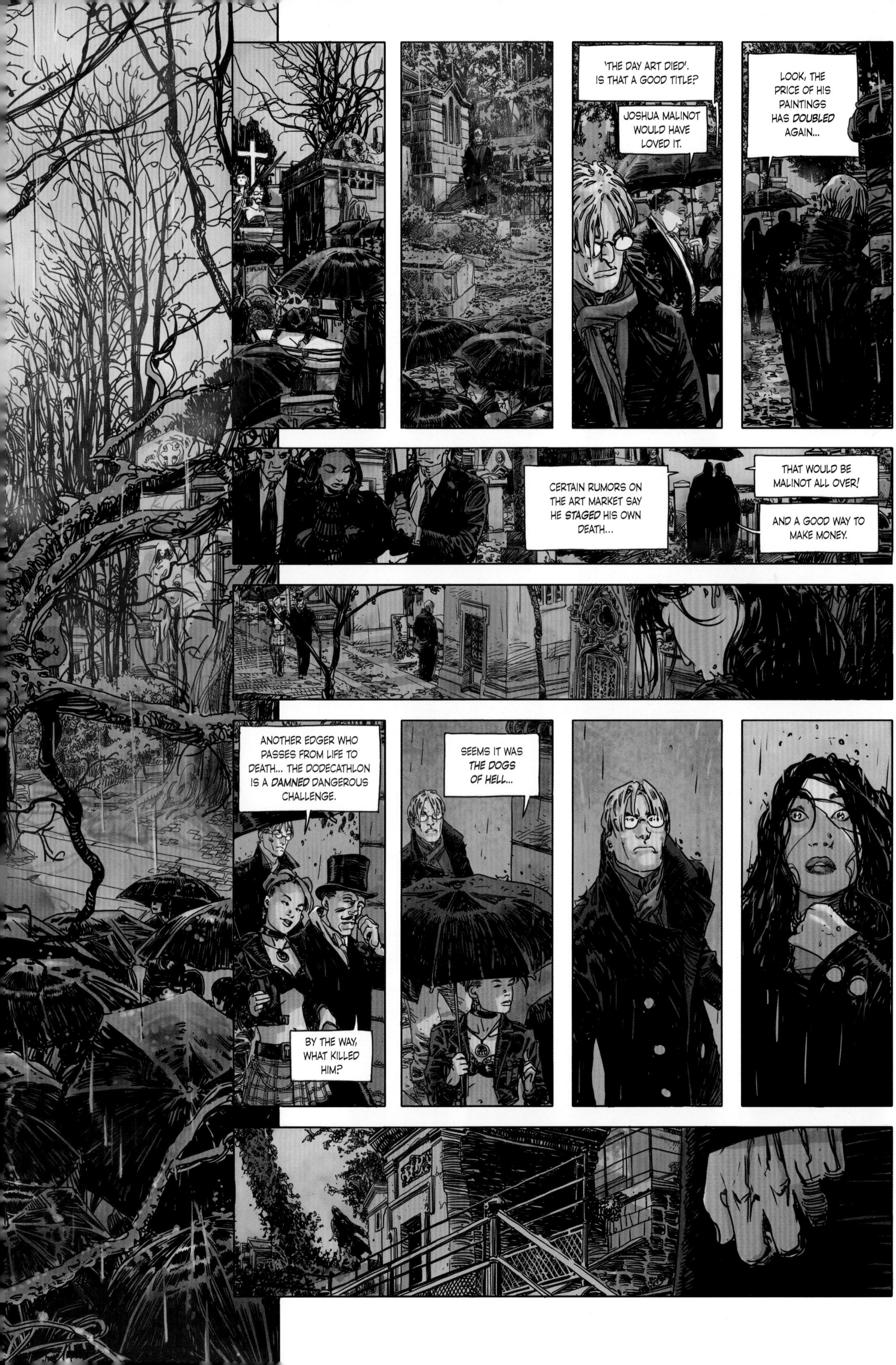

'THE DAY ART DIED'. IS THAT A GOOD TITLE?
JOSHUA MALINOT WOULD HAVE LOVED IT.
LOOK, THE PRICE OF HIS PAINTINGS HAS DOUBLED AGAIN...
CERTAIN RUMORS ON THE ART MARKET SAY HE STAGED HIS OWN DEATH...
THAT WOULD BE MALINOT ALL OVER!
AND A GOOD WAY TO MAKE MONEY.
ANOTHER EDGER WHO PASSES FROM LIFE TO DEATH... THE DODECATHLON IS A DAMNED DANGEROUS CHALLENGE.
BY THE WAY, WHAT KILLED HIM?
SEEMS IT WAS THE DOGS OF HELL...

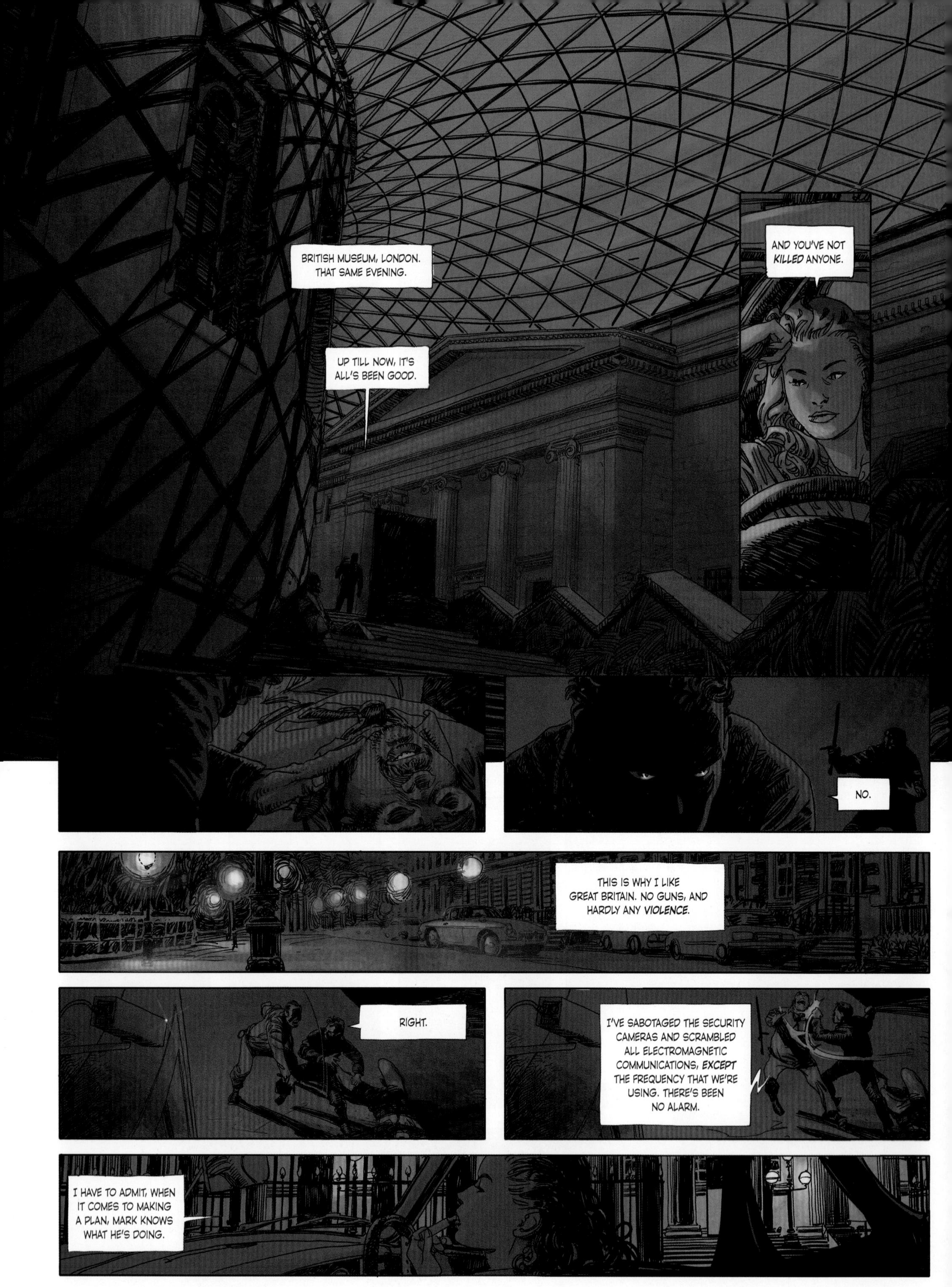
BRITISH MUSEUM, LONDON. THAT SAME EVENING.
UP TILL NOW, IT'S ALL'S BEEN GOOD.
AND YOU'VE NOT KILLED ANYONE.
NO.
THIS IS WHY I LIKE GREAT BRITAIN. NO GUNS, AND HARDLY ANY VIOLENCE.
RIGHT.
I'VE SABOTAGED THE SECURITY CAMERAS AND SCRAMBLED ALL ELECTROMAGNETIC COMMUNICATIONS, EXCEPT THE FREQUENCY THAT WE'RE USING. THERE'S BEEN NO ALARM.
I HAVE TO ADMIT, WHEN IT COMES TO MAKING A PLAN, MARK KNOWS WHAT HE'S DOING.

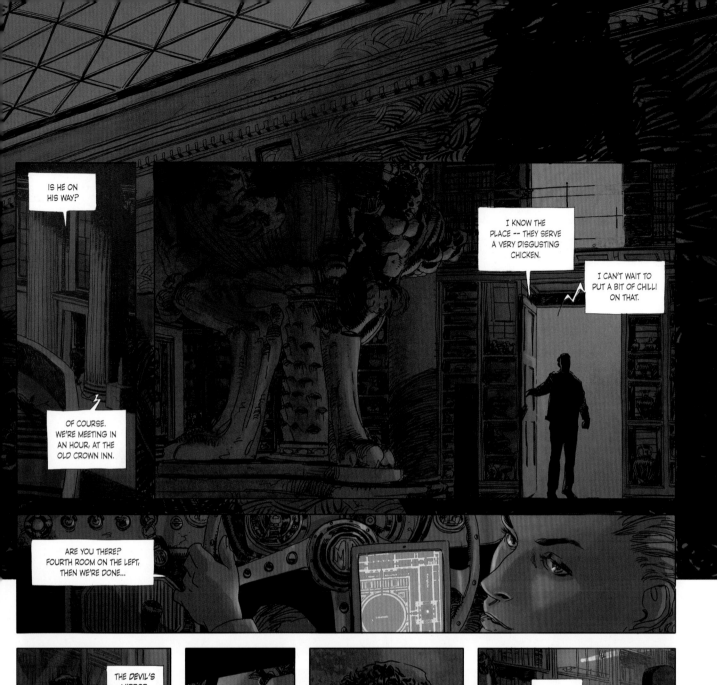

IS HE ON HIS WAY?

I KNOW THE PLACE -- THEY SERVE A VERY DISGUSTING CHICKEN.

I CAN'T WAIT TO PUT A BIT OF CHILLI ON THAT.

OF COURSE. WE'RE MEETING IN AN HOUR, AT THE OLD CROWN INN.

ARE YOU THERE? FOURTH ROOM ON THE LEFT, THEN WE'RE DONE...

THE DEVIL'S MIRROR.

WE LOST TWO PEOPLE IN OUR FIRST TRIAL AND ALMOST LOST OUR LIVES IN ALL THE OTHERS. THIS TIME WAS EASY. YOU REMEMBER THAT THING WITH LENIN'S MUMMY? JESUS, THAT WAS UGLY.

THERE'S NO POINT.

IT'S A FAKE.

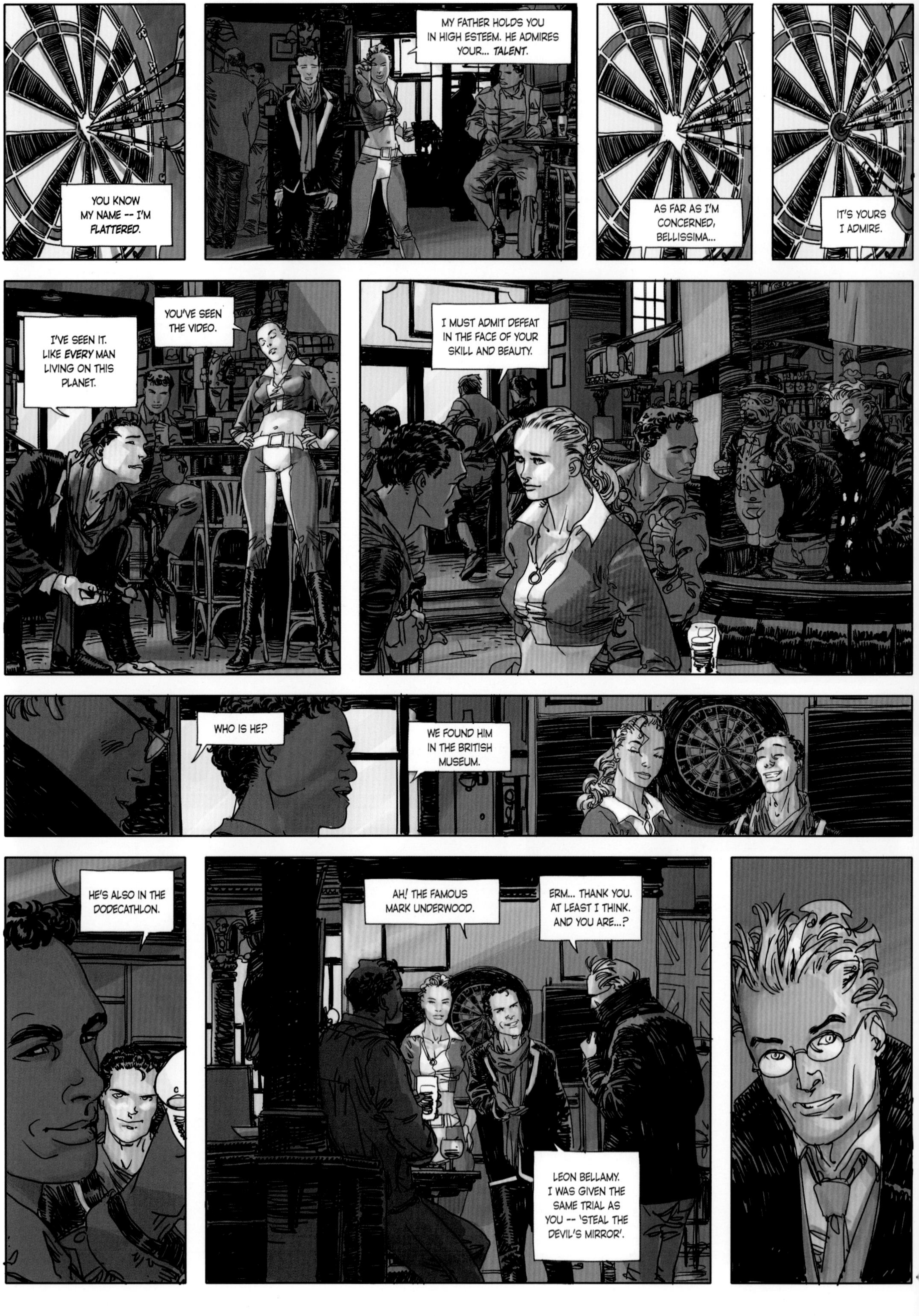
YOU KNOW MY NAME -- I'M *FLATTERED*.
MY FATHER HOLDS YOU IN HIGH ESTEEM. HE ADMIRES YOUR... *TALENT*.
AS FAR AS I'M CONCERNED, BELLISSIMA...
IT'S YOURS I ADMIRE.
YOU'VE SEEN THE VIDEO.
I'VE SEEN IT. LIKE **EVERY** MAN LIVING ON THIS PLANET.
I MUST ADMIT DEFEAT IN THE FACE OF YOUR SKILL AND BEAUTY.
WHO IS HE?
WE FOUND HIM IN THE BRITISH MUSEUM.
HE'S ALSO IN THE DODECATHLON.
AH! THE FAMOUS MARK UNDERWOOD.
ERM... THANK YOU. AT LEAST I THINK. AND YOU ARE...?
LEON BELLAMY. I WAS GIVEN THE SAME TRIAL AS YOU -- 'STEAL THE DEVIL'S MIRROR'.

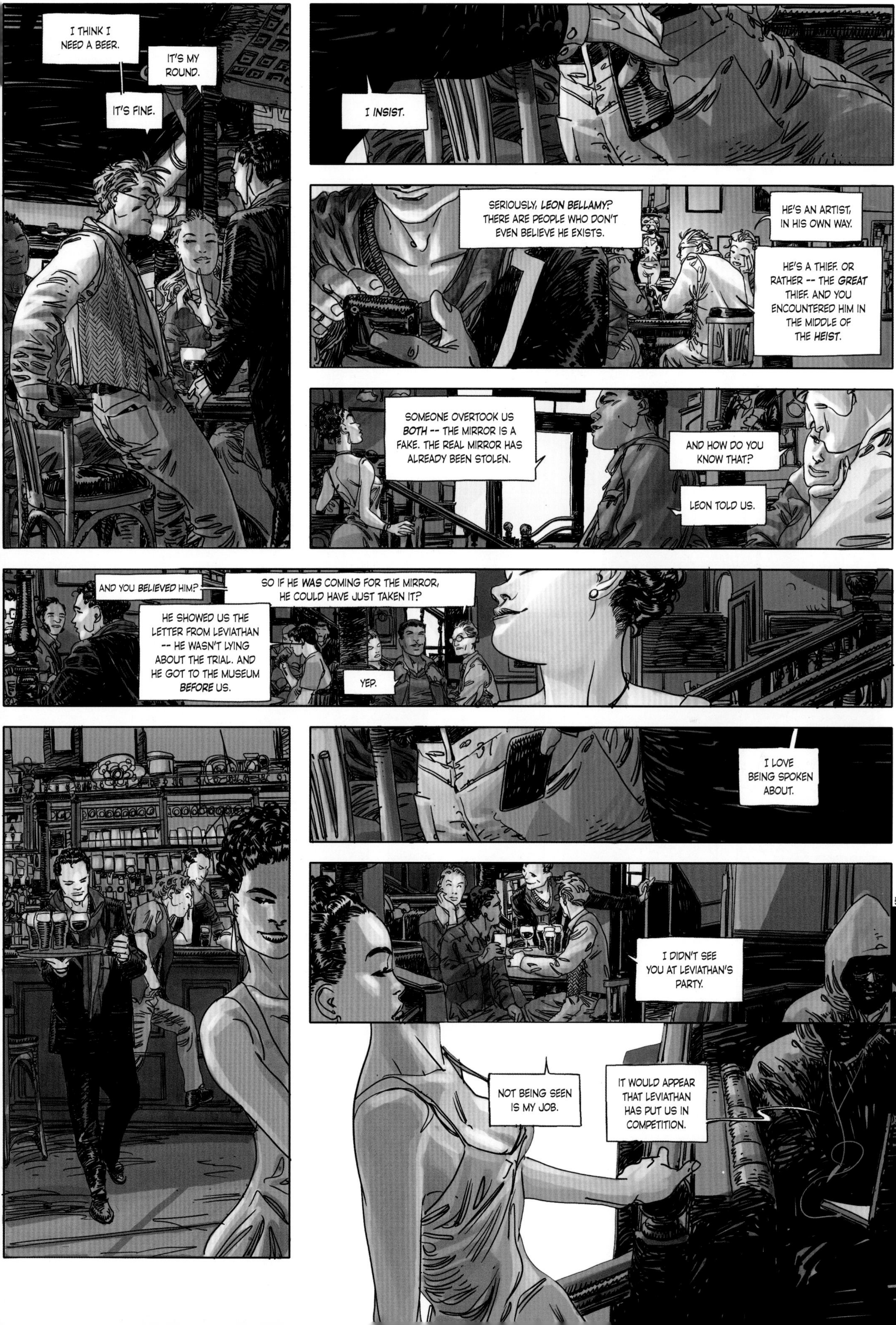
I THINK I NEED A BEER.
IT'S MY ROUND.
IT'S FINE.
I *INSIST*.
SERIOUSLY, *LEON BELLAMY*? THERE ARE PEOPLE WHO DON'T EVEN BELIEVE HE EXISTS.
HE'S AN ARTIST, IN HIS OWN WAY.
HE'S A THIEF. OR RATHER -- THE *GREAT* THIEF. AND YOU ENCOUNTERED HIM IN THE MIDDLE OF THE *HEIST*.
SOMEONE OVERTOOK US *BOTH* -- THE MIRROR IS A FAKE. THE REAL MIRROR HAS ALREADY BEEN STOLEN.
AND HOW DO YOU KNOW THAT?
LEON TOLD US.
AND YOU *BELIEVED* HIM?
HE SHOWED US THE LETTER FROM LEVIATHAN -- HE WASN'T LYING ABOUT THE TRIAL. AND HE GOT TO THE MUSEUM *BEFORE* US.
SO IF HE *WAS* COMING FOR THE MIRROR, HE COULD HAVE JUST TAKEN IT?
YEP.
I LOVE BEING SPOKEN ABOUT.
I DIDN'T SEE YOU AT LEVIATHAN'S PARTY.
NOT BEING SEEN IS MY JOB.
IT WOULD APPEAR THAT LEVIATHAN HAS PUT US IN COMPETITION.

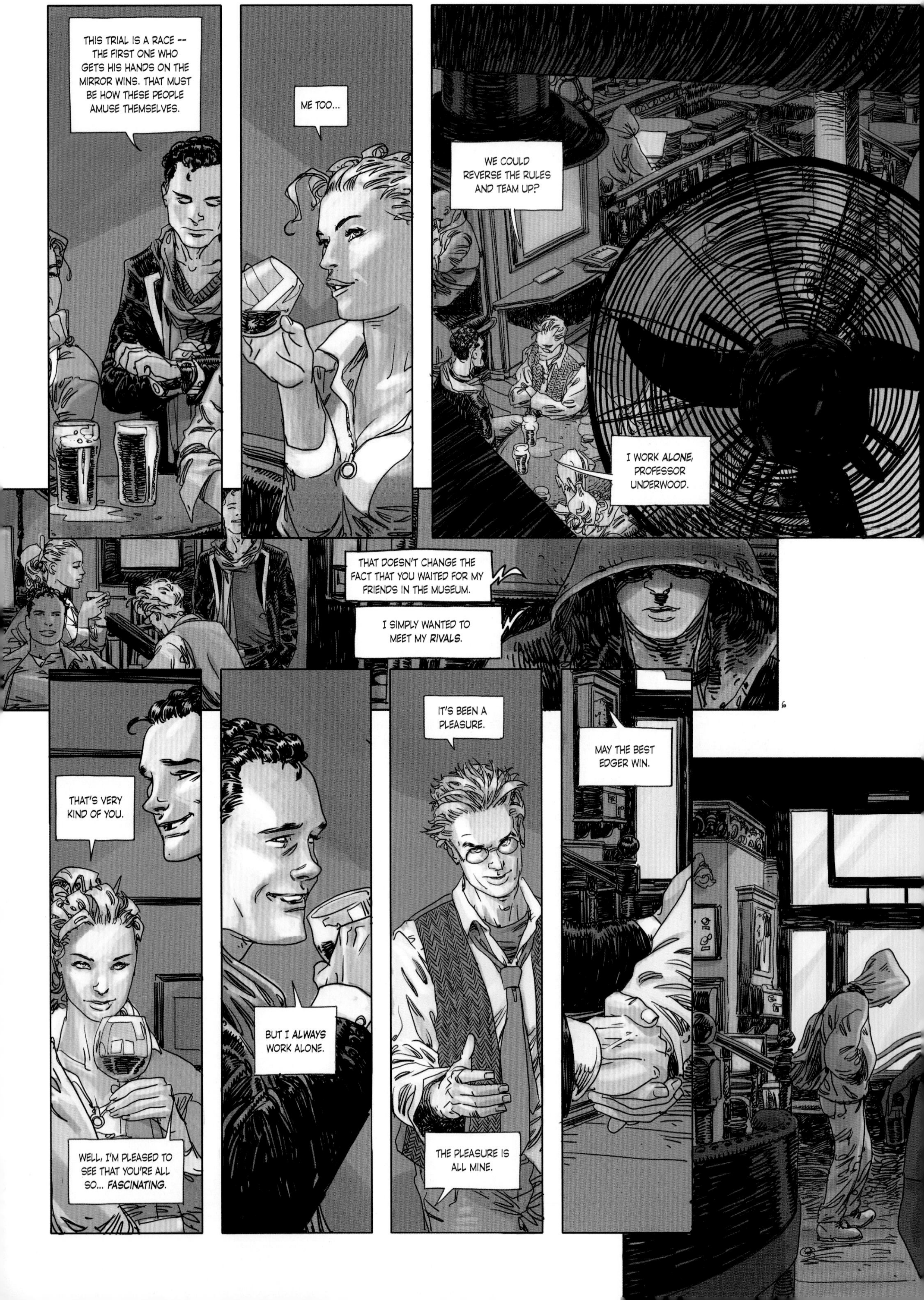
THIS TRIAL IS A RACE -- THE FIRST ONE WHO GETS HIS HANDS ON THE MIRROR WINS. THAT MUST BE HOW THESE PEOPLE AMUSE THEMSELVES.
ME TOO...
WE COULD REVERSE THE RULES AND TEAM UP?
I WORK ALONE, PROFESSOR UNDERWOOD.
THAT DOESN'T CHANGE THE FACT THAT YOU WAITED FOR MY FRIENDS IN THE MUSEUM.
I SIMPLY WANTED TO MEET MY RIVALS.
THAT'S VERY KIND OF YOU.
WELL, I'M PLEASED TO SEE THAT YOU'RE ALL SO... FASCINATING.
BUT I ALWAYS WORK ALONE.
IT'S BEEN A PLEASURE.
THE PLEASURE IS ALL MINE.
MAY THE BEST EDGER WIN.
6

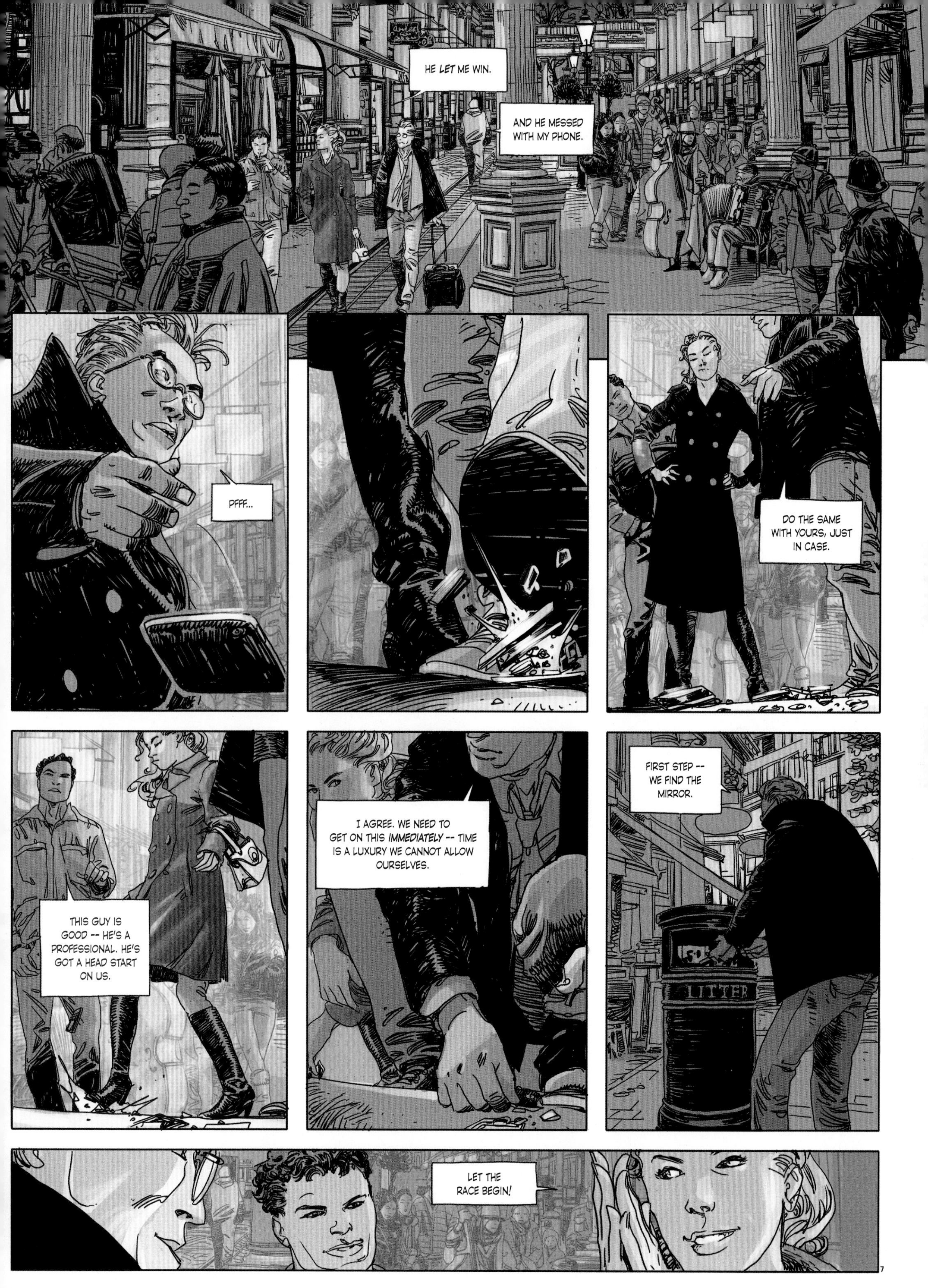
HE LET ME WIN.
AND HE MESSED WITH MY PHONE.
PFFF...
DO THE SAME WITH YOURS, JUST IN CASE.
THIS GUY IS GOOD -- HE'S A PROFESSIONAL. HE'S GOT A HEAD START ON US.
I AGREE. WE NEED TO GET ON THIS *IMMEDIATELY* -- TIME IS A LUXURY WE CANNOT ALLOW OURSELVES.
FIRST STEP -- WE FIND THE MIRROR.
LITTER
LET THE RACE BEGIN!

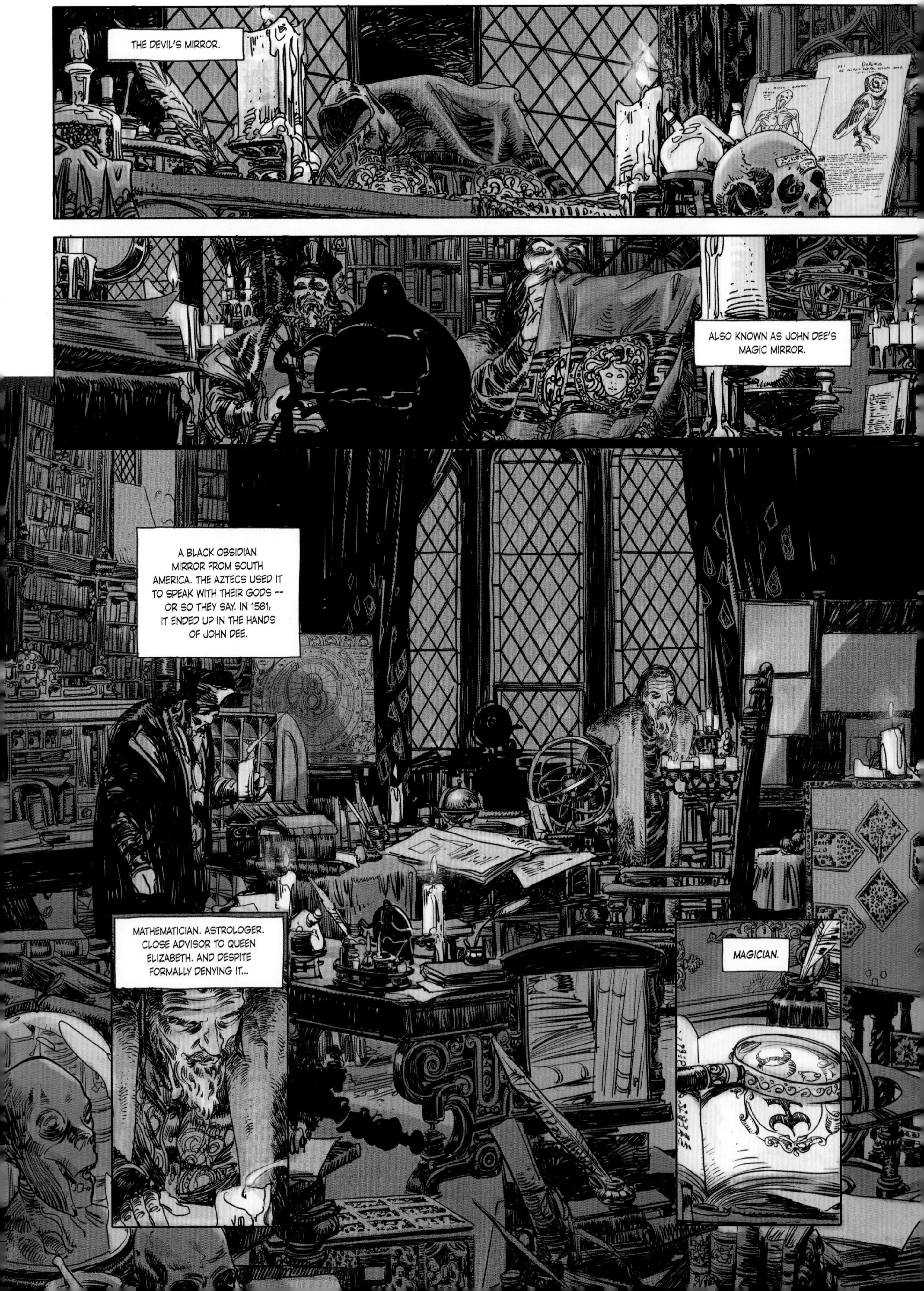
THE DEVIL'S MIRROR.
ALSO KNOWN AS JOHN DEE'S MAGIC MIRROR.
A BLACK OBSIDIAN MIRROR FROM SOUTH AMERICA. THE AZTECS USED IT TO SPEAK WITH THEIR GODS -- OR SO THEY SAY. IN 1581, IT ENDED UP IN THE HANDS OF JOHN DEE.
MATHEMATICIAN. ASTROLOGER. CLOSE ADVISOR TO QUEEN ELIZABETH. AND DESPITE FORMALLY DENYING IT...
MAGICIAN.

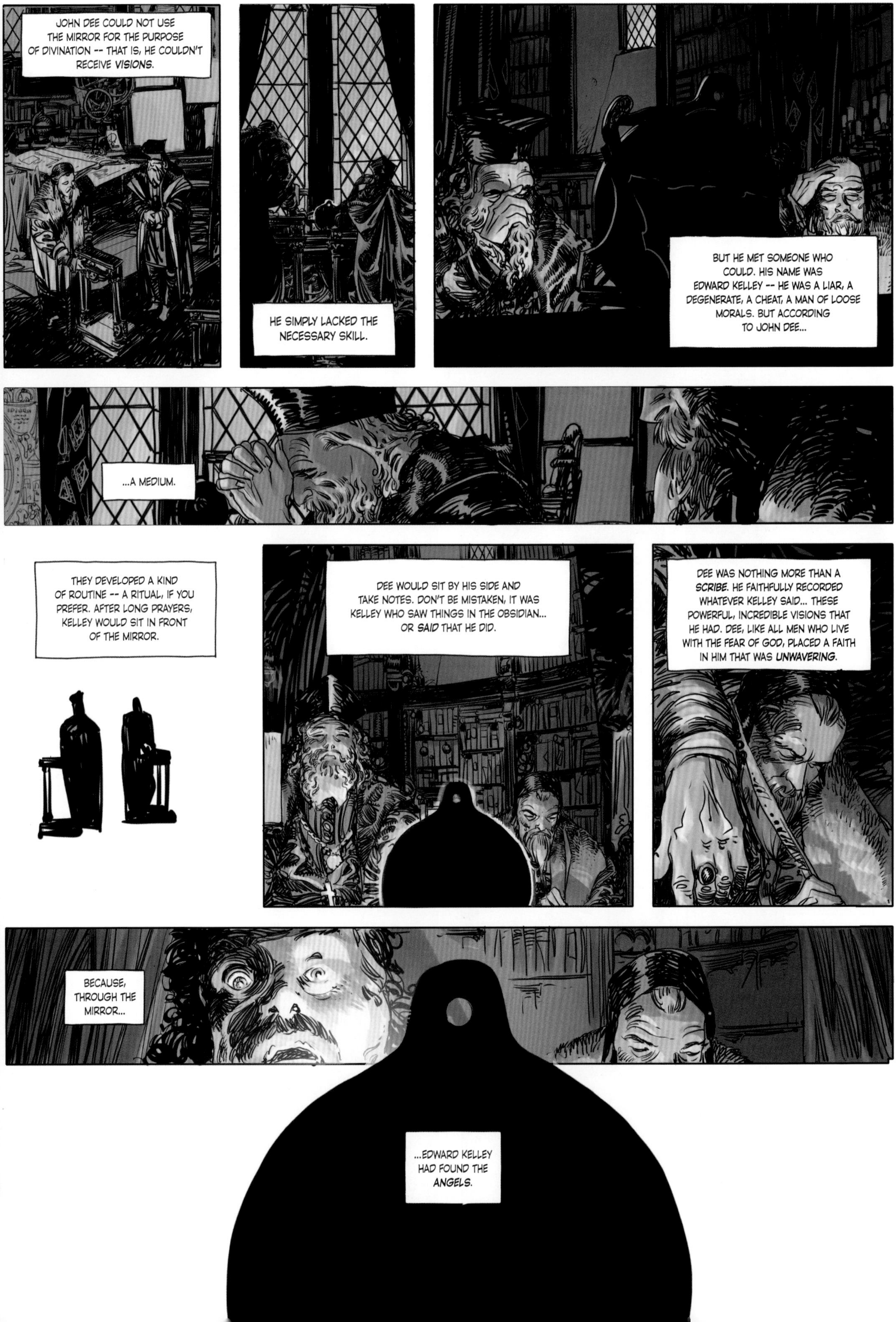
JOHN DEE COULD NOT USE THE MIRROR FOR THE PURPOSE OF DIVINATION -- THAT IS, HE COULDN'T RECEIVE VISIONS.
HE SIMPLY LACKED THE NECESSARY SKILL.
BUT HE MET SOMEONE WHO COULD. HIS NAME WAS EDWARD KELLEY -- HE WAS A LIAR, A DEGENERATE, A CHEAT, A MAN OF LOOSE MORALS. BUT ACCORDING TO JOHN DEE...
...A MEDIUM.
THEY DEVELOPED A KIND OF ROUTINE -- A RITUAL, IF YOU PREFER. AFTER LONG PRAYERS, KELLEY WOULD SIT IN FRONT OF THE MIRROR.
DEE WOULD SIT BY HIS SIDE AND TAKE NOTES. DON'T BE MISTAKEN, IT WAS KELLEY WHO SAW THINGS IN THE OBSIDIAN... OR SAID THAT HE DID.
DEE WAS NOTHING MORE THAN A SCRIBE. HE FAITHFULLY RECORDED WHATEVER KELLEY SAID... THESE POWERFUL, INCREDIBLE VISIONS THAT HE HAD. DEE, LIKE ALL MEN WHO LIVE WITH THE FEAR OF GOD, PLACED A FAITH IN HIM THAT WAS UNWAVERING.
BECAUSE, THROUGH THE MIRROR...
...EDWARD KELLEY HAD FOUND THE ANGELS.

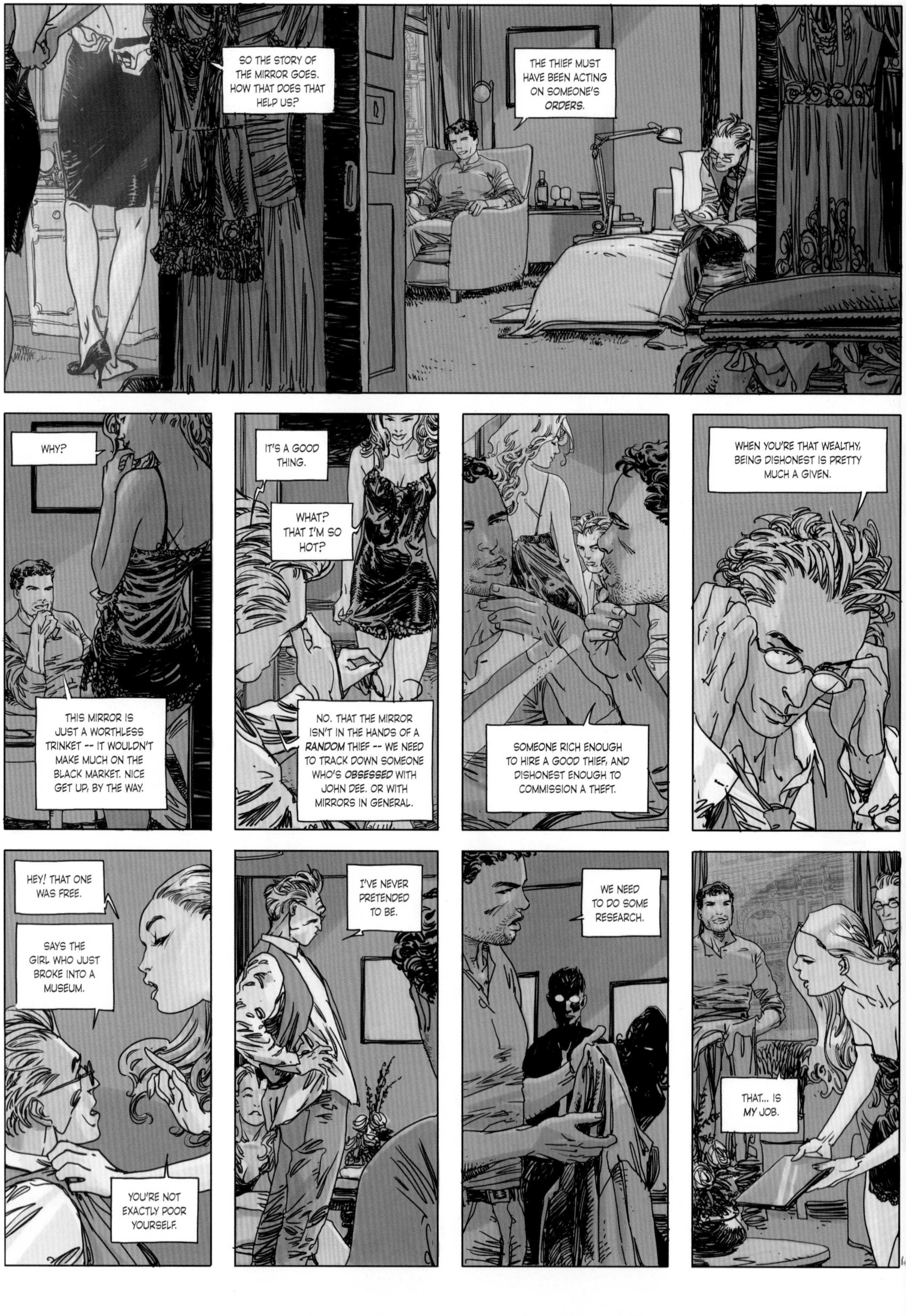
SO THE STORY OF THE MIRROR GOES. HOW THAT DOES THAT HELP US?
THE THIEF MUST HAVE BEEN ACTING ON SOMEONE'S *ORDERS*.
WHY?
THIS MIRROR IS JUST A WORTHLESS TRINKET -- IT WOULDN'T MAKE MUCH ON THE BLACK MARKET. NICE GET UP, BY THE WAY.
IT'S A GOOD THING.
WHAT? THAT I'M SO HOT?
NO. THAT THE MIRROR ISN'T IN THE HANDS OF A *RANDOM* THIEF -- WE NEED TO TRACK DOWN SOMEONE WHO'S *OBSESSED* WITH JOHN DEE. OR WITH MIRRORS IN GENERAL.
SOMEONE RICH ENOUGH TO HIRE A GOOD THIEF, AND DISHONEST ENOUGH TO COMMISSION A THEFT.
WHEN YOU'RE THAT WEALTHY, BEING DISHONEST IS PRETTY MUCH A GIVEN.
HEY! THAT ONE WAS FREE.
SAYS THE GIRL WHO JUST BROKE INTO A MUSEUM.
YOU'RE NOT EXACTLY POOR YOURSELF.
I'VE NEVER PRETENDED TO BE.
WE NEED TO DO SOME RESEARCH.
THAT... IS *MY* JOB.

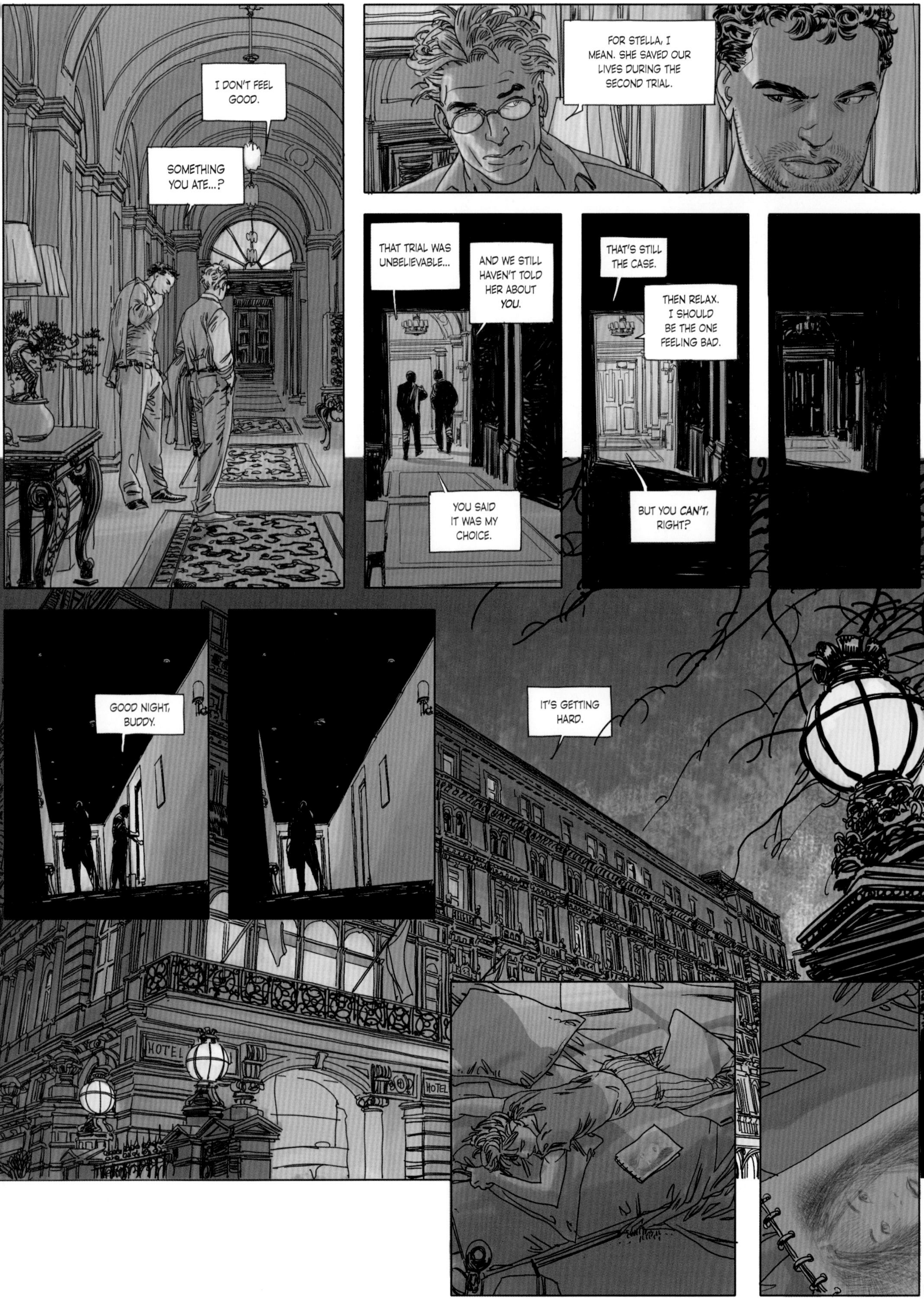
I DON'T FEEL GOOD.
SOMETHING YOU ATE...?
FOR STELLA, I MEAN. SHE SAVED OUR LIVES DURING THE SECOND TRIAL.
THAT TRIAL WAS UNBELIEVABLE...
AND WE STILL HAVEN'T TOLD HER ABOUT *YOU*.
YOU SAID IT WAS MY CHOICE.
THAT'S STILL THE CASE.
THEN RELAX. I SHOULD BE THE ONE FEELING BAD.
BUT YOU **CAN'T**, RIGHT?
GOOD NIGHT, BUDDY.
IT'S GETTING HARD.
HOTEL
HOTEL

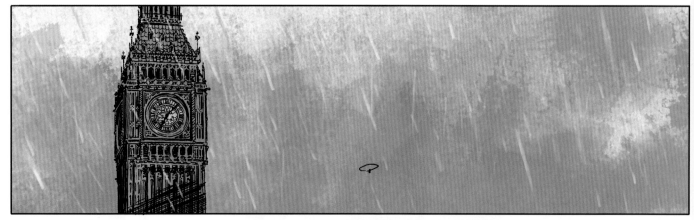

YES?

IT'S STELLA. I'VE SENT YOU AN EMAIL WITH NAMES.

LOOK AT THIS -- EMMA CROSSING-JONES, LADY OF LOVESTONE. PASSIONATE ABOUT ELIZABETHAN ART, AND INCIDENTALLY, BORING TO DEATH.

OR JOHN COLLINS -- AMERICAN MATHEMATICIAN, BASED IN HONG KONG. THIS GUY COLLECTS MIRRORS AND OBJECTS LINKED TO JOHN DEE.

THAT'S HIM.

HOW CAN YOU BE SO SURE?

HE AND I HAVE A HISTORY -- IT CAN'T BE A COINCIDENCE.

AND BY HISTORY YOU MEAN...?

HISTORY.

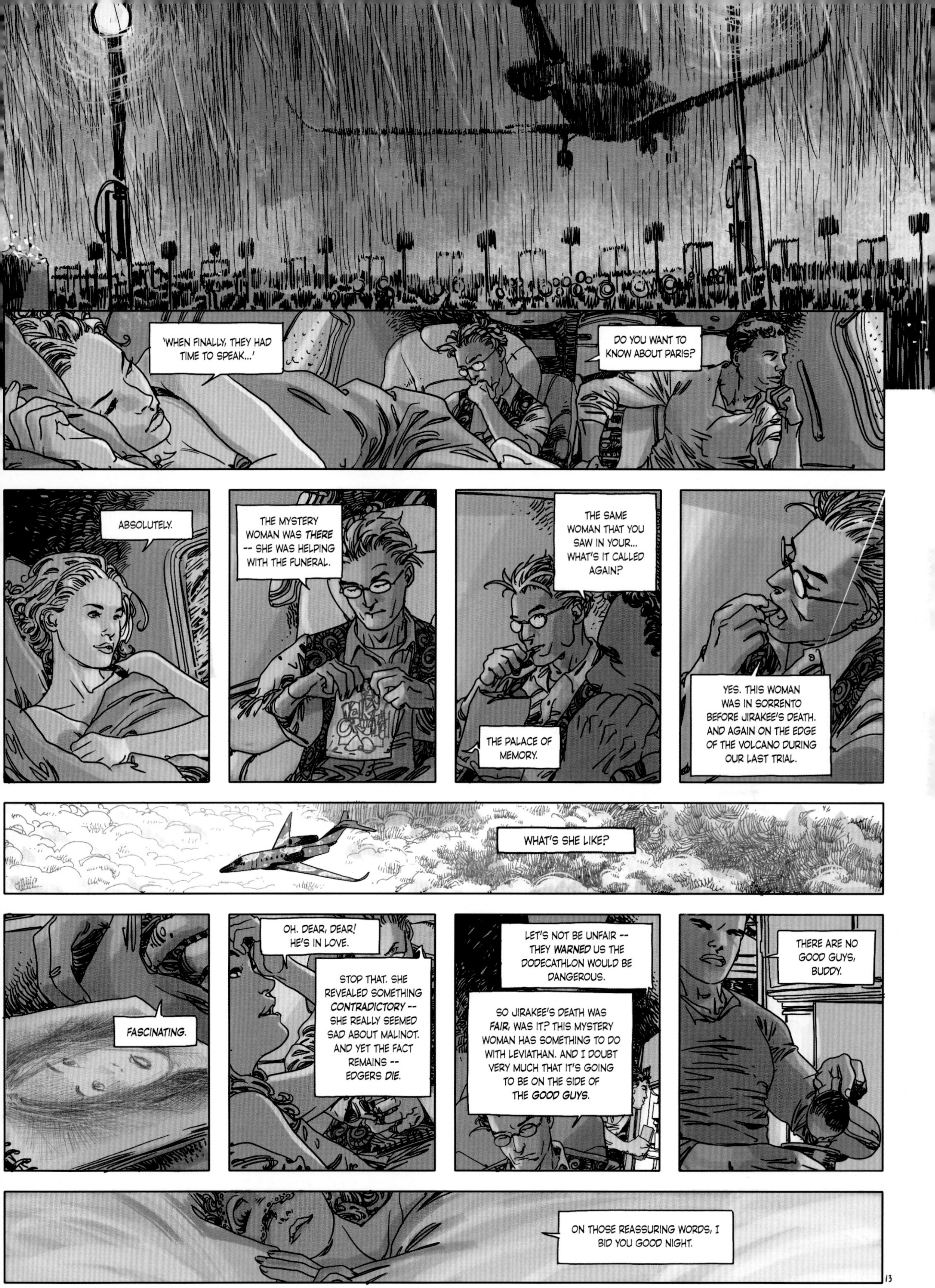
'WHEN FINALLY, THEY HAD TIME TO SPEAK...'
DO YOU WANT TO KNOW ABOUT PARIS?
ABSOLUTELY.
THE MYSTERY WOMAN WAS *THERE* -- SHE WAS HELPING WITH THE FUNERAL.
THE SAME WOMAN THAT YOU SAW IN YOUR... WHAT'S IT CALLED AGAIN?
THE PALACE OF MEMORY.
YES. THIS WOMAN WAS IN SORRENTO BEFORE JIRAKEE'S DEATH. AND AGAIN ON THE EDGE OF THE VOLCANO DURING OUR LAST TRIAL.
WHAT'S SHE LIKE?
FASCINATING.
OH. DEAR, DEAR! HE'S IN LOVE.
STOP THAT. SHE REVEALED SOMETHING *CONTRADICTORY* -- SHE REALLY SEEMED SAD ABOUT MALINOT. AND YET THE FACT REMAINS -- EDGERS *DIE*.
LET'S NOT BE UNFAIR -- THEY *WARNED* US THE DODECATHLON WOULD BE DANGEROUS.
SO JIRAKEE'S DEATH WAS *FAIR*, WAS IT? THIS MYSTERY WOMAN HAS SOMETHING TO DO WITH LEVIATHAN. AND I DOUBT VERY MUCH THAT IT'S GOING TO BE ON THE SIDE OF THE *GOOD GUYS*.
THERE ARE NO GOOD GUYS, BUDDY.
ON THOSE REASSURING WORDS, I BID YOU GOOD NIGHT.

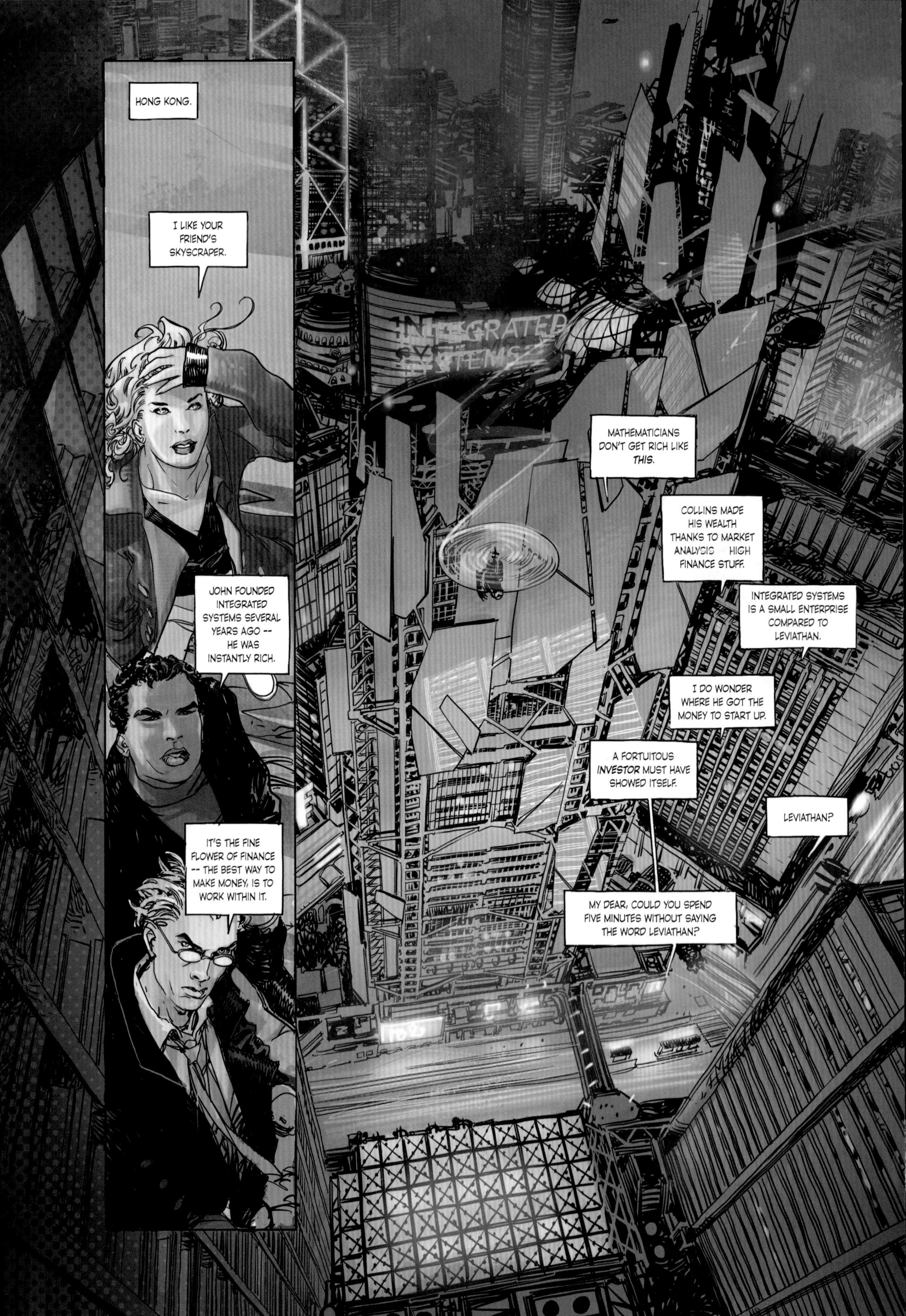

HONG KONG.
I LIKE YOUR FRIEND'S SKYSCRAPER.
JOHN FOUNDED INTEGRATED SYSTEMS SEVERAL YEARS AGO -- HE WAS INSTANTLY RICH.
IT'S THE FINE FLOWER OF FINANCE -- THE BEST WAY TO MAKE MONEY, IS TO WORK WITHIN IT.
INTEGRATED SYSTEMS
MATHEMATICIANS DON'T GET RICH LIKE *THIS*.
COLLINS MADE HIS WEALTH THANKS TO MARKET ANALYSIS HIGH FINANCE STUFF.
INTEGRATED SYSTEMS IS A SMALL ENTERPRISE COMPARED TO LEVIATHAN.
I DO WONDER WHERE HE GOT THE MONEY TO START UP.
A FORTUITOUS ***INVESTOR*** MUST HAVE SHOWED ITSELF.
LEVIATHAN?
MY DEAR, COULD YOU SPEND FIVE MINUTES WITHOUT SAYING THE WORD LEVIATHAN?

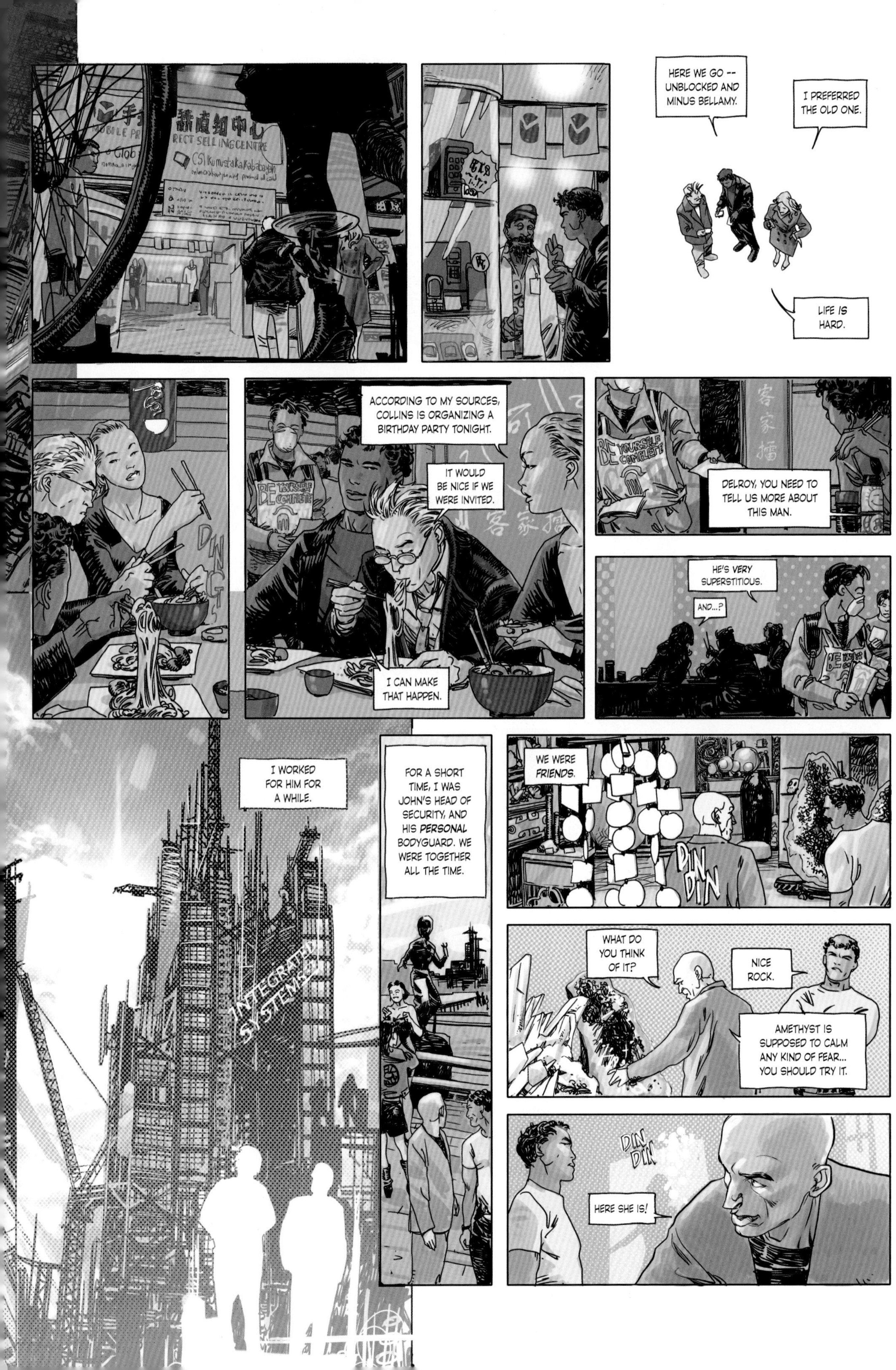

HERE WE GO -- UNBLOCKED AND MINUS BELLAMY.
I PREFERRED THE OLD ONE.
LIFE IS HARD.
ACCORDING TO MY SOURCES, COLLINS IS ORGANIZING A BIRTHDAY PARTY TONIGHT.
IT WOULD BE NICE IF WE WERE INVITED.
I CAN MAKE THAT HAPPEN.
DELROY, YOU NEED TO TELL US MORE ABOUT THIS MAN.
HE'S VERY SUPERSTITIOUS.
AND...?
I WORKED FOR HIM FOR A WHILE.
INTEGRATED SYSTEMS
FOR A SHORT TIME, I WAS JOHN'S HEAD OF SECURITY, AND HIS PERSONAL BODYGUARD. WE WERE TOGETHER ALL THE TIME.
WE WERE FRIENDS.
DIN DIN
WHAT DO YOU THINK OF IT?
NICE ROCK.
AMETHYST IS SUPPOSED TO CALM ANY KIND OF FEAR... YOU SHOULD TRY IT.
DIN DIN
HERE SHE IS!

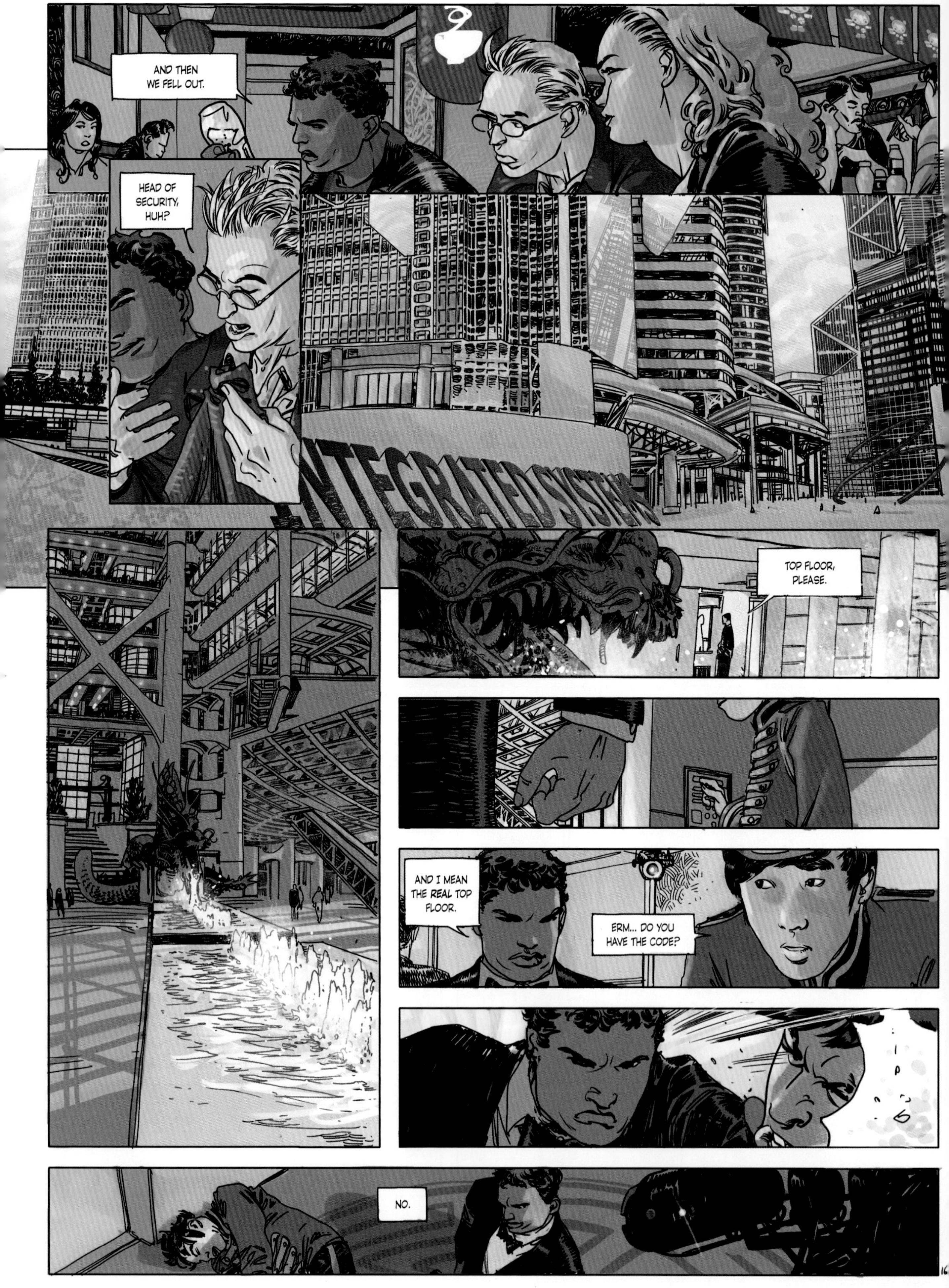

AND THEN WE FELL OUT.
HEAD OF SECURITY, HUH?
INTEGRATED SYSTEMS
TOP FLOOR, PLEASE.
AND I MEAN THE REAL TOP FLOOR.
ERM... DO YOU HAVE THE CODE?
NO.

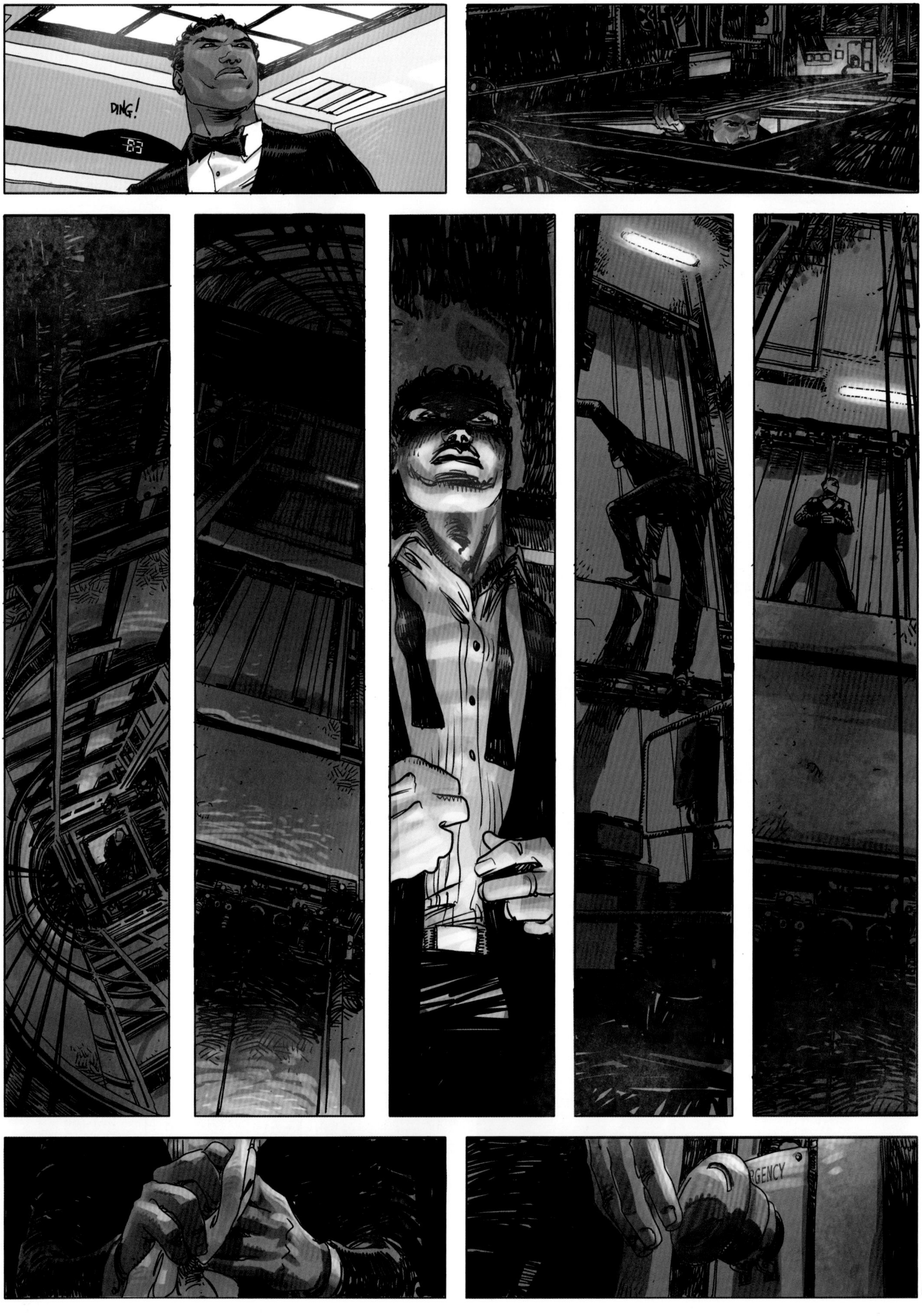
DING!
RGENCY

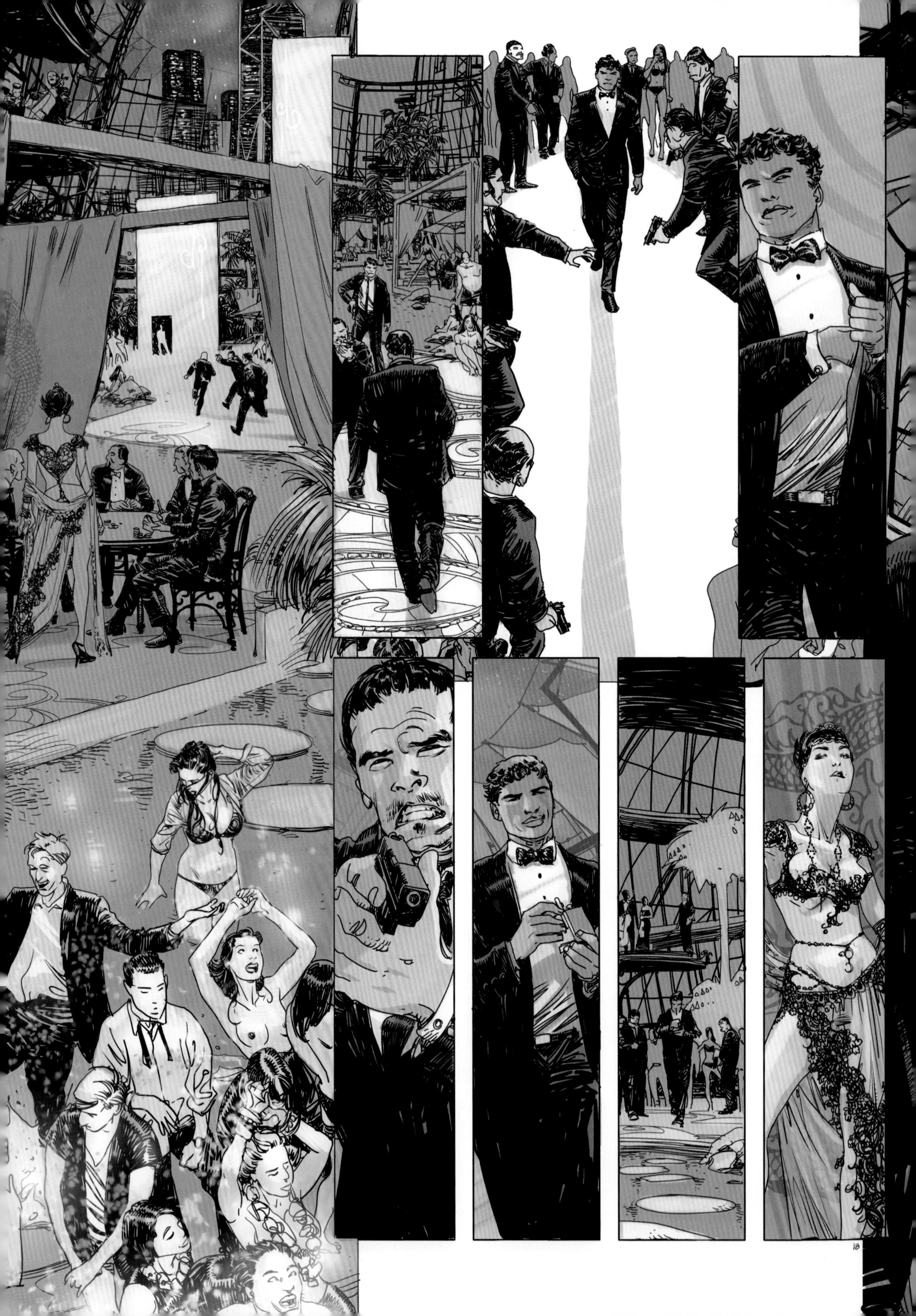

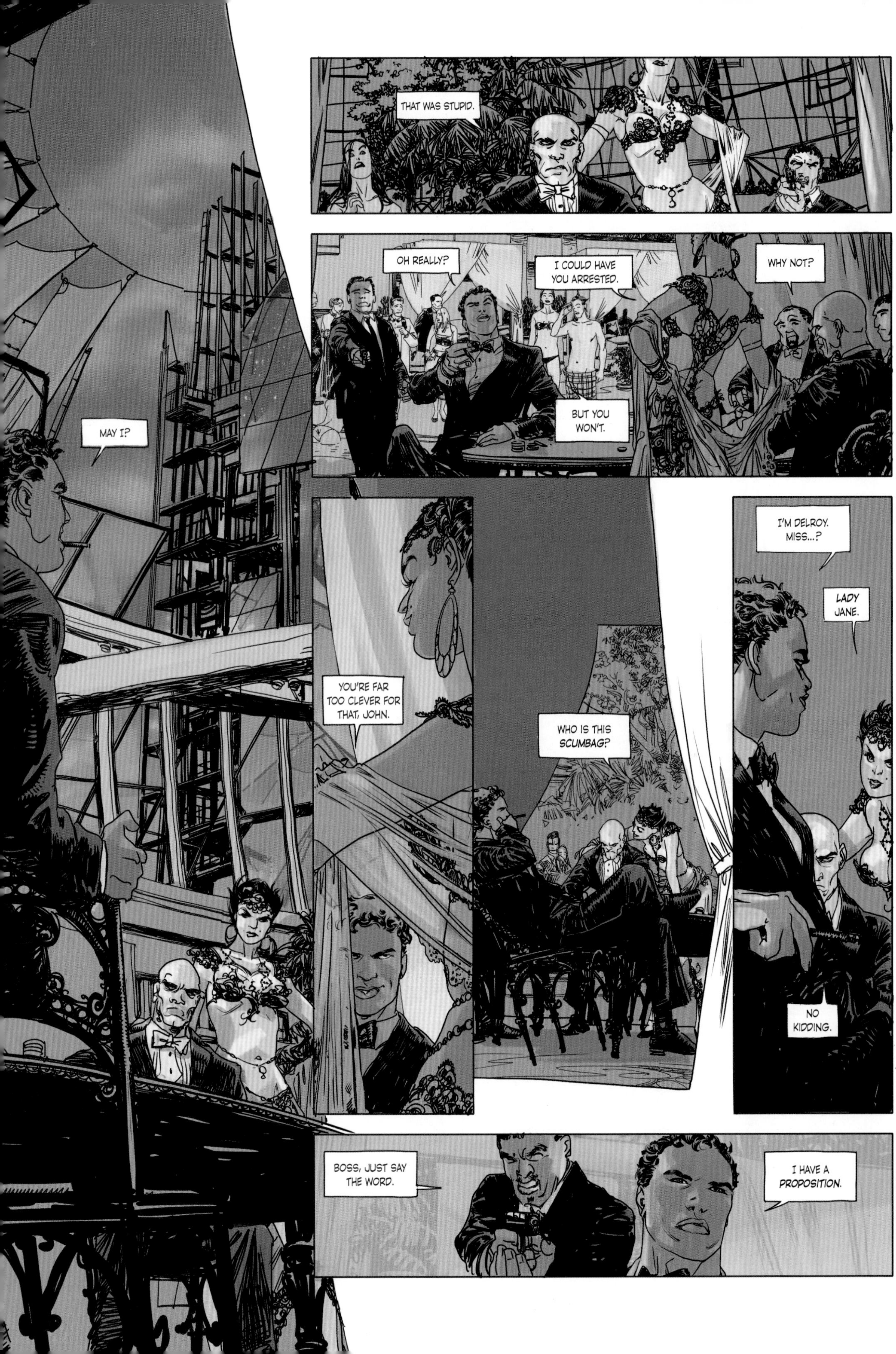

THAT WAS STUPID.
OH REALLY?
I COULD HAVE YOU ARRESTED.
WHY NOT?
BUT YOU WON'T.
MAY I?
YOU'RE FAR TOO CLEVER FOR THAT, JOHN.
WHO IS THIS SCUMBAG?
I'M DELROY. MISS...?
LADY JANE.
NO KIDDING.
BOSS, JUST SAY THE WORD.
I HAVE A PROPOSITION.

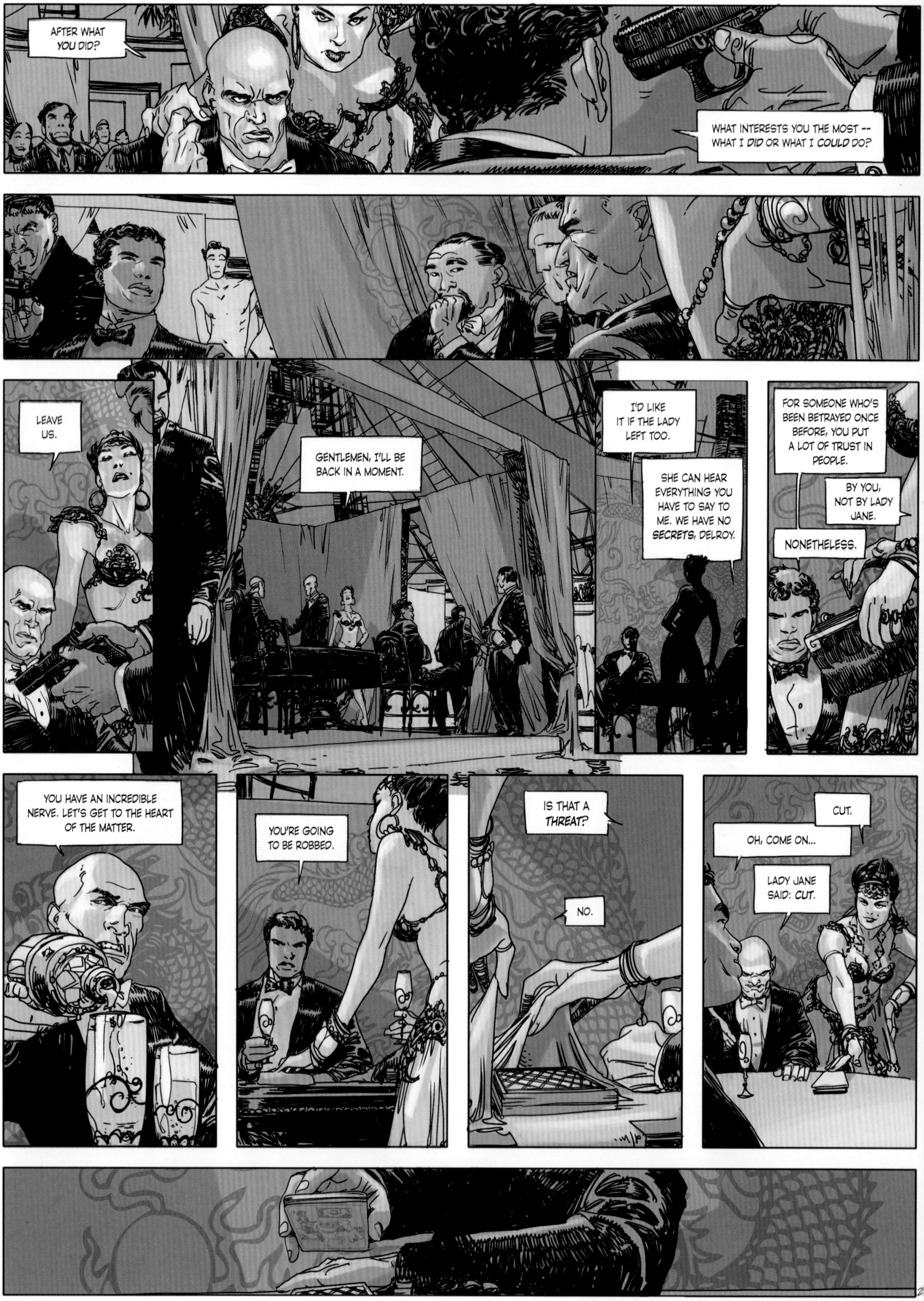
AFTER WHAT YOU DID?
WHAT INTERESTS YOU THE MOST -- WHAT I DID OR WHAT I COULD DO?
LEAVE US.
GENTLEMEN, I'LL BE BACK IN A MOMENT.
I'D LIKE IT IF THE LADY LEFT TOO.
SHE CAN HEAR EVERYTHING YOU HAVE TO SAY TO ME. WE HAVE NO SECRETS, DELROY.
FOR SOMEONE WHO'S BEEN BETRAYED ONCE BEFORE, YOU PUT A LOT OF TRUST IN PEOPLE.
BY YOU, NOT BY LADY JANE.
NONETHELESS.
YOU HAVE AN INCREDIBLE NERVE. LET'S GET TO THE HEART OF THE MATTER.
YOU'RE GOING TO BE ROBBED.
IS THAT A THREAT?
NO.
CUT.
OH, COME ON...
LADY JANE SAID: CUT.

WHAT SIGN ARE YOU?

I DON'T KNOW.

YOU DON'T KNOW WHEN YOU WERE BORN? YOU MUST HAVE HAD A *TERRIBLE* CHILDHOOD.

I'VE SEEN WORSE.

WHO WANTS TO ROB ME?

LEON BELLAMY.

REALLY? AND WHAT COULD HE POSSIBLY BE AFTER?

THE DEVIL'S MIRROR.

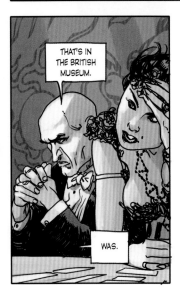

THAT'S IN THE BRITISH MUSEUM.

WAS.

AT SOME POINT, YOU HAD IT STOLEN, AND NOW, SOMEONE HAS TASKED BELLAMY TO TAKE IT HIMSELF.

WHO?

DELROY EDGER

ALEXANDRA GRETCHKO EDGER

HONESTLY, I DON'T KNOW.

21

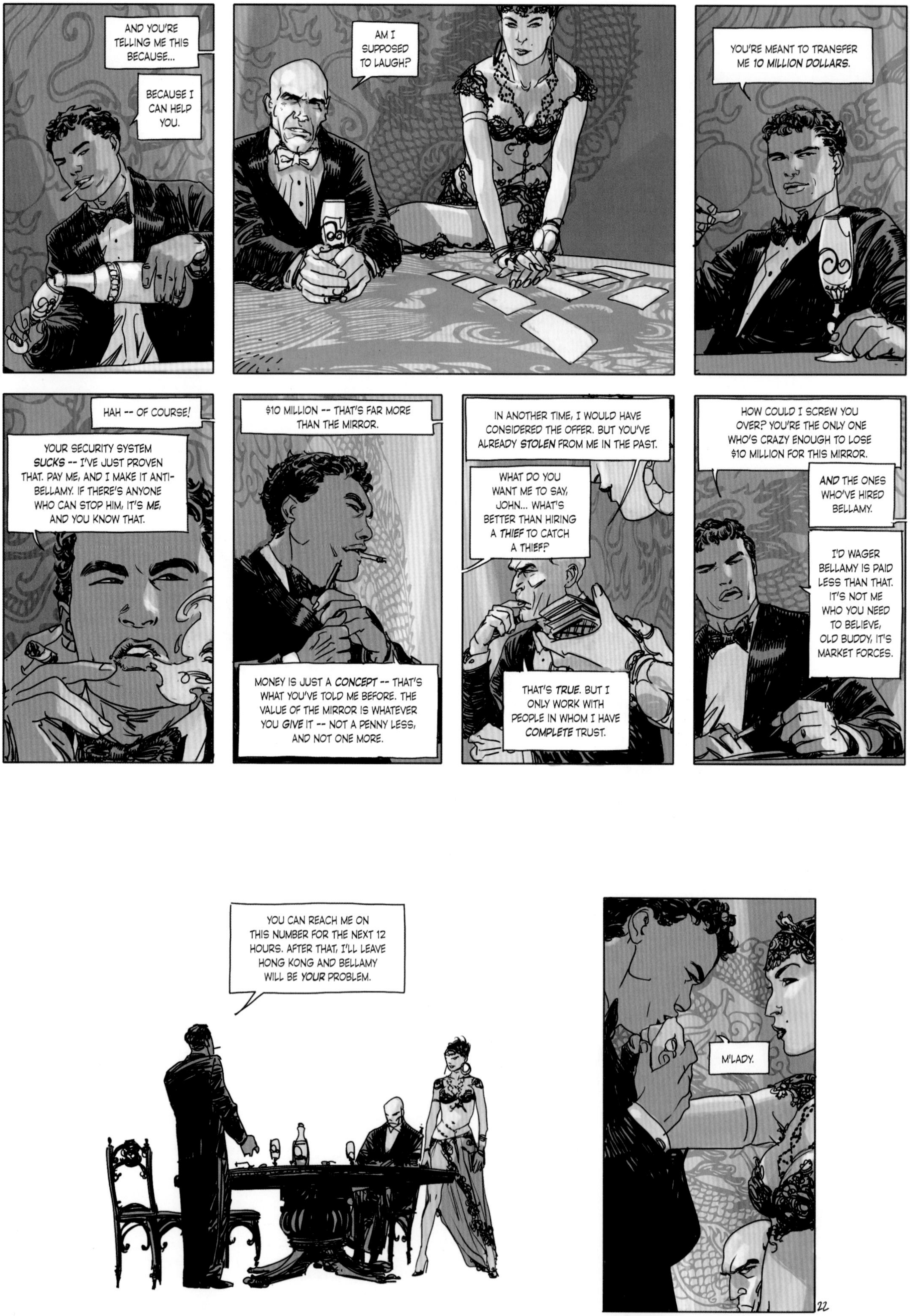
AND YOU'RE TELLING ME THIS BECAUSE...
BECAUSE I CAN HELP YOU.
AM I SUPPOSED TO LAUGH?
YOU'RE MEANT TO TRANSFER ME *10 MILLION DOLLARS*.
HAH -- OF COURSE!
YOUR SECURITY SYSTEM *SUCKS* -- I'VE JUST PROVEN THAT. PAY ME, AND I MAKE IT ANTI-BELLAMY. IF THERE'S ANYONE WHO CAN STOP HIM, IT'S *ME*, AND YOU KNOW THAT.
$10 MILLION -- THAT'S FAR MORE THAN THE MIRROR.
MONEY IS JUST A *CONCEPT* -- THAT'S WHAT YOU'VE TOLD ME BEFORE. THE VALUE OF THE MIRROR IS WHATEVER YOU *GIVE* IT -- NOT A PENNY LESS, AND NOT ONE MORE.
IN ANOTHER TIME, I WOULD HAVE CONSIDERED THE OFFER. BUT YOU'VE ALREADY *STOLEN* FROM ME IN THE PAST.
WHAT DO YOU WANT ME TO SAY, JOHN... WHAT'S BETTER THAN HIRING A *THIEF* TO CATCH A THIEF?
THAT'S *TRUE*. BUT I ONLY WORK WITH PEOPLE IN WHOM I HAVE *COMPLETE* TRUST.
HOW COULD I SCREW YOU OVER? YOU'RE THE ONLY ONE WHO'S CRAZY ENOUGH TO LOSE $10 MILLION FOR THIS MIRROR.
AND THE ONES WHO'VE HIRED BELLAMY.
I'D WAGER BELLAMY IS PAID LESS THAN THAT. IT'S NOT ME WHO YOU NEED TO BELIEVE, OLD BUDDY, IT'S MARKET FORCES.
YOU CAN REACH ME ON THIS NUMBER FOR THE NEXT 12 HOURS. AFTER THAT, I'LL LEAVE HONG KONG AND BELLAMY WILL BE *YOUR* PROBLEM.
M'LADY.

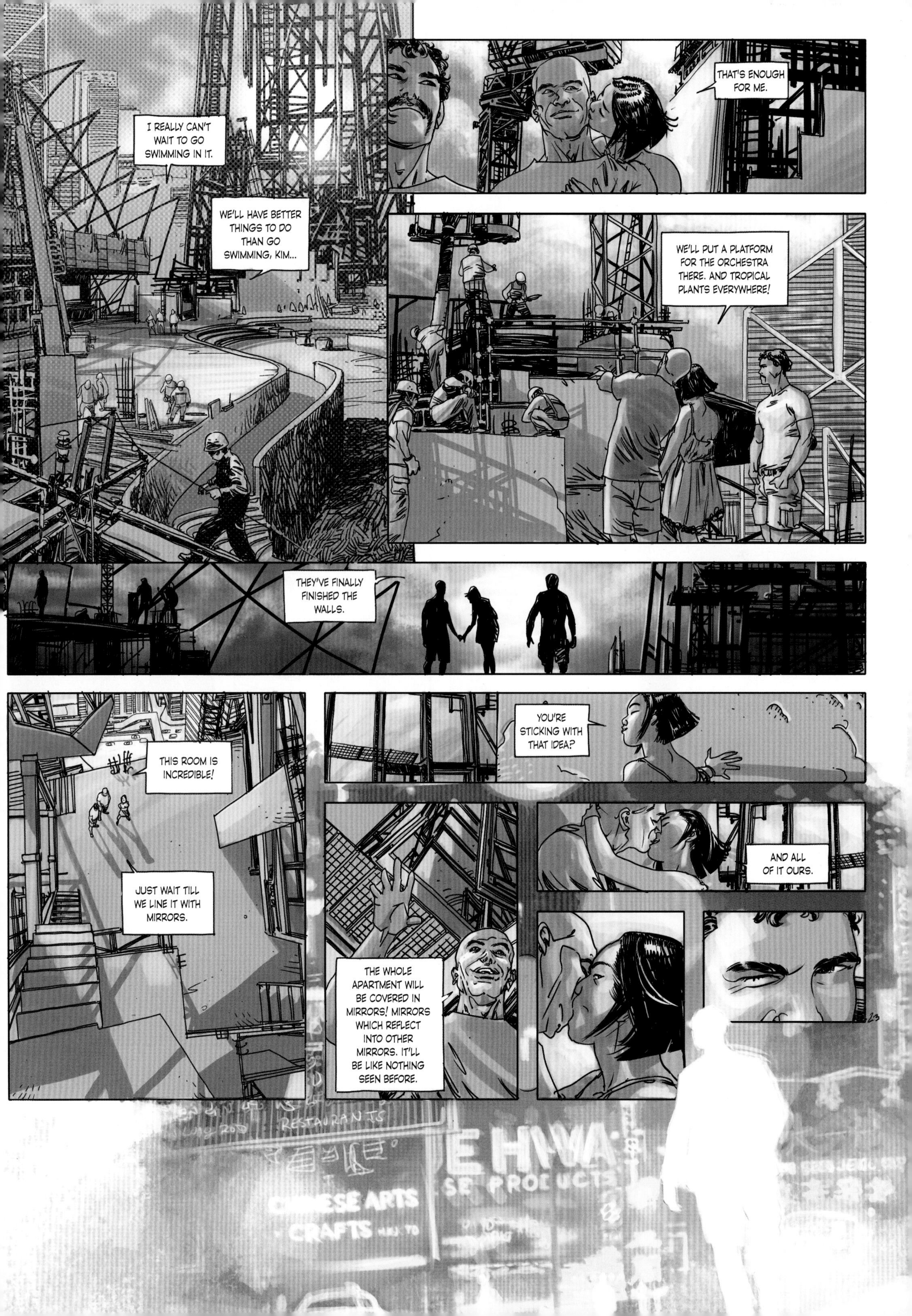
I REALLY CAN'T WAIT TO GO SWIMMING IN IT.
WE'LL HAVE BETTER THINGS TO DO THAN GO SWIMMING, KIM...
THAT'S ENOUGH FOR ME.
WE'LL PUT A PLATFORM FOR THE ORCHESTRA THERE. AND TROPICAL PLANTS EVERYWHERE!
THEY'VE FINALLY FINISHED THE WALLS.
THIS ROOM IS INCREDIBLE!
JUST WAIT TILL WE LINE IT WITH MIRRORS.
YOU'RE STICKING WITH THAT IDEA?
THE WHOLE APARTMENT WILL BE COVERED IN MIRRORS! MIRRORS WHICH REFLECT INTO OTHER MIRRORS. IT'LL BE LIKE NOTHING SEEN BEFORE.
AND ALL OF IT OURS.
RESTAURANTS
CHINESE ARTS
CRAFTS

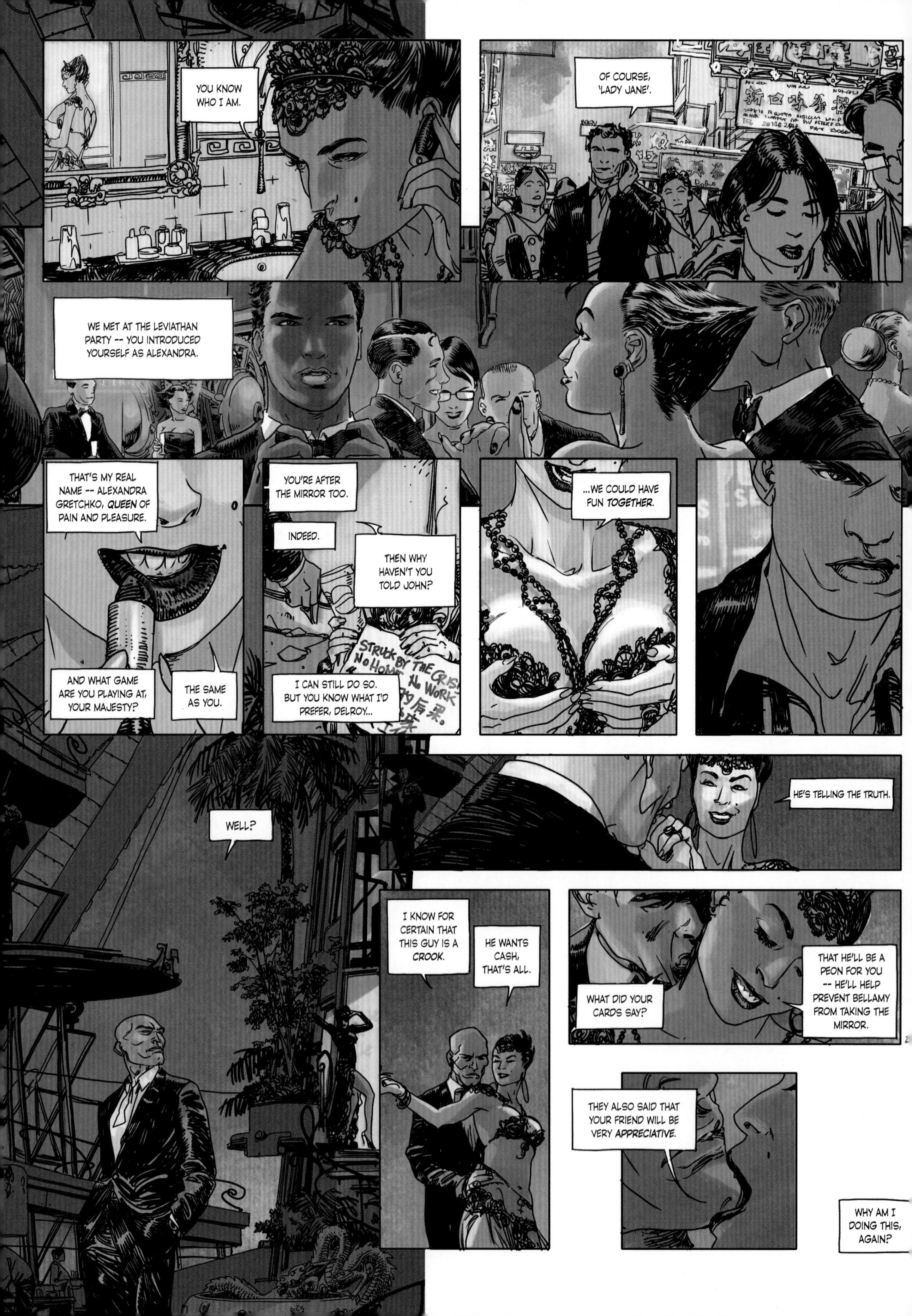
YOU KNOW WHO I AM.
OF COURSE, 'LADY JANE'.
WE MET AT THE LEVIATHAN PARTY -- YOU INTRODUCED YOURSELF AS ALEXANDRA.
THAT'S MY REAL NAME -- ALEXANDRA GRETCHKO, QUEEN OF PAIN AND PLEASURE.
AND WHAT GAME ARE YOU PLAYING AT, YOUR MAJESTY?
THE SAME AS YOU.
YOU'RE AFTER THE MIRROR TOO.
INDEED.
THEN WHY HAVEN'T YOU TOLD JOHN?
I CAN STILL DO SO. BUT YOU KNOW WHAT I'D PREFER, DELROY...
...WE COULD HAVE FUN TOGETHER.
WELL?
HE'S TELLING THE TRUTH.
I KNOW FOR CERTAIN THAT THIS GUY IS A CROOK.
HE WANTS CASH, THAT'S ALL.
WHAT DID YOUR CARDS SAY?
THAT HE'LL BE A PEON FOR YOU -- HE'LL HELP PREVENT BELLAMY FROM TAKING THE MIRROR.
THEY ALSO SAID THAT YOUR FRIEND WILL BE VERY APPRECIATIVE.
WHY AM I DOING THIS, AGAIN?

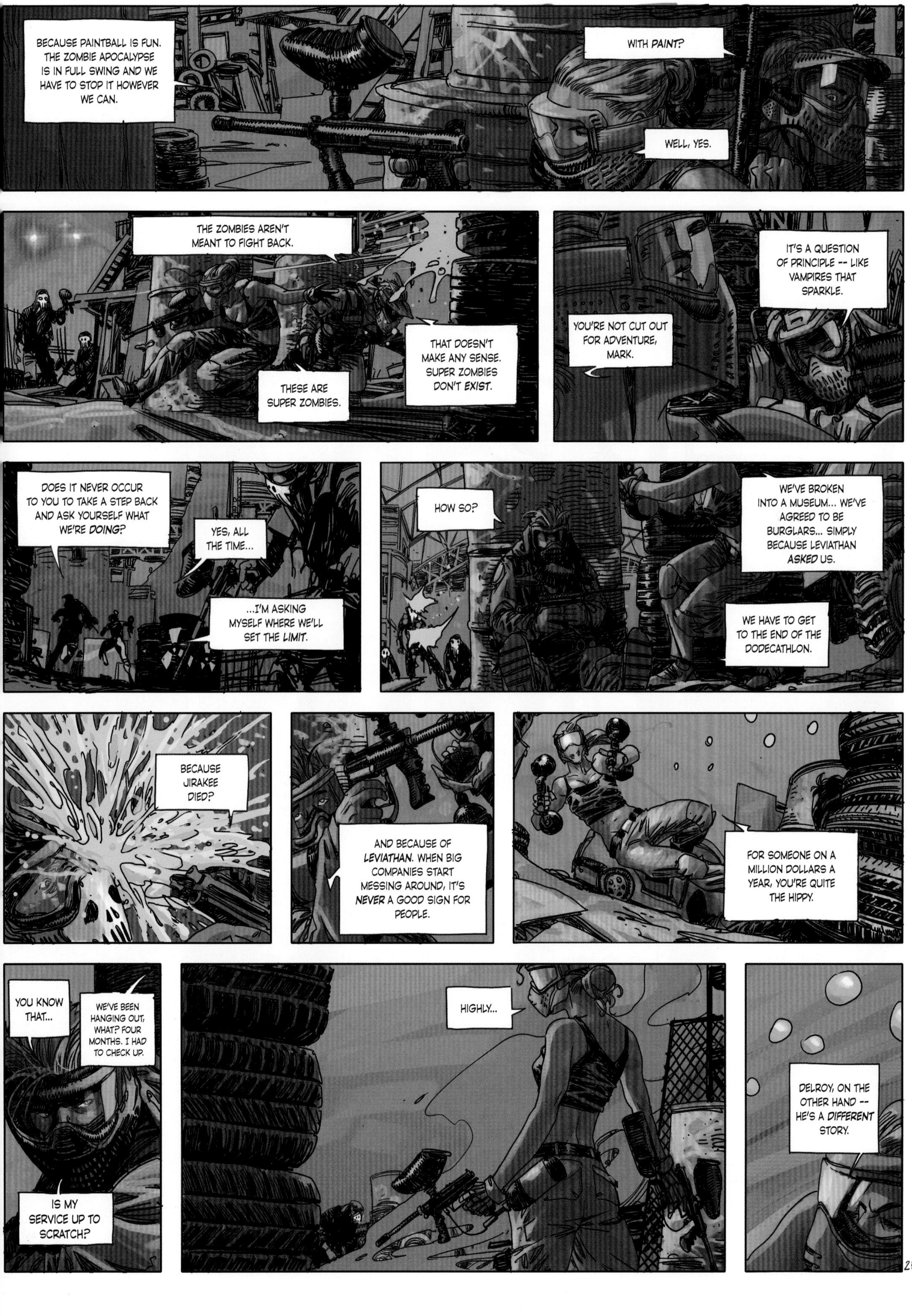

BECAUSE PAINTBALL IS FUN. THE ZOMBIE APOCALYPSE IS IN FULL SWING AND WE HAVE TO STOP IT HOWEVER WE CAN.
WITH *PAINT?*
WELL, YES.
THE ZOMBIES AREN'T MEANT TO FIGHT BACK.
THESE ARE SUPER ZOMBIES.
THAT DOESN'T MAKE ANY SENSE. SUPER ZOMBIES DON'T *EXIST*.
IT'S A QUESTION OF PRINCIPLE -- LIKE VAMPIRES THAT SPARKLE.
YOU'RE NOT CUT OUT FOR ADVENTURE, MARK.
DOES IT NEVER OCCUR TO YOU TO TAKE A STEP BACK AND ASK YOURSELF WHAT WE'RE *DOING?*
YES, ALL THE TIME...
...I'M ASKING MYSELF WHERE WE'LL SET THE *LIMIT*.
HOW SO?
WE'VE BROKEN INTO A MUSEUM... WE'VE AGREED TO BE BURGLARS... SIMPLY BECAUSE LEVIATHAN *ASKED* US.
WE HAVE TO GET TO THE END OF THE DODECATHLON.
BECAUSE JIRAKEE DIED?
AND BECAUSE OF *LEVIATHAN*. WHEN BIG COMPANIES START MESSING AROUND, IT'S *NEVER* A GOOD SIGN FOR PEOPLE.
FOR SOMEONE ON A MILLION DOLLARS A YEAR, YOU'RE QUITE THE HIPPY.
YOU KNOW THAT...
WE'VE BEEN HANGING OUT, WHAT? FOUR MONTHS. I HAD TO CHECK UP.
IS MY SERVICE UP TO SCRATCH?
HIGHLY...
DELROY, ON THE OTHER HAND -- HE'S A *DIFFERENT* STORY.

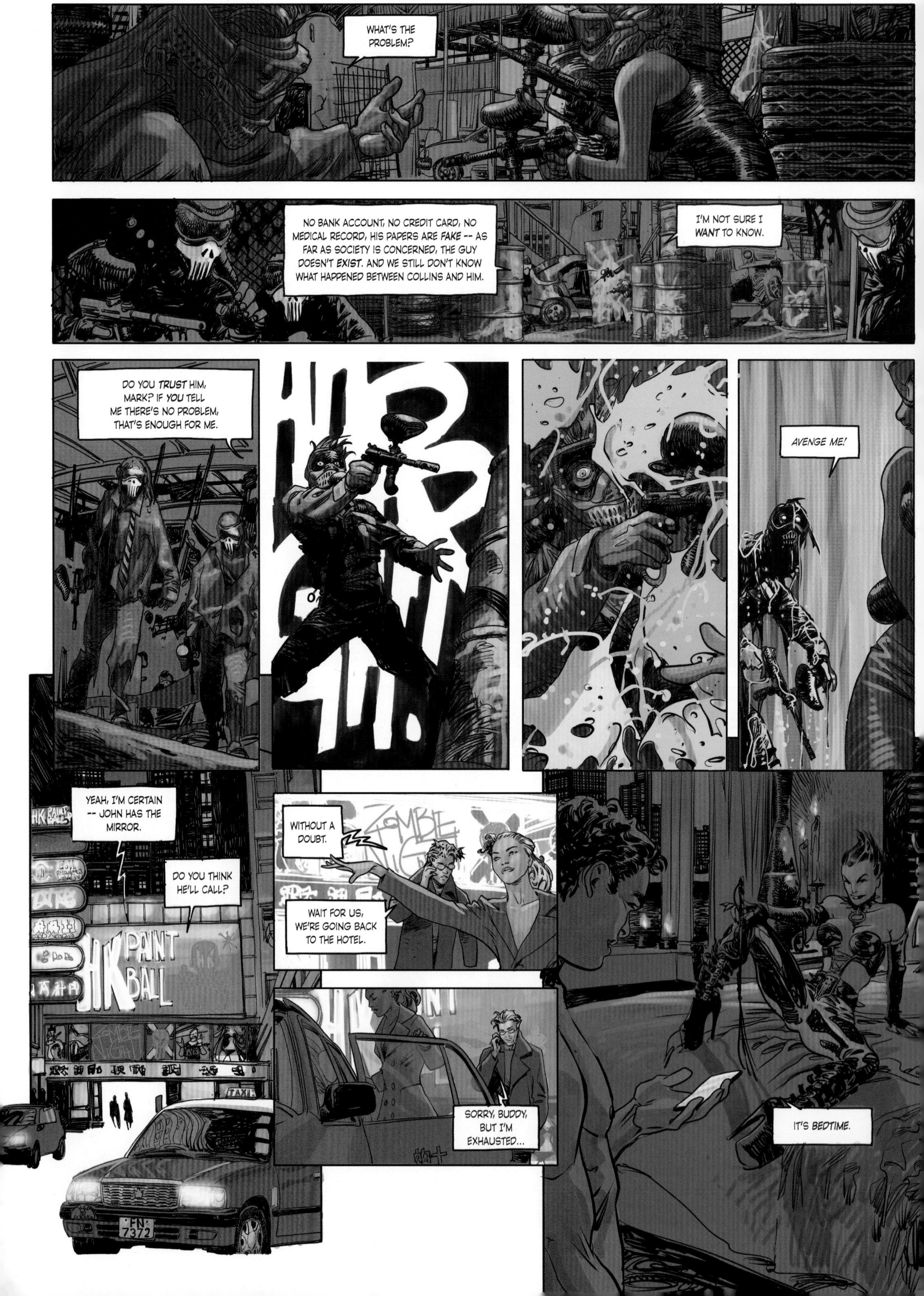
WHAT'S THE PROBLEM?
NO BANK ACCOUNT, NO CREDIT CARD, NO MEDICAL RECORD, HIS PAPERS ARE FAKE -- AS FAR AS SOCIETY IS CONCERNED, THE GUY DOESN'T EXIST. AND WE STILL DON'T KNOW WHAT HAPPENED BETWEEN COLLINS AND HIM.
I'M NOT SURE I WANT TO KNOW.
DO YOU TRUST HIM, MARK? IF YOU TELL ME THERE'S NO PROBLEM, THAT'S ENOUGH FOR ME.
AVENGE ME!
YEAH, I'M CERTAIN -- JOHN HAS THE MIRROR.
DO YOU THINK HE'LL CALL?
HK PAINT BALL
WITHOUT A DOUBT.
WAIT FOR US, WE'RE GOING BACK TO THE HOTEL.
SORRY, BUDDY, BUT I'M EXHAUSTED...
IT'S BEDTIME.
TAXI
FN 7372

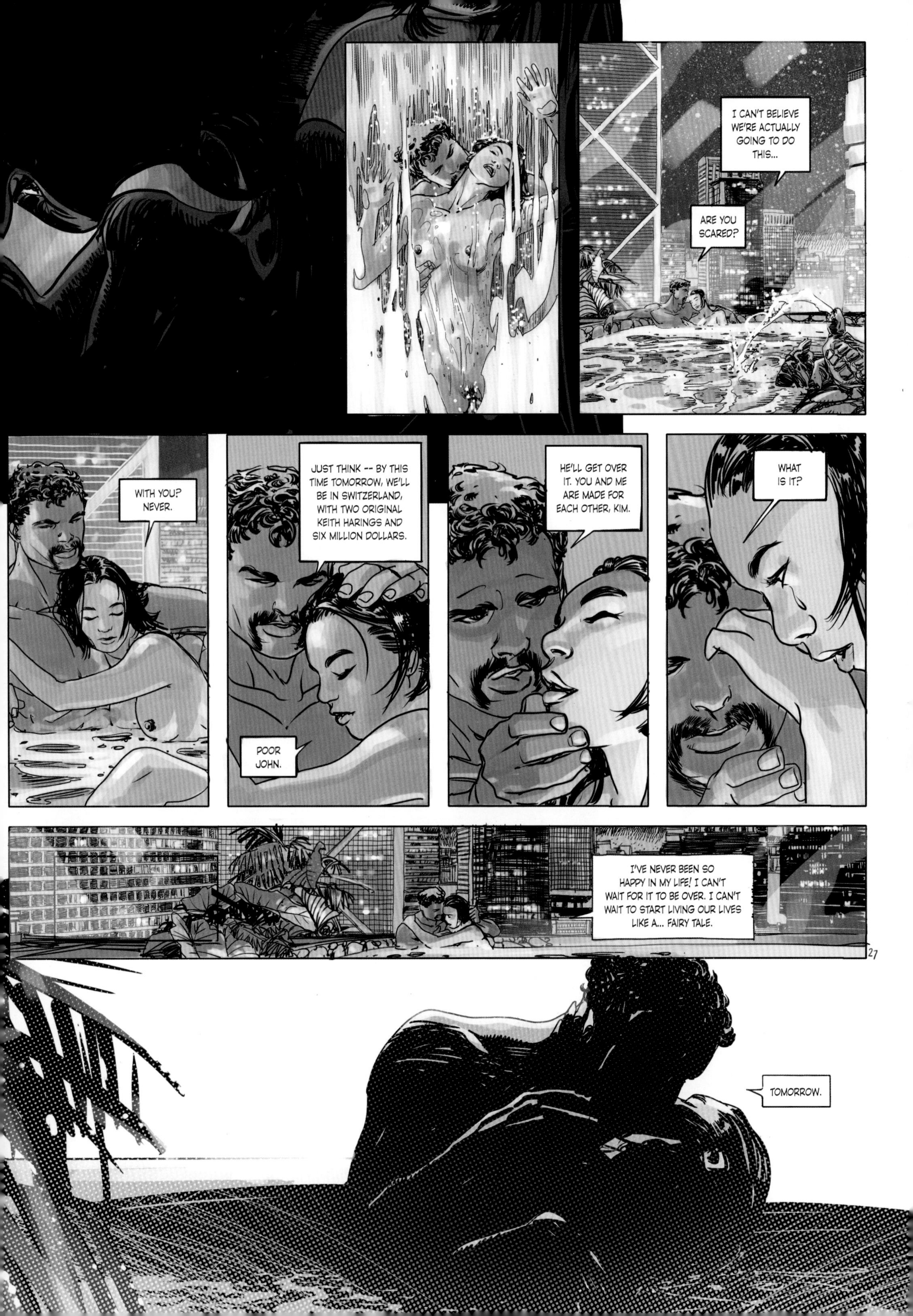
I CAN'T BELIEVE WE'RE ACTUALLY GOING TO DO THIS...
ARE YOU SCARED?
WITH YOU? NEVER.
JUST THINK -- BY THIS TIME TOMORROW, WE'LL BE IN SWITZERLAND, WITH TWO ORIGINAL KEITH HARINGS AND SIX MILLION DOLLARS.
POOR JOHN.
HE'LL GET OVER IT. YOU AND ME ARE MADE FOR EACH OTHER, KIM.
WHAT IS IT?
I'VE NEVER BEEN SO HAPPY IN MY LIFE! I CAN'T WAIT FOR IT TO BE OVER. I CAN'T WAIT TO START LIVING OUR LIVES LIKE A... FAIRY TALE.
TOMORROW.

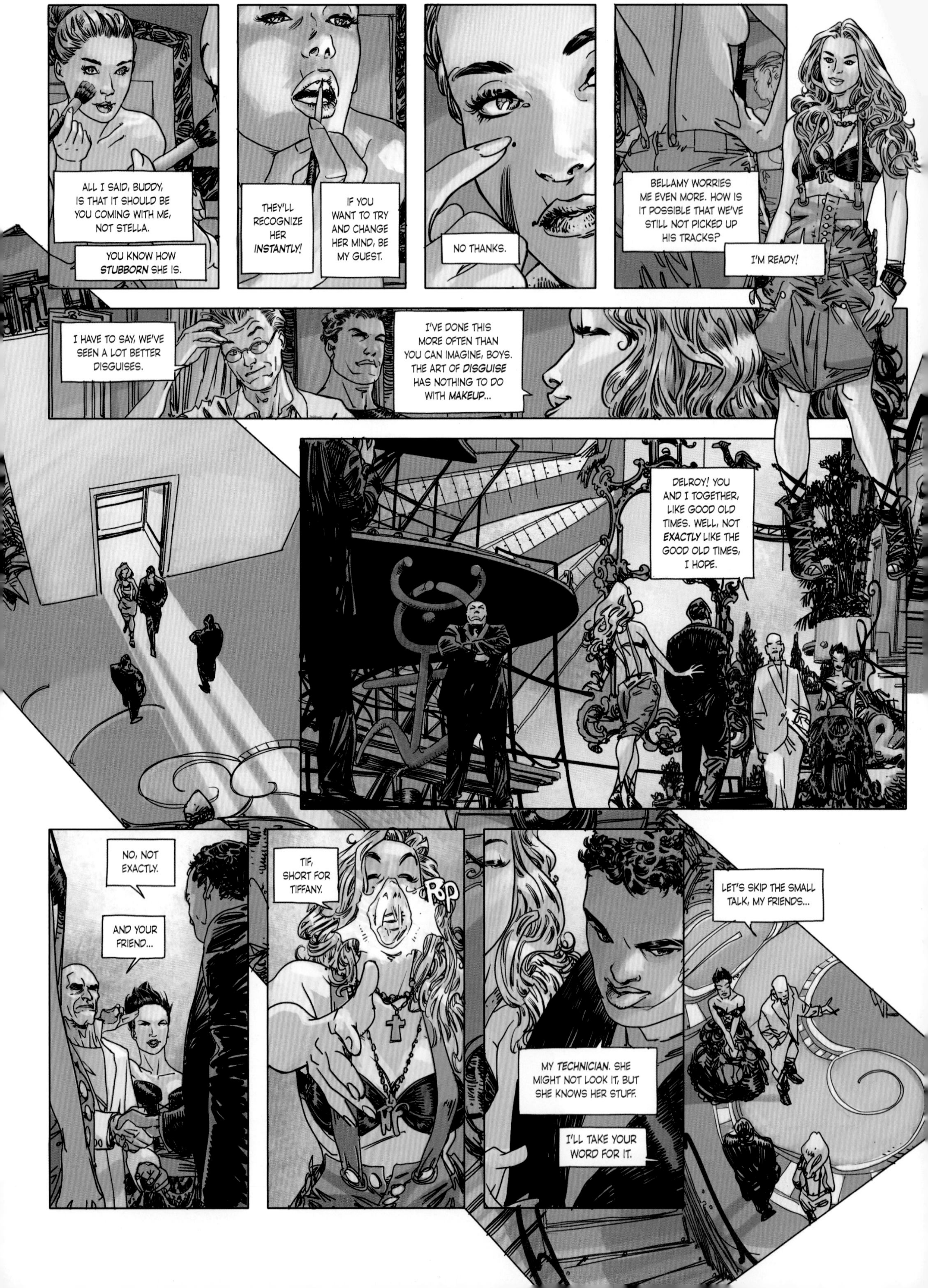
ALL I SAID, BUDDY, IS THAT IT SHOULD BE YOU COMING WITH ME, NOT STELLA.
YOU KNOW HOW STUBBORN SHE IS.
THEY'LL RECOGNIZE HER INSTANTLY!
IF YOU WANT TO TRY AND CHANGE HER MIND, BE MY GUEST.
NO THANKS.
BELLAMY WORRIES ME EVEN MORE. HOW IS IT POSSIBLE THAT WE'VE STILL NOT PICKED UP HIS TRACKS?
I'M READY!
I HAVE TO SAY, WE'VE SEEN A LOT BETTER DISGUISES.
I'VE DONE THIS MORE OFTEN THAN YOU CAN IMAGINE, BOYS. THE ART OF DISGUISE HAS NOTHING TO DO WITH MAKEUP...
DELROY! YOU AND I TOGETHER, LIKE GOOD OLD TIMES. WELL, NOT EXACTLY LIKE THE GOOD OLD TIMES, I HOPE.
NO, NOT EXACTLY.
AND YOUR FRIEND...
TIF, SHORT FOR TIFFANY.
POP
MY TECHNICIAN. SHE MIGHT NOT LOOK IT, BUT SHE KNOWS HER STUFF.
I'LL TAKE YOUR WORD FOR IT.
LET'S SKIP THE SMALL TALK, MY FRIENDS...

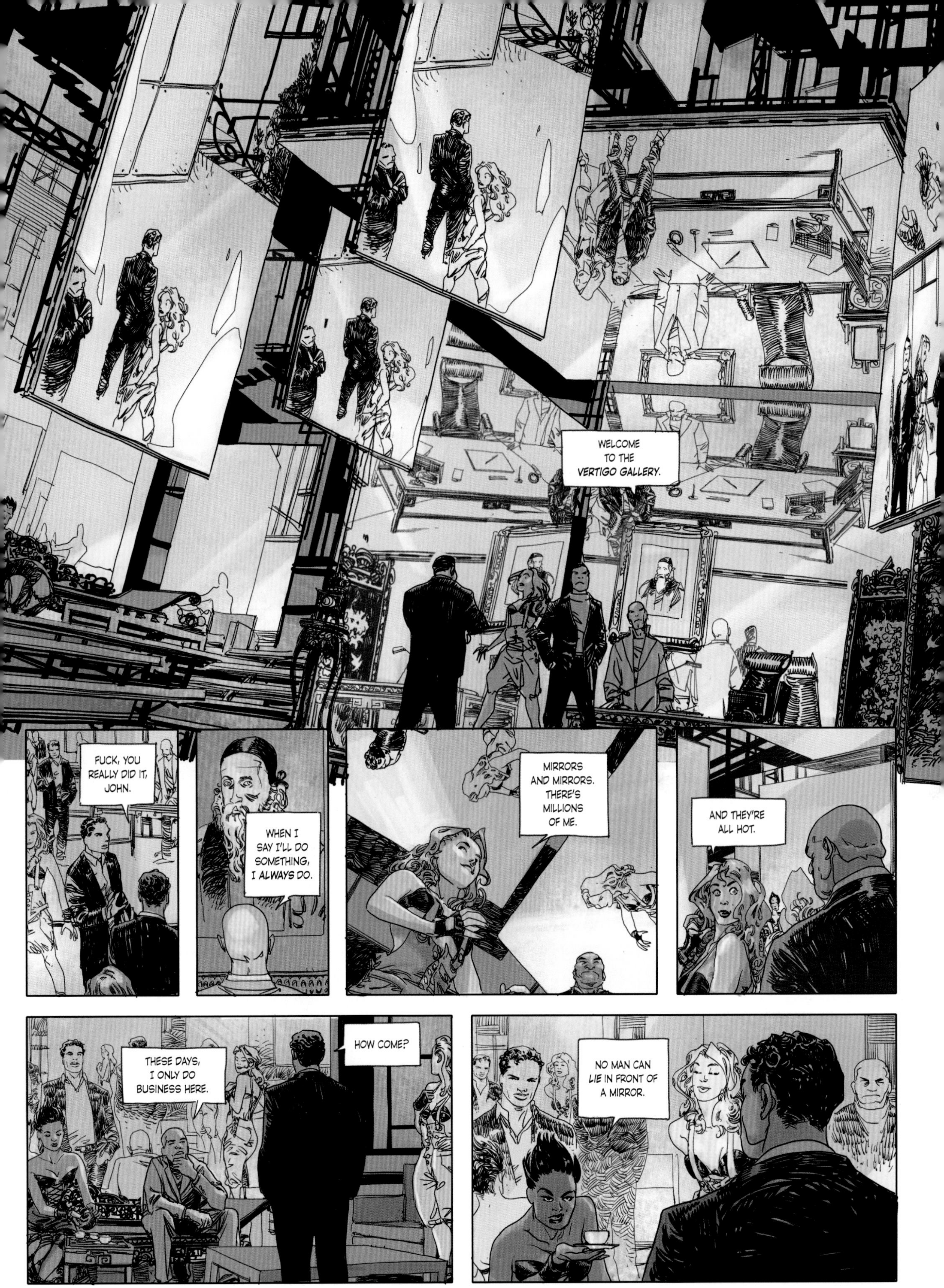
WELCOME TO THE VERTIGO GALLERY.
FUCK, YOU REALLY DID IT, JOHN.
WHEN I SAY I'LL DO SOMETHING, I *ALWAYS* DO.
MIRRORS AND MIRRORS. THERE'S MILLIONS OF ME.
AND THEY'RE ALL HOT.
THESE DAYS, I ONLY DO BUSINESS HERE.
HOW COME?
NO MAN CAN *LIE* IN FRONT OF A MIRROR.

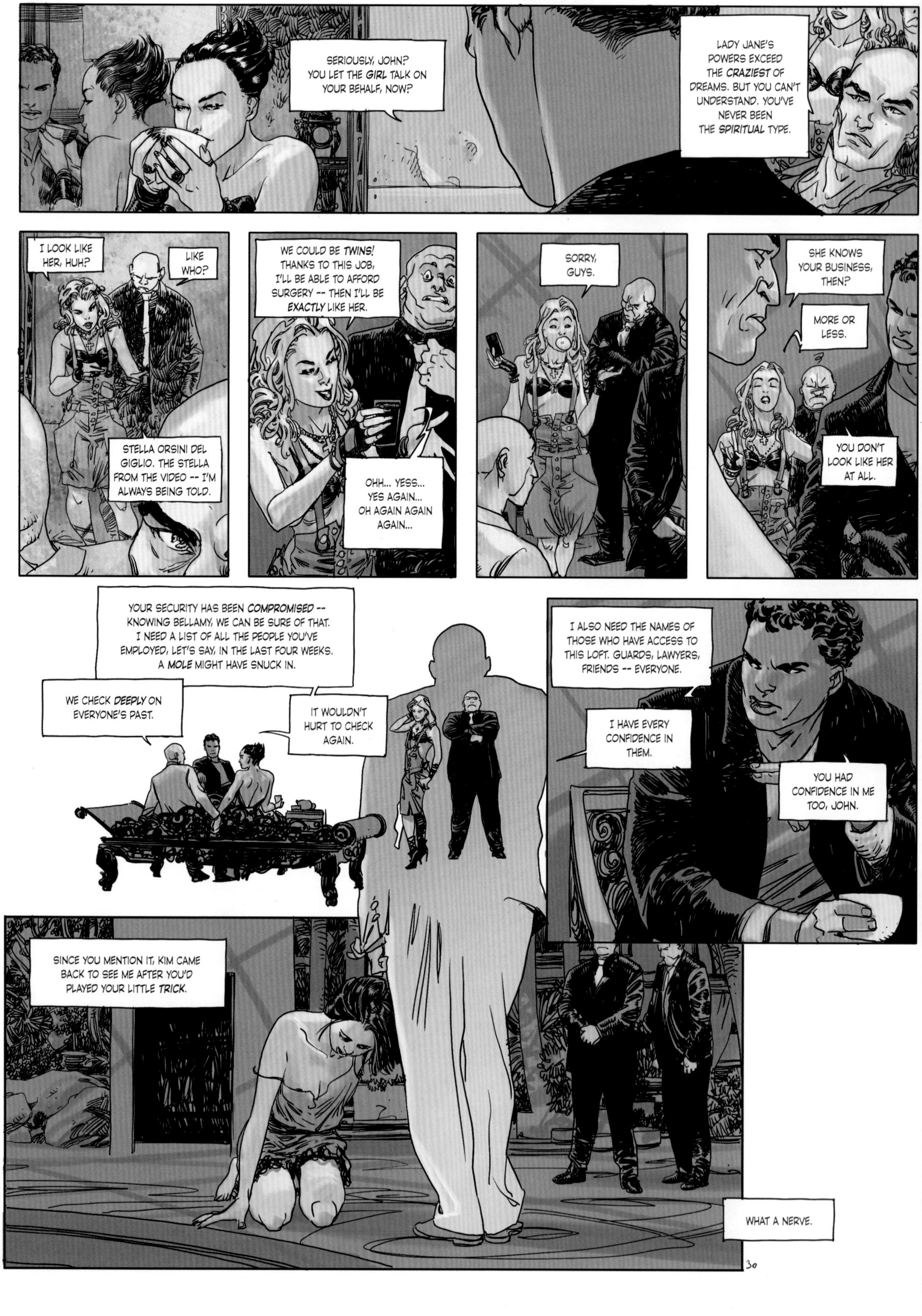
SERIOUSLY, JOHN? YOU LET THE GIRL TALK ON YOUR BEHALF, NOW?
LADY JANE'S POWERS EXCEED THE CRAZIEST OF DREAMS. BUT YOU CAN'T UNDERSTAND. YOU'VE NEVER BEEN THE SPIRITUAL TYPE.
I LOOK LIKE HER, HUH?
LIKE WHO?
STELLA ORSINI DEL GIGLIO. THE STELLA FROM THE VIDEO -- I'M ALWAYS BEING TOLD.
WE COULD BE TWINS! THANKS TO THIS JOB, I'LL BE ABLE TO AFFORD SURGERY -- THEN I'LL BE EXACTLY LIKE HER.
OHH... YESS... YES AGAIN... OH AGAIN AGAIN AGAIN...
SORRY, GUYS.
SHE KNOWS YOUR BUSINESS, THEN?
MORE OR LESS.
YOU DON'T LOOK LIKE HER AT ALL.
YOUR SECURITY HAS BEEN COMPROMISED -- KNOWING BELLAMY, WE CAN BE SURE OF THAT. I NEED A LIST OF ALL THE PEOPLE YOU'VE EMPLOYED, LET'S SAY, IN THE LAST FOUR WEEKS. A MOLE MIGHT HAVE SNUCK IN.
WE CHECK DEEPLY ON EVERYONE'S PAST.
IT WOULDN'T HURT TO CHECK AGAIN.
I ALSO NEED THE NAMES OF THOSE WHO HAVE ACCESS TO THIS LOFT. GUARDS, LAWYERS, FRIENDS -- EVERYONE.
I HAVE EVERY CONFIDENCE IN THEM.
YOU HAD CONFIDENCE IN ME TOO, JOHN.
SINCE YOU MENTION IT, KIM CAME BACK TO SEE ME AFTER YOU'D PLAYED YOUR LITTLE TRICK.
WHAT A NERVE.

INDEED.

WHAT DID YOU DO?

I DON'T ACCEPT RETURNS.

GOOD.

COME, LET ME SHOW YOU THE REST.

AS YOU KNOW, YOU NEED TO ENTER A *SECRET CODE* IN THE ELEVATOR TO GET HERE. THE BELLBOY DOESN'T HAVE IT -- ONLY THE HIGHEST LEVEL GUARDS KNOW IT.

I DIDN'T NEED A CODE THE FIRST TIME.

I'M PAYING YOU TO ENSURE THAT DOESN'T HAPPEN AGAIN.

NOW THE STAIRWELL...

...IS LOCATED BEHIND A *REINFORCED* DOOR. YOU ALSO NEED A CODE TO OPEN IT, *DIFFERENT* FROM THE ELEVATOR CODE.

THERE ARE ALSO MANY SECURITY CAMERAS -- SOME OF THEM VISIBLE, OTHERS CONCEALED BEHIND MIRRORS.

WHAT WAS ON THE *LAST FLOOR* -- BEFORE THIS ONE?

OFFICES.

FIVE GUARDS PATROL THE LOFT, 24 HOURS A DAY, SEVEN DAYS A WEEK.

AND THERE ARE PLENTY MORE SCATTERED AROUND THE BUILDING.

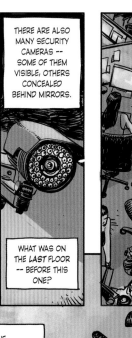

FRANKLY, JOHN. IT'S ALL A BIT *LIGHT*.

I KEEP THE MOST *PRECIOUS* PIECES OF MY COLLECTION IN A PARTICULAR PART OF THE HOUSE. A PRIVATE *MUSEUM*, SO TO SPEAK.

I TOTALLY LOOK LIKE HER.

THIS GLASS DOOR IS CUSTOM MADE -- AS STRONG AS STEEL AND A HUNDRED TIMES MORE EXPENSIVE. IT OPENS WITH A CODE ONLY I KNOW. WHICH OF COURSE I'LL CHANGE THE MINUTE YOU'VE LEFT.

OF COURSE.

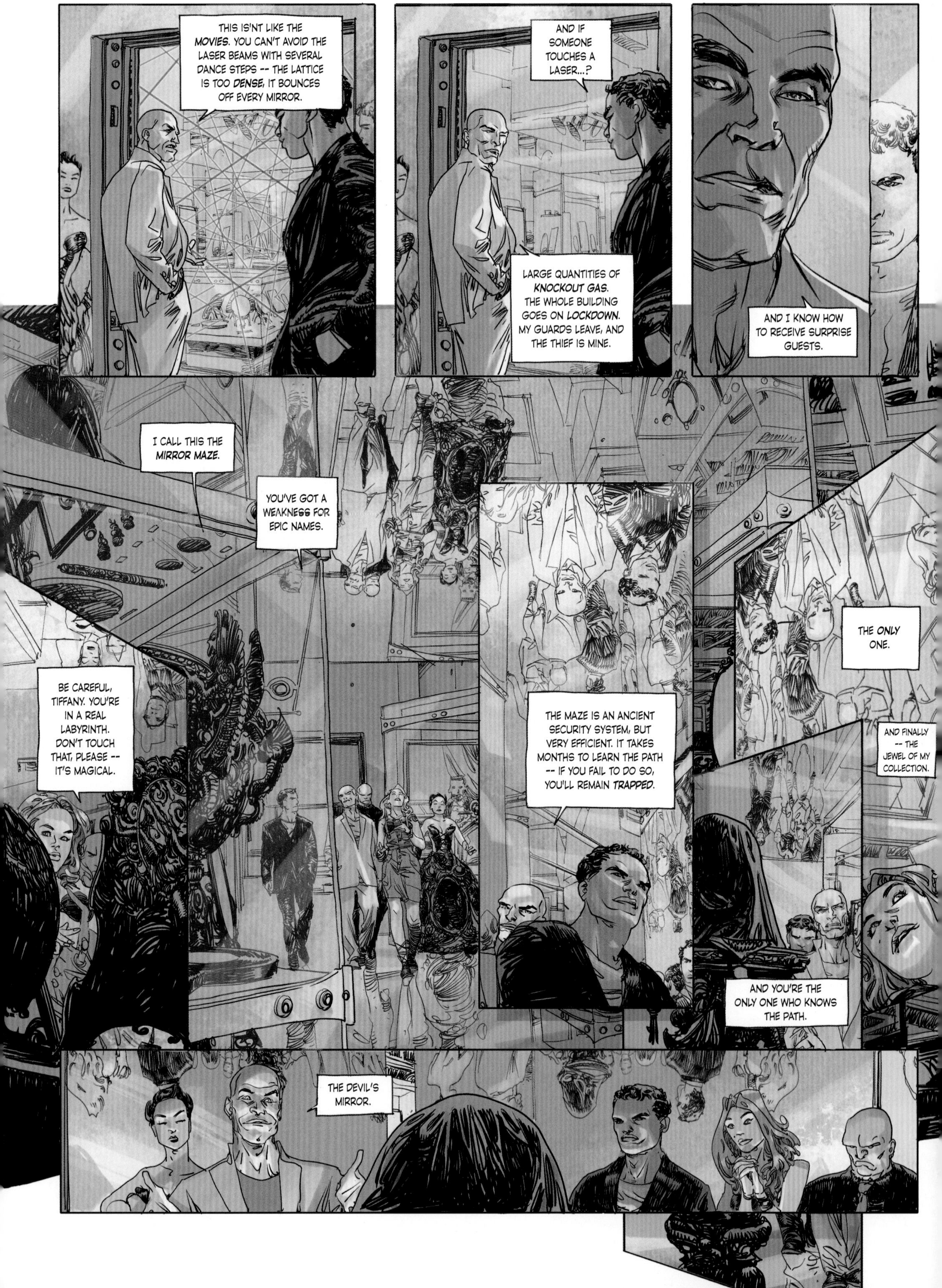
THIS IS'NT LIKE THE MOVIES. YOU CAN'T AVOID THE LASER BEAMS WITH SEVERAL DANCE STEPS -- THE LATTICE IS TOO DENSE, IT BOUNCES OFF EVERY MIRROR.
AND IF SOMEONE TOUCHES A LASER...?
LARGE QUANTITIES OF KNOCKOUT GAS. THE WHOLE BUILDING GOES ON LOCKDOWN. MY GUARDS LEAVE, AND THE THIEF IS MINE.
AND I KNOW HOW TO RECEIVE SURPRISE GUESTS.
I CALL THIS THE MIRROR MAZE.
YOU'VE GOT A WEAKNESS FOR EPIC NAMES.
BE CAREFUL, TIFFANY. YOU'RE IN A REAL LABYRINTH. DON'T TOUCH THAT, PLEASE -- IT'S MAGICAL.
THE MAZE IS AN ANCIENT SECURITY SYSTEM, BUT VERY EFFICIENT. IT TAKES MONTHS TO LEARN THE PATH -- IF YOU FAIL TO DO SO, YOU'LL REMAIN TRAPPED.
THE ONLY ONE.
AND YOU'RE THE ONLY ONE WHO KNOWS THE PATH.
AND FINALLY -- THE JEWEL OF MY COLLECTION.
THE DEVIL'S MIRROR.

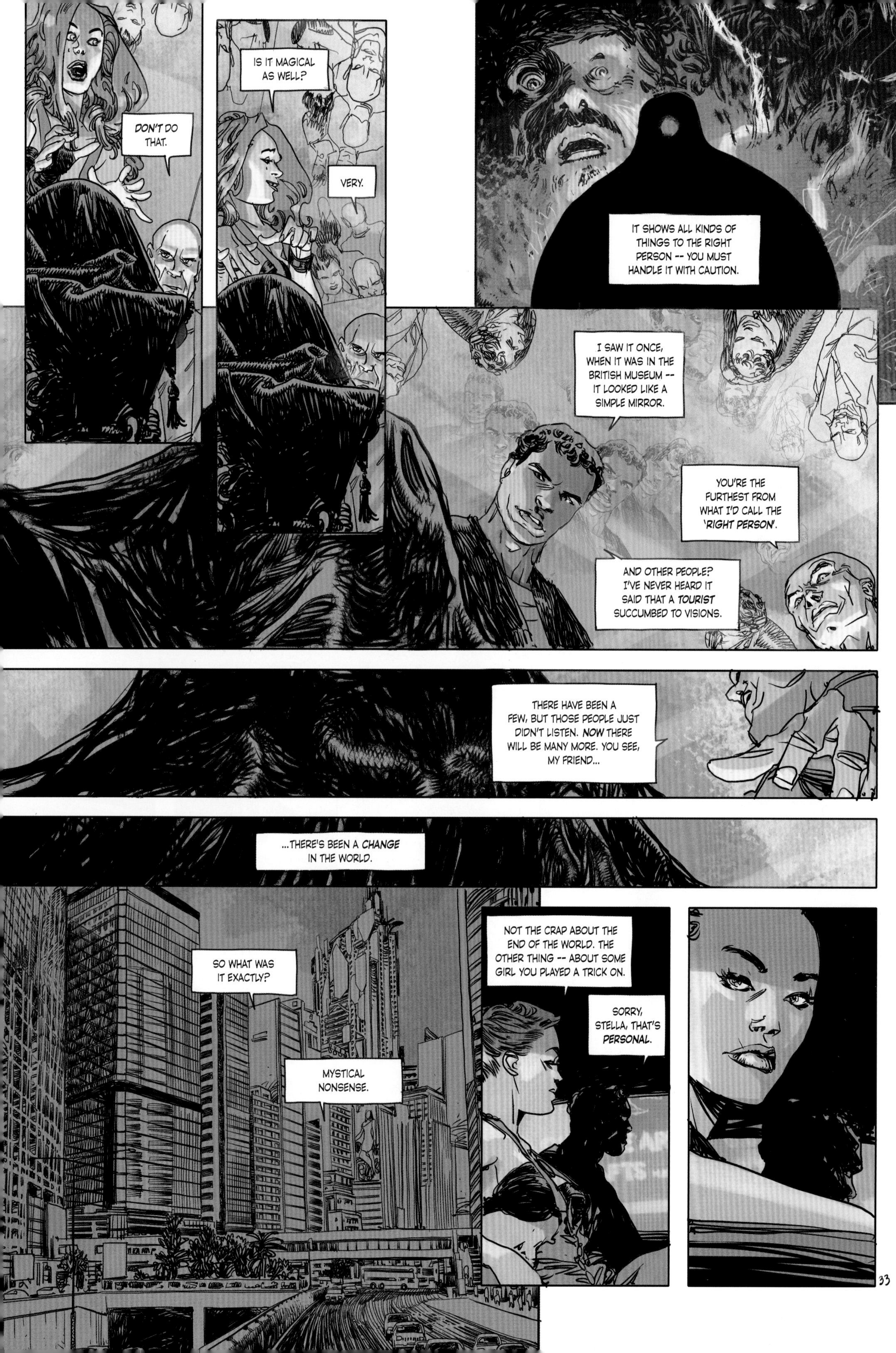
DON'T DO THAT.
IS IT MAGICAL AS WELL?
VERY.
IT SHOWS ALL KINDS OF THINGS TO THE RIGHT PERSON -- YOU MUST HANDLE IT WITH CAUTION.
I SAW IT ONCE, WHEN IT WAS IN THE BRITISH MUSEUM -- IT LOOKED LIKE A SIMPLE MIRROR.
YOU'RE THE FURTHEST FROM WHAT I'D CALL THE 'RIGHT PERSON'.
AND OTHER PEOPLE? I'VE NEVER HEARD IT SAID THAT A TOURIST SUCCUMBED TO VISIONS.
THERE HAVE BEEN A FEW, BUT THOSE PEOPLE JUST DIDN'T LISTEN. NOW THERE WILL BE MANY MORE. YOU SEE, MY FRIEND...
...THERE'S BEEN A CHANGE IN THE WORLD.
SO WHAT WAS IT EXACTLY?
MYSTICAL NONSENSE.
NOT THE CRAP ABOUT THE END OF THE WORLD. THE OTHER THING -- ABOUT SOME GIRL YOU PLAYED A TRICK ON.
SORRY, STELLA, THAT'S PERSONAL.

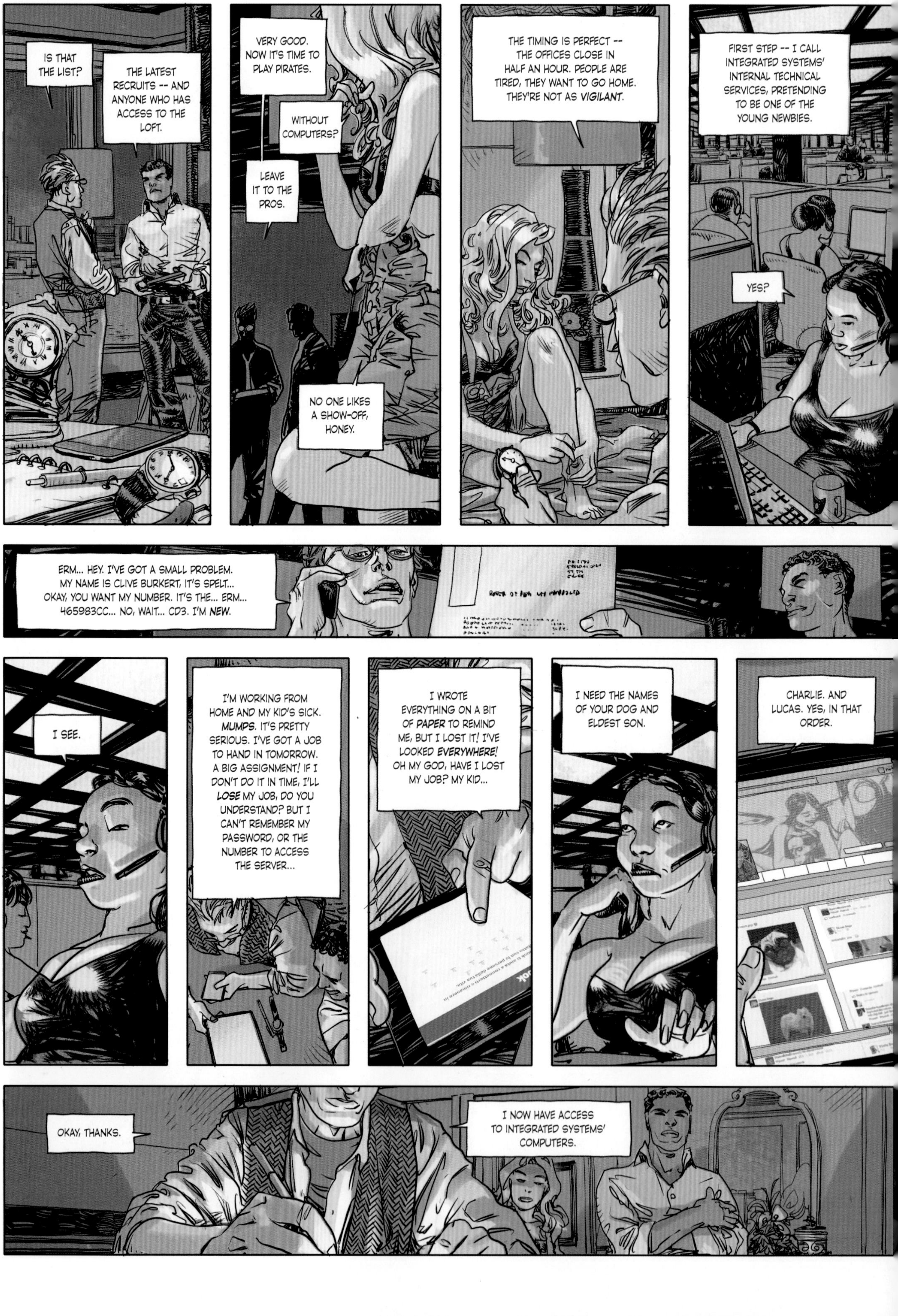
IS THAT THE LIST?
THE LATEST RECRUITS -- AND ANYONE WHO HAS ACCESS TO THE LOFT.
VERY GOOD. NOW IT'S TIME TO PLAY PIRATES.
WITHOUT COMPUTERS?
LEAVE IT TO THE PROS.
NO ONE LIKES A SHOW-OFF, HONEY.
THE TIMING IS PERFECT -- THE OFFICES CLOSE IN HALF AN HOUR. PEOPLE ARE TIRED, THEY WANT TO GO HOME. THEY'RE NOT AS VIGILANT.
FIRST STEP -- I CALL INTEGRATED SYSTEMS' INTERNAL TECHNICAL SERVICES, PRETENDING TO BE ONE OF THE YOUNG NEWBIES.
YES?
ERM... HEY. I'VE GOT A SMALL PROBLEM. MY NAME IS CLIVE BURKERT, IT'S SPELT... OKAY, YOU WANT MY NUMBER. IT'S THE... ERM... 465983CC... NO, WAIT... CD3. I'M NEW.
I SEE.
I'M WORKING FROM HOME AND MY KID'S SICK. MUMPS. IT'S PRETTY SERIOUS. I'VE GOT A JOB TO HAND IN TOMORROW. A BIG ASSIGNMENT! IF I DON'T DO IT IN TIME, I'LL LOSE MY JOB, DO YOU UNDERSTAND? BUT I CAN'T REMEMBER MY PASSWORD, OR THE NUMBER TO ACCESS THE SERVER...
I WROTE EVERYTHING ON A BIT OF PAPER TO REMIND ME, BUT I LOST IT! I'VE LOOKED EVERYWHERE! OH MY GOD, HAVE I LOST MY JOB? MY KID...
I NEED THE NAMES OF YOUR DOG AND ELDEST SON.
CHARLIE. AND LUCAS. YES, IN THAT ORDER.
OKAY, THANKS.
I NOW HAVE ACCESS TO INTEGRATED SYSTEMS' COMPUTERS.

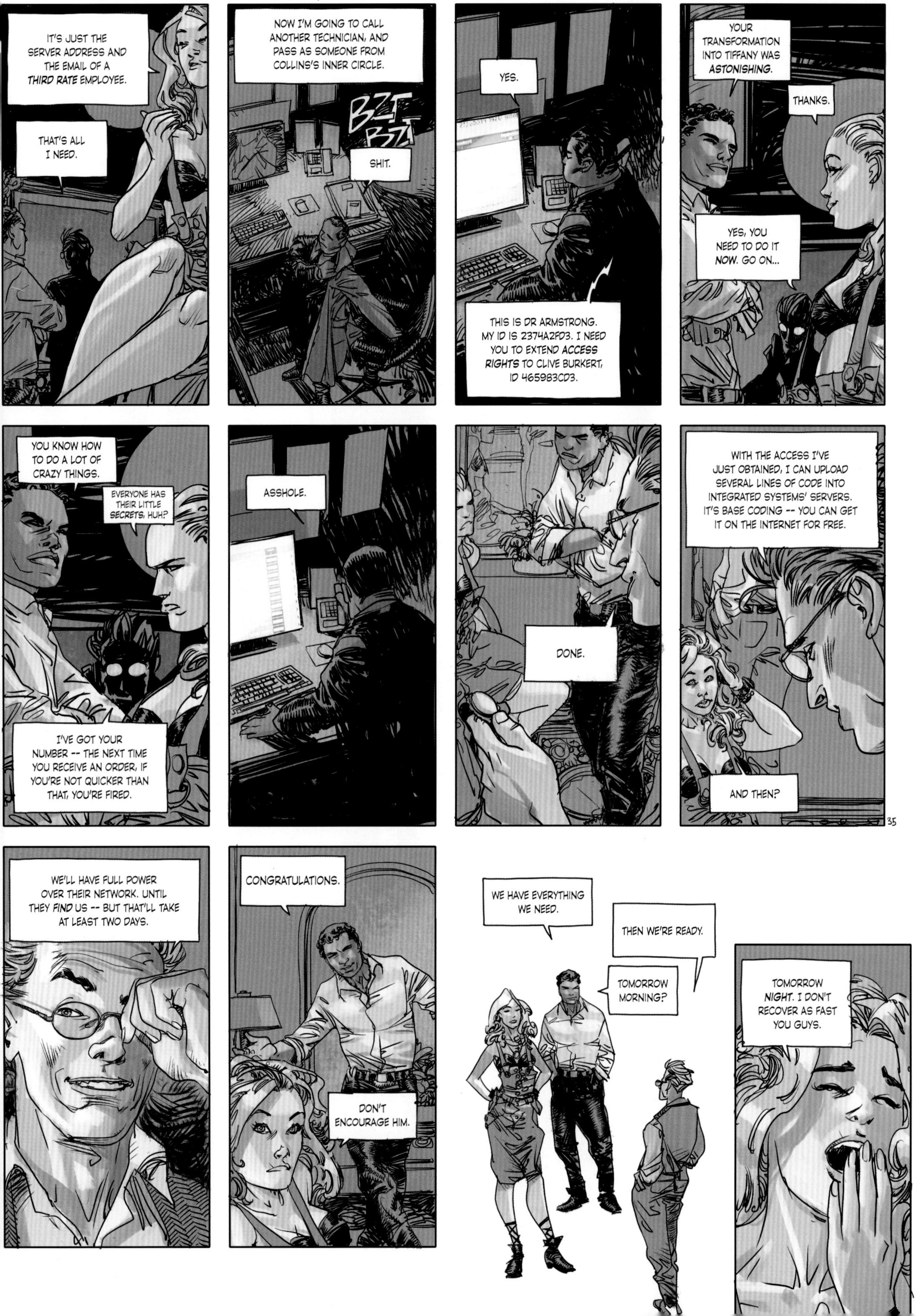
IT'S JUST THE SERVER ADDRESS AND THE EMAIL OF A THIRD RATE EMPLOYEE.
THAT'S ALL I NEED.
NOW I'M GOING TO CALL ANOTHER TECHNICIAN, AND PASS AS SOMEONE FROM COLLINS'S INNER CIRCLE.
BZZ BZZ
SHIT.
YES.
THIS IS DR ARMSTRONG. MY ID IS 2374A2FD3. I NEED YOU TO EXTEND ACCESS RIGHTS TO CLIVE BURKERT, ID 465983CD3.
YOUR TRANSFORMATION INTO TIFFANY WAS ASTONISHING.
THANKS.
YES, YOU NEED TO DO IT NOW. GO ON...
YOU KNOW HOW TO DO A LOT OF CRAZY THINGS.
EVERYONE HAS THEIR LITTLE SECRETS, HUH?
I'VE GOT YOUR NUMBER -- THE NEXT TIME YOU RECEIVE AN ORDER, IF YOU'RE NOT QUICKER THAN THAT, YOU'RE FIRED.
ASSHOLE.
DONE.
WITH THE ACCESS I'VE JUST OBTAINED, I CAN UPLOAD SEVERAL LINES OF CODE INTO INTEGRATED SYSTEMS' SERVERS. IT'S BASE CODING -- YOU CAN GET IT ON THE INTERNET FOR FREE.
AND THEN?
WE'LL HAVE FULL POWER OVER THEIR NETWORK. UNTIL THEY FIND US -- BUT THAT'LL TAKE AT LEAST TWO DAYS.
CONGRATULATIONS.
DON'T ENCOURAGE HIM.
WE HAVE EVERYTHING WE NEED.
THEN WE'RE READY.
TOMORROW MORNING?
TOMORROW NIGHT. I DON'T RECOVER AS FAST YOU GUYS.

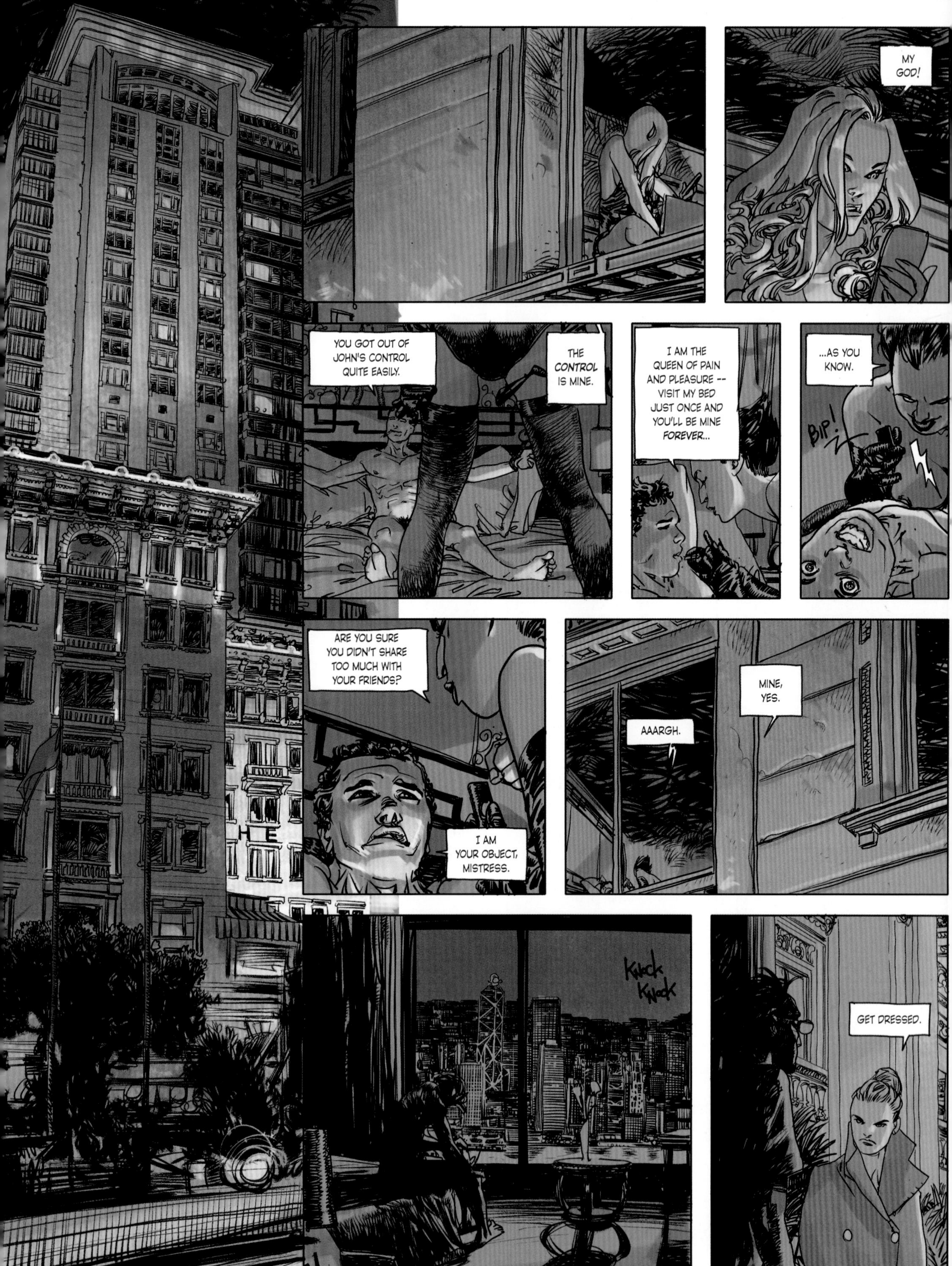
MY GOD!
YOU GOT OUT OF JOHN'S CONTROL QUITE EASILY.
THE CONTROL IS MINE.
I AM THE QUEEN OF PAIN AND PLEASURE -- VISIT MY BED JUST ONCE AND YOU'LL BE MINE FOREVER...
...AS YOU KNOW.
BIP!
ARE YOU SURE YOU DIDN'T SHARE TOO MUCH WITH YOUR FRIENDS?
I AM YOUR OBJECT, MISTRESS.
AAARGH.
MINE, YES.
KNOCK KNOCK
GET DRESSED.

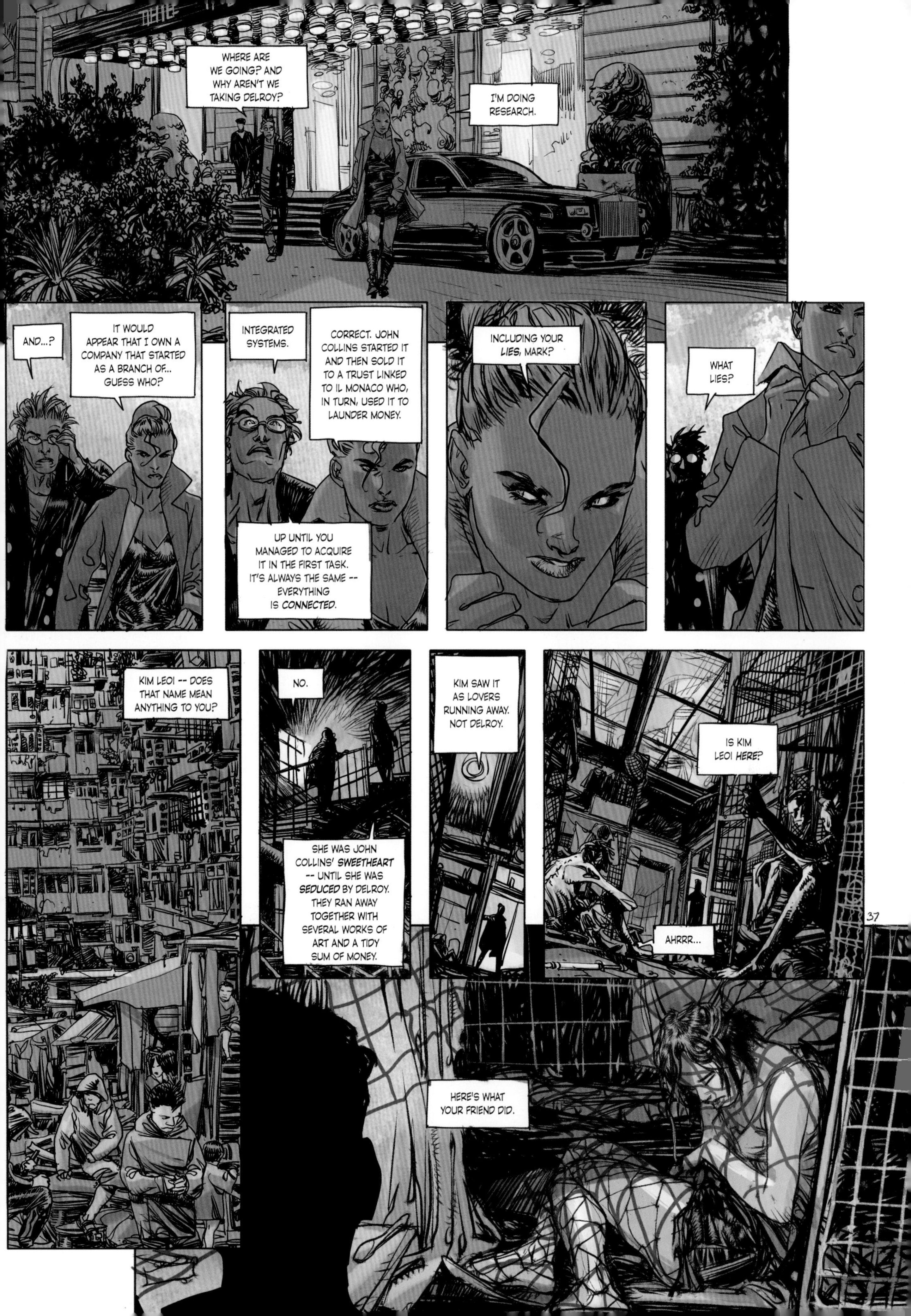

WHERE ARE WE GOING? AND WHY AREN'T WE TAKING DELROY?
I'M DOING RESEARCH.
AND...?
IT WOULD APPEAR THAT I OWN A COMPANY THAT STARTED AS A BRANCH OF... GUESS WHO?
INTEGRATED SYSTEMS.
CORRECT. JOHN COLLINS STARTED IT AND THEN SOLD IT TO A TRUST LINKED TO IL MONACO WHO, IN TURN, USED IT TO LAUNDER MONEY.
UP UNTIL YOU MANAGED TO ACQUIRE IT IN THE FIRST TASK. IT'S ALWAYS THE SAME -- EVERYTHING IS *CONNECTED*.
INCLUDING YOUR *LIES*, MARK?
WHAT LIES?
KIM LEOI -- DOES THAT NAME MEAN ANYTHING TO YOU?
NO.
SHE WAS JOHN COLLINS' ***SWEETHEART*** -- UNTIL SHE WAS ***SEDUCED*** BY DELROY. THEY RAN AWAY TOGETHER WITH SEVERAL WORKS OF ART AND A TIDY SUM OF MONEY.
KIM SAW IT AS LOVERS RUNNING AWAY. NOT DELROY.
IS KIM LEOI *HERE*?
AHRRR...
HERE'S WHAT YOUR FRIEND DID.

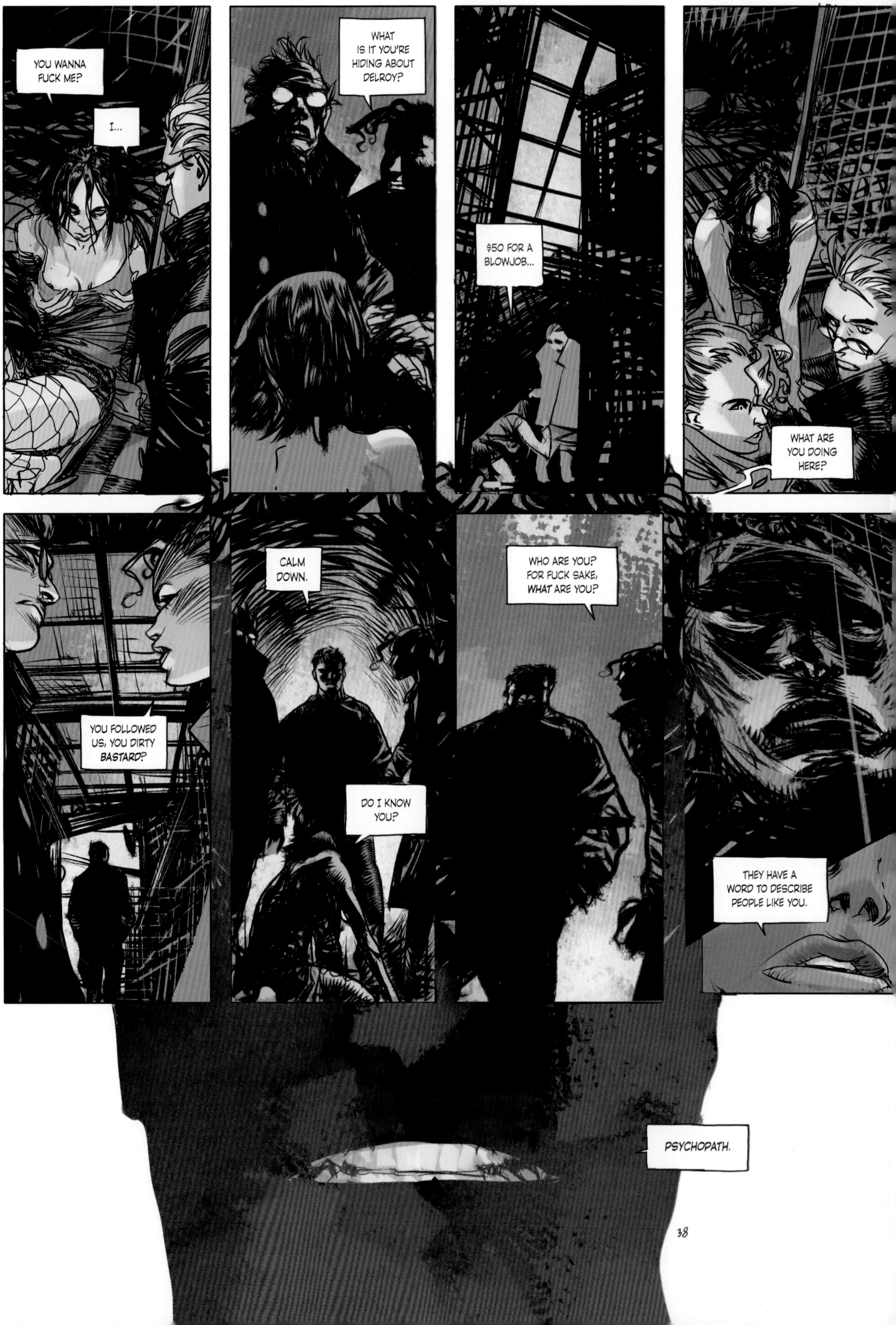
YOU WANNA FUCK ME?
I...
WHAT IS IT YOU'RE HIDING ABOUT DELROY?
$50 FOR A BLOWJOB...
WHAT ARE YOU DOING HERE?
YOU FOLLOWED US, YOU DIRTY BASTARD?
CALM DOWN.
DO I KNOW YOU?
WHO ARE YOU? FOR FUCK SAKE, WHAT ARE YOU?
THEY HAVE A WORD TO DESCRIBE PEOPLE LIKE YOU.
PSYCHOPATH.

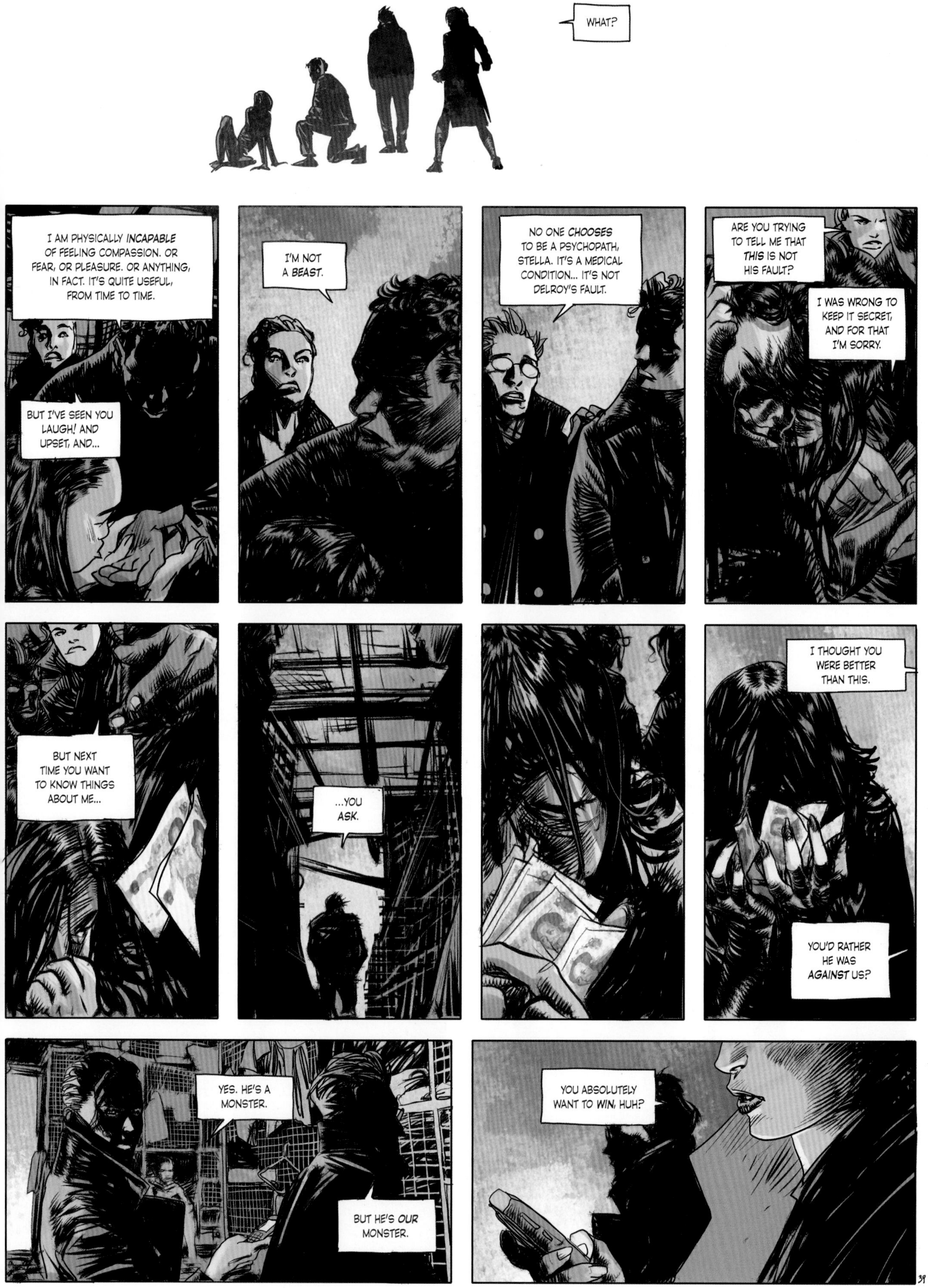
WHAT?
I AM PHYSICALLY INCAPABLE OF FEELING COMPASSION. OR FEAR, OR PLEASURE. OR ANYTHING, IN FACT. IT'S QUITE USEFUL, FROM TIME TO TIME.
BUT I'VE SEEN YOU LAUGH! AND UPSET, AND...
I'M NOT A BEAST.
NO ONE CHOOSES TO BE A PSYCHOPATH, STELLA. IT'S A MEDICAL CONDITION... IT'S NOT DELROY'S FAULT.
ARE YOU TRYING TO TELL ME THAT THIS IS NOT HIS FAULT?
I WAS WRONG TO KEEP IT SECRET, AND FOR THAT I'M SORRY.
BUT NEXT TIME YOU WANT TO KNOW THINGS ABOUT ME...
...YOU ASK.
I THOUGHT YOU WERE BETTER THAN THIS.
YOU'D RATHER HE WAS AGAINST US?
YES. HE'S A MONSTER.
BUT HE'S OUR MONSTER.
YOU ABSOLUTELY WANT TO WIN, HUH?

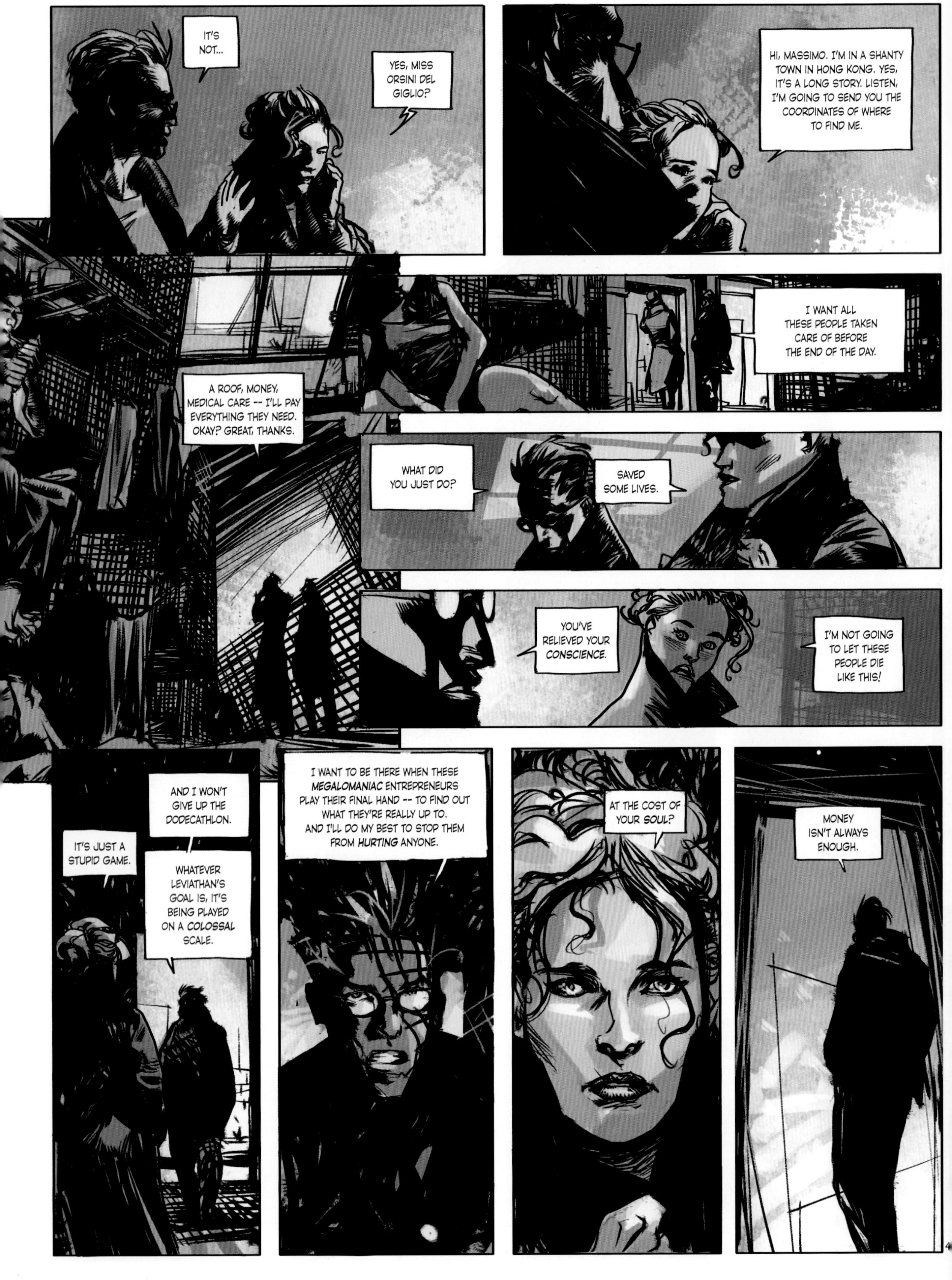
IT'S NOT...
YES, MISS ORSINI DEL GIGLIO?
HI, MASSIMO. I'M IN A SHANTY TOWN IN HONG KONG. YES, IT'S A LONG STORY. LISTEN, I'M GOING TO SEND YOU THE COORDINATES OF WHERE TO FIND ME.
I WANT ALL THESE PEOPLE TAKEN CARE OF BEFORE THE END OF THE DAY.
A ROOF, MONEY, MEDICAL CARE -- I'LL PAY EVERYTHING THEY NEED. OKAY? GREAT, THANKS.
WHAT DID YOU JUST DO?
SAVED SOME LIVES.
YOU'VE RELIEVED YOUR *CONSCIENCE*.
I'M NOT GOING TO LET THESE PEOPLE DIE LIKE THIS!
IT'S JUST A STUPID GAME.
AND I WON'T GIVE UP THE DODECATHLON.
WHATEVER LEVIATHAN'S GOAL IS, IT'S BEING PLAYED ON A *COLOSSAL* SCALE.
I WANT TO BE THERE WHEN THESE *MEGALOMANIAC* ENTREPRENEURS PLAY THEIR FINAL HAND -- TO FIND OUT WHAT THEY'RE REALLY UP TO. AND I'LL DO MY BEST TO STOP THEM FROM *HURTING* ANYONE.
AT THE COST OF YOUR *SOUL*?
MONEY ISN'T ALWAYS ENOUGH.

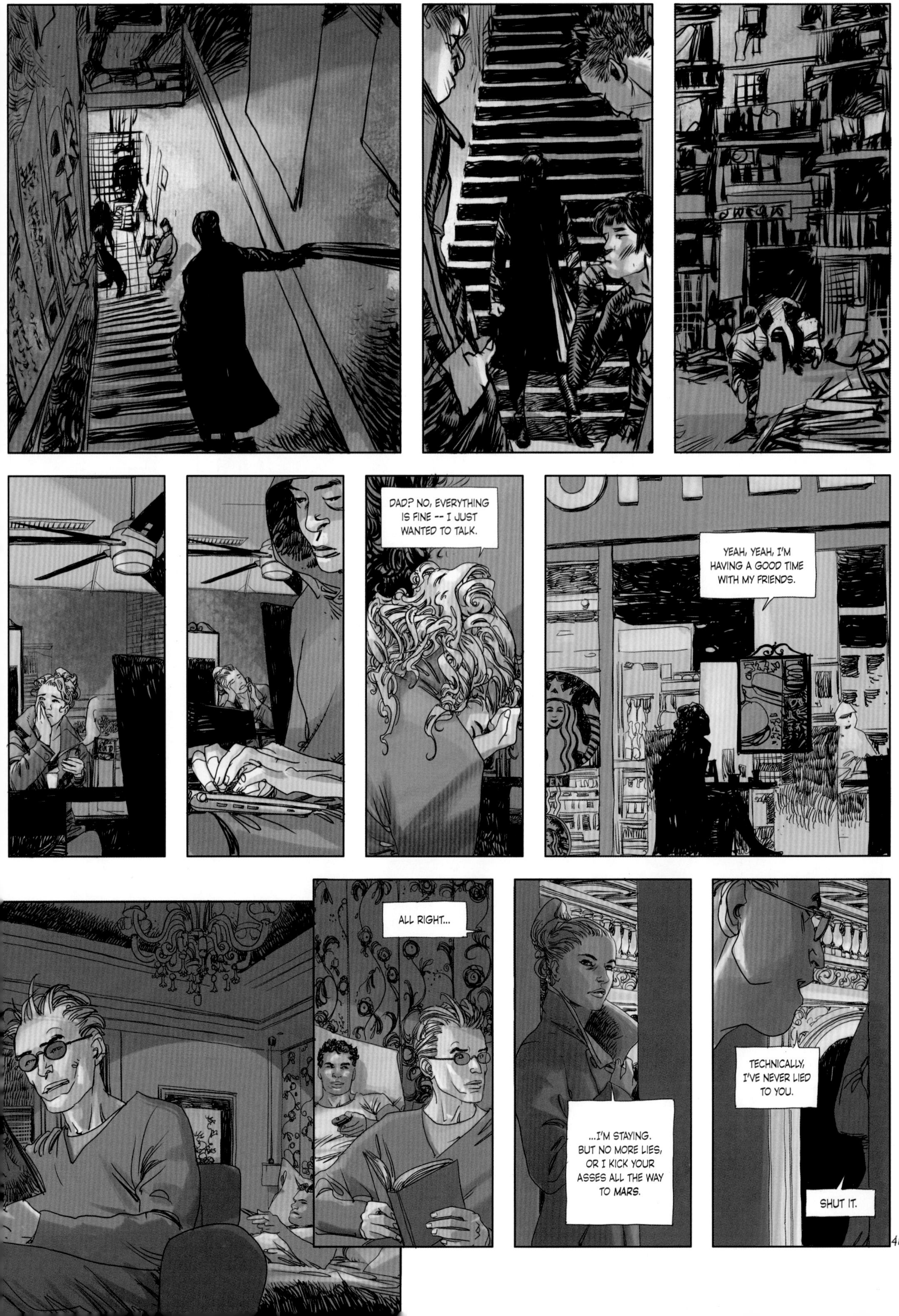

DAD? NO, EVERYTHING IS FINE -- I JUST WANTED TO TALK.
YEAH, YEAH, I'M HAVING A GOOD TIME WITH MY FRIENDS.
ALL RIGHT...
...I'M STAYING. BUT NO MORE LIES, OR I KICK YOUR ASSES ALL THE WAY TO MARS.
TECHNICALLY, I'VE NEVER LIED TO YOU.
SHUT IT.

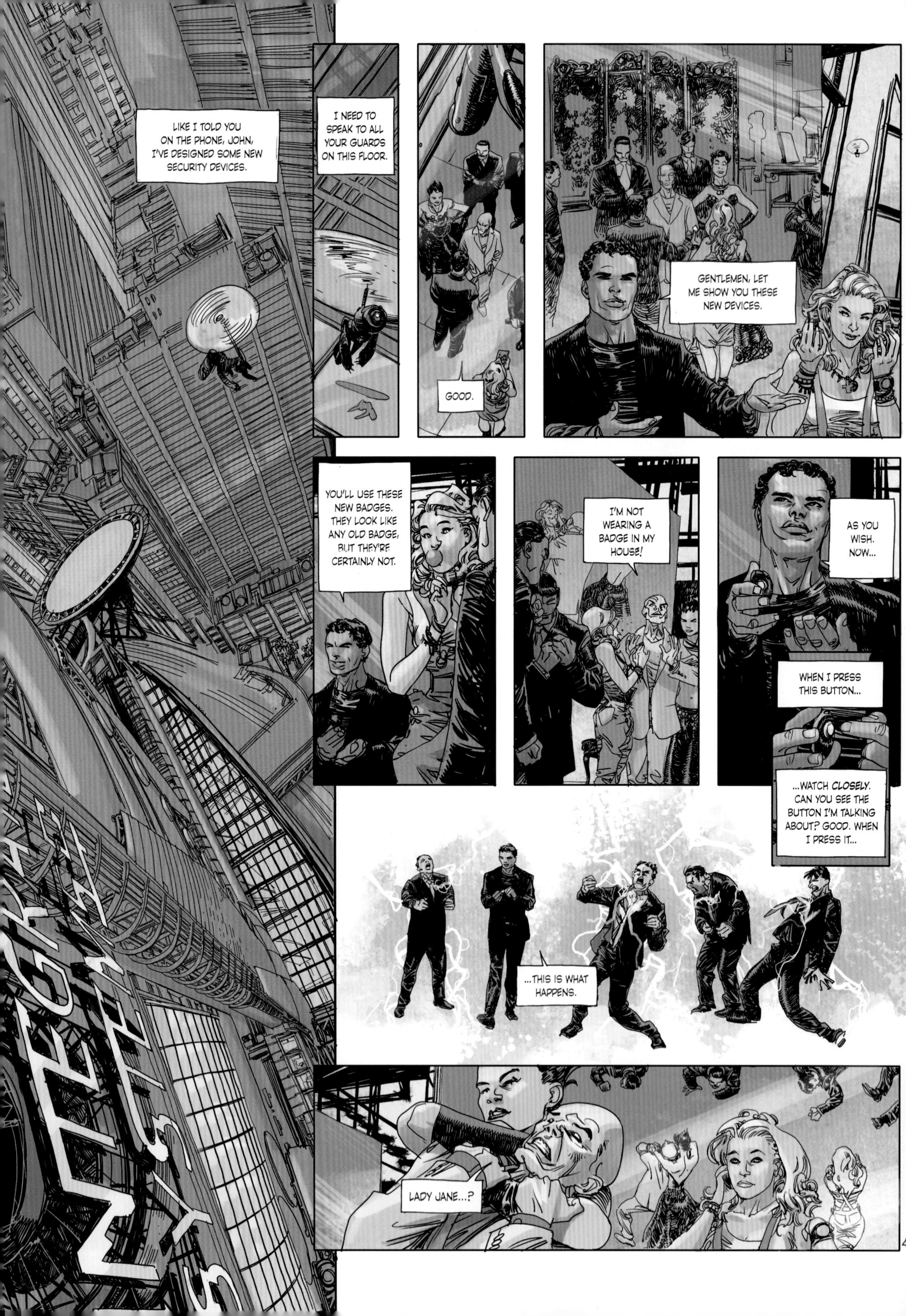
LIKE I TOLD YOU ON THE PHONE, JOHN, I'VE DESIGNED SOME NEW SECURITY DEVICES.
I NEED TO SPEAK TO ALL YOUR GUARDS ON THIS FLOOR.
GOOD.
GENTLEMEN, LET ME SHOW YOU THESE NEW DEVICES.
YOU'LL USE THESE NEW BADGES. THEY LOOK LIKE ANY OLD BADGE, BUT THEY'RE CERTAINLY NOT.
I'M NOT WEARING A BADGE IN MY HOUSE!
AS YOU WISH. NOW...
WHEN I PRESS THIS BUTTON...
...WATCH CLOSELY. CAN YOU SEE THE BUTTON I'M TALKING ABOUT? GOOD. WHEN I PRESS IT...
...THIS IS WHAT HAPPENS.
LADY JANE...?

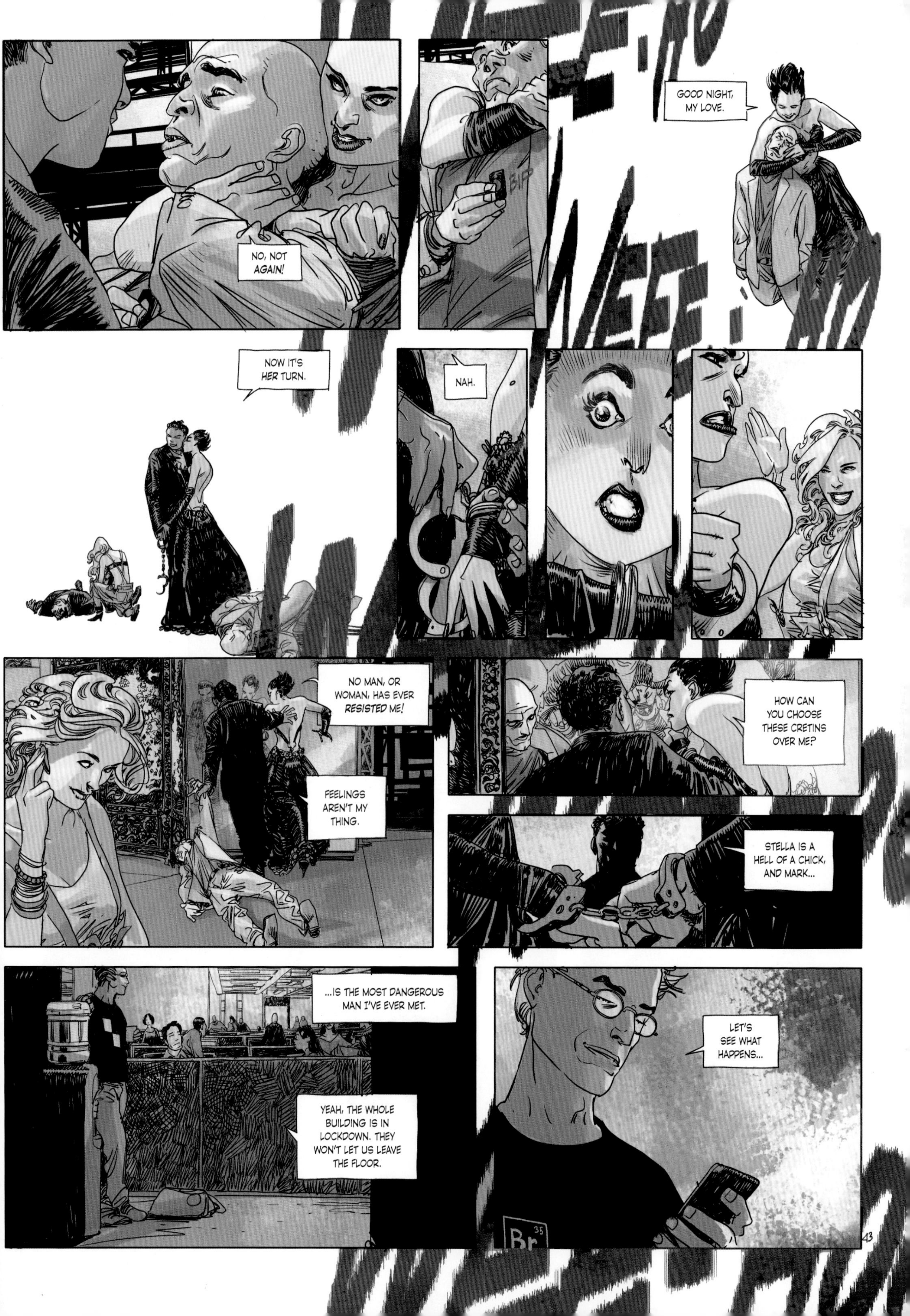
NO, NOT AGAIN!
GOOD NIGHT, MY LOVE.
NOW IT'S HER TURN.
NAH.
NO MAN, OR WOMAN, HAS EVER RESISTED ME!
FEELINGS AREN'T MY THING.
HOW CAN YOU CHOOSE THESE CRETINS OVER ME?
STELLA IS A HELL OF A CHICK, AND MARK...
...IS THE MOST DANGEROUS MAN I'VE EVER MET.
YEAH, THE WHOLE BUILDING IS IN LOCKDOWN. THEY WON'T LET US LEAVE THE FLOOR.
LET'S SEE WHAT HAPPENS...

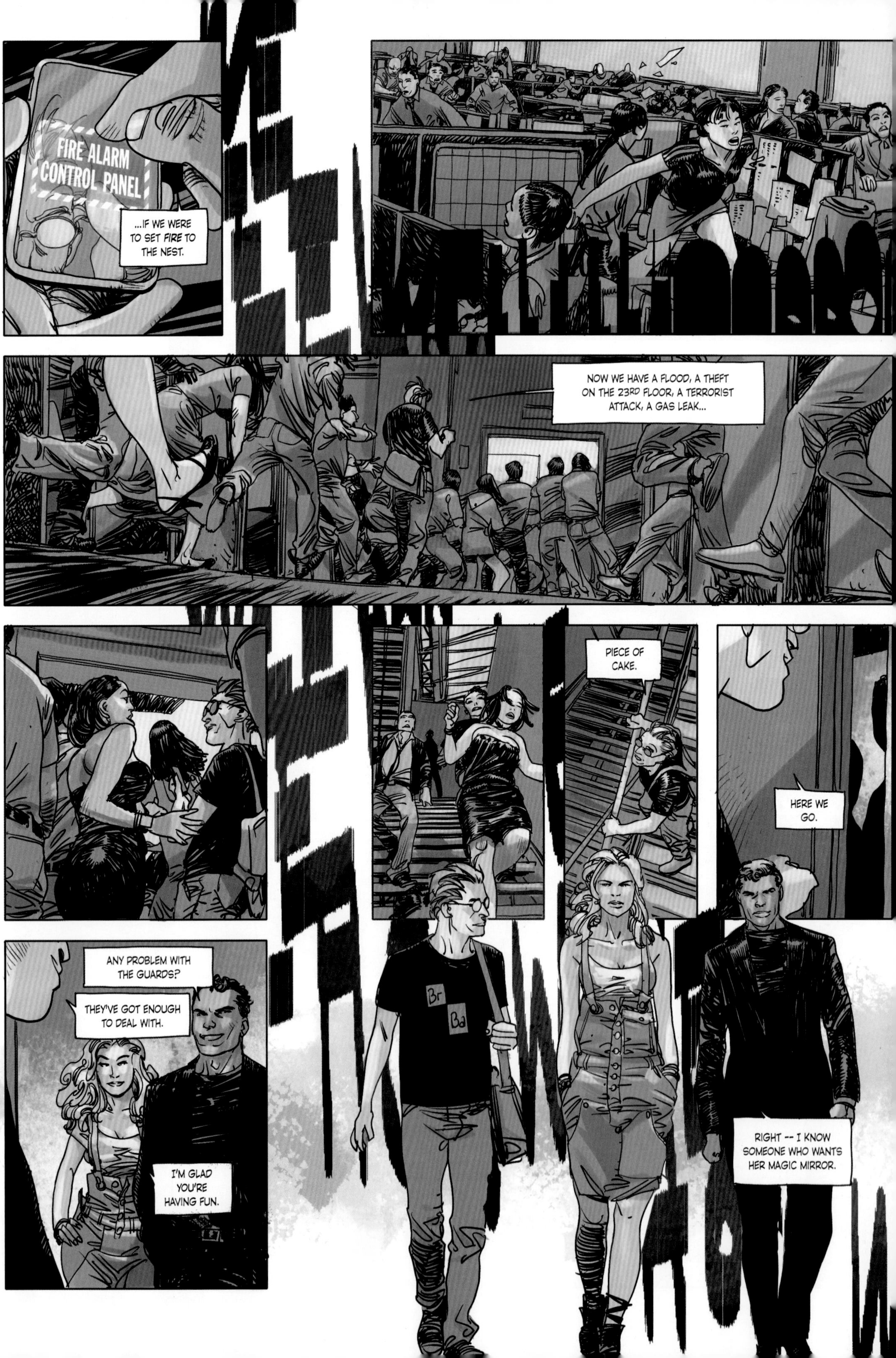
FIRE ALARM CONTROL PANEL
...IF WE WERE TO SET FIRE TO THE NEST.
NOW WE HAVE A FLOOD, A THEFT ON THE 23RD FLOOR, A TERRORIST ATTACK, A GAS LEAK...
PIECE OF CAKE.
HERE WE GO.
ANY PROBLEM WITH THE GUARDS?
THEY'VE GOT ENOUGH TO DEAL WITH.
I'M GLAD YOU'RE HAVING FUN.
Br
Ba
RIGHT -- I KNOW SOMEONE WHO WANTS HER MAGIC MIRROR.

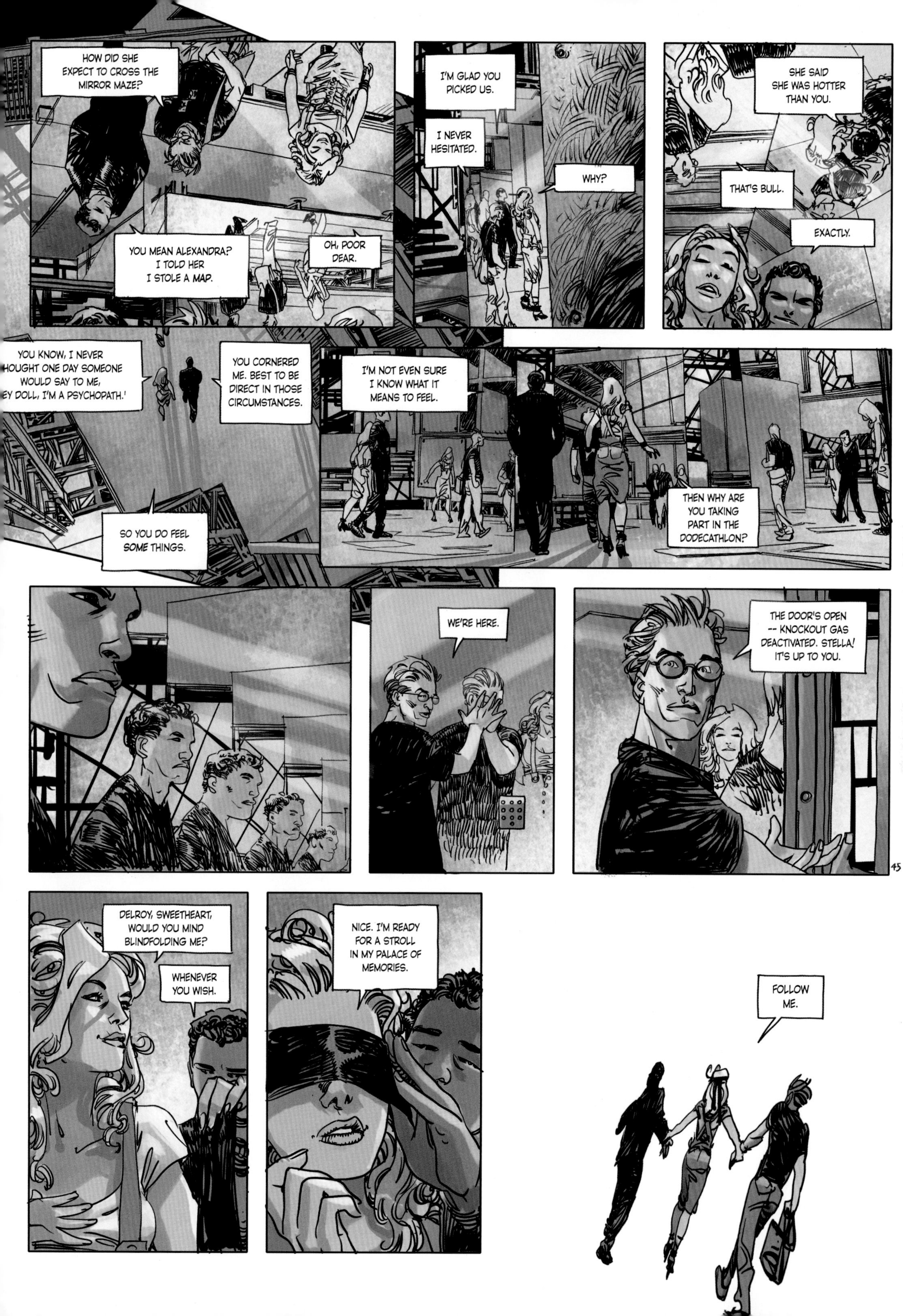
HOW DID SHE EXPECT TO CROSS THE MIRROR MAZE?
YOU MEAN ALEXANDRA? I TOLD HER I STOLE A MAP.
OH, POOR DEAR.
I'M GLAD YOU PICKED US.
I NEVER HESITATED.
WHY?
SHE SAID SHE WAS HOTTER THAN YOU.
THAT'S BULL.
EXACTLY.
YOU KNOW, I NEVER HOUGHT ONE DAY SOMEONE WOULD SAY TO ME, EY DOLL, I'M A PSYCHOPATH.'
YOU CORNERED ME. BEST TO BE DIRECT IN THOSE CIRCUMSTANCES.
SO YOU DO FEEL SOME THINGS.
I'M NOT EVEN SURE I KNOW WHAT IT MEANS TO FEEL.
THEN WHY ARE YOU TAKING PART IN THE DODECATHLON?
WE'RE HERE.
THE DOOR'S OPEN -- KNOCKOUT GAS DEACTIVATED. STELLA! IT'S UP TO YOU.
DELROY, SWEETHEART, WOULD YOU MIND BLINDFOLDING ME?
WHENEVER YOU WISH.
NICE. I'M READY FOR A STROLL IN MY PALACE OF MEMORIES.
FOLLOW ME.

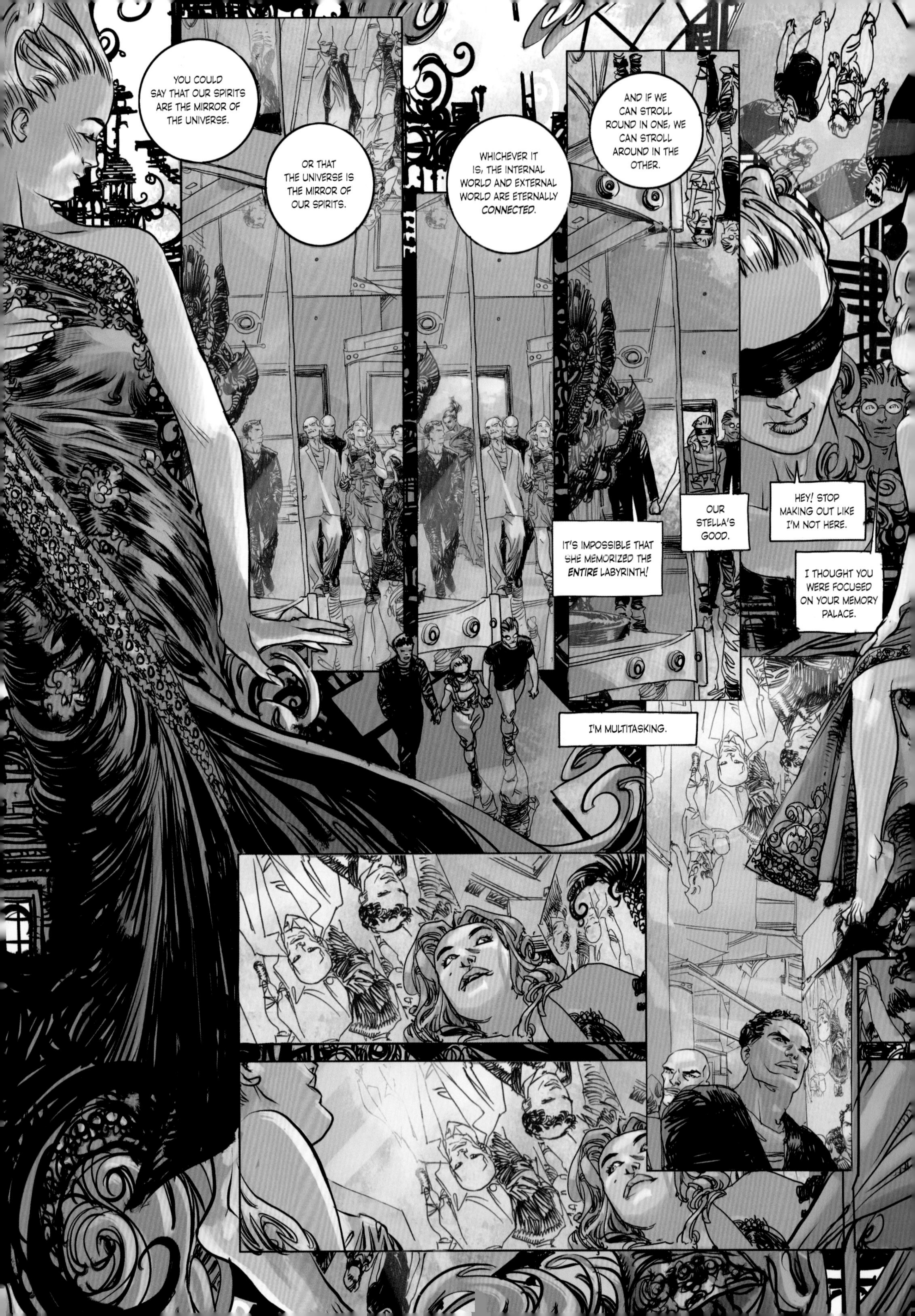

YOU COULD SAY THAT OUR SPIRITS ARE THE MIRROR OF THE UNIVERSE.
OR THAT THE UNIVERSE IS THE MIRROR OF OUR SPIRITS.
WHICHEVER IT IS, THE INTERNAL WORLD AND EXTERNAL WORLD ARE ETERNALLY *CONNECTED*.
AND IF WE CAN STROLL ROUND IN ONE, WE CAN STROLL AROUND IN THE OTHER.
IT'S IMPOSSIBLE THAT SHE MEMORIZED THE ***ENTIRE*** LABYRINTH!
OUR STELLA'S GOOD.
HEY! STOP MAKING OUT LIKE I'M NOT HERE.
I THOUGHT YOU WERE FOCUSED ON YOUR MEMORY PALACE.
I'M MULTITASKING.

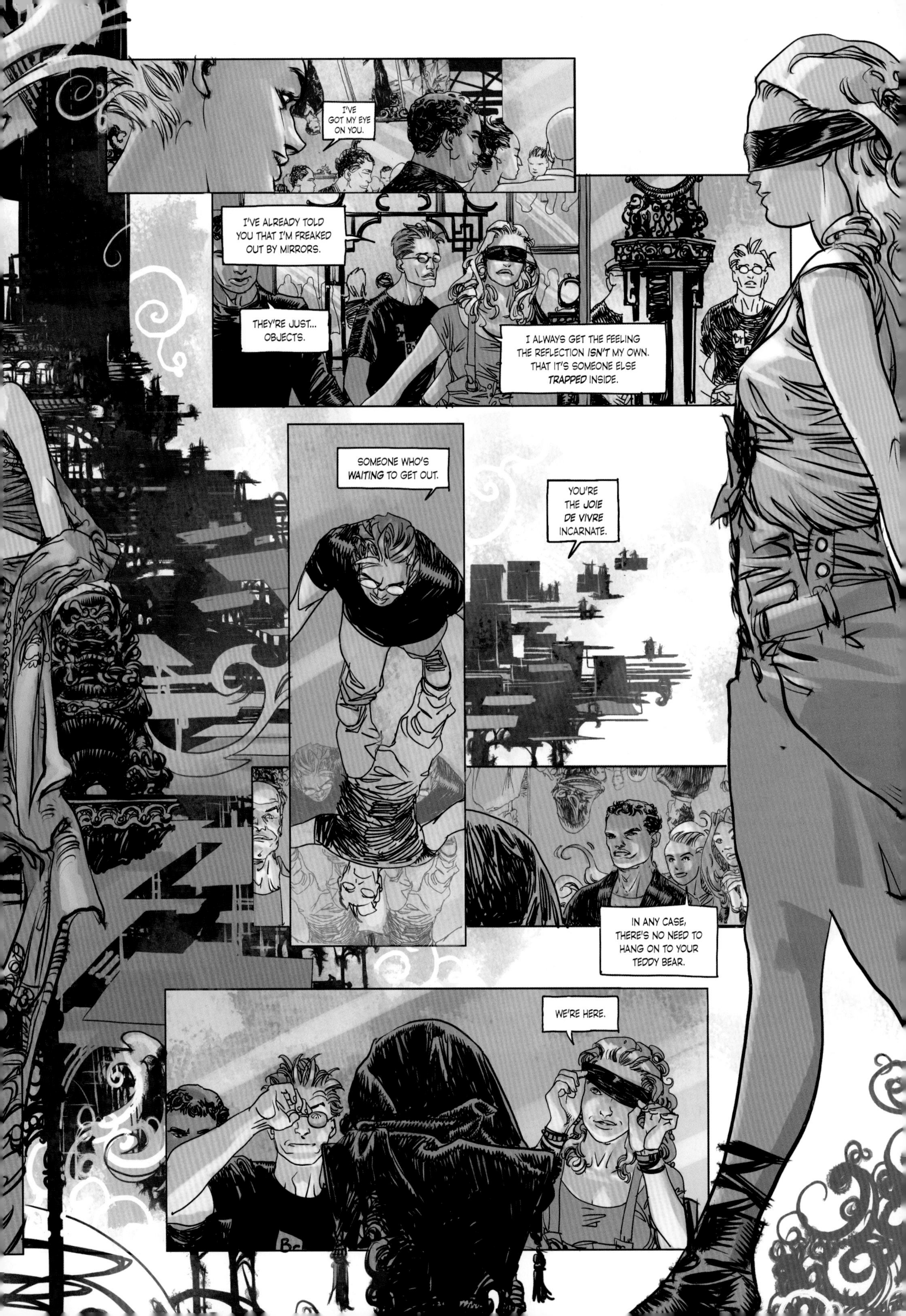
I'VE GOT MY EYE ON YOU.
I'VE ALREADY TOLD YOU THAT I'M FREAKED OUT BY MIRRORS.
THEY'RE JUST... OBJECTS.
I ALWAYS GET THE FEELING THE REFLECTION ISN'T MY OWN. THAT IT'S SOMEONE ELSE TRAPPED INSIDE.
SOMEONE WHO'S WAITING TO GET OUT.
YOU'RE THE JOIE DE VIVRE INCARNATE.
IN ANY CASE, THERE'S NO NEED TO HANG ON TO YOUR TEDDY BEAR.
WE'RE HERE.

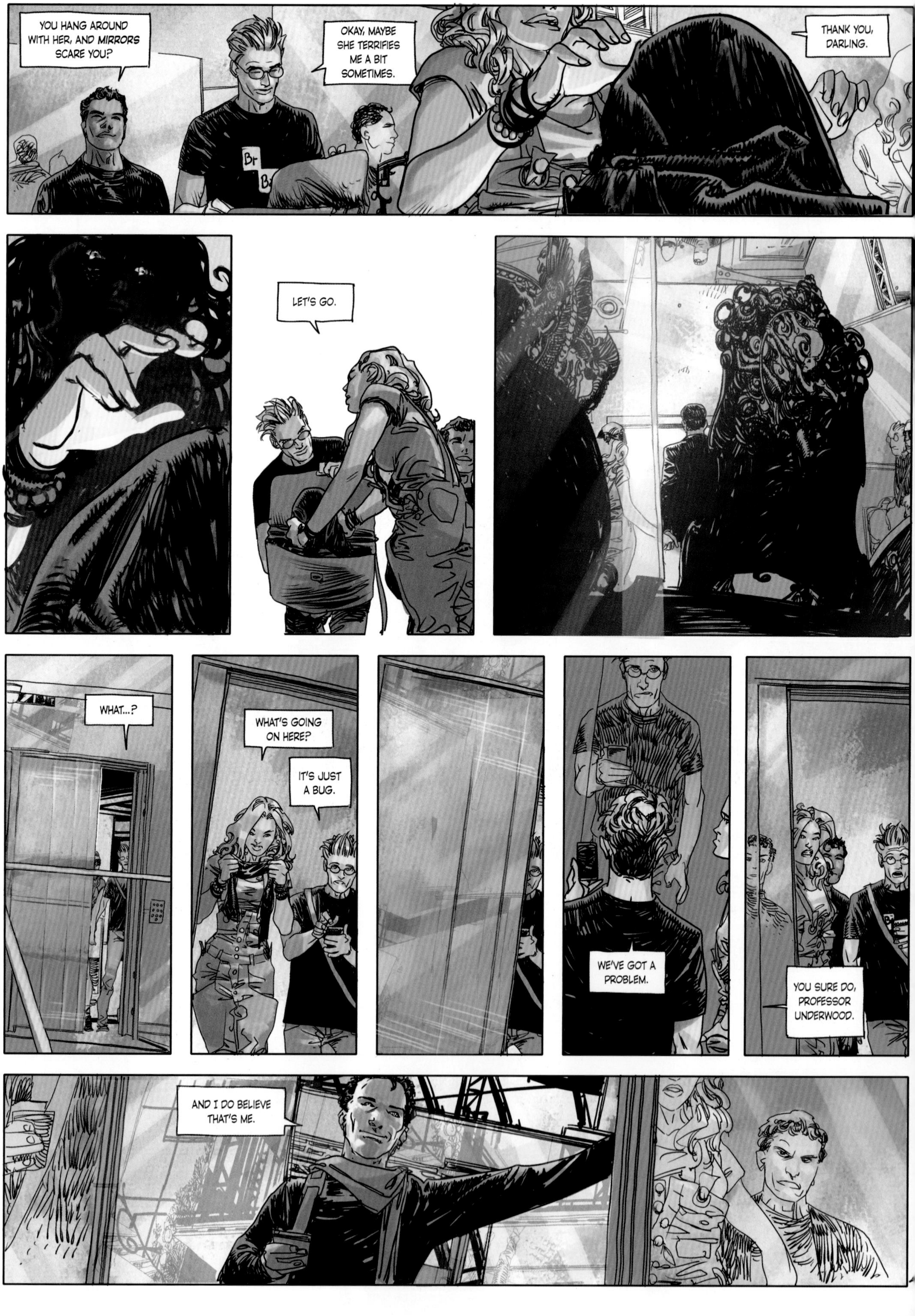
YOU HANG AROUND WITH HER, AND MIRRORS SCARE YOU?
OKAY, MAYBE SHE TERRIFIES ME A BIT SOMETIMES.
THANK YOU, DARLING.
LET'S GO.
WHAT...?
WHAT'S GOING ON HERE?
IT'S JUST A BUG.
WE'VE GOT A PROBLEM.
YOU SURE DO, PROFESSOR UNDERWOOD.
AND I DO BELIEVE THAT'S ME.

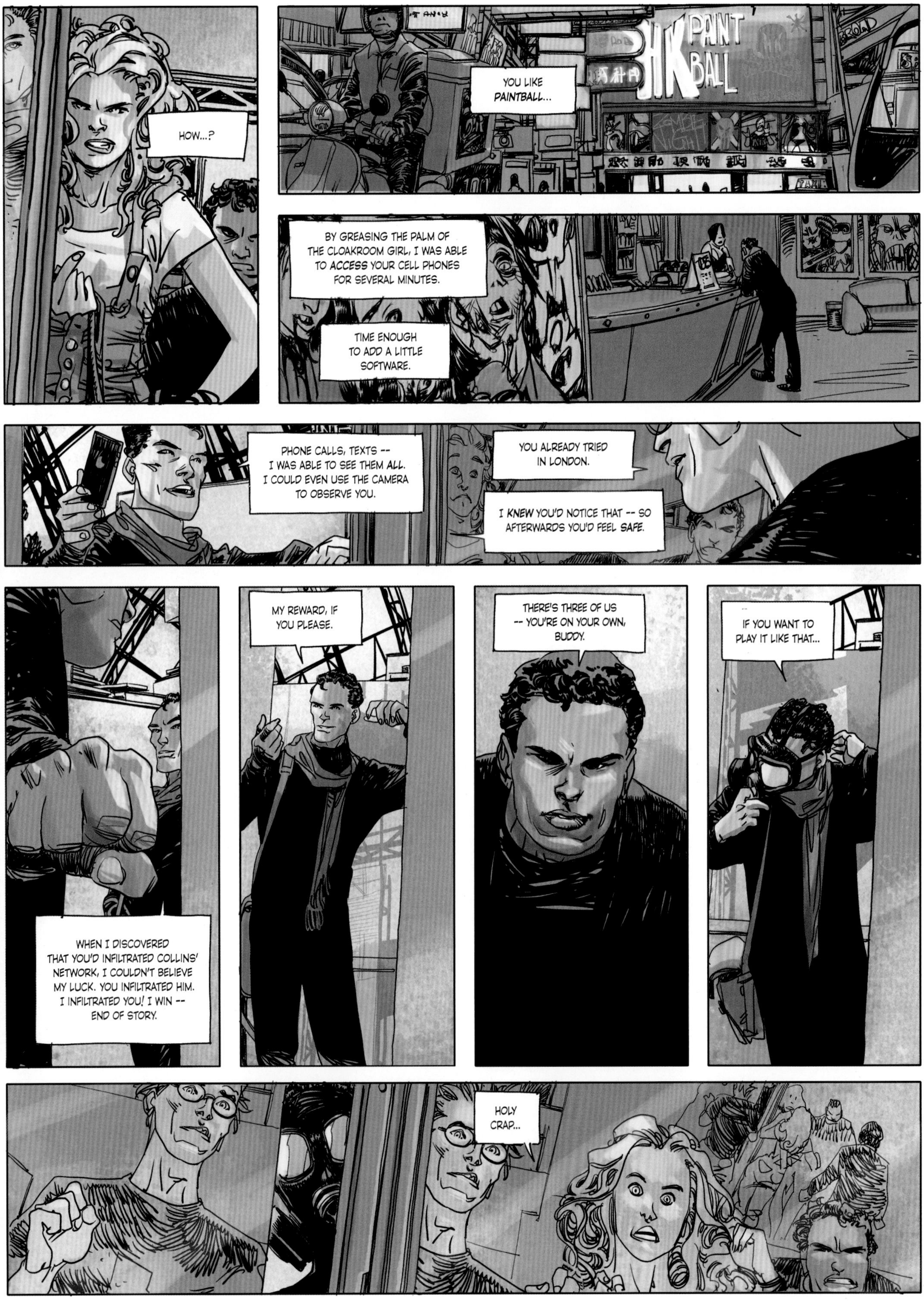
HOW...?
YOU LIKE PAINTBALL...
BY GREASING THE PALM OF THE CLOAKROOM GIRL, I WAS ABLE TO ACCESS YOUR CELL PHONES FOR SEVERAL MINUTES.
TIME ENOUGH TO ADD A LITTLE SOFTWARE.
PHONE CALLS, TEXTS -- I WAS ABLE TO SEE THEM ALL. I COULD EVEN USE THE CAMERA TO OBSERVE YOU.
YOU ALREADY TRIED IN LONDON.
I KNEW YOU'D NOTICE THAT -- SO AFTERWARDS YOU'D FEEL SAFE.
WHEN I DISCOVERED THAT YOU'D INFILTRATED COLLINS' NETWORK, I COULDN'T BELIEVE MY LUCK. YOU INFILTRATED HIM. I INFILTRATED YOU! I WIN -- END OF STORY.
MY REWARD, IF YOU PLEASE.
THERE'S THREE OF US -- YOU'RE ON YOUR OWN, BUDDY.
IF YOU WANT TO PLAY IT LIKE THAT...
HOLY CRAP...

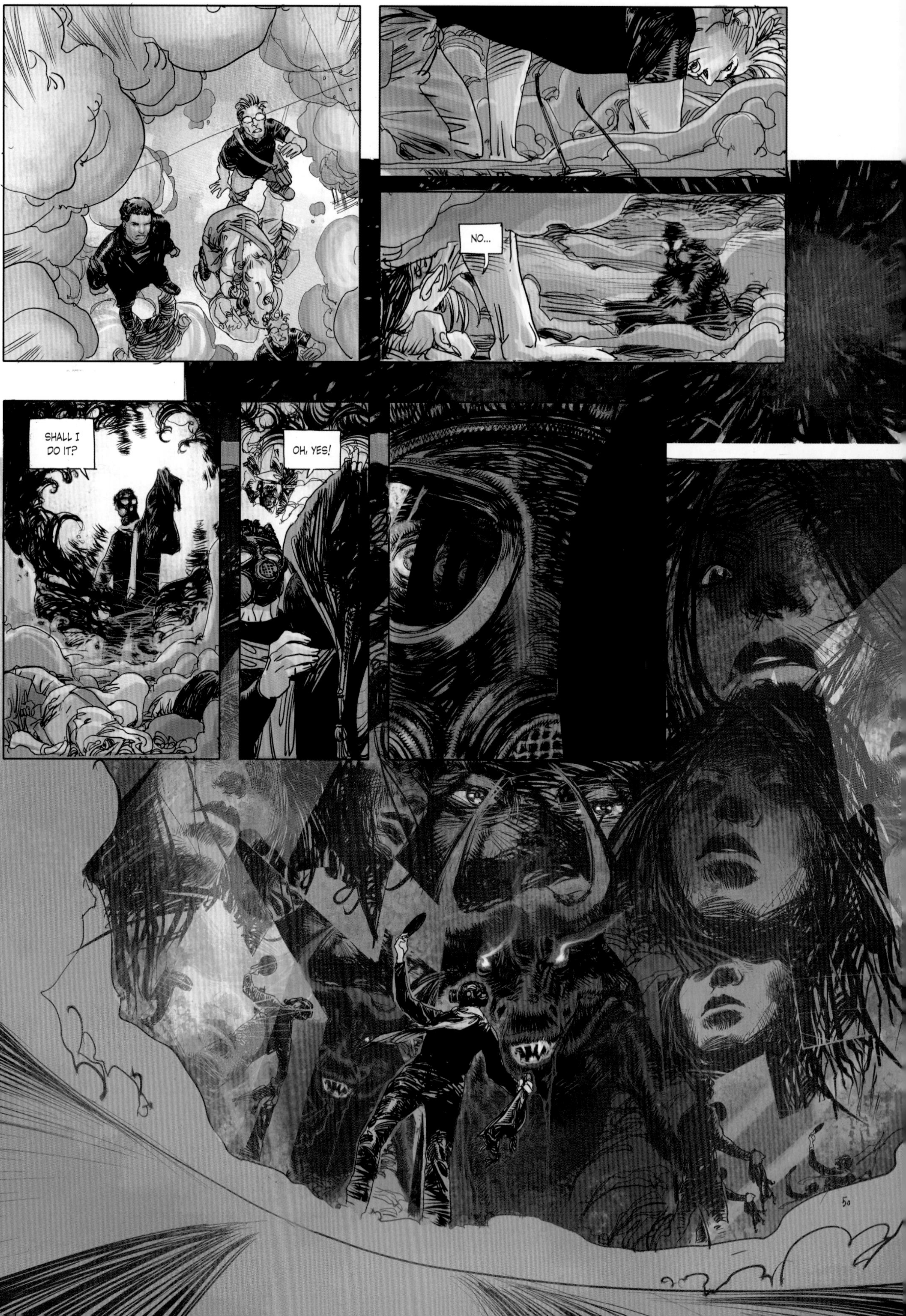
NO...
SHALL I DO IT?
OH, YES!

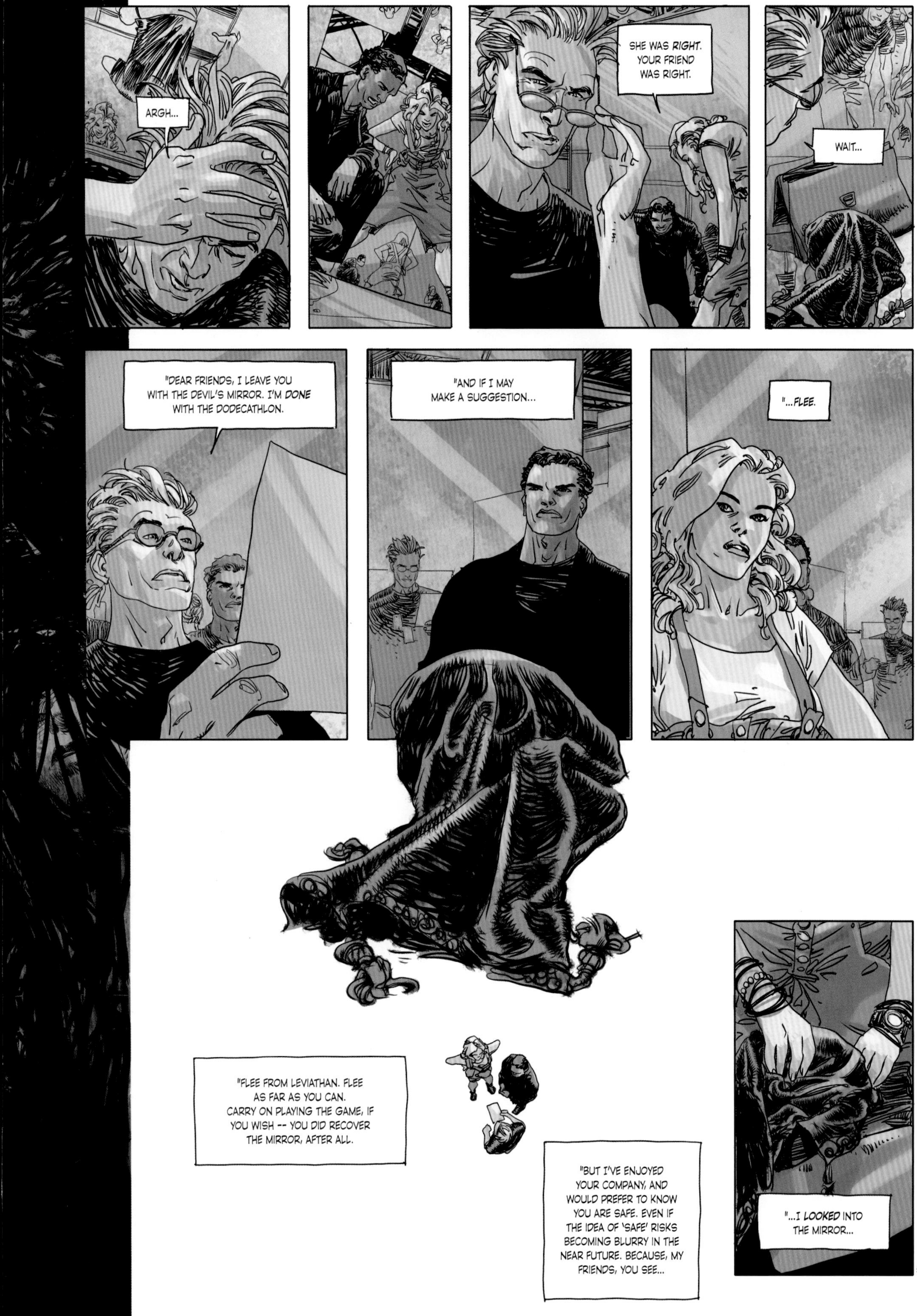

ARGH...
SHE WAS *RIGHT*. YOUR FRIEND WAS RIGHT.
WAIT...
"DEAR FRIENDS, I LEAVE YOU WITH THE DEVIL'S MIRROR. I'M *DONE* WITH THE DODECATHLON.
"AND IF I MAY MAKE A SUGGESTION...
"...*FLEE*.
"FLEE FROM LEVIATHAN. FLEE AS FAR AS YOU CAN. CARRY ON PLAYING THE GAME, IF YOU WISH -- YOU DID RECOVER THE MIRROR, AFTER ALL.
"BUT I'VE ENJOYED YOUR COMPANY, AND WOULD PREFER TO KNOW YOU ARE SAFE. EVEN IF THE IDEA OF 'SAFE' RISKS BECOMING BLURRY IN THE NEAR FUTURE. BECAUSE, MY FRIENDS, YOU SEE...
"...I *LOOKED* INTO THE MIRROR...

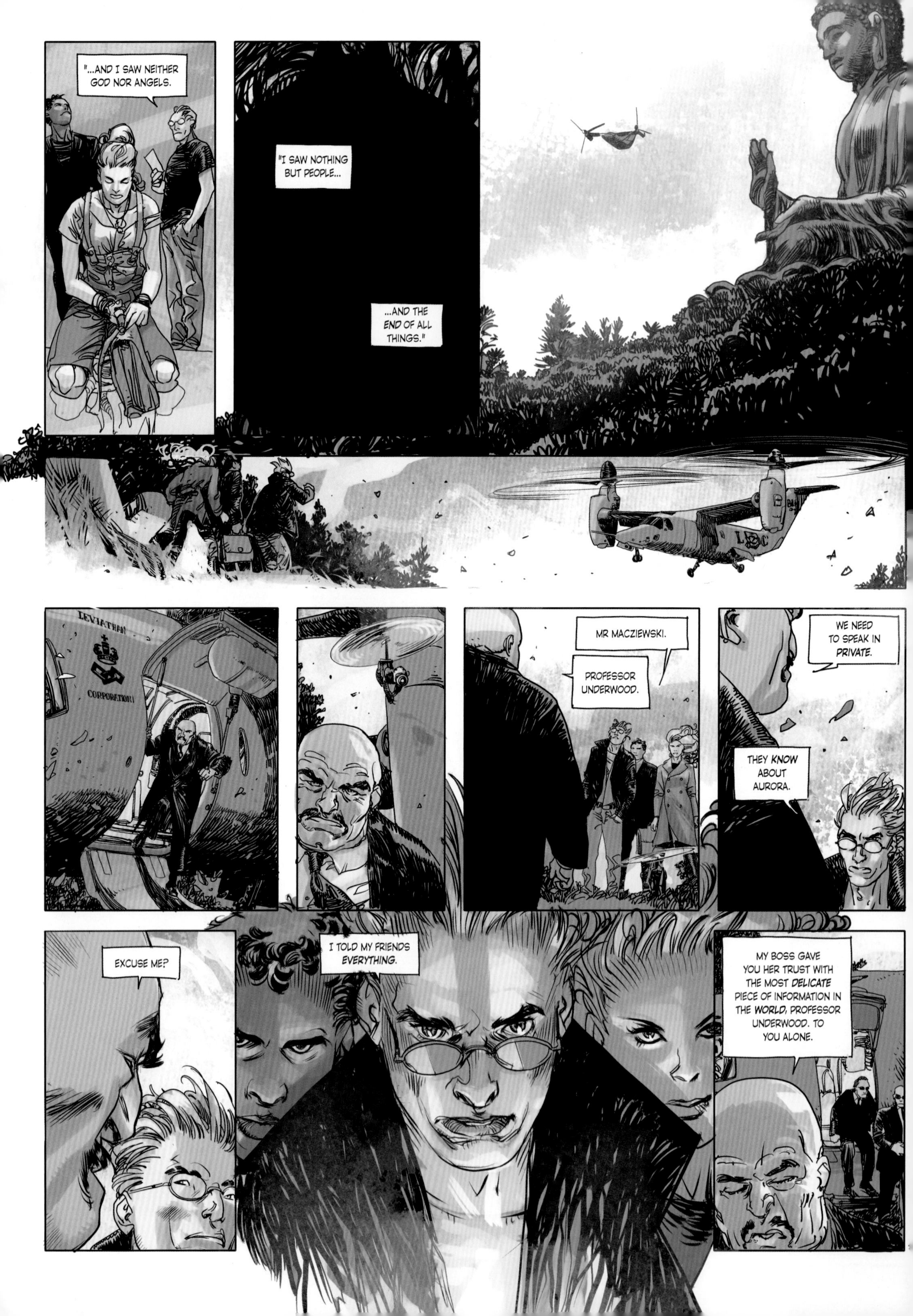
"...AND I SAW NEITHER GOD NOR ANGELS.
"I SAW NOTHING BUT PEOPLE...
...AND THE END OF ALL THINGS."
LEVIATHAN
CORPORATION
MR MACZIEWSKI.
PROFESSOR UNDERWOOD.
WE NEED TO SPEAK IN PRIVATE.
THEY KNOW ABOUT AURORA.
EXCUSE ME?
I TOLD MY FRIENDS EVERYTHING.
MY BOSS GAVE YOU HER TRUST WITH THE MOST DELICATE PIECE OF INFORMATION IN THE WORLD, PROFESSOR UNDERWOOD. TO YOU ALONE.

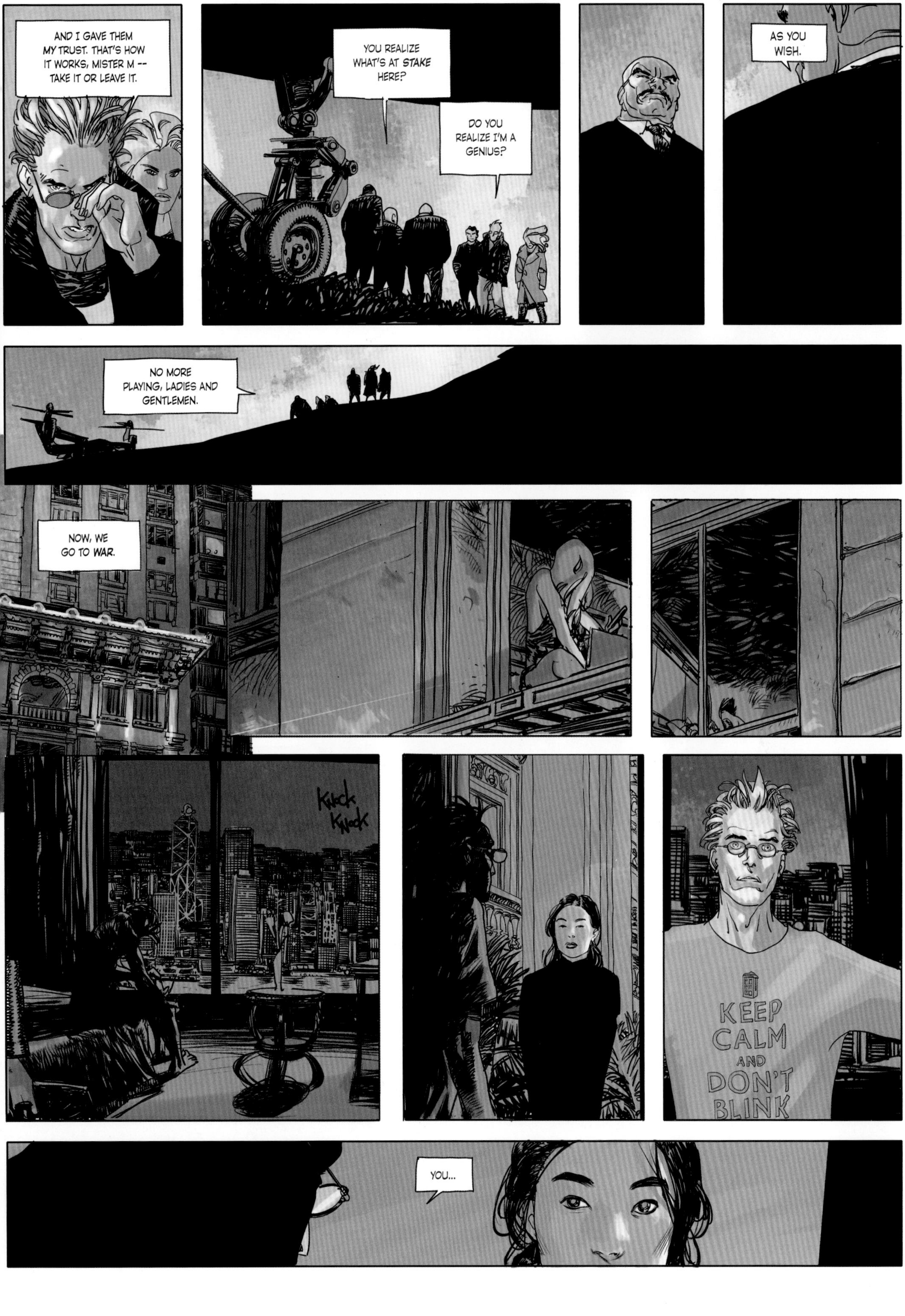
AND I GAVE THEM MY TRUST. THAT'S HOW IT WORKS, MISTER M -- TAKE IT OR LEAVE IT.
YOU REALIZE WHAT'S AT STAKE HERE?
DO YOU REALIZE I'M A GENIUS?
AS YOU WISH.
NO MORE PLAYING, LADIES AND GENTLEMEN.
NOW, WE GO TO WAR.
KNOCK KNOCK
KEEP CALM AND DON'T BLINK
YOU...

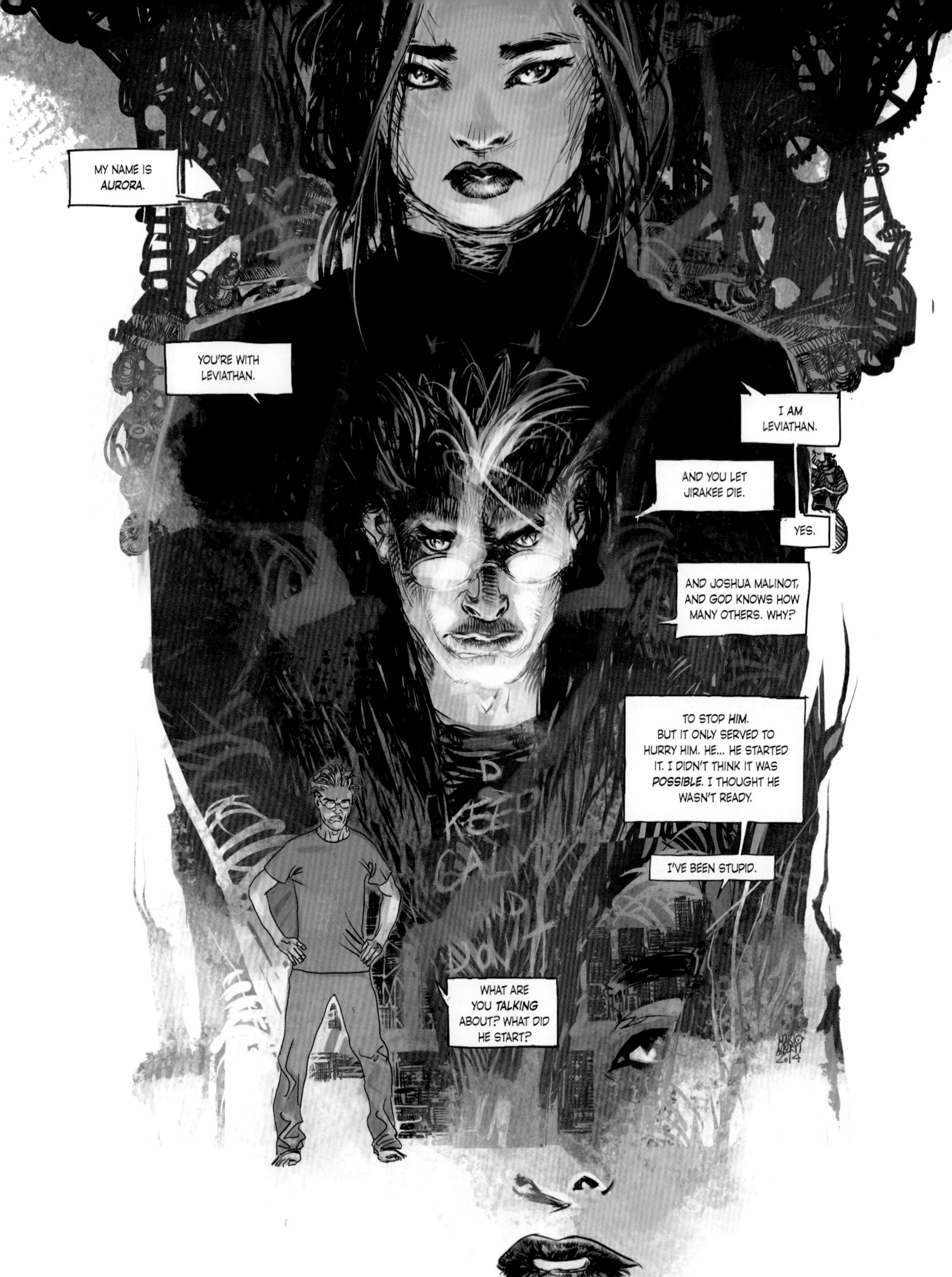
MY NAME IS AURORA.
YOU'RE WITH LEVIATHAN.
I AM LEVIATHAN.
AND YOU LET JIRAKEE DIE.
YES.
AND JOSHUA MALINOT, AND GOD KNOWS HOW MANY OTHERS. WHY?
TO STOP HIM. BUT IT ONLY SERVED TO HURRY HIM. HE... HE STARTED IT. I DIDN'T THINK IT WAS POSSIBLE. I THOUGHT HE WASN'T READY.
I'VE BEEN STUPID.
WHAT ARE YOU TALKING ABOUT? WHAT DID HE START?

LEON BELLAMY IS GOING TO WIN.

END OF CHAPTER THREE

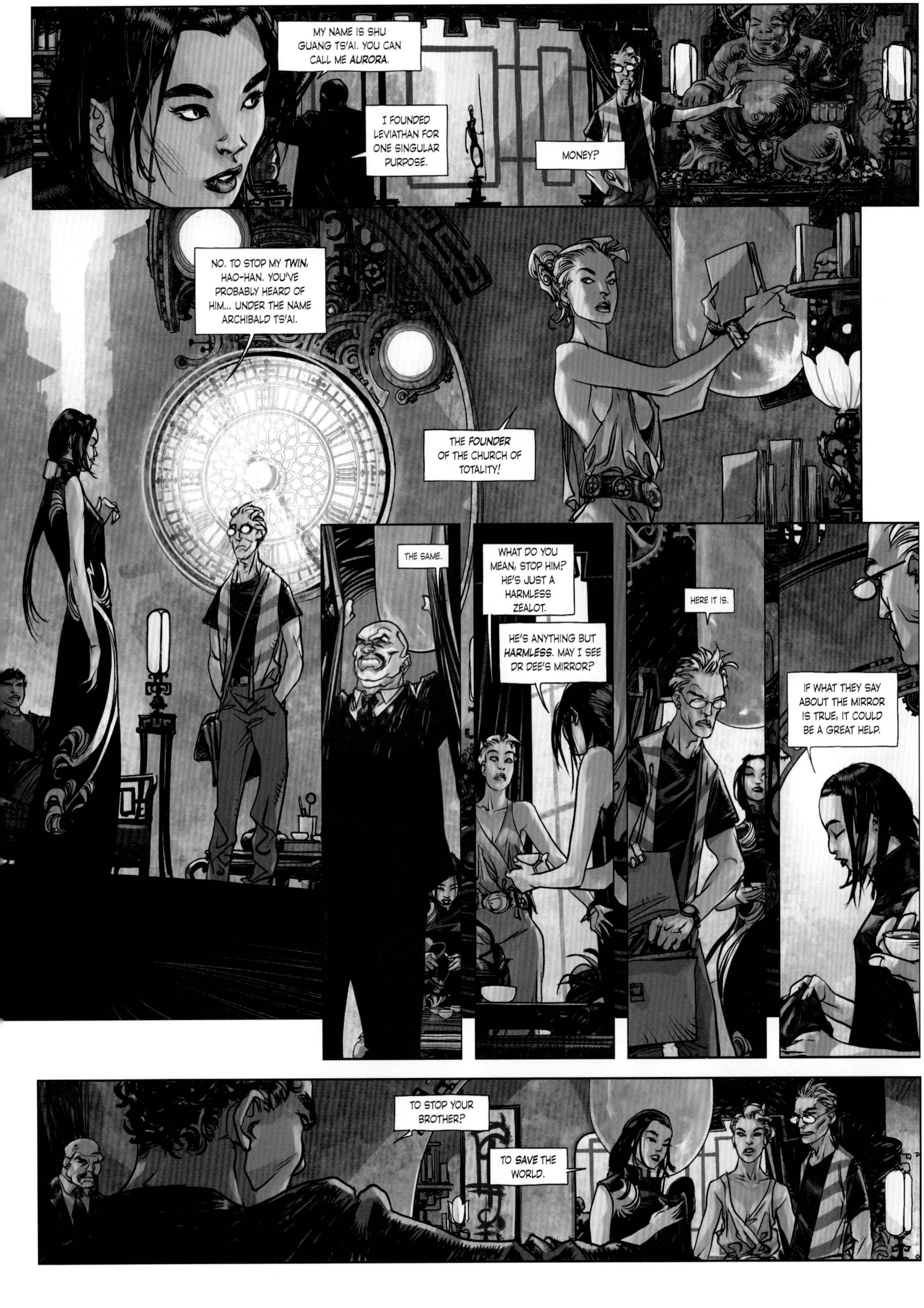
MY NAME IS SHU GUANG TS'AI. YOU CAN CALL ME AURORA.
I FOUNDED LEVIATHAN FOR ONE SINGULAR PURPOSE.
MONEY?
NO. TO STOP MY TWIN, HAO-HAN. YOU'VE PROBABLY HEARD OF HIM... UNDER THE NAME ARCHIBALD TS'AI.
THE FOUNDER OF THE CHURCH OF TOTALITY!
THE SAME.
WHAT DO YOU MEAN, STOP HIM? HE'S JUST A HARMLESS ZEALOT.
HE'S ANYTHING BUT HARMLESS. MAY I SEE DR DEE'S MIRROR?
HERE IT IS.
IF WHAT THEY SAY ABOUT THE MIRROR IS TRUE, IT COULD BE A GREAT HELP.
TO STOP YOUR BROTHER?
TO SAVE THE WORLD.

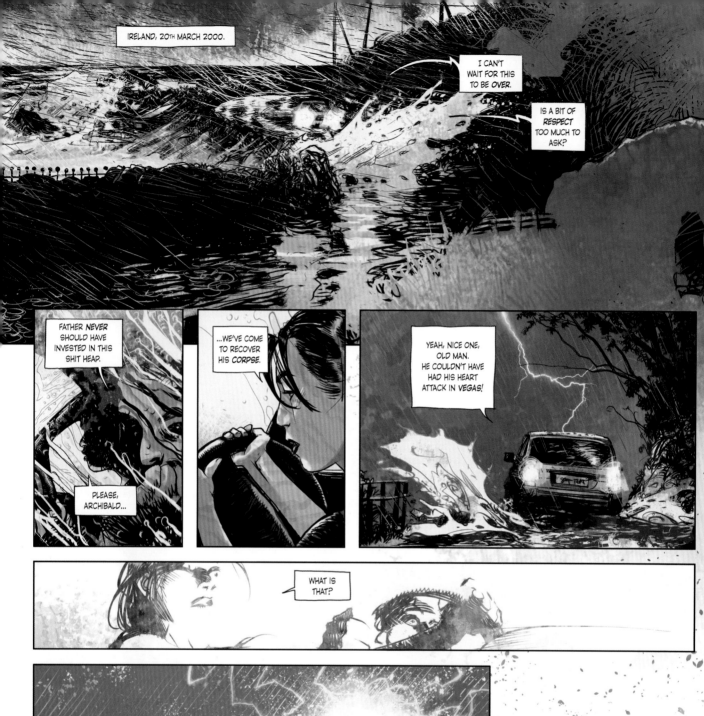

IRELAND, 20TH MARCH 2000.

I CAN'T WAIT FOR THIS TO BE OVER.

IS A BIT OF RESPECT TOO MUCH TO ASK?

FATHER NEVER SHOULD HAVE INVESTED IN THIS SHIT HEAP.

PLEASE, ARCHIBALD...

...WE'VE COME TO RECOVER HIS CORPSE.

YEAH, NICE ONE, OLD MAN. HE COULDN'T HAVE HAD HIS HEART ATTACK IN VEGAS!

WHAT IS THAT?

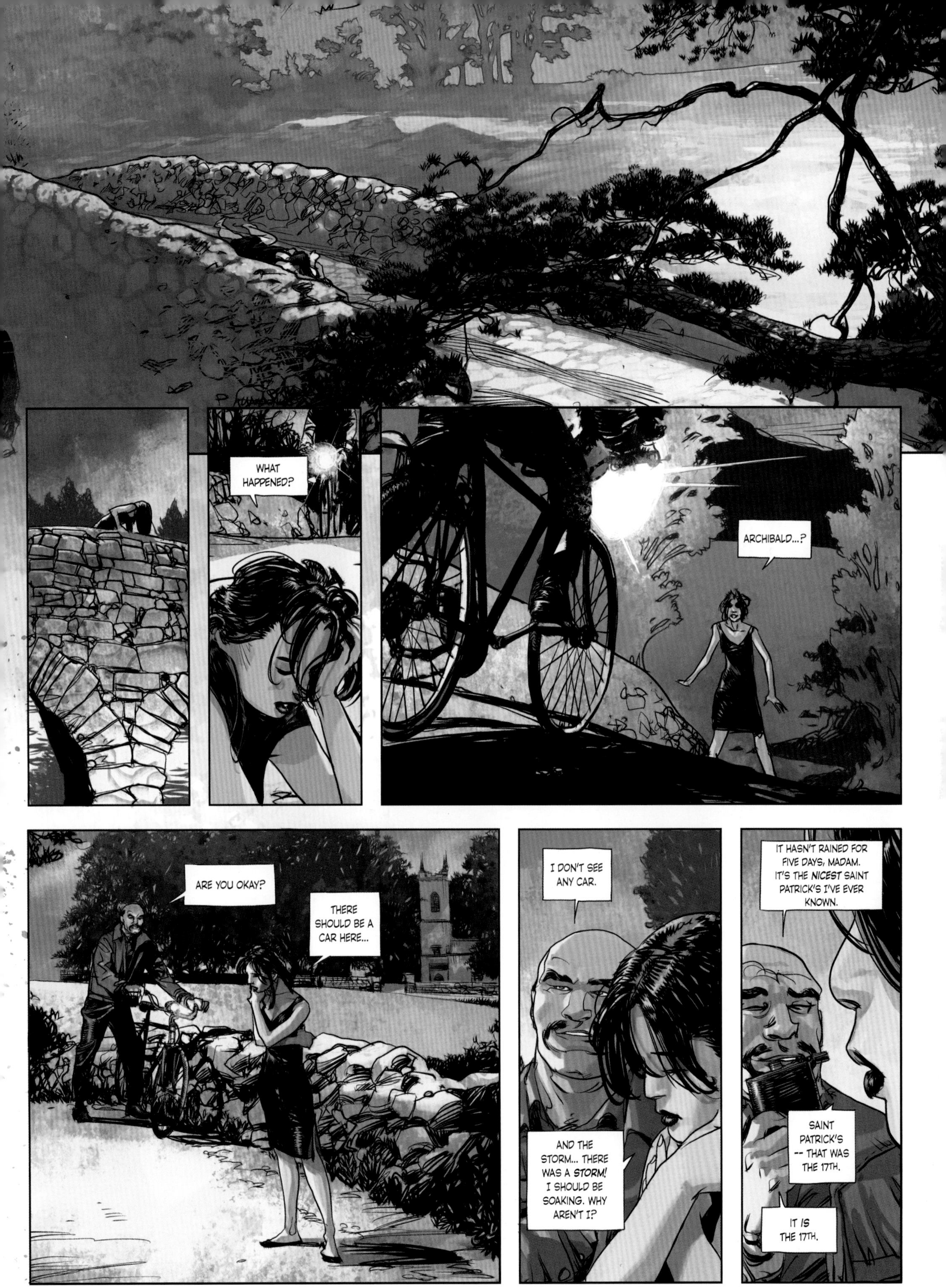
WHAT HAPPENED?
ARCHIBALD...?
ARE YOU OKAY?
THERE SHOULD BE A CAR HERE...
I DON'T SEE ANY CAR.
AND THE STORM... THERE WAS A STORM! I SHOULD BE SOAKING. WHY AREN'T I?
IT HASN'T RAINED FOR FIVE DAYS, MADAM. IT'S THE NICEST SAINT PATRICK'S I'VE EVER KNOWN.
SAINT PATRICK'S -- THAT WAS THE 17TH.
IT IS THE 17TH.

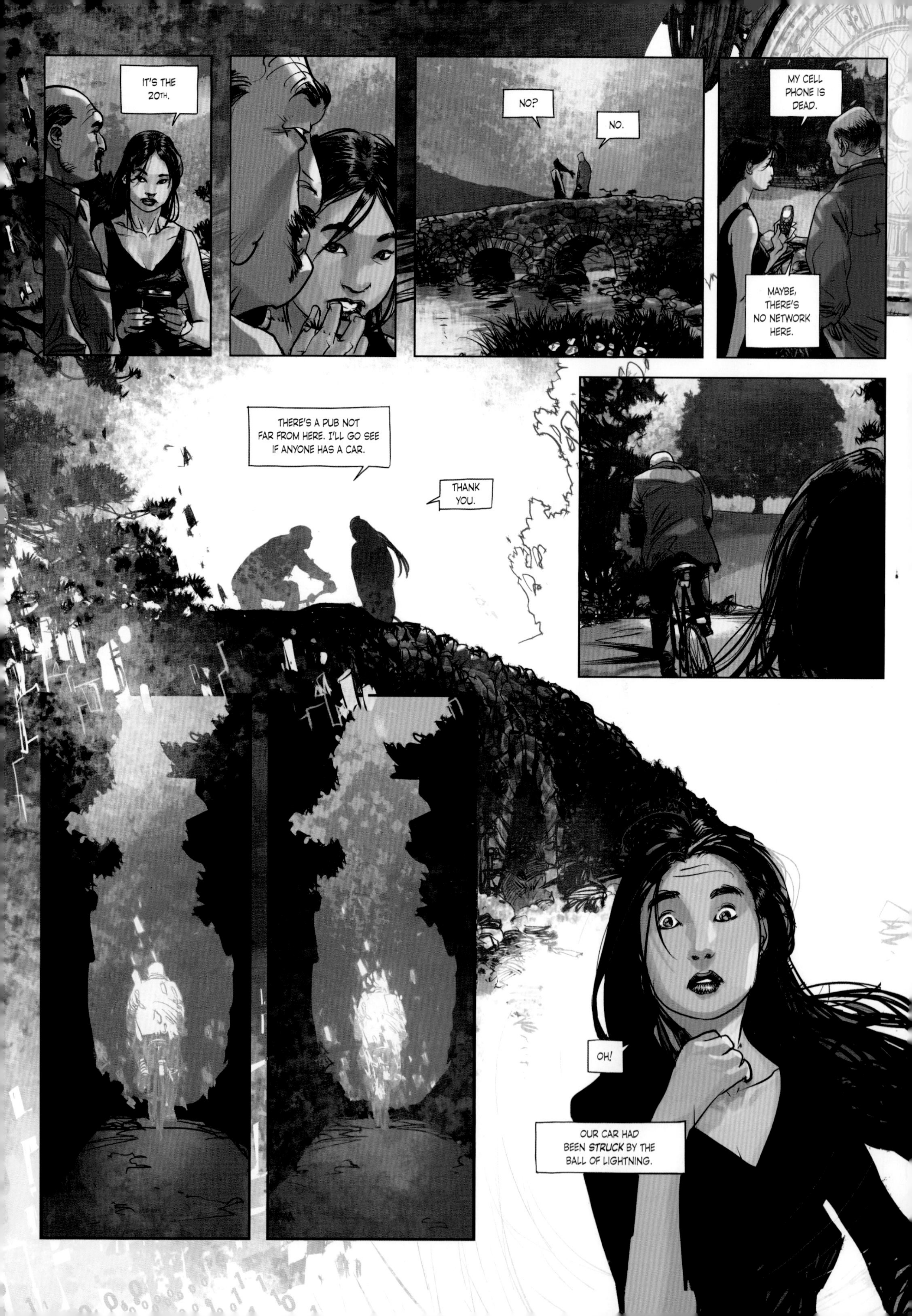
IT'S THE 20TH.
NO?
NO.
MY CELL PHONE IS DEAD.
MAYBE, THERE'S NO NETWORK HERE.
THERE'S A PUB NOT FAR FROM HERE. I'LL GO SEE IF ANYONE HAS A CAR.
THANK YOU.
OH!
OUR CAR HAD BEEN STRUCK BY THE BALL OF LIGHTNING.

A STRANGE METEOROLOGICAL PHENOMENON WHICH WE KNOW VERY LITTLE ABOUT.

IT WAS MORE THAN JUST *TERRIFYING*. THE LIGHTNING DIDN'T JUST STRIKE ARCHIBALD AND I...

IT EXPELLED US OUT OF *TIME*.

IT SENT ME THREE DAYS INTO THE PAST. I LOST CONSCIOUSNESS ON THE 20TH, AND WOKE UP ON THE 17TH. AT LEAST, THAT'S WHAT I FIRST BELIEVED.

IT BECAME MORE *COMPLICATED* THAN THAT.

TIME, SPACE, THE ENTIRETY OF THE UNIVERSE IS MADE UP OF WHAT WE CALL *INFORMATION*. PROFESSOR ITOU, YOUR OLD COLLEAGUE, WAS THE LEADING EXPERT ON THE SUBJECT.

HIROSHI WAS A *BASTARD*.

THAT'S TRUE.

THE LIGHTNING CREATED A *BUBBLE* OF INFORMATION AROUND ME. IF THAT INFORMATION COMES INTO CONTACT WITH ME -- AND IS *LINKED* TO AN ACTIVE CONSCIOUSNESS -- IT TRAVELS *THREE DAYS* INTO ITS OWN PAST.

LET'S SAY THAT I BELIEVE YOU. SO WHAT? IF WE LIVE THREE DAYS IN THE PAST, NOTHING *CHANGES* FROM OUR POINT OF VIEW. WE JUST CONTINUE OUR LIVES, LIKE DOC IN *BACK TO THE FUTURE 3*.

WE'RE IN CONTACT WITH YOU RIGHT NOW.

YOU ARE NOW IN YOUR *PAST*.

I WISH IT WAS THAT SIMPLE.

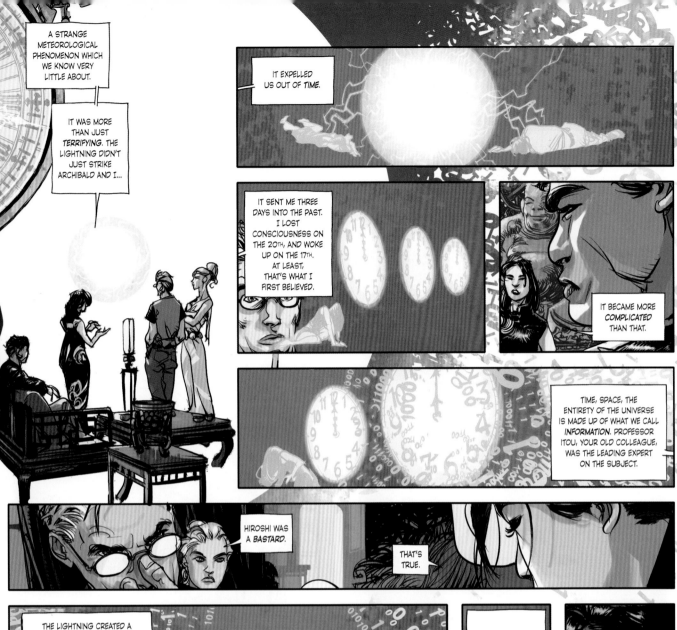

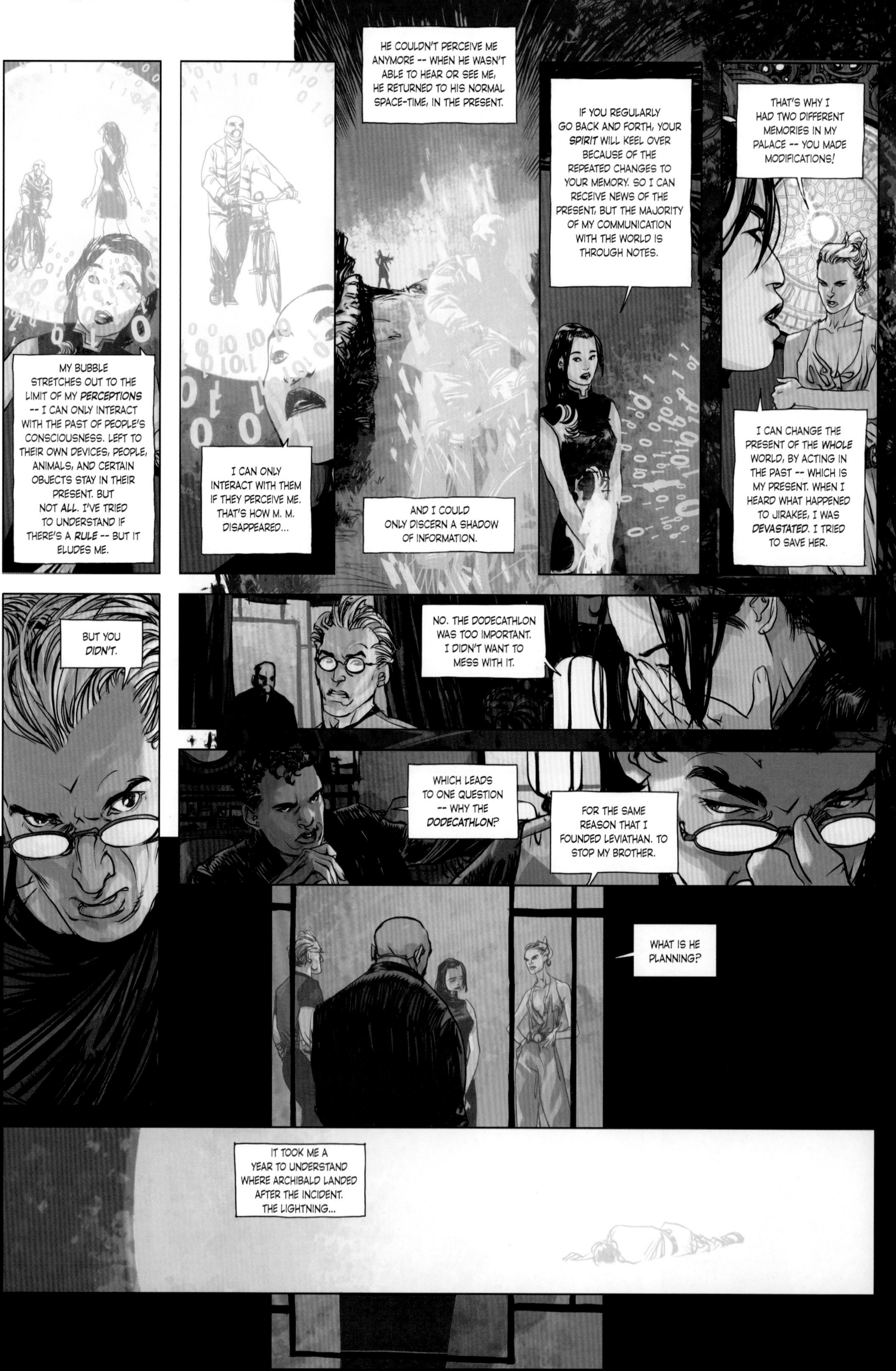
MY BUBBLE STRETCHES OUT TO THE LIMIT OF MY *PERCEPTIONS* -- I CAN ONLY INTERACT WITH THE PAST OF PEOPLE'S CONSCIOUSNESS. LEFT TO THEIR OWN DEVICES, PEOPLE, ANIMALS, AND CERTAIN OBJECTS STAY IN THEIR PRESENT. BUT NOT *ALL*. I'VE TRIED TO UNDERSTAND IF THERE'S A *RULE* -- BUT IT ELUDES ME.
I CAN ONLY INTERACT WITH THEM IF THEY PERCEIVE ME. THAT'S HOW M. M. DISAPPEARED...
HE COULDN'T PERCEIVE ME ANYMORE -- WHEN HE WASN'T ABLE TO HEAR OR SEE ME, HE RETURNED TO HIS NORMAL SPACE-TIME, IN THE PRESENT.
AND I COULD ONLY DISCERN A SHADOW OF INFORMATION.
IF YOU REGULARLY GO BACK AND FORTH, YOUR *SPIRIT* WILL KEEL OVER BECAUSE OF THE REPEATED CHANGES TO YOUR MEMORY. SO I CAN RECEIVE NEWS OF THE PRESENT, BUT THE MAJORITY OF MY COMMUNICATION WITH THE WORLD IS THROUGH NOTES.
THAT'S WHY I HAD TWO DIFFERENT MEMORIES IN MY PALACE -- YOU MADE MODIFICATIONS!
I CAN CHANGE THE PRESENT OF THE *WHOLE* WORLD, BY ACTING IN THE PAST -- WHICH IS MY PRESENT. WHEN I HEARD WHAT HAPPENED TO JIRAKEE, I WAS *DEVASTATED*. I TRIED TO SAVE HER.
BUT YOU *DIDN'T*.
NO. THE DODECATHLON WAS TOO IMPORTANT. I DIDN'T WANT TO MESS WITH IT.
WHICH LEADS TO ONE QUESTION -- WHY THE *DODECATHLON?*
FOR THE SAME REASON THAT I FOUNDED LEVIATHAN. TO STOP MY BROTHER.
WHAT IS HE PLANNING?
IT TOOK ME A YEAR TO UNDERSTAND WHERE ARCHIBALD LANDED AFTER THE INCIDENT. THE LIGHTNING...

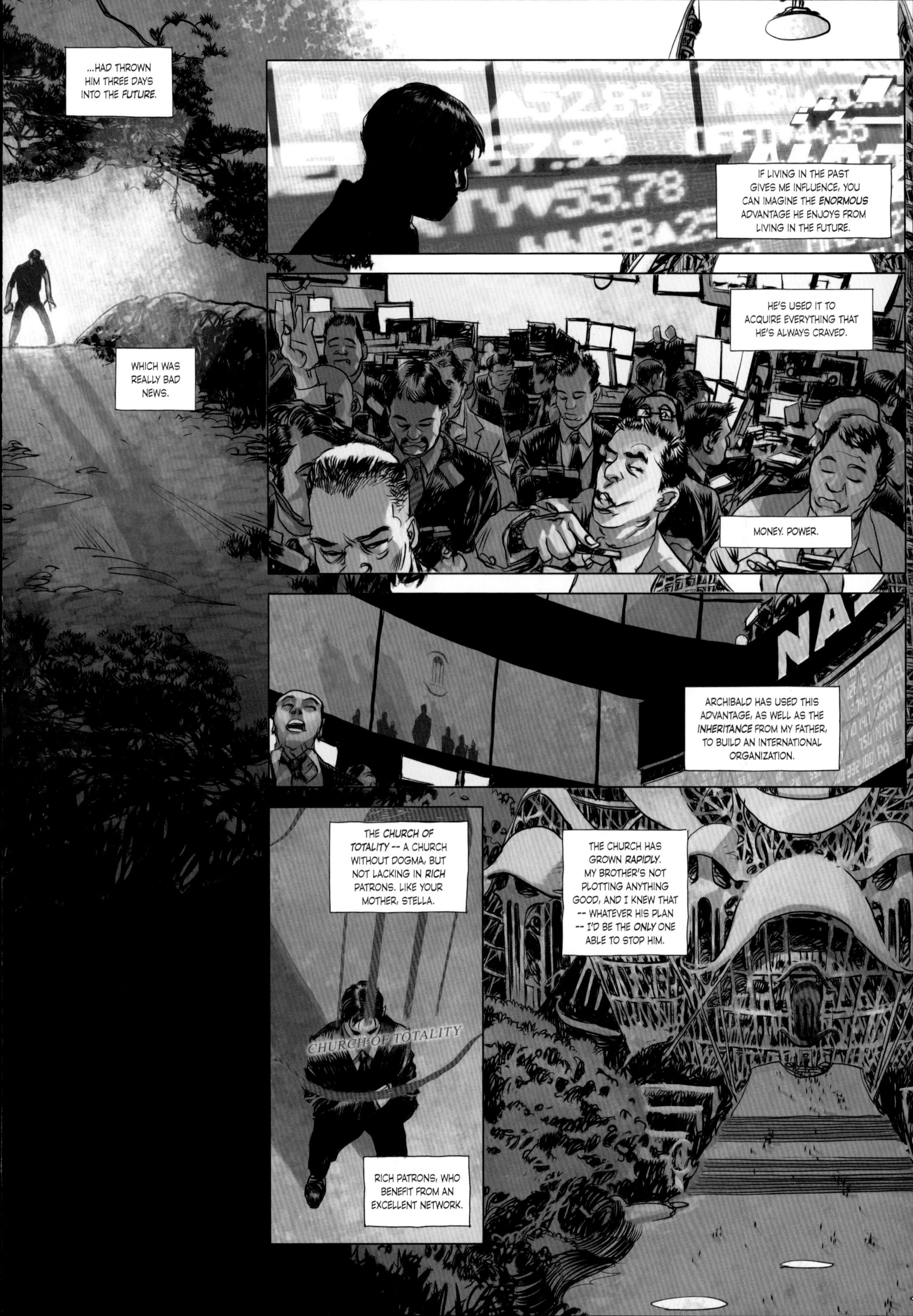
...HAD THROWN HIM THREE DAYS INTO THE *FUTURE*.
IF LIVING IN THE PAST GIVES ME INFLUENCE, YOU CAN IMAGINE THE *ENORMOUS* ADVANTAGE HE ENJOYS FROM LIVING IN THE FUTURE.
WHICH WAS REALLY BAD NEWS.
HE'S USED IT TO ACQUIRE EVERYTHING THAT HE'S ALWAYS CRAVED.
MONEY. POWER.
ARCHIBALD HAS USED THIS ADVANTAGE, AS WELL AS THE *INHERITANCE* FROM MY FATHER, TO BUILD AN INTERNATIONAL ORGANIZATION.
THE *CHURCH OF TOTALITY* -- A CHURCH WITHOUT DOGMA, BUT NOT LACKING IN *RICH* PATRONS. LIKE YOUR MOTHER, STELLA.
CHURCH OF TOTALITY
RICH PATRONS, WHO BENEFIT FROM AN EXCELLENT NETWORK.
THE CHURCH HAS GROWN *RAPIDLY*. MY BROTHER'S NOT PLOTTING ANYTHING GOOD, AND I KNEW THAT -- WHATEVER HIS PLAN -- I'D BE THE *ONLY* ONE ABLE TO STOP HIM.

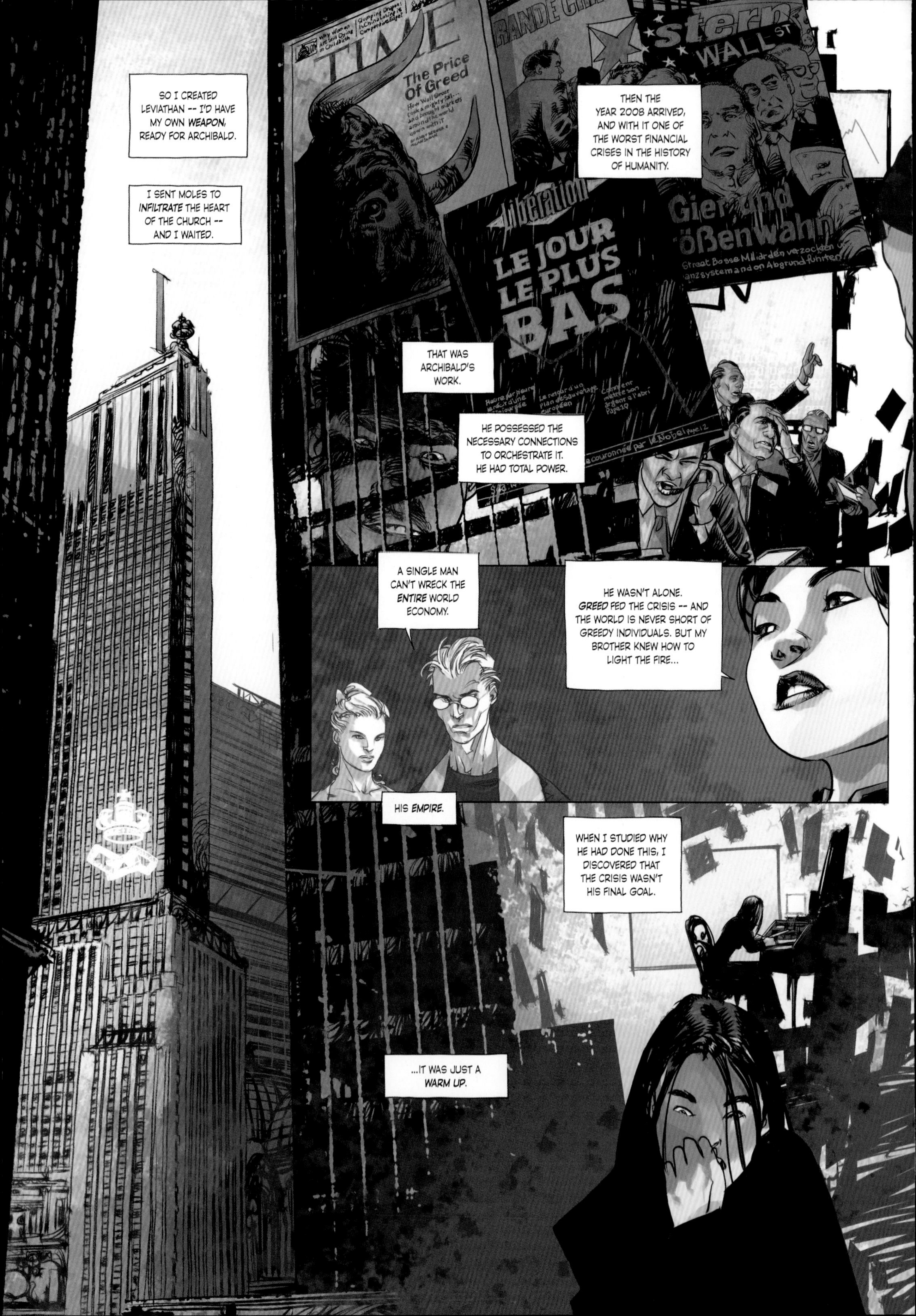

SO I CREATED LEVIATHAN -- I'D HAVE MY OWN WEAPON, READY FOR ARCHIBALD.
I SENT MOLES TO INFILTRATE THE HEART OF THE CHURCH -- AND I WAITED.
TIME
The Price Of Greed
THEN THE YEAR 2008 ARRIVED, AND WITH IT ONE OF THE WORST FINANCIAL CRISES IN THE HISTORY OF HUMANITY.
stern
WALL ST
Libération
LE JOUR LE PLUS BAS
THAT WAS ARCHIBALD'S WORK.
HE POSSESSED THE NECESSARY CONNECTIONS TO ORCHESTRATE IT. HE HAD TOTAL POWER.
A SINGLE MAN CAN'T WRECK THE ENTIRE WORLD ECONOMY.
HE WASN'T ALONE. GREED FED THE CRISIS -- AND THE WORLD IS NEVER SHORT OF GREEDY INDIVIDUALS. BUT MY BROTHER KNEW HOW TO LIGHT THE FIRE...
HIS EMPIRE.
WHEN I STUDIED WHY HE HAD DONE THIS, I DISCOVERED THAT THE CRISIS WASN'T HIS FINAL GOAL.
...IT WAS JUST A WARM UP.

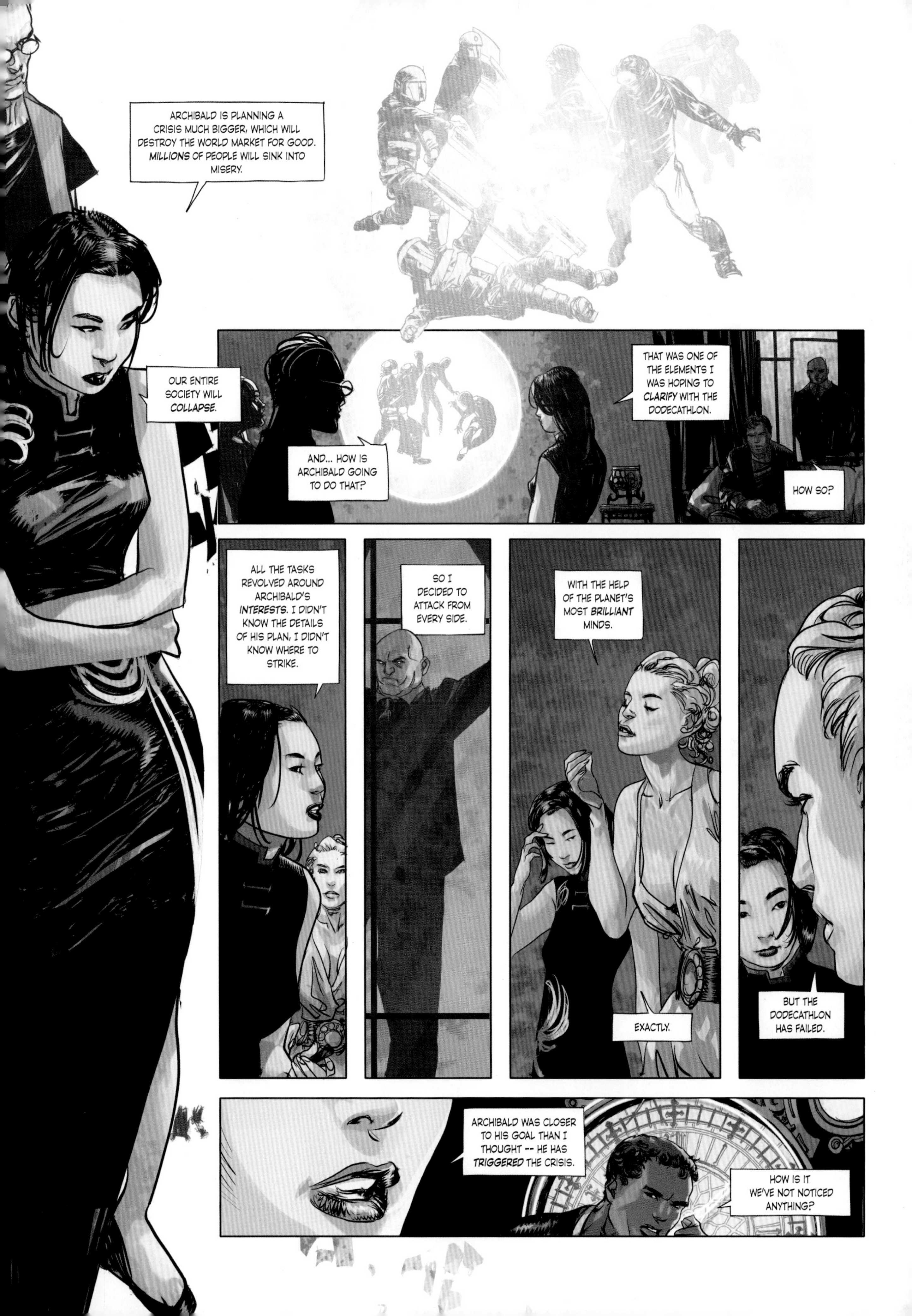

ARCHIBALD IS PLANNING A CRISIS MUCH BIGGER, WHICH WILL DESTROY THE WORLD MARKET FOR GOOD. MILLIONS OF PEOPLE WILL SINK INTO MISERY.
OUR ENTIRE SOCIETY WILL COLLAPSE.
AND... HOW IS ARCHIBALD GOING TO DO THAT?
THAT WAS ONE OF THE ELEMENTS I WAS HOPING TO CLARIFY WITH THE DODECATHLON.
HOW SO?
ALL THE TASKS REVOLVED AROUND ARCHIBALD'S INTERESTS. I DIDN'T KNOW THE DETAILS OF HIS PLAN, I DIDN'T KNOW WHERE TO STRIKE.
SO I DECIDED TO ATTACK FROM EVERY SIDE.
WITH THE HELP OF THE PLANET'S MOST BRILLIANT MINDS.
EXACTLY.
BUT THE DODECATHLON HAS FAILED.
ARCHIBALD WAS CLOSER TO HIS GOAL THAN I THOUGHT -- HE HAS TRIGGERED THE CRISIS.
HOW IS IT WE'VE NOT NOTICED ANYTHING?

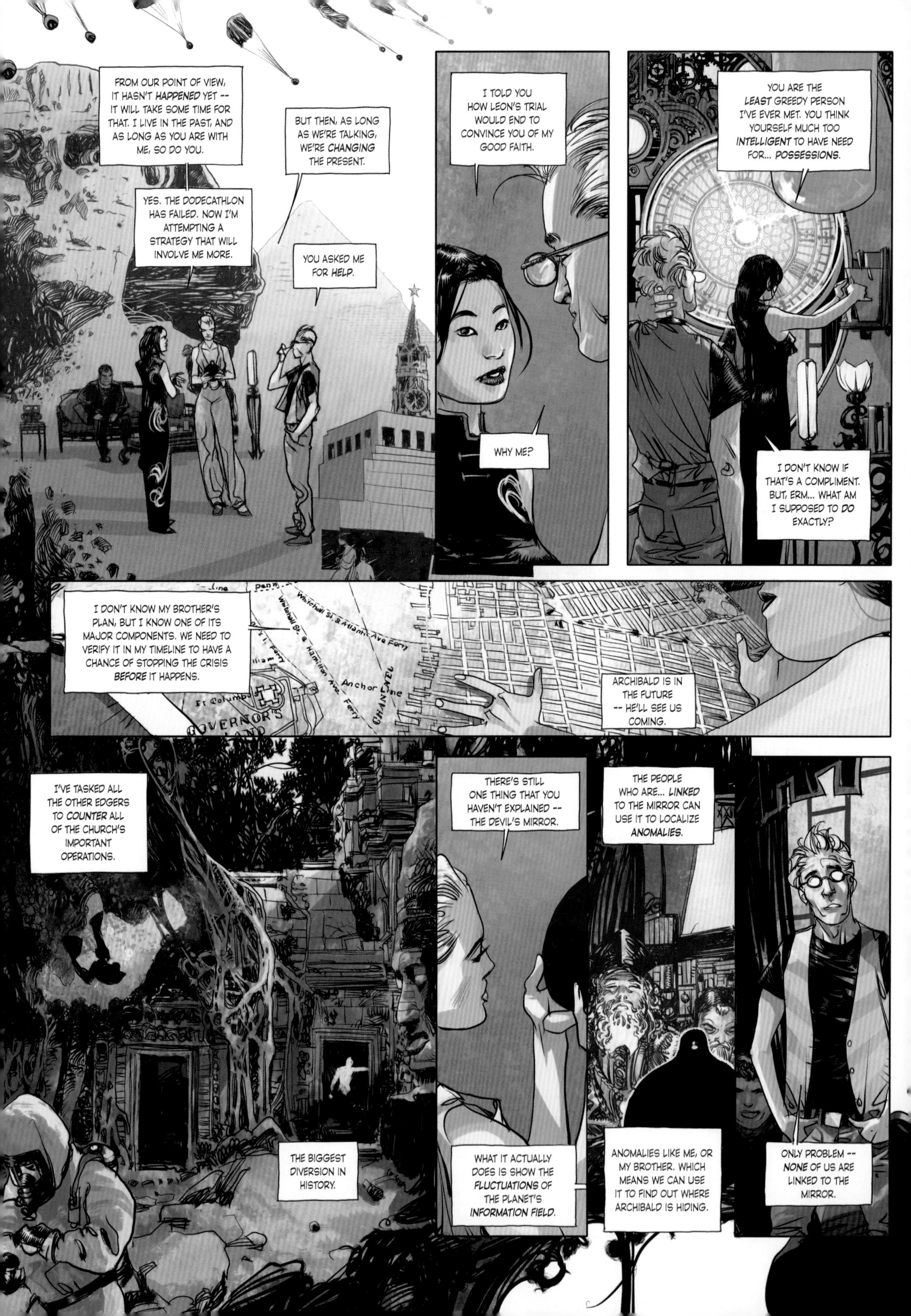
FROM OUR POINT OF VIEW, IT HASN'T HAPPENED YET -- IT WILL TAKE SOME TIME FOR THAT. I LIVE IN THE PAST, AND AS LONG AS YOU ARE WITH ME, SO DO YOU.
YES. THE DODECATHLON HAS FAILED. NOW I'M ATTEMPTING A STRATEGY THAT WILL INVOLVE ME MORE.
BUT THEN, AS LONG AS WE'RE TALKING, WE'RE CHANGING THE PRESENT.
YOU ASKED ME FOR HELP.
I TOLD YOU HOW LEON'S TRIAL WOULD END TO CONVINCE YOU OF MY GOOD FAITH.
WHY ME?
YOU ARE THE LEAST GREEDY PERSON I'VE EVER MET. YOU THINK YOURSELF MUCH TOO INTELLIGENT TO HAVE NEED FOR... POSSESSIONS.
I DON'T KNOW IF THAT'S A COMPLIMENT. BUT, ERM... WHAT AM I SUPPOSED TO DO EXACTLY?
I DON'T KNOW MY BROTHER'S PLAN, BUT I KNOW ONE OF ITS MAJOR COMPONENTS. WE NEED TO VERIFY IT IN MY TIMELINE TO HAVE A CHANCE OF STOPPING THE CRISIS BEFORE IT HAPPENS.
ARCHIBALD IS IN THE FUTURE -- HE'LL SEE US COMING.
I'VE TASKED ALL THE OTHER EDGERS TO COUNTER ALL OF THE CHURCH'S IMPORTANT OPERATIONS.
THE BIGGEST DIVERSION IN HISTORY.
THERE'S STILL ONE THING THAT YOU HAVEN'T EXPLAINED -- THE DEVIL'S MIRROR.
WHAT IT ACTUALLY DOES IS SHOW THE FLUCTUATIONS OF THE PLANET'S INFORMATION FIELD.
THE PEOPLE WHO ARE... LINKED TO THE MIRROR CAN USE IT TO LOCALIZE ANOMALIES.
ANOMALIES LIKE ME, OR MY BROTHER. WHICH MEANS WE CAN USE IT TO FIND OUT WHERE ARCHIBALD IS HIDING.
ONLY PROBLEM -- NONE OF US ARE LINKED TO THE MIRROR.

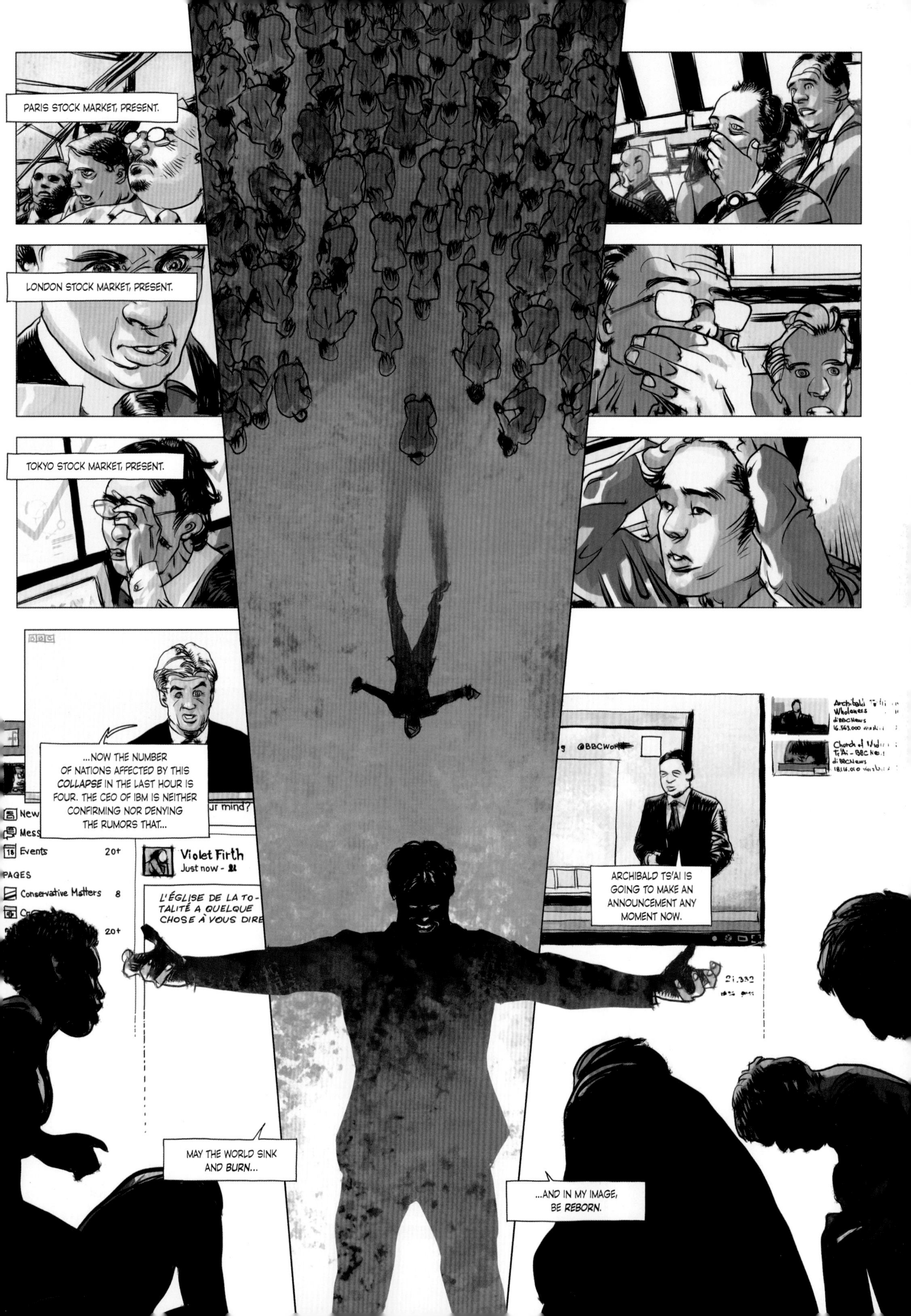
PARIS STOCK MARKET, PRESENT.
LONDON STOCK MARKET, PRESENT.
TOKYO STOCK MARKET, PRESENT.
...NOW THE NUMBER OF NATIONS AFFECTED BY THIS *COLLAPSE* IN THE LAST HOUR IS FOUR. THE CEO OF IBM IS NEITHER CONFIRMING NOR DENYING THE RUMORS THAT...
Events 20+
PAGES
Conservative Matters 8
Violet Firth
Just now
L'ÉGLISE DE LA TOTALITÉ A QUELQUE CHOSE À VOUS DIRE
@BBCWor
ARCHIBALD TS'AI IS GOING TO MAKE AN ANNOUNCEMENT ANY MOMENT NOW.
MAY THE WORLD SINK AND *BURN*...
...AND IN MY IMAGE, BE *REBORN*.

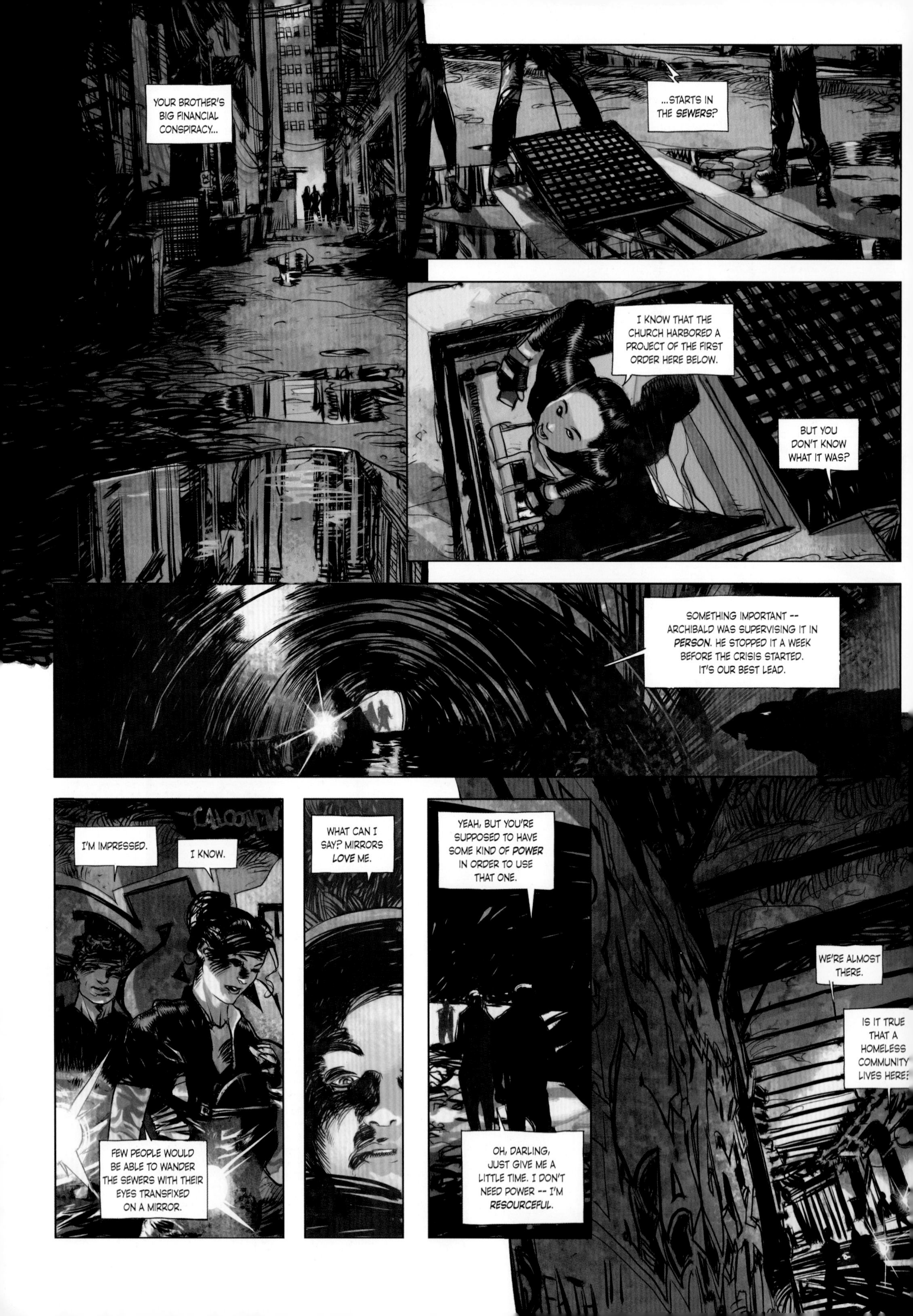
YOUR BROTHER'S BIG FINANCIAL CONSPIRACY...
...STARTS IN THE SEWERS?
I KNOW THAT THE CHURCH HARBORED A PROJECT OF THE FIRST ORDER HERE BELOW.
BUT YOU DON'T KNOW WHAT IT WAS?
SOMETHING IMPORTANT -- ARCHIBALD WAS SUPERVISING IT IN PERSON. HE STOPPED IT A WEEK BEFORE THE CRISIS STARTED. IT'S OUR BEST LEAD.
I'M IMPRESSED.
I KNOW.
FEW PEOPLE WOULD BE ABLE TO WANDER THE SEWERS WITH THEIR EYES TRANSFIXED ON A MIRROR.
WHAT CAN I SAY? MIRRORS LOVE ME.
YEAH, BUT YOU'RE SUPPOSED TO HAVE SOME KIND OF POWER IN ORDER TO USE THAT ONE.
OH, DARLING, JUST GIVE ME A LITTLE TIME. I DON'T NEED POWER -- I'M RESOURCEFUL.
WE'RE ALMOST THERE.
IS IT TRUE THAT A HOMELESS COMMUNITY LIVES HERE?

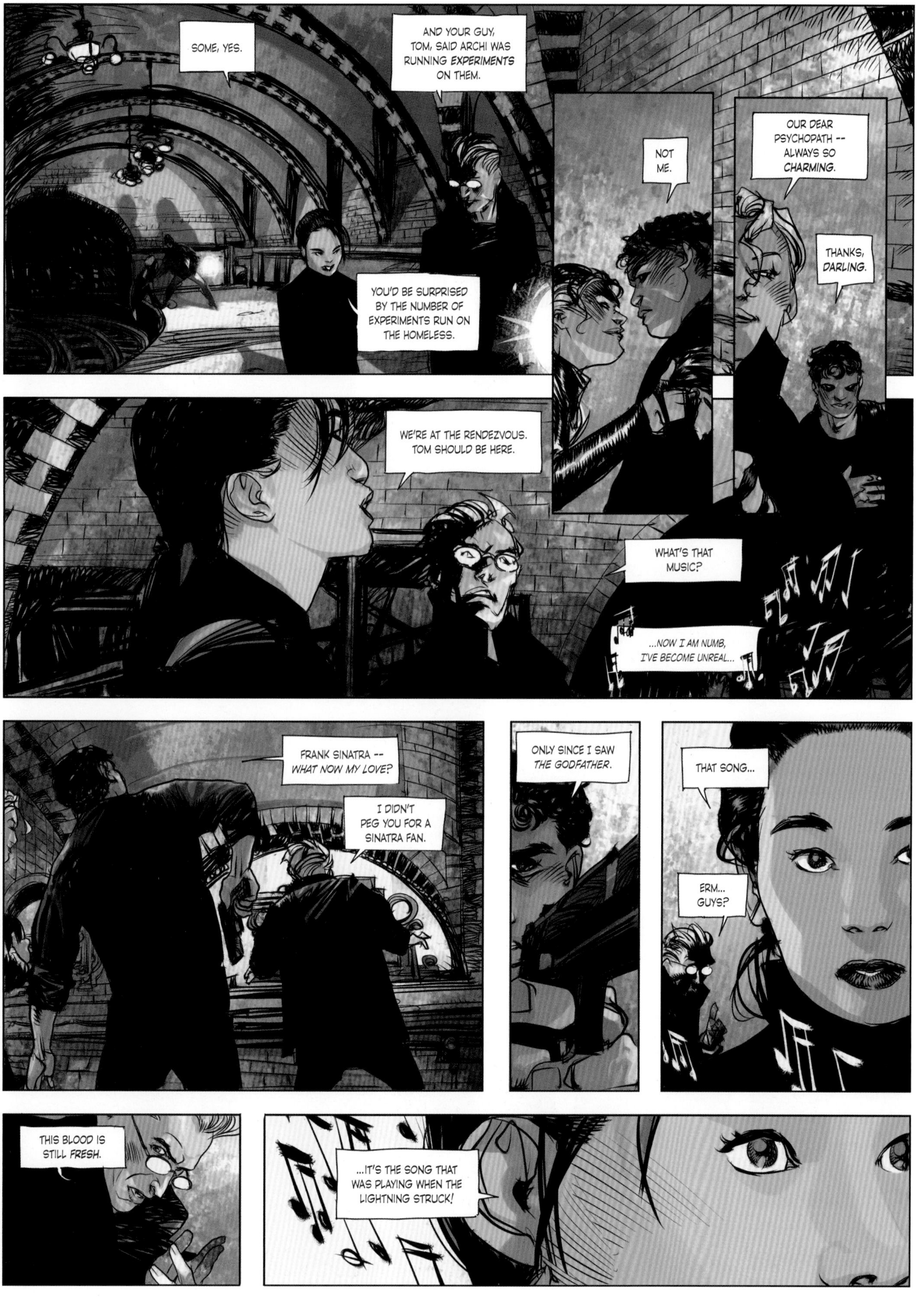
SOME, YES.
AND YOUR GUY, TOM, SAID ARCHI WAS RUNNING EXPERIMENTS ON THEM.
YOU'D BE SURPRISED BY THE NUMBER OF EXPERIMENTS RUN ON THE HOMELESS.
NOT ME.
OUR DEAR PSYCHOPATH -- ALWAYS SO CHARMING.
THANKS, DARLING.
WE'RE AT THE RENDEZVOUS. TOM SHOULD BE HERE.
WHAT'S THAT MUSIC?
...NOW I AM NUMB, I'VE BECOME UNREAL...
FRANK SINATRA -- WHAT NOW MY LOVE?
I DIDN'T PEG YOU FOR A SINATRA FAN.
ONLY SINCE I SAW THE GODFATHER.
THAT SONG...
ERM... GUYS?
THIS BLOOD IS STILL FRESH.
...IT'S THE SONG THAT WAS PLAYING WHEN THE LIGHTNING STRUCK!

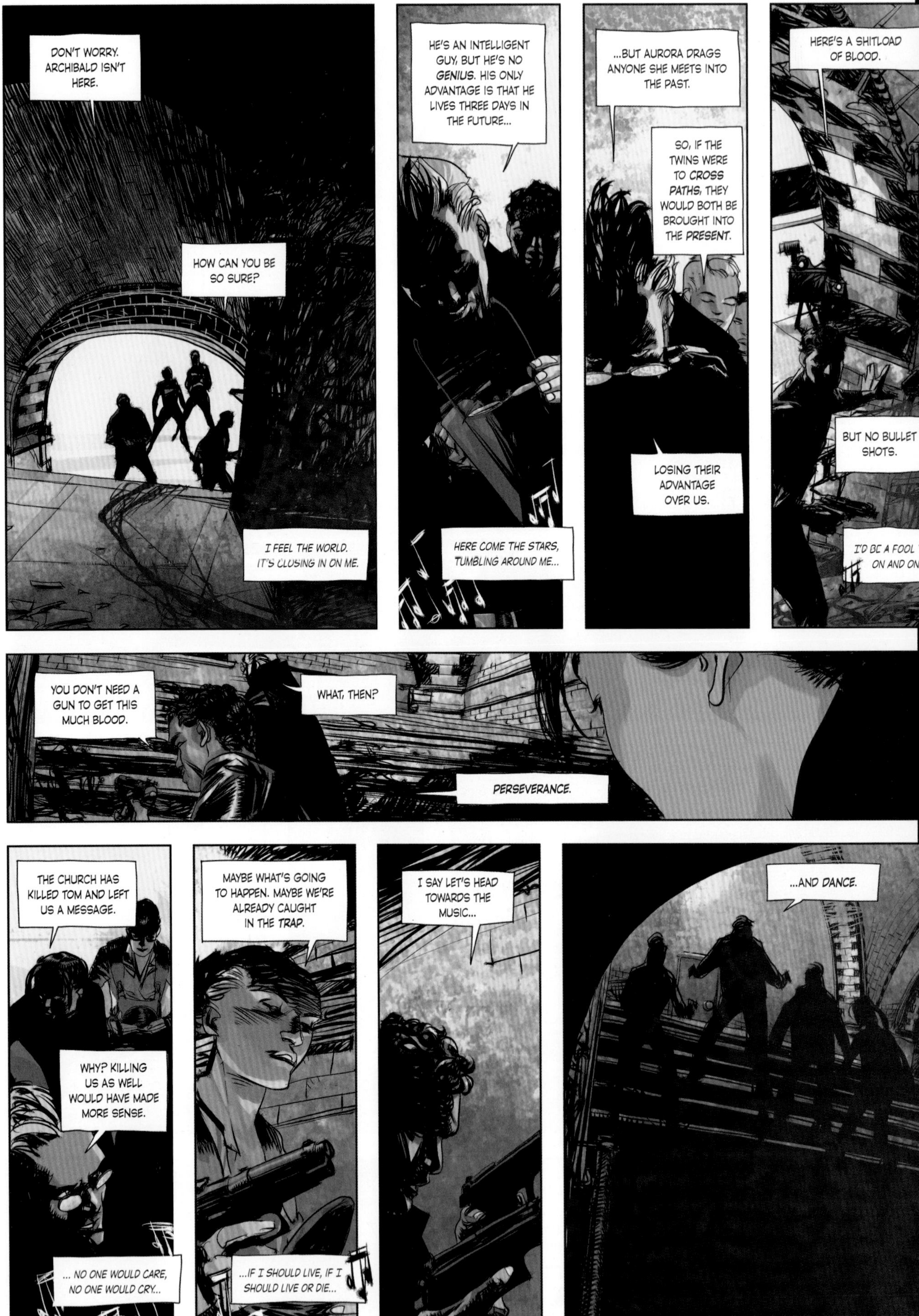

DON'T WORRY. ARCHIBALD ISN'T HERE.
HOW CAN YOU BE SO SURE?
I FEEL THE WORLD. IT'S CLOSING IN ON ME.
HE'S AN INTELLIGENT GUY, BUT HE'S NO GENIUS. HIS ONLY ADVANTAGE IS THAT HE LIVES THREE DAYS IN THE FUTURE...
HERE COME THE STARS, TUMBLING AROUND ME...
...BUT AURORA DRAGS ANYONE SHE MEETS INTO THE PAST.
SO, IF THE TWINS WERE TO CROSS PATHS, THEY WOULD BOTH BE BROUGHT INTO THE PRESENT.
LOSING THEIR ADVANTAGE OVER US.
HERE'S A SHITLOAD OF BLOOD.
BUT NO BULLET SHOTS.
I'D BE A FOOL TO GO ON AND ON...
YOU DON'T NEED A GUN TO GET THIS MUCH BLOOD.
WHAT, THEN?
PERSEVERANCE.
THE CHURCH HAS KILLED TOM AND LEFT US A MESSAGE.
WHY? KILLING US AS WELL WOULD HAVE MADE MORE SENSE.
... NO ONE WOULD CARE, NO ONE WOULD CRY...
MAYBE WHAT'S GOING TO HAPPEN. MAYBE WE'RE ALREADY CAUGHT IN THE TRAP.
...IF I SHOULD LIVE, IF I SHOULD LIVE OR DIE...
I SAY LET'S HEAD TOWARDS THE MUSIC...
...AND DANCE.

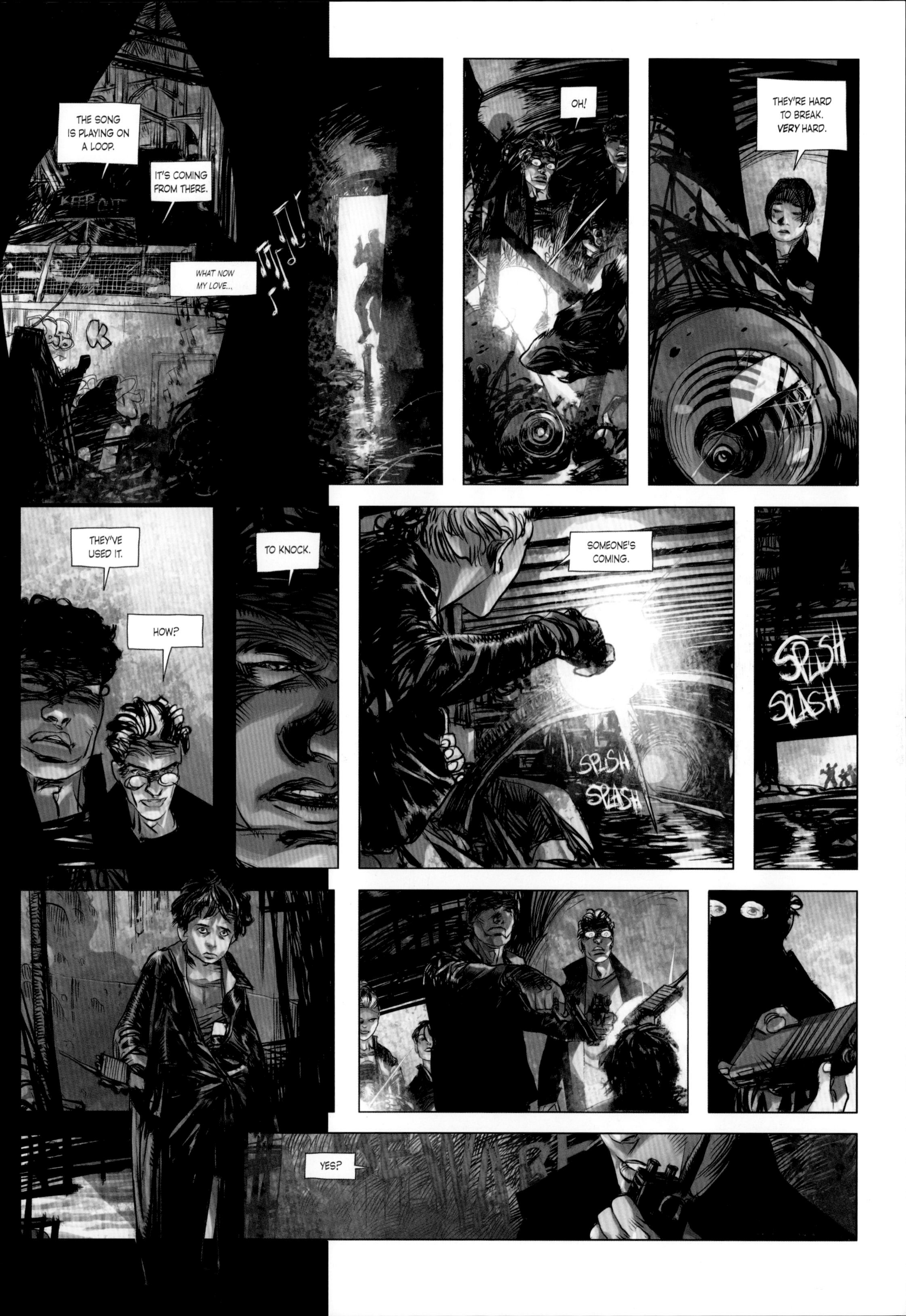

THE SONG IS PLAYING ON A LOOP.
IT'S COMING FROM THERE.
WHAT NOW MY LOVE...
OH!
THEY'RE HARD TO BREAK. VERY HARD.
THEY'VE USED IT.
HOW?
TO KNOCK.
SOMEONE'S COMING.
SPLSH SPLASH
SPLSH SPLASH
YES?

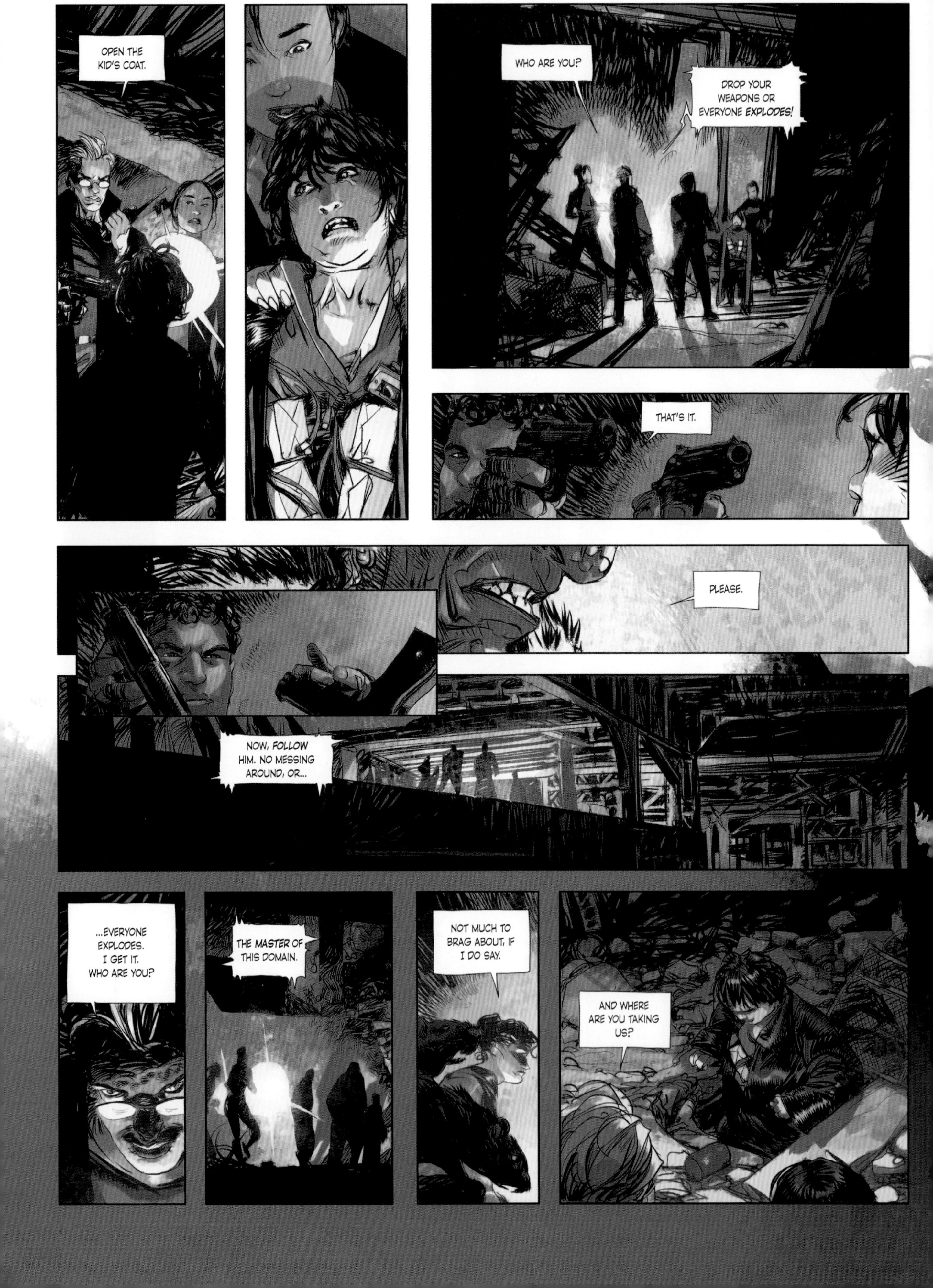
OPEN THE KID'S COAT.
WHO ARE YOU?
DROP YOUR WEAPONS OR EVERYONE EXPLODES!
THAT'S IT.
PLEASE.
NOW, FOLLOW HIM. NO MESSING AROUND, OR...
...EVERYONE EXPLODES. I GET IT. WHO ARE YOU?
THE MASTER OF THIS DOMAIN.
NOT MUCH TO BRAG ABOUT, IF I DO SAY.
AND WHERE ARE YOU TAKING US?

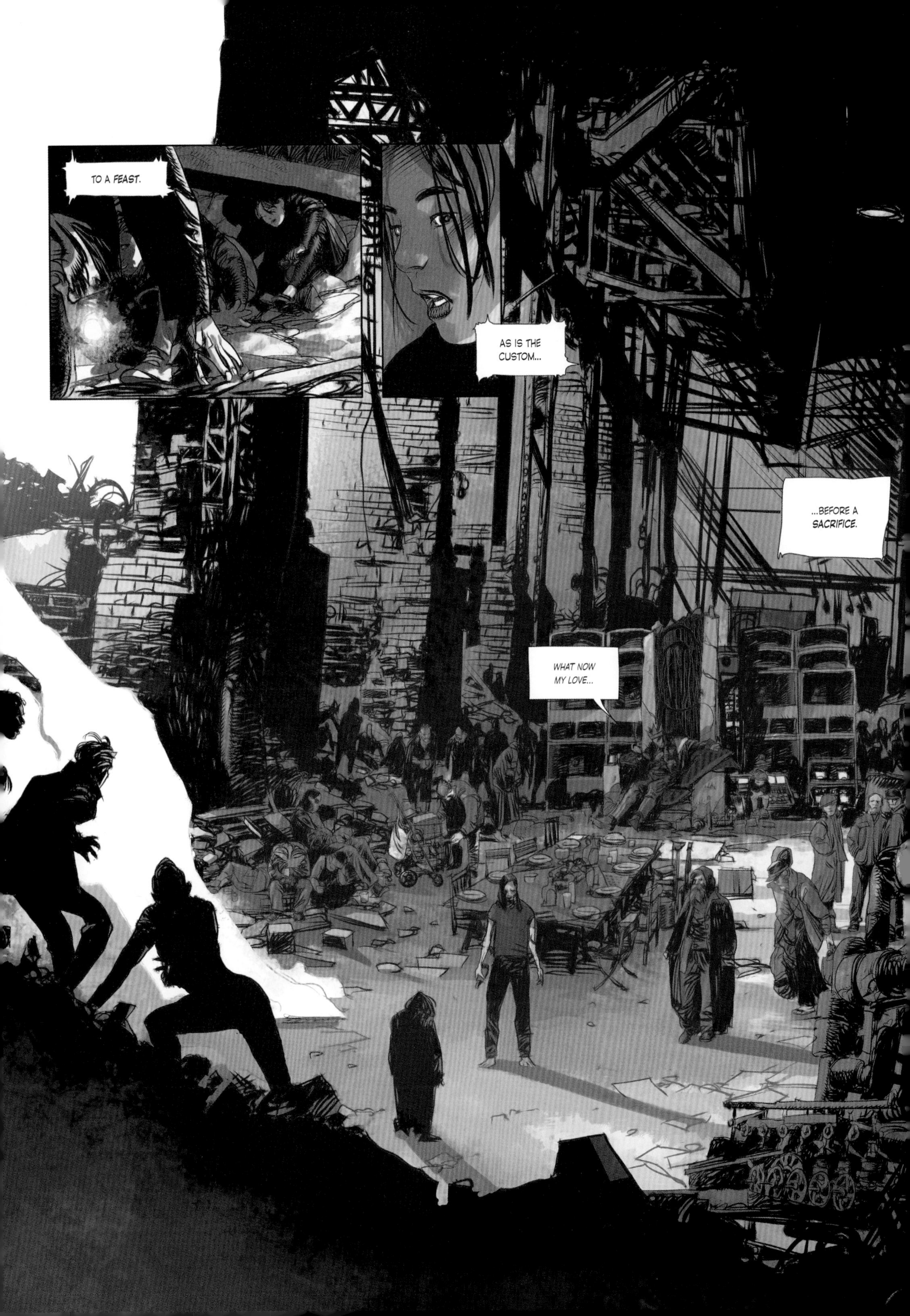
TO A FEAST.
AS IS THE CUSTOM...
...BEFORE A SACRIFICE.
WHAT NOW MY LOVE...

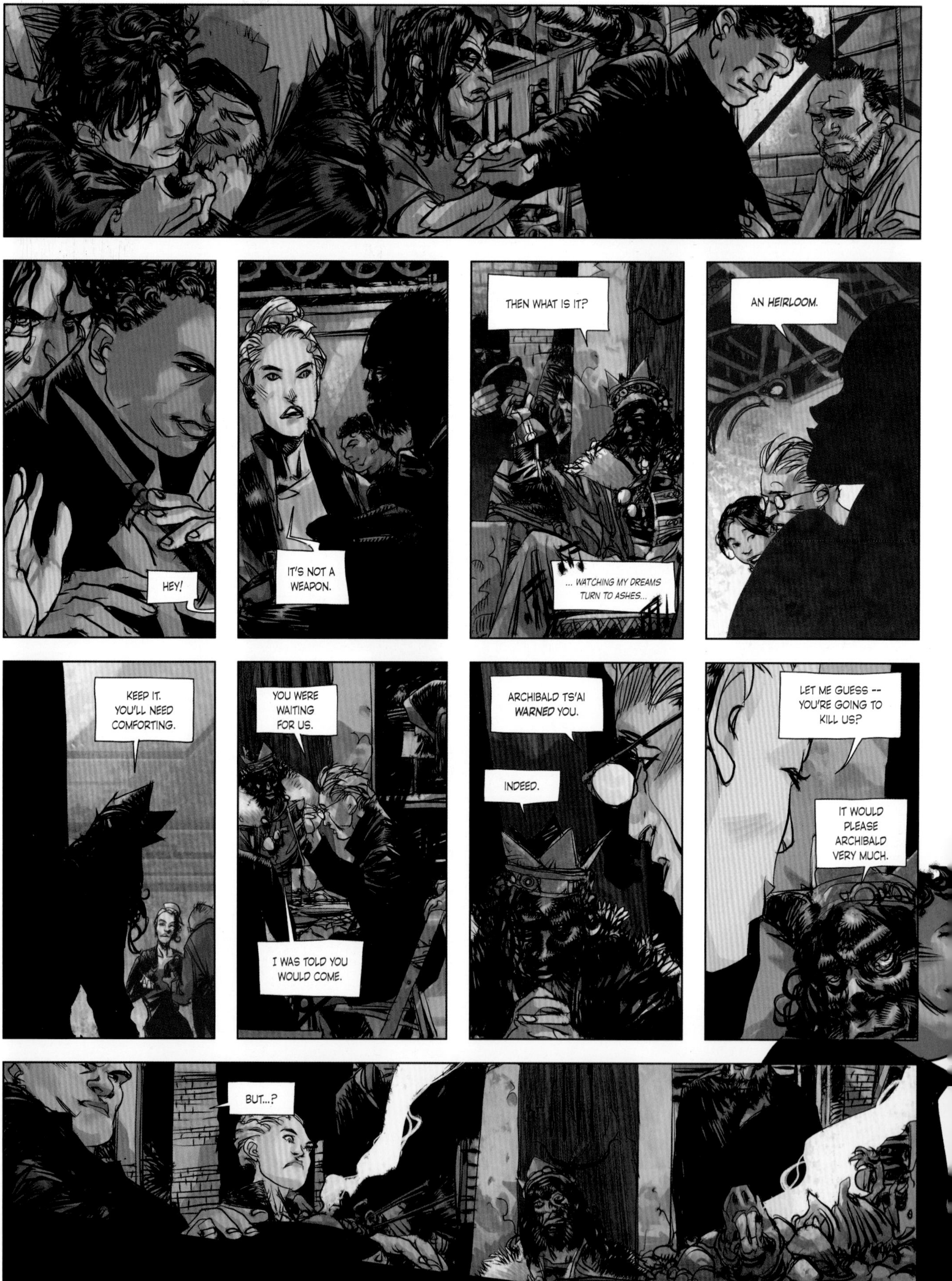
HEY!
IT'S NOT A WEAPON.
THEN WHAT IS IT?
... WATCHING MY DREAMS TURN TO ASHES...
AN HEIRLOOM.
KEEP IT. YOU'LL NEED COMFORTING.
YOU WERE WAITING FOR US.
I WAS TOLD YOU WOULD COME.
ARCHIBALD TS'AI WARNED YOU.
INDEED.
LET ME GUESS -- YOU'RE GOING TO KILL US?
IT WOULD PLEASE ARCHIBALD VERY MUCH.
BUT...?

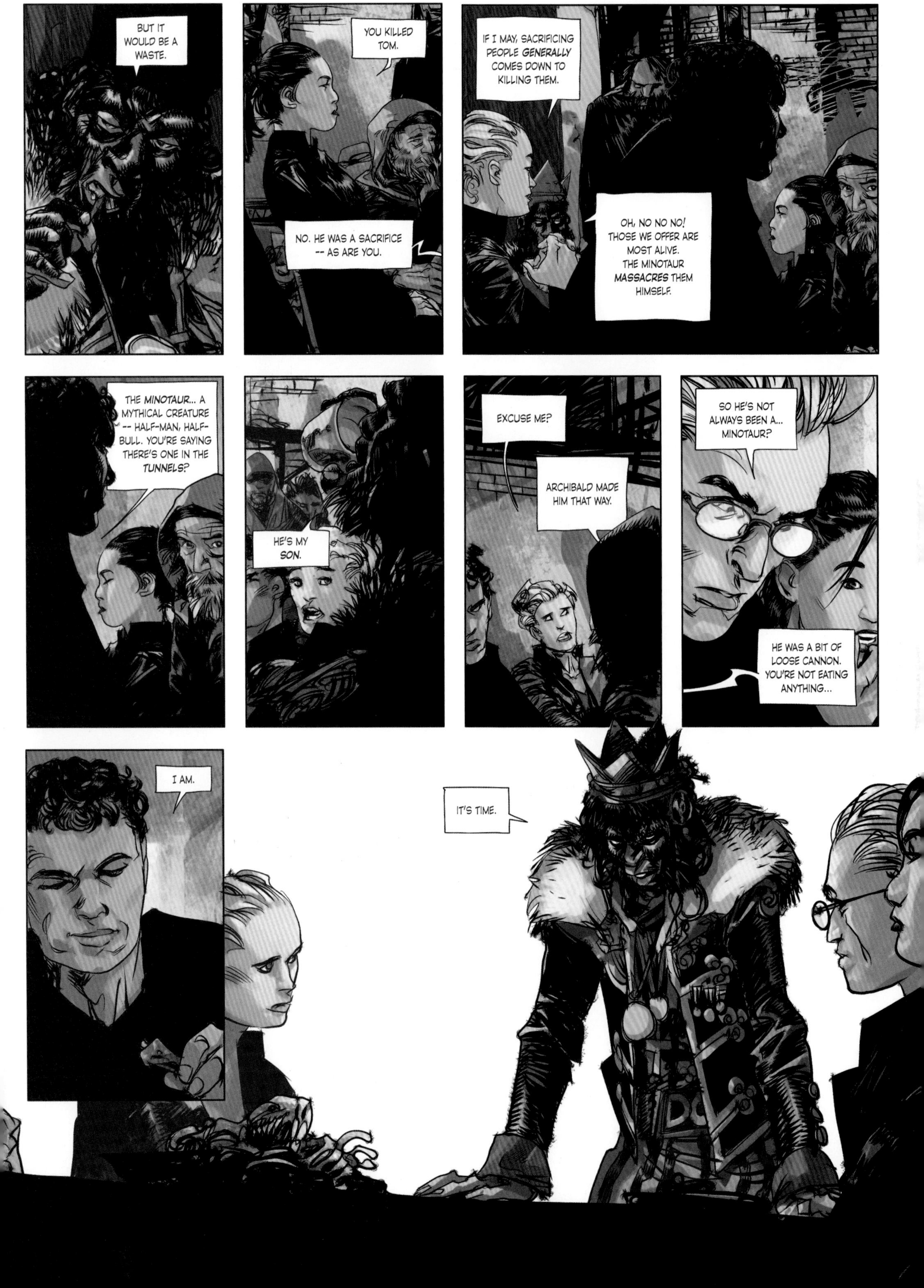
BUT IT WOULD BE A WASTE.
YOU KILLED TOM.
NO. HE WAS A SACRIFICE -- AS ARE YOU.
IF I MAY, SACRIFICING PEOPLE GENERALLY COMES DOWN TO KILLING THEM.
OH, NO NO NO! THOSE WE OFFER ARE MOST ALIVE. THE MINOTAUR MASSACRES THEM HIMSELF.
THE MINOTAUR... A MYTHICAL CREATURE -- HALF-MAN, HALF-BULL. YOU'RE SAYING THERE'S ONE IN THE TUNNELS?
HE'S MY SON.
EXCUSE ME?
ARCHIBALD MADE HIM THAT WAY.
SO HE'S NOT ALWAYS BEEN A... MINOTAUR?
HE WAS A BIT OF LOOSE CANNON. YOU'RE NOT EATING ANYTHING...
I AM.
IT'S TIME.

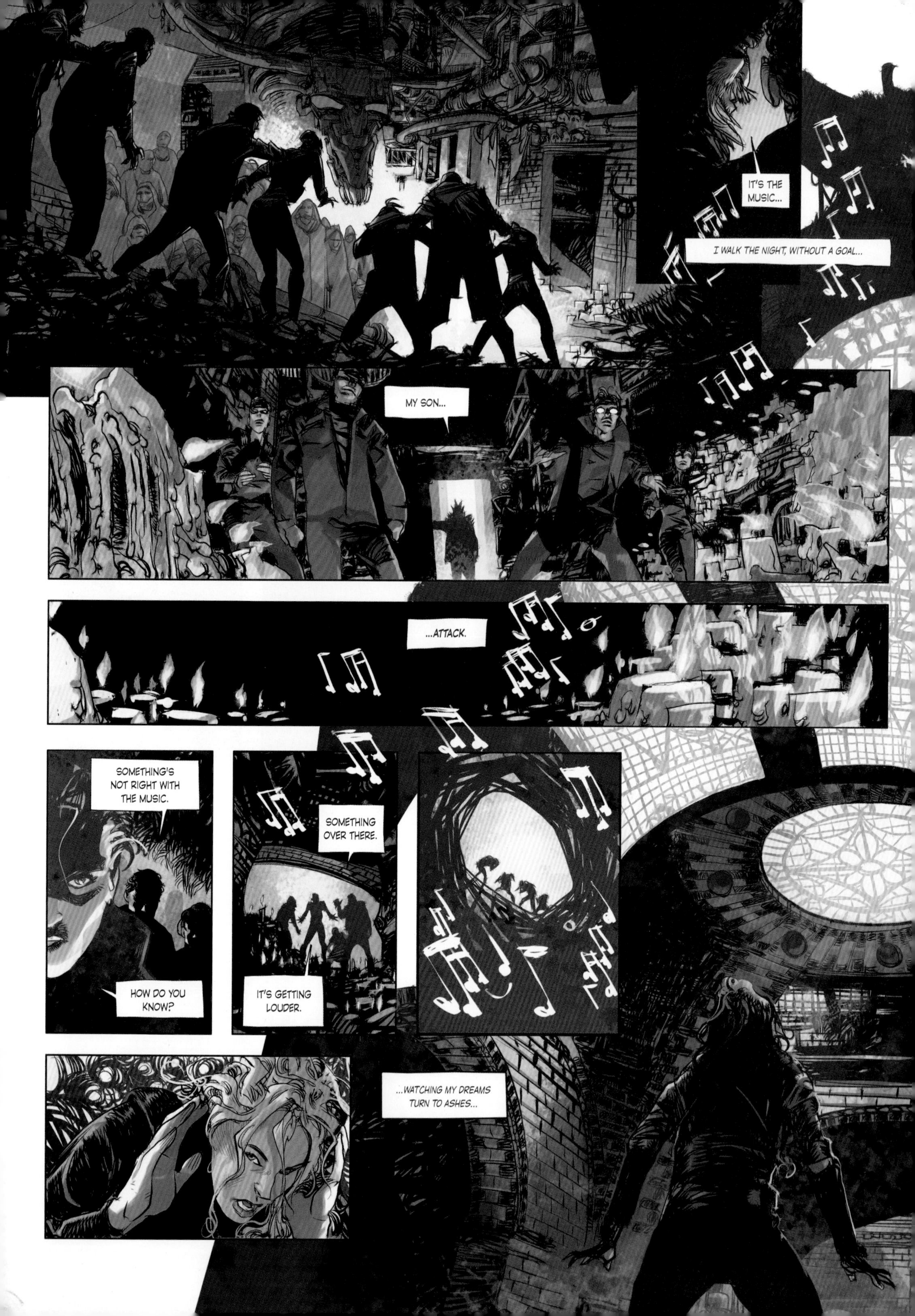

IT'S THE MUSIC...
I WALK THE NIGHT, WITHOUT A GOAL...
MY SON...
...ATTACK.
SOMETHING'S NOT RIGHT WITH THE MUSIC.
HOW DO YOU KNOW?
SOMETHING OVER THERE.
IT'S GETTING LOUDER.
...WATCHING MY DREAMS TURN TO ASHES...

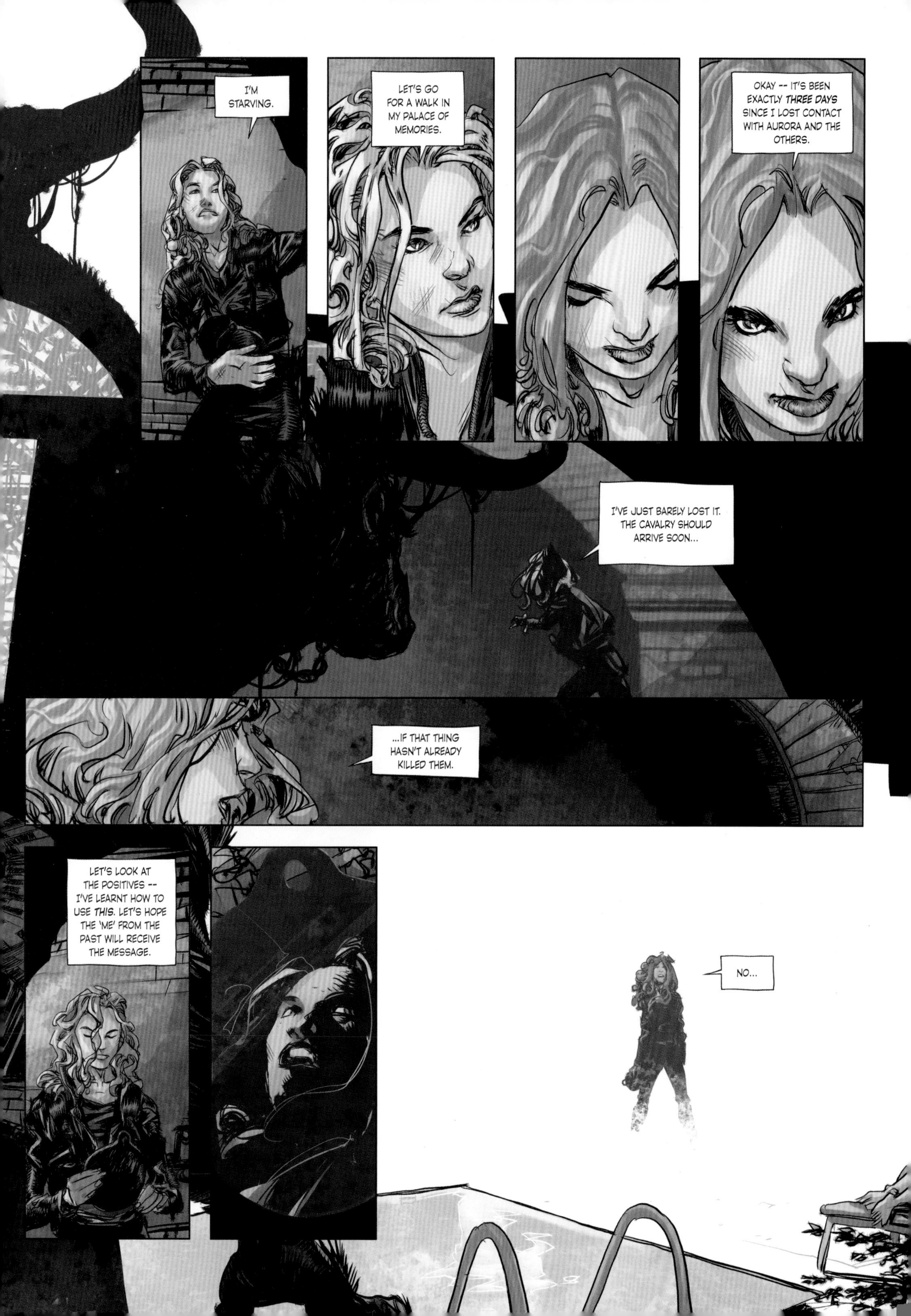
I'M STARVING.
LET'S GO FOR A WALK IN MY PALACE OF MEMORIES.
OKAY -- IT'S BEEN EXACTLY THREE DAYS SINCE I LOST CONTACT WITH AURORA AND THE OTHERS.
I'VE JUST BARELY LOST IT. THE CAVALRY SHOULD ARRIVE SOON...
...IF THAT THING HASN'T ALREADY KILLED THEM.
LET'S LOOK AT THE POSITIVES -- I'VE LEARNT HOW TO USE THIS. LET'S HOPE THE 'ME' FROM THE PAST WILL RECEIVE THE MESSAGE.
NO...

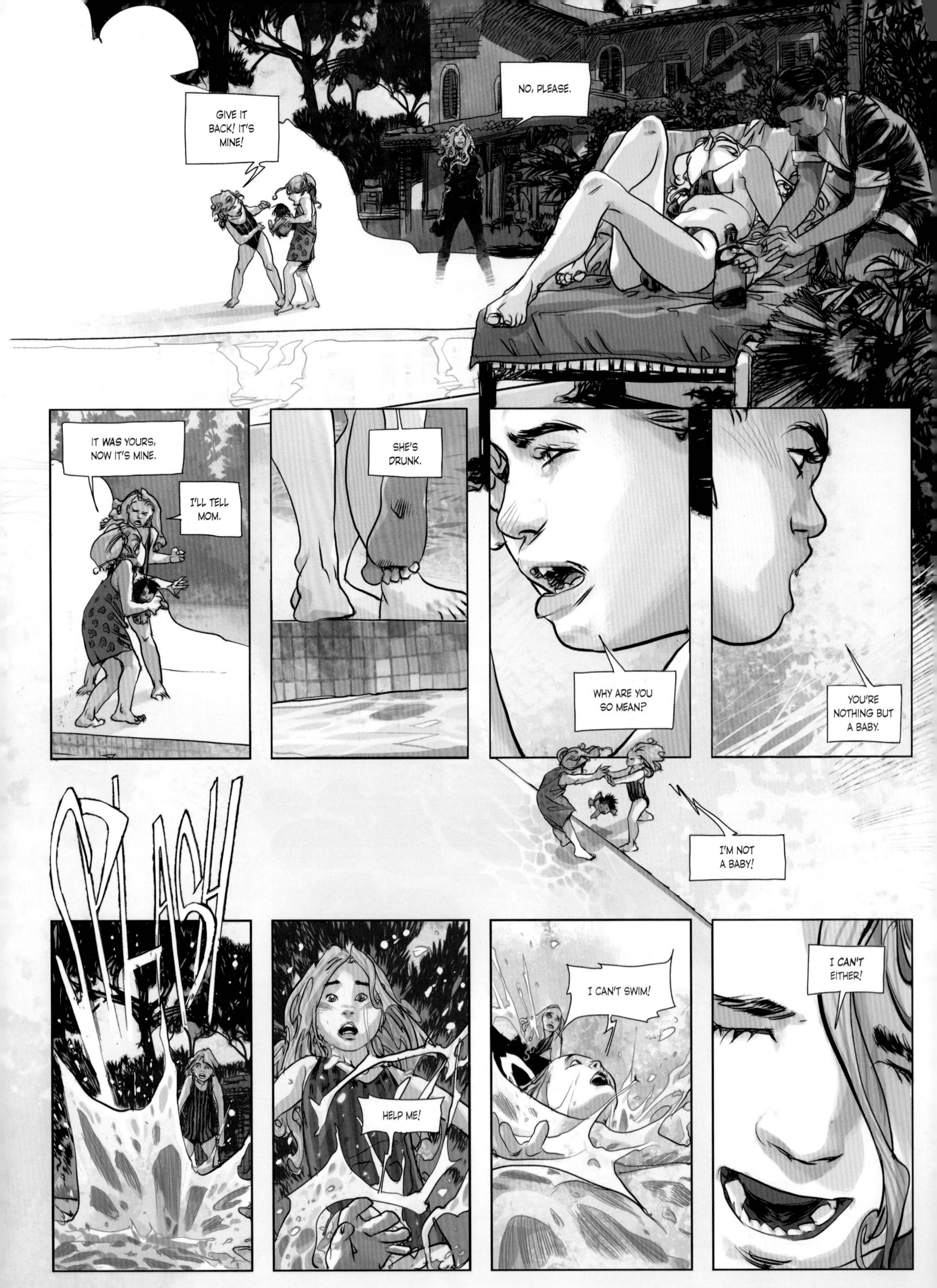
GIVE IT BACK! IT'S MINE!
NO, PLEASE.
IT WAS YOURS, NOW IT'S MINE.
I'LL TELL MOM.
SHE'S DRUNK.
WHY ARE YOU SO MEAN?
YOU'RE NOTHING BUT A BABY.
I'M NOT A BABY!
SPLASH
HELP ME!
I CAN'T SWIM!
I CAN'T EITHER!

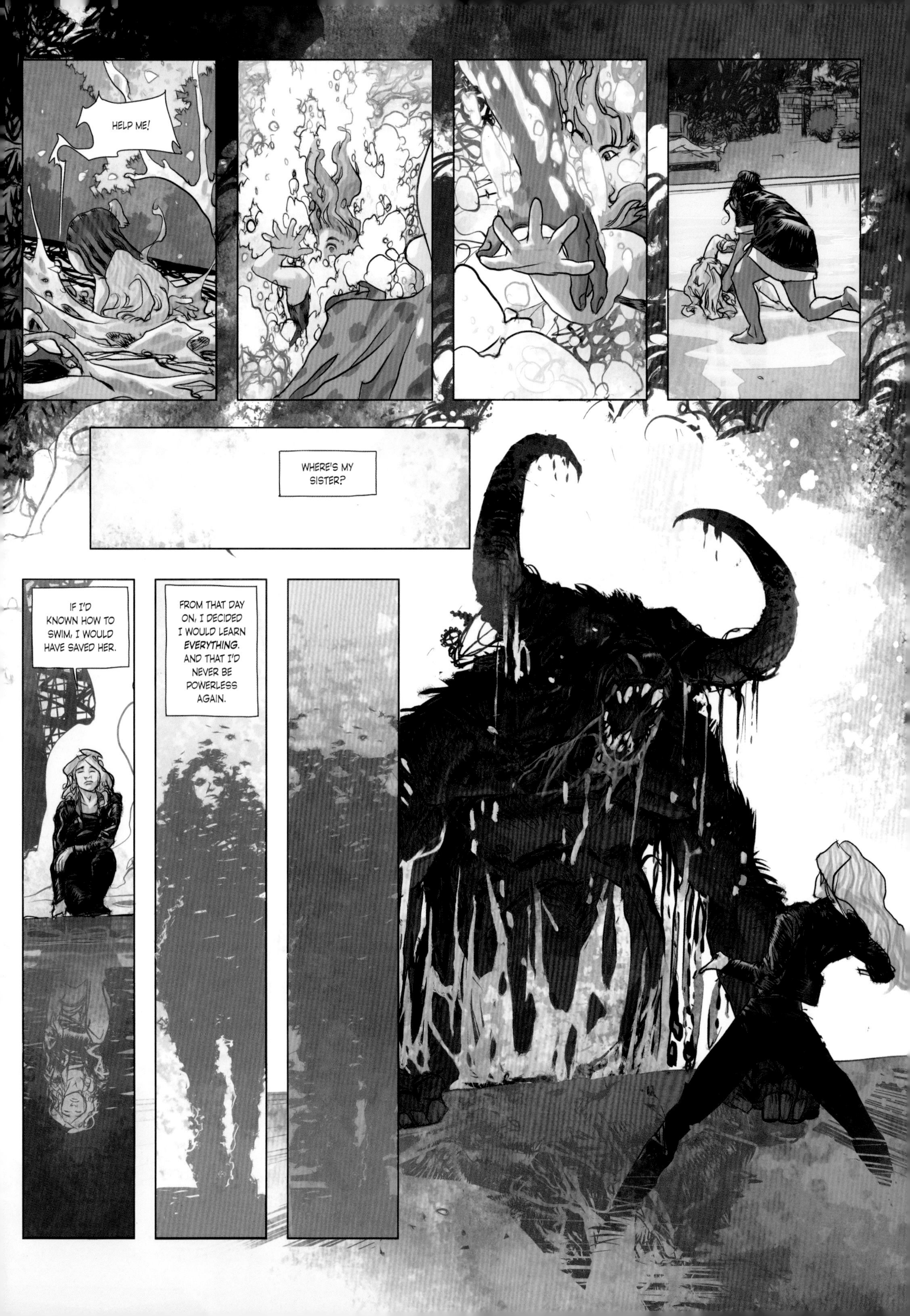
HELP ME!
WHERE'S MY SISTER?
IF I'D KNOWN HOW TO SWIM, I WOULD HAVE SAVED HER.
FROM THAT DAY ON, I DECIDED I WOULD LEARN **EVERYTHING**. AND THAT I'D NEVER BE POWERLESS AGAIN.

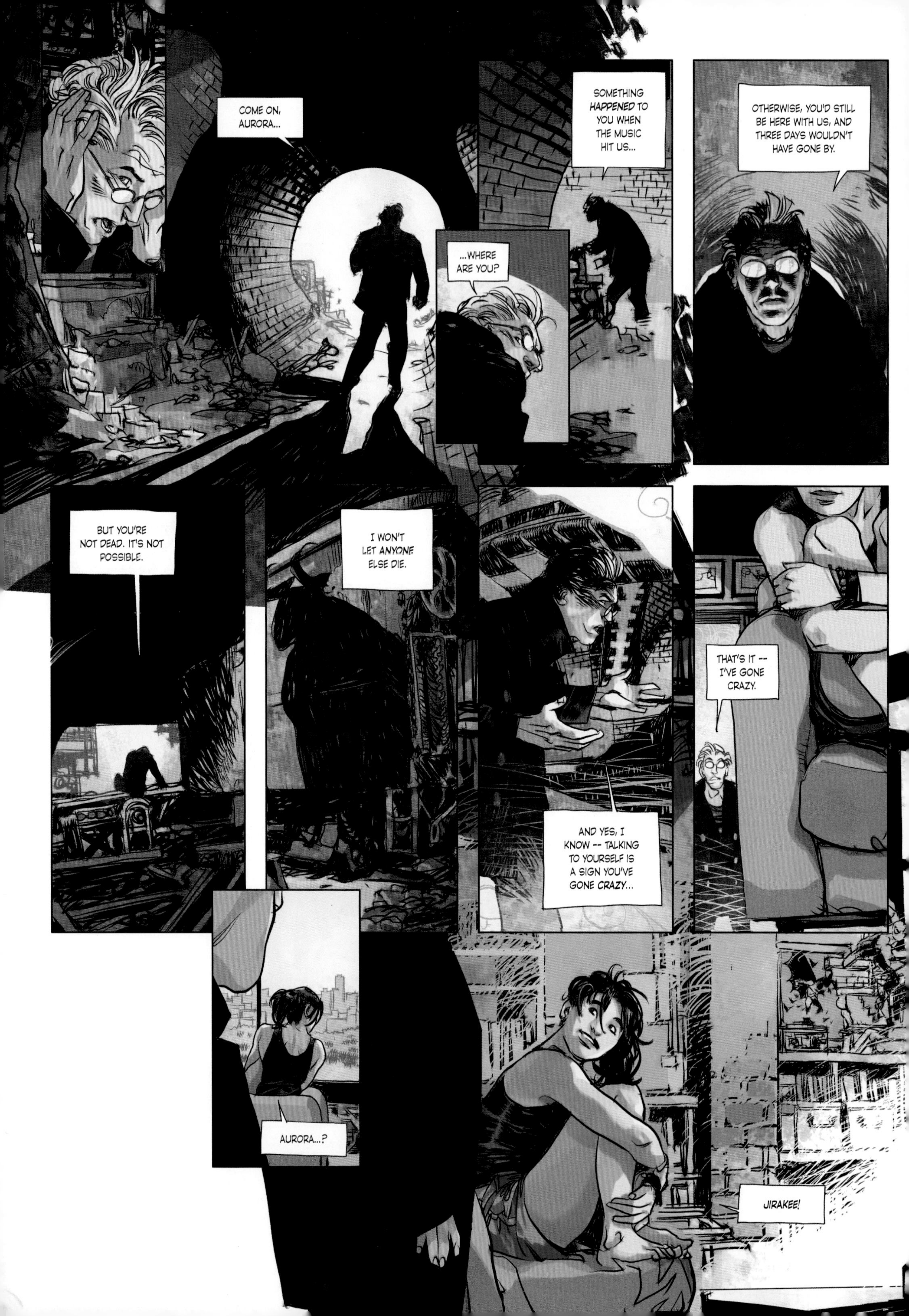
COME ON, AURORA...
...WHERE ARE YOU?
SOMETHING HAPPENED TO YOU WHEN THE MUSIC HIT US...
OTHERWISE, YOU'D STILL BE HERE WITH US, AND THREE DAYS WOULDN'T HAVE GONE BY.
BUT YOU'RE NOT DEAD. IT'S NOT POSSIBLE.
I WON'T LET ANYONE ELSE DIE.
AND YES, I KNOW -- TALKING TO YOURSELF IS A SIGN YOU'VE GONE CRAZY...
THAT'S IT -- I'VE GONE CRAZY.
AURORA...?
JIRAKEE!

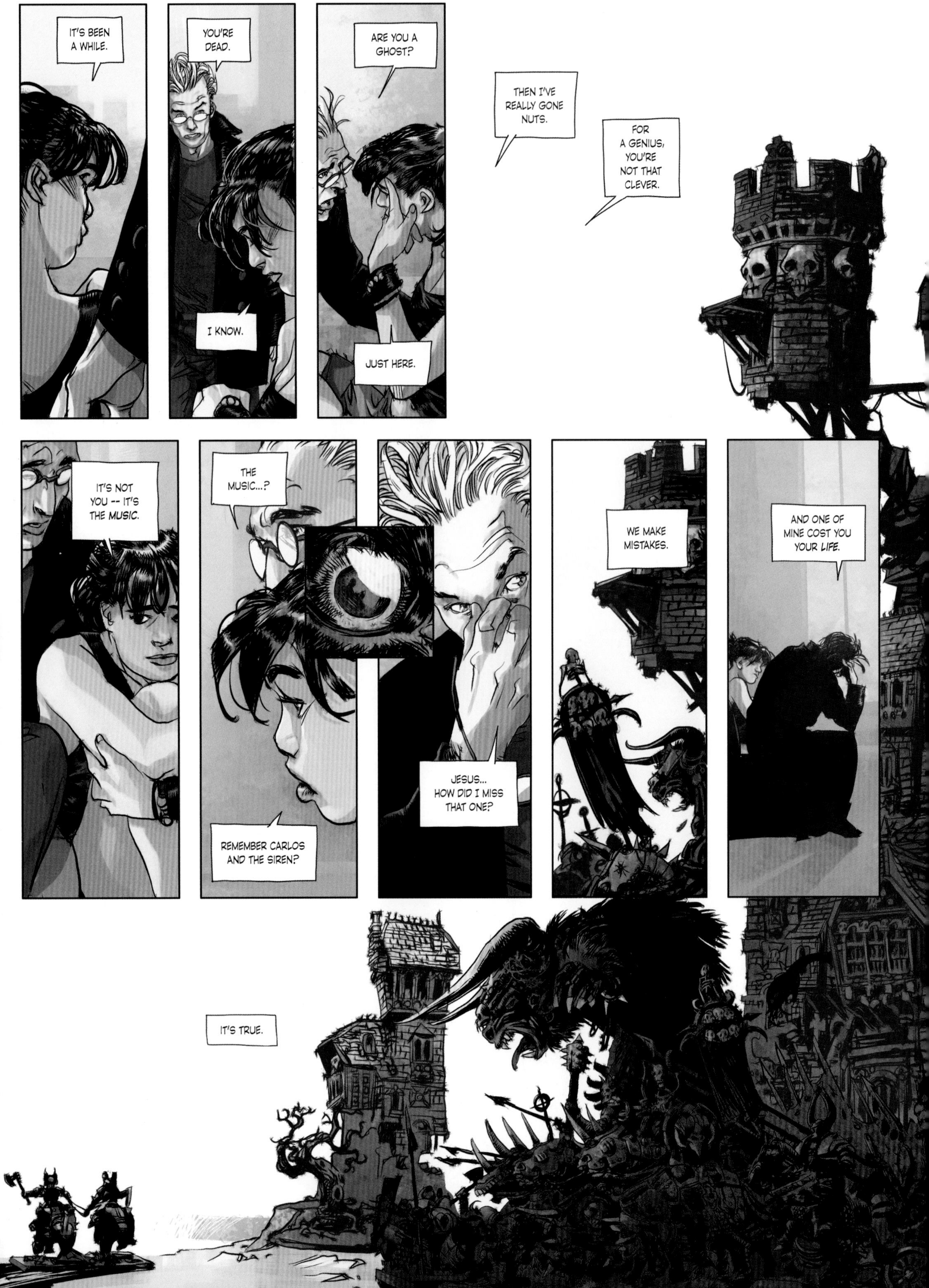
IT'S BEEN A WHILE.
YOU'RE DEAD.
I KNOW.
ARE YOU A GHOST?
JUST HERE.
THEN I'VE REALLY GONE NUTS.
FOR A GENIUS, YOU'RE NOT THAT CLEVER.
IT'S NOT YOU -- IT'S THE MUSIC.
THE MUSIC...?
REMEMBER CARLOS AND THE SIREN?
JESUS... HOW DID I MISS THAT ONE?
WE MAKE MISTAKES.
AND ONE OF MINE COST YOU YOUR LIFE.
IT'S TRUE.

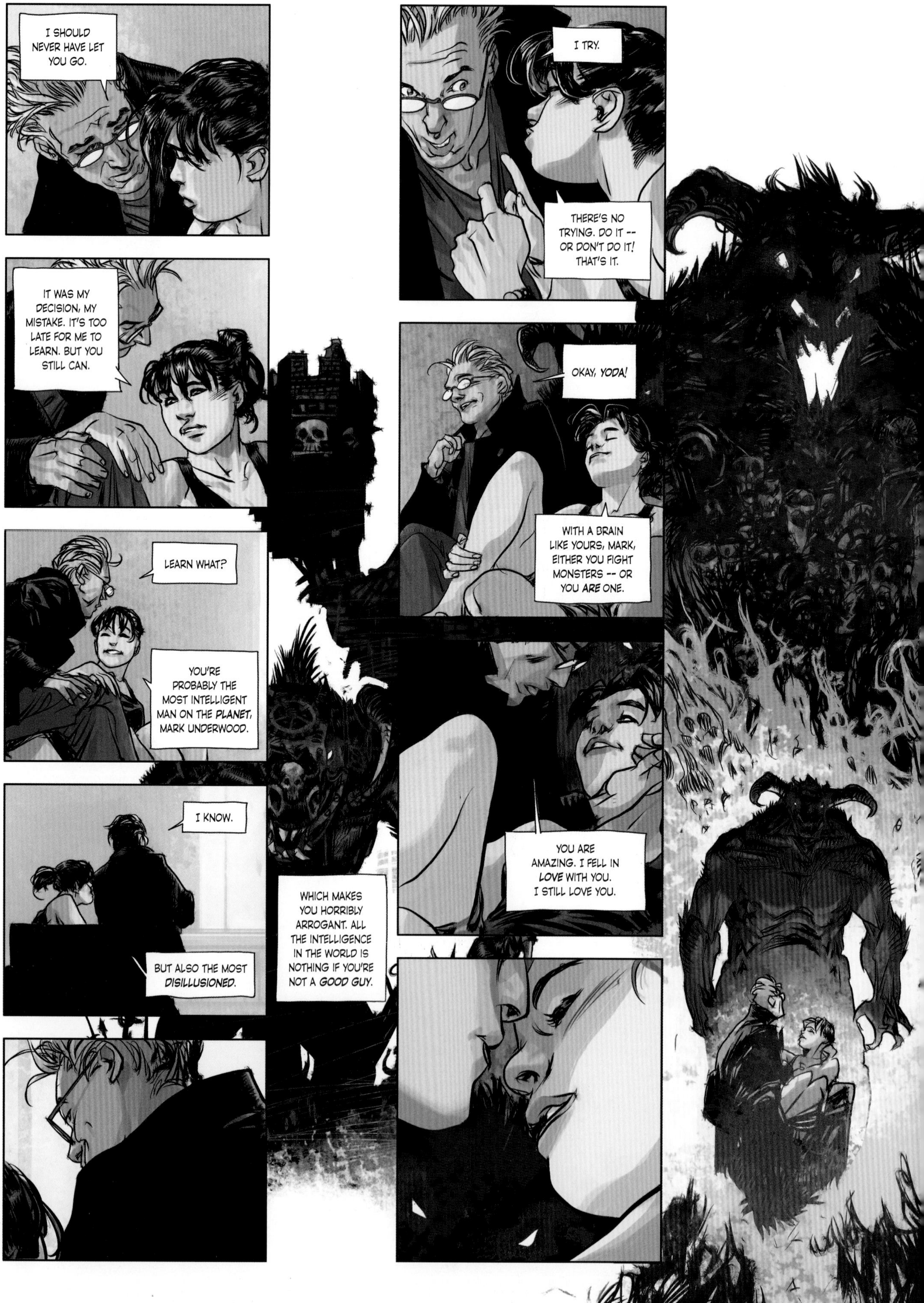
I SHOULD NEVER HAVE LET YOU GO.
IT WAS MY DECISION, MY MISTAKE. IT'S TOO LATE FOR ME TO LEARN. BUT YOU STILL CAN.
LEARN WHAT?
YOU'RE PROBABLY THE MOST INTELLIGENT MAN ON THE *PLANET*, MARK UNDERWOOD.
I KNOW.
BUT ALSO THE MOST *DISILLUSIONED*.
WHICH MAKES YOU HORRIBLY ARROGANT. ALL THE INTELLIGENCE IN THE WORLD IS NOTHING IF YOU'RE NOT A *GOOD GUY*.
I TRY.
THERE'S NO TRYING. DO IT -- OR DON'T DO IT! THAT'S IT.
OKAY, *YODA!*
WITH A BRAIN LIKE YOURS, MARK, EITHER YOU FIGHT MONSTERS -- OR YOU *ARE* ONE.
YOU ARE AMAZING. I FELL IN *LOVE* WITH YOU. I STILL LOVE YOU.

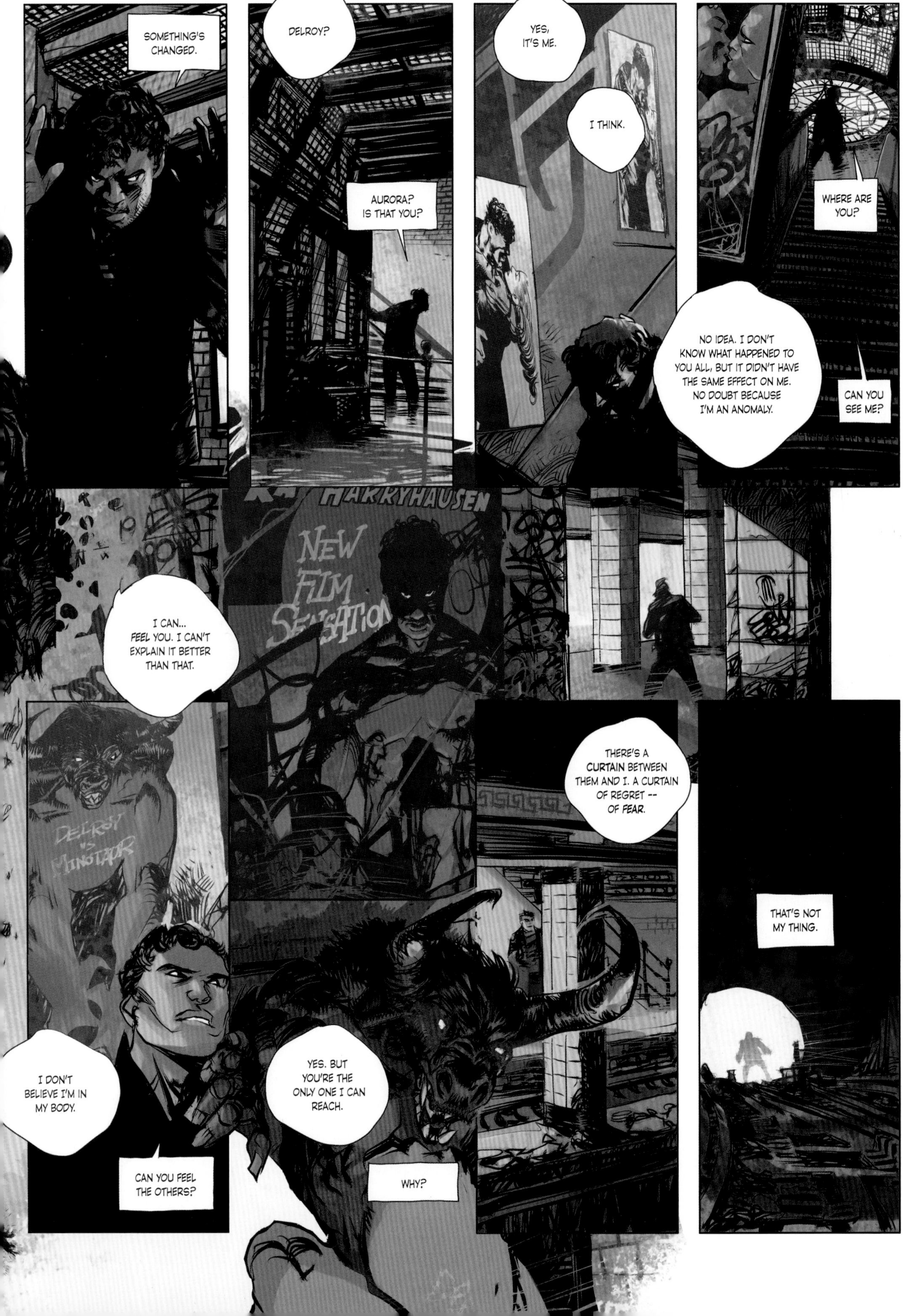

SOMETHING'S CHANGED.
DELROY?
AURORA? IS THAT YOU?
YES, IT'S ME.
I THINK.
WHERE ARE YOU?
NO IDEA. I DON'T KNOW WHAT HAPPENED TO YOU ALL, BUT IT DIDN'T HAVE THE SAME EFFECT ON ME. NO DOUBT BECAUSE I'M AN ANOMALY.
CAN YOU SEE ME?
HARRYHAUSEN
NEW FILM SENSATION
I CAN... FEEL YOU. I CAN'T EXPLAIN IT BETTER THAN THAT.
DELROY vs MINOTAUR
I DON'T BELIEVE I'M IN MY BODY.
CAN YOU FEEL THE OTHERS?
YES. BUT YOU'RE THE ONLY ONE I CAN REACH.
WHY?
THERE'S A CURTAIN BETWEEN THEM AND I. A CURTAIN OF REGRET -- OF FEAR.
THAT'S NOT MY THING.

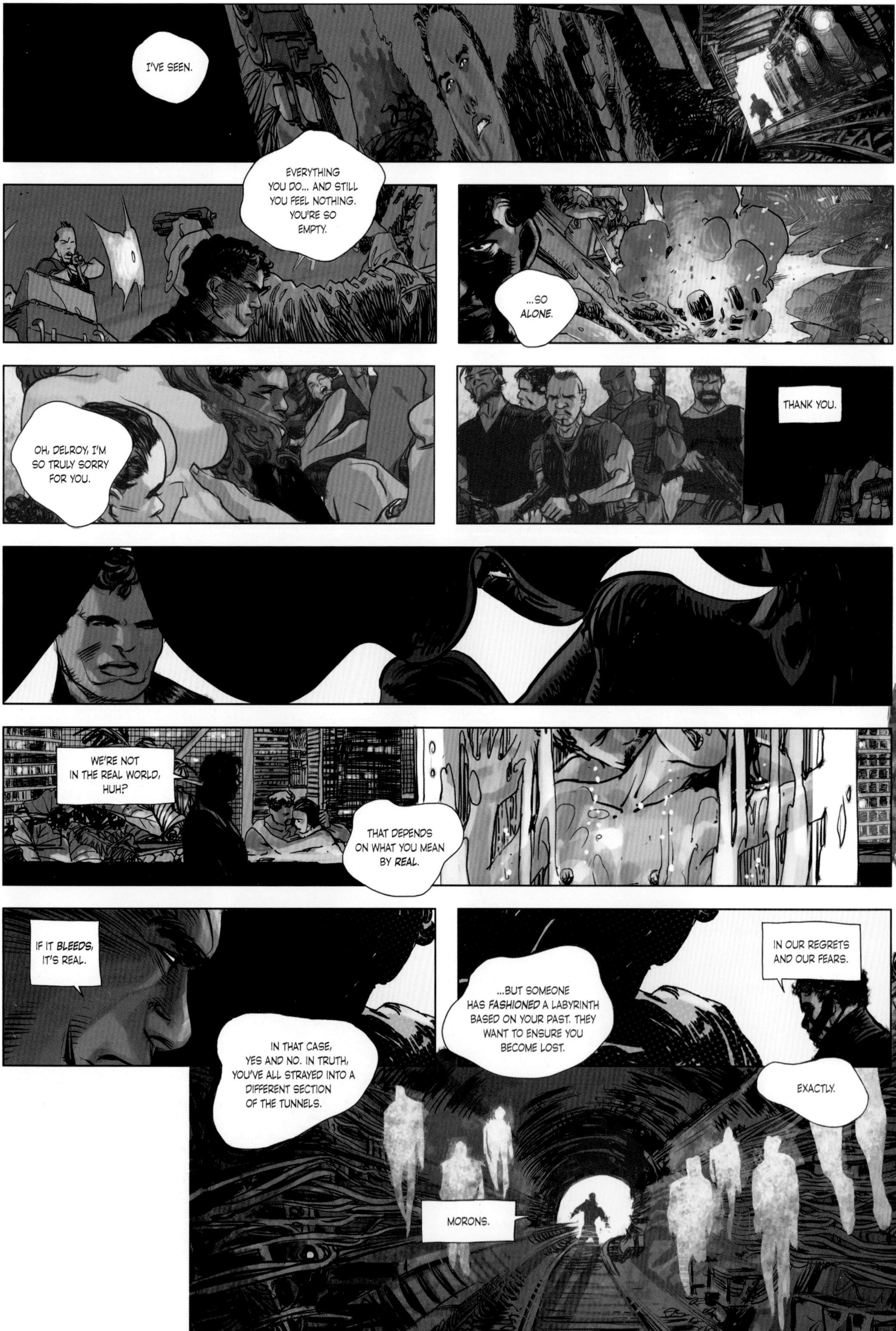
I'VE SEEN.
EVERYTHING YOU DO... AND STILL YOU FEEL NOTHING. YOU'RE SO EMPTY.
...SO ALONE.
OH, DELROY, I'M SO TRULY SORRY FOR YOU.
THANK YOU.
WE'RE NOT IN THE REAL WORLD, HUH?
THAT DEPENDS ON WHAT YOU MEAN BY REAL.
IF IT BLEEDS, IT'S REAL.
IN THAT CASE, YES AND NO. IN TRUTH, YOU'VE ALL STRAYED INTO A DIFFERENT SECTION OF THE TUNNELS.
...BUT SOMEONE HAS FASHIONED A LABYRINTH BASED ON YOUR PAST. THEY WANT TO ENSURE YOU BECOME LOST.
IN OUR REGRETS AND OUR FEARS.
EXACTLY.
MORONS.

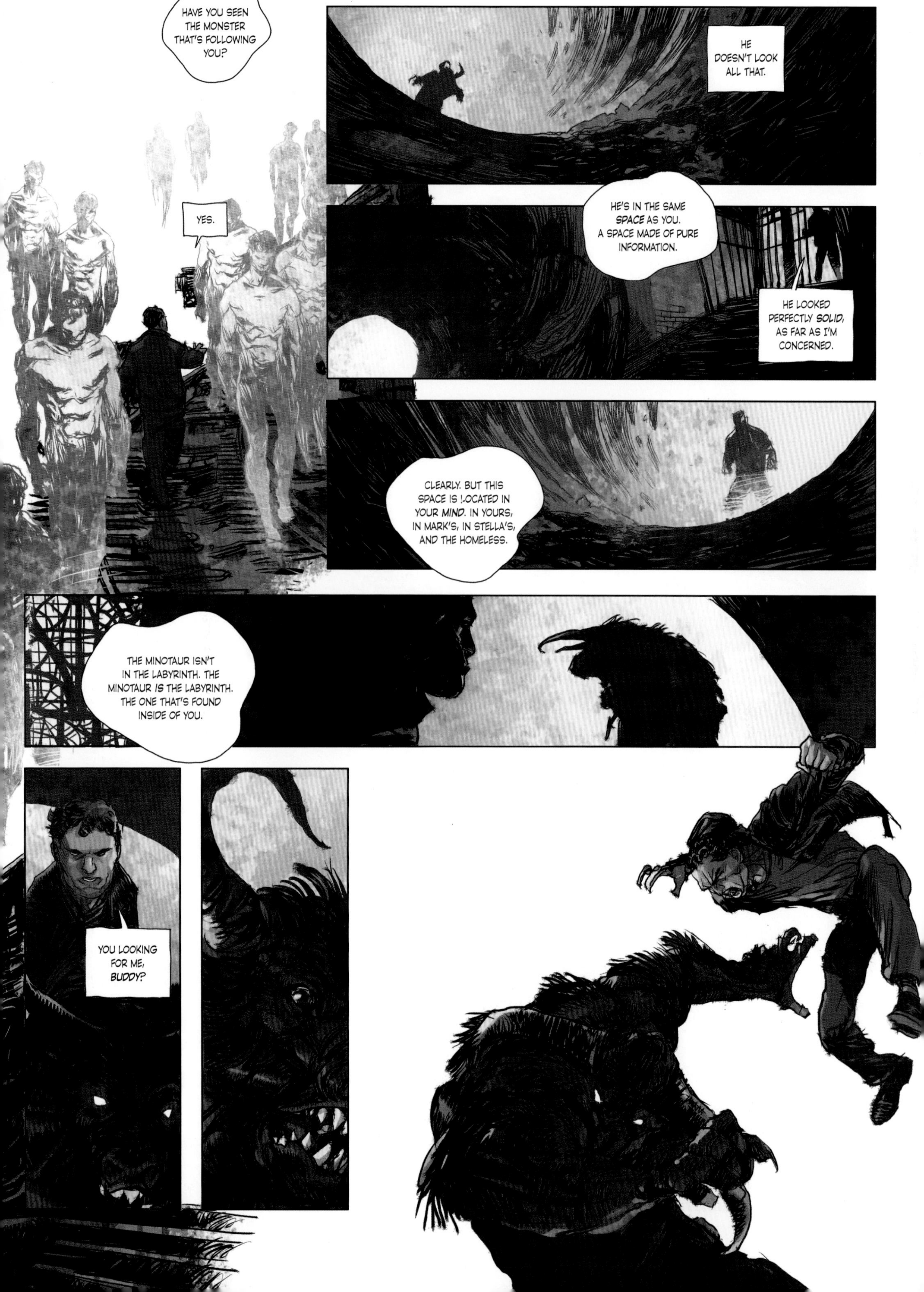
HAVE YOU SEEN THE MONSTER THAT'S FOLLOWING YOU?
HE DOESN'T LOOK ALL THAT.
YES.
HE'S IN THE SAME *SPACE* AS YOU. A SPACE MADE OF PURE INFORMATION.
HE LOOKED PERFECTLY *SOLID*, AS FAR AS I'M CONCERNED.
CLEARLY. BUT THIS SPACE IS LOCATED IN YOUR *MIND*. IN YOURS, IN MARK'S, IN STELLA'S, AND THE HOMELESS.
THE MINOTAUR ISN'T IN THE LABYRINTH. THE MINOTAUR *IS* THE LABYRINTH. THE ONE THAT'S FOUND INSIDE OF YOU.
YOU LOOKING FOR ME, *BUDDY*?

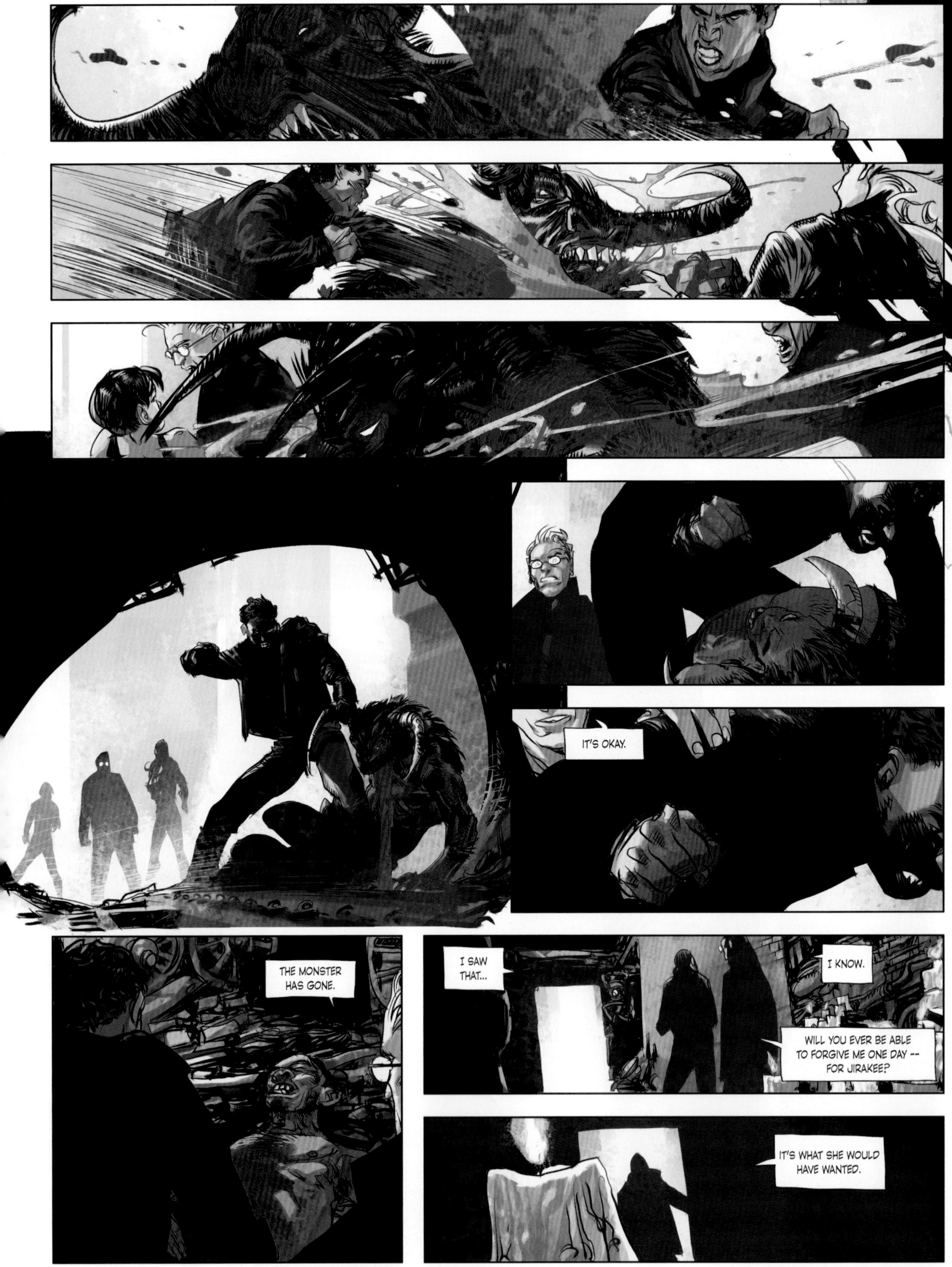
IT'S OKAY.
THE MONSTER HAS GONE.
I SAW THAT...
I KNOW.
WILL YOU EVER BE ABLE TO FORGIVE ME ONE DAY -- FOR JIRAKEE?
IT'S WHAT SHE WOULD HAVE WANTED.

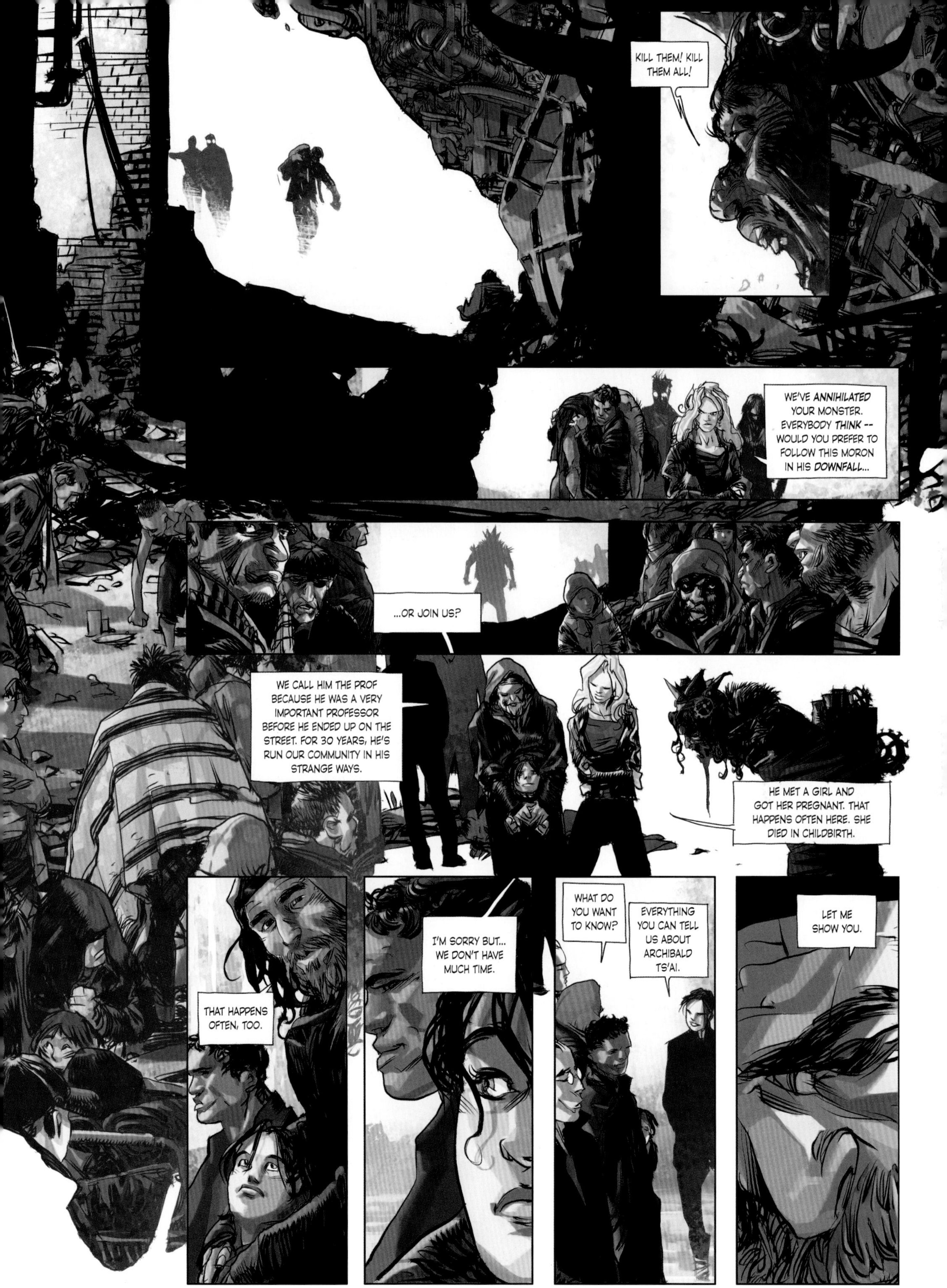
KILL THEM! KILL THEM ALL!
WE'VE ANNIHILATED YOUR MONSTER. EVERYBODY THINK -- WOULD YOU PREFER TO FOLLOW THIS MORON IN HIS DOWNFALL...
...OR JOIN US?
WE CALL HIM THE PROF BECAUSE HE WAS A VERY IMPORTANT PROFESSOR BEFORE HE ENDED UP ON THE STREET. FOR 30 YEARS, HE'S RUN OUR COMMUNITY IN HIS STRANGE WAYS.
HE MET A GIRL AND GOT HER PREGNANT. THAT HAPPENS OFTEN HERE. SHE DIED IN CHILDBIRTH.
THAT HAPPENS OFTEN, TOO.
I'M SORRY BUT... WE DON'T HAVE MUCH TIME.
WHAT DO YOU WANT TO KNOW?
EVERYTHING YOU CAN TELL US ABOUT ARCHIBALD TS'AI.
LET ME SHOW YOU.

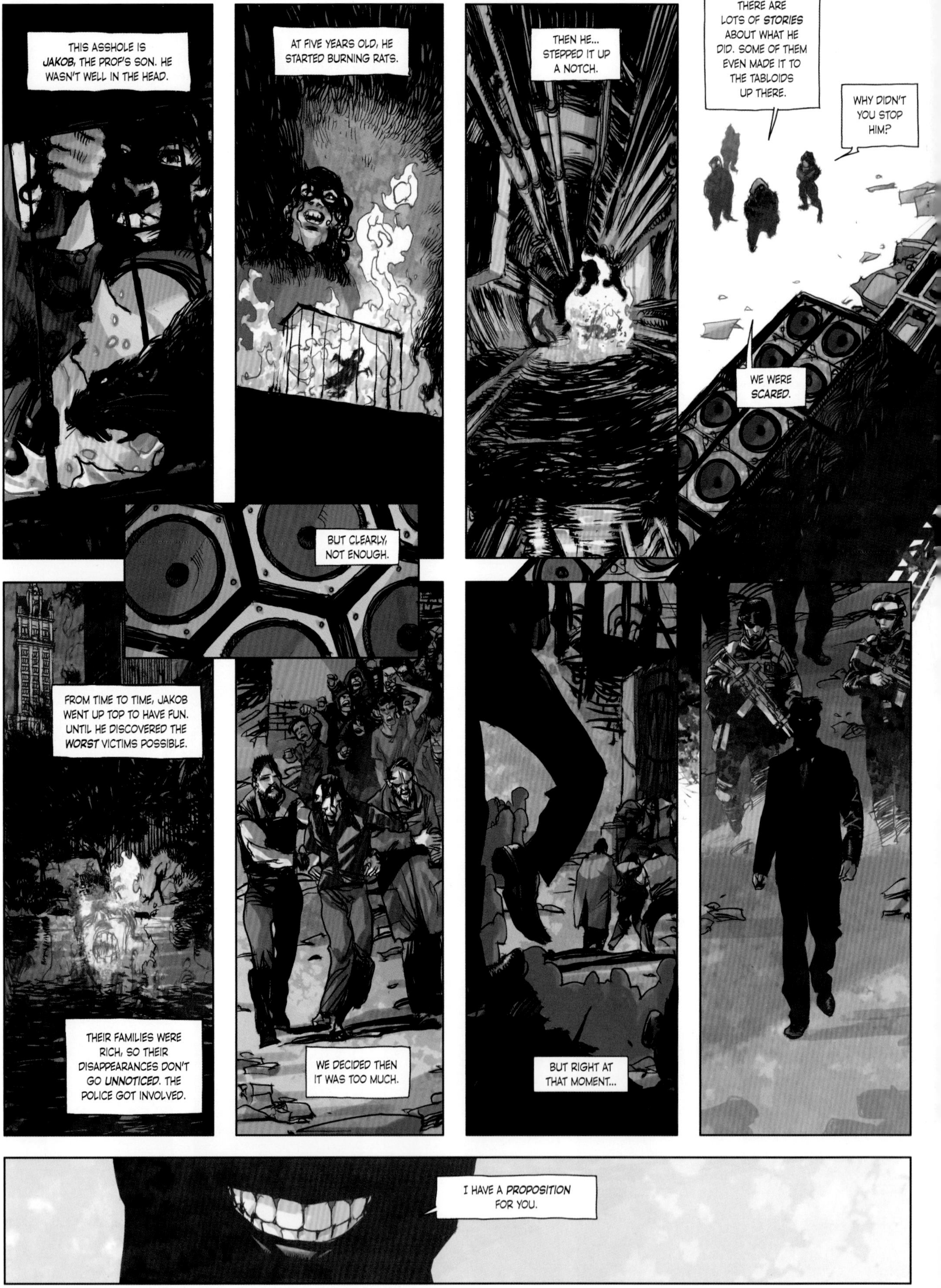

THIS ASSHOLE IS *JAKOB*, THE PROF'S SON. HE WASN'T WELL IN THE HEAD.
AT FIVE YEARS OLD, HE STARTED BURNING RATS.
THEN HE... STEPPED IT UP A NOTCH.
THERE ARE LOTS OF *STORIES* ABOUT WHAT HE DID. SOME OF THEM EVEN MADE IT TO THE TABLOIDS UP THERE.
WHY DIDN'T YOU STOP HIM?
WE WERE *SCARED*.
BUT CLEARLY, NOT ENOUGH.
FROM TIME TO TIME, JAKOB WENT UP TOP TO HAVE FUN. UNTIL HE DISCOVERED THE *WORST* VICTIMS POSSIBLE.
THEIR FAMILIES WERE RICH, SO THEIR DISAPPEARANCES DON'T GO *UNNOTICED*. THE POLICE GOT INVOLVED.
WE DECIDED THEN IT WAS TOO MUCH.
BUT RIGHT AT THAT MOMENT...
I HAVE A *PROPOSITION* FOR YOU.

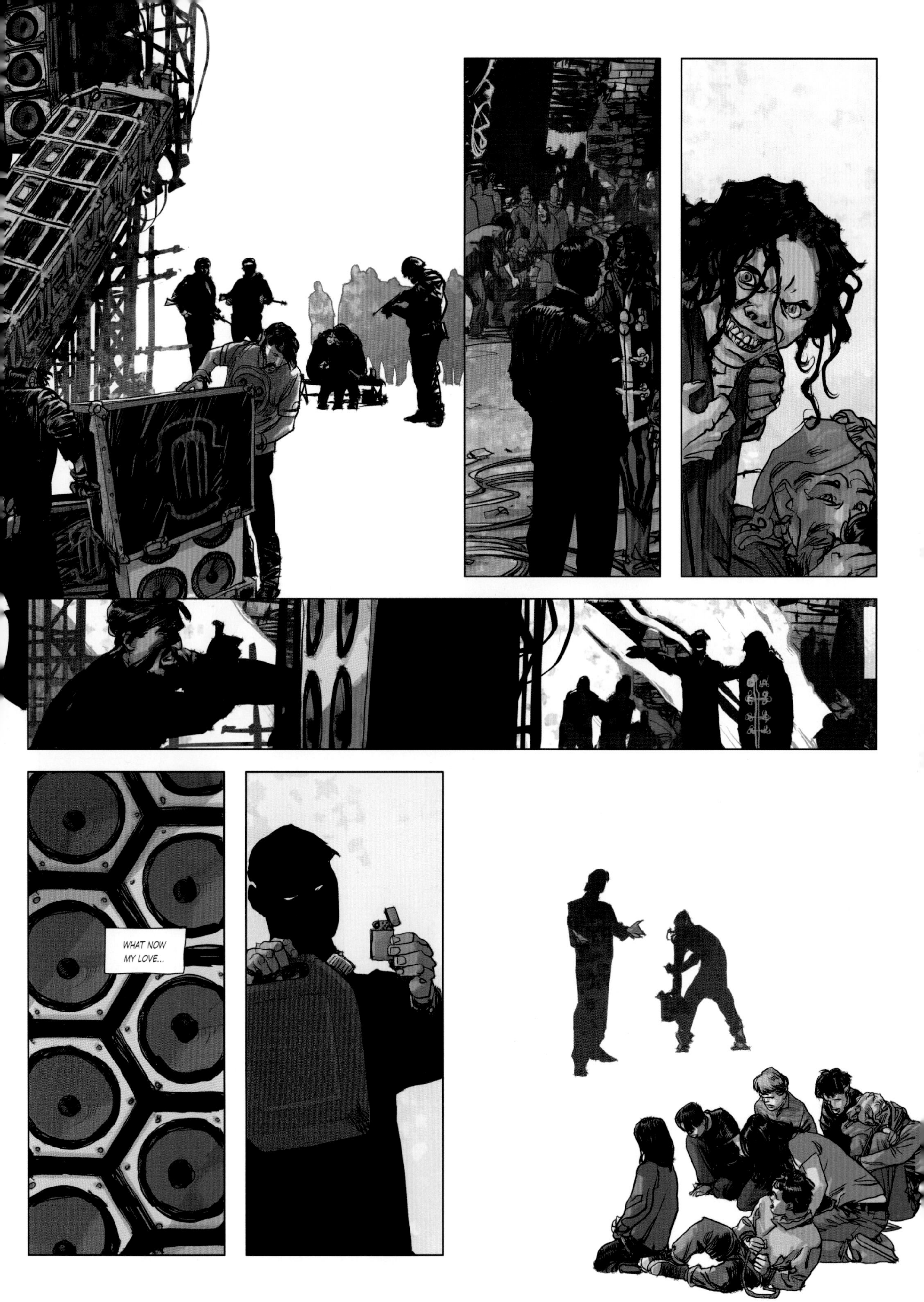
WHAT NOW
MY LOVE...

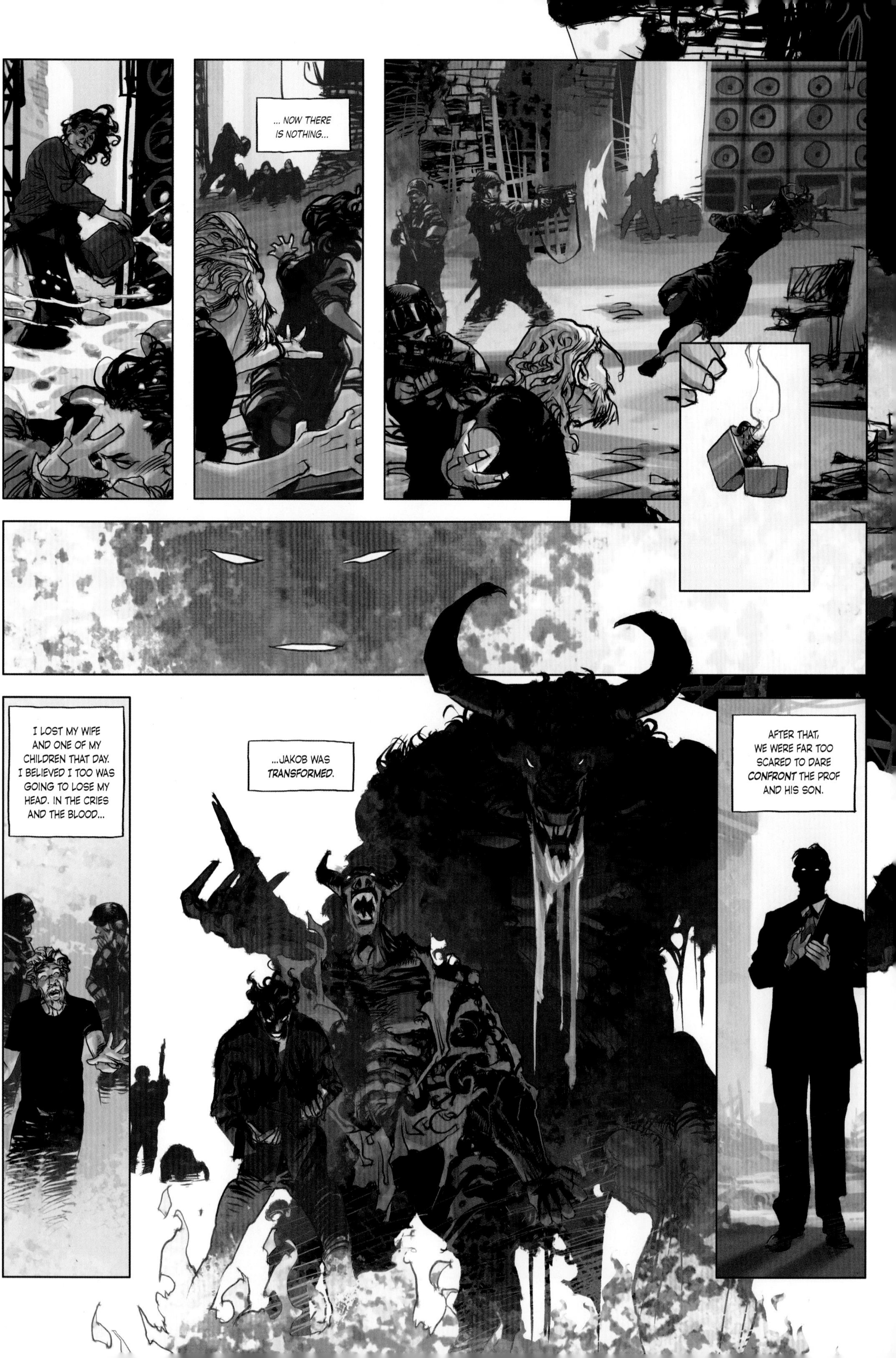
... NOW THERE IS NOTHING...
I LOST MY WIFE AND ONE OF MY CHILDREN THAT DAY. I BELIEVED I TOO WAS GOING TO LOSE MY HEAD. IN THE CRIES AND THE BLOOD...
...JAKOB WAS *TRANSFORMED*.
AFTER THAT, WE WERE FAR TOO SCARED TO DARE ***CONFRONT*** THE PROF AND HIS SON.

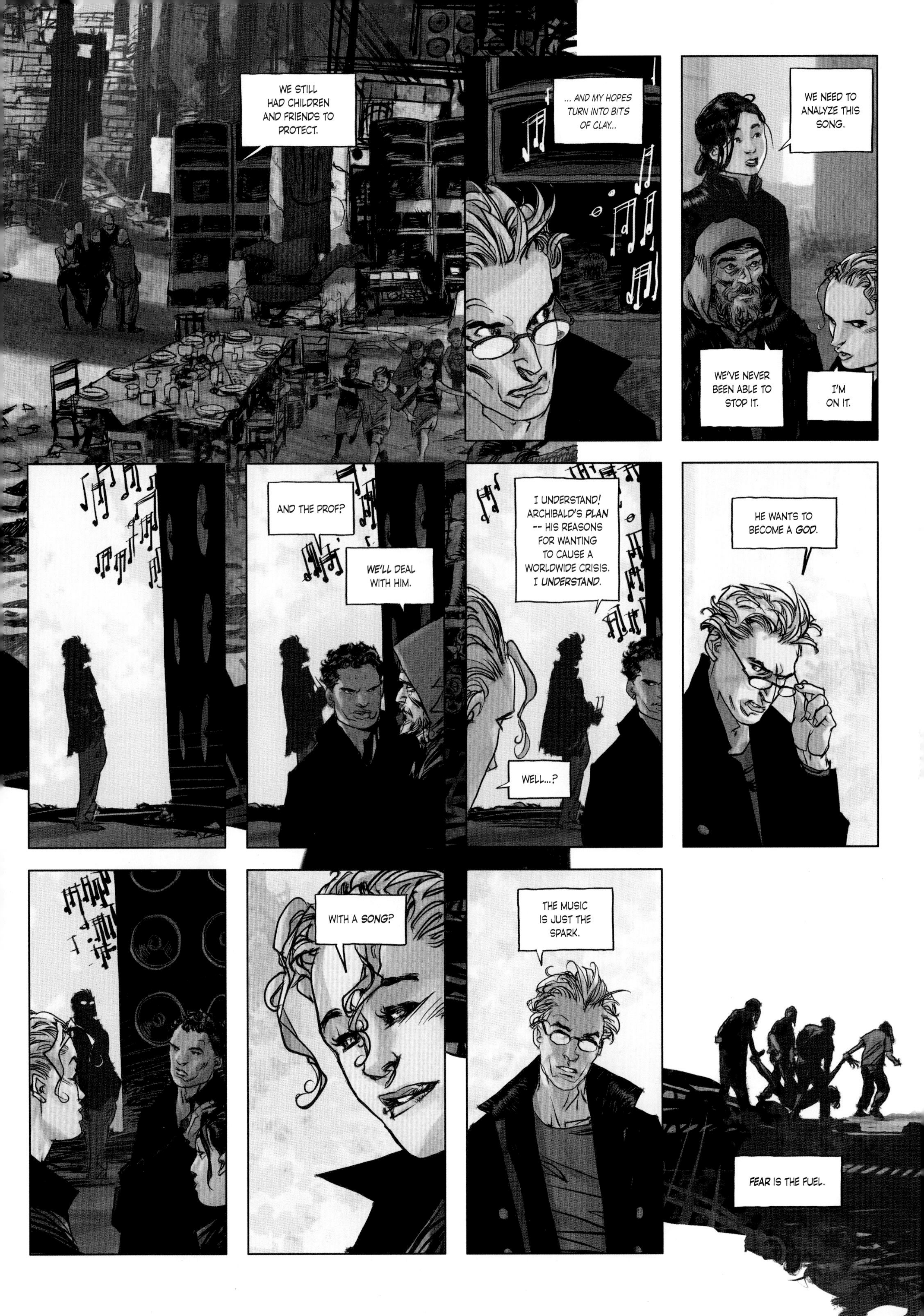

WE STILL HAD CHILDREN AND FRIENDS TO PROTECT.
... AND MY HOPES TURN INTO BITS OF CLAY...
WE NEED TO ANALYZE THIS SONG.
WE'VE NEVER BEEN ABLE TO STOP IT.
I'M ON IT.
AND THE PROF?
WE'LL DEAL WITH HIM.
I UNDERSTAND! ARCHIBALD'S PLAN -- HIS REASONS FOR WANTING TO CAUSE A WORLDWIDE CRISIS. I UNDERSTAND.
WELL...?
HE WANTS TO BECOME A GOD.
WITH A SONG?
THE MUSIC IS JUST THE SPARK.
FEAR IS THE FUEL.

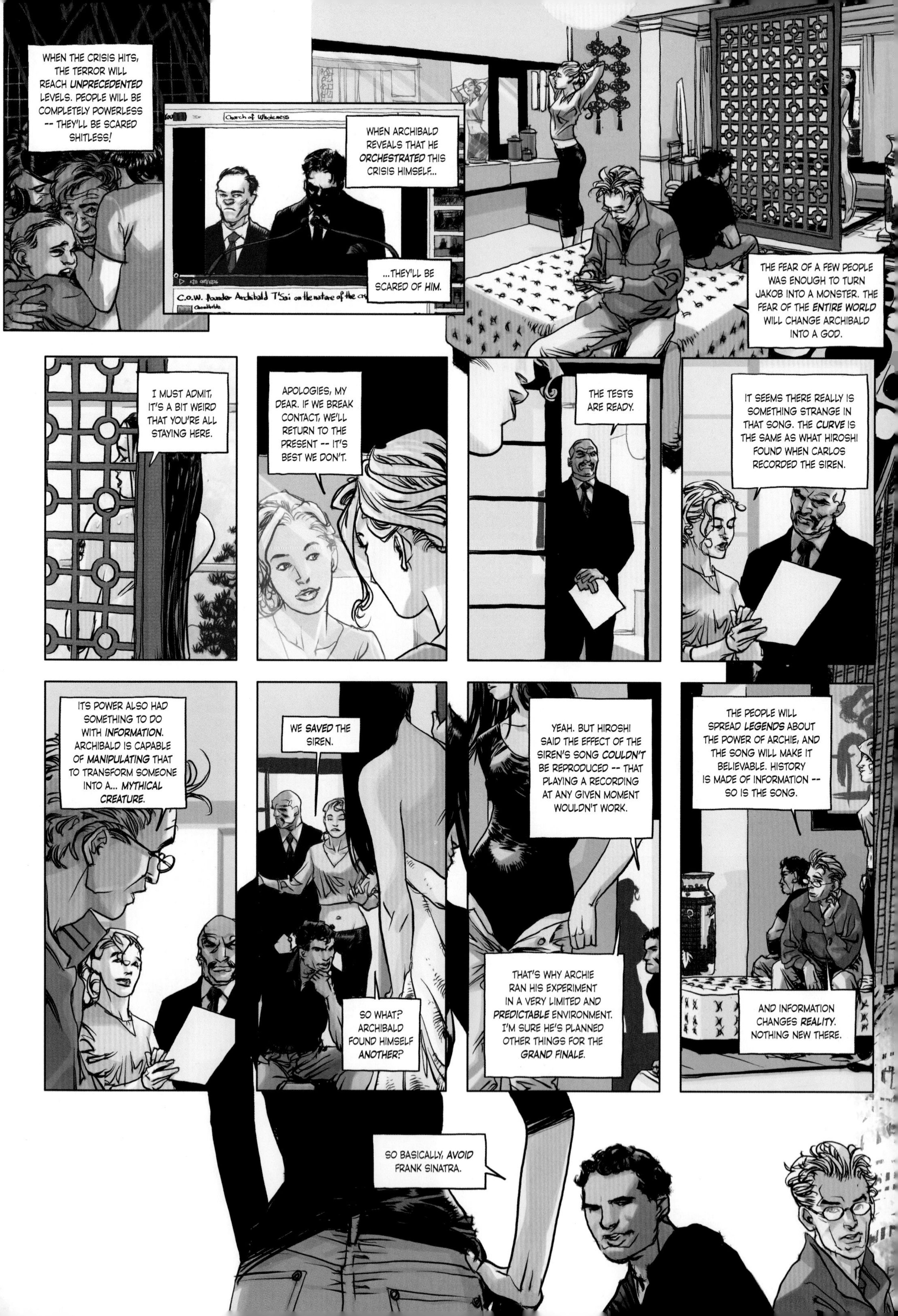
WHEN THE CRISIS HITS, THE TERROR WILL REACH *UNPRECEDENTED* LEVELS. PEOPLE WILL BE COMPLETELY POWERLESS -- THEY'LL BE SCARED SHITLESS!
Church of Wholeness
WHEN ARCHIBALD REVEALS THAT HE *ORCHESTRATED* THIS CRISIS HIMSELF...
...THEY'LL BE SCARED OF *HIM*.
C.O.W. founder Archibald T'Sai on the nature of the
THE FEAR OF A FEW PEOPLE WAS ENOUGH TO TURN JAKOB INTO A MONSTER. THE FEAR OF THE *ENTIRE WORLD* WILL CHANGE ARCHIBALD INTO A GOD.
I MUST ADMIT, IT'S A BIT WEIRD THAT YOU'RE ALL STAYING HERE.
APOLOGIES, MY DEAR. IF WE BREAK CONTACT, WE'LL RETURN TO THE PRESENT -- IT'S BEST WE DON'T.
THE TESTS ARE READY.
IT SEEMS THERE REALLY IS SOMETHING STRANGE IN THAT SONG. THE *CURVE* IS THE SAME AS WHAT HIROSHI FOUND WHEN CARLOS RECORDED THE SIREN.
ITS POWER ALSO HAD SOMETHING TO DO WITH *INFORMATION*. ARCHIBALD IS CAPABLE OF *MANIPULATING* THAT TO TRANSFORM SOMEONE INTO A... *MYTHICAL CREATURE*.
WE *SAVED* THE SIREN.
SO WHAT? ARCHIBALD FOUND HIMSELF *ANOTHER*?
YEAH. BUT HIROSHI SAID THE EFFECT OF THE SIREN'S SONG *COULDN'T* BE REPRODUCED -- THAT PLAYING A RECORDING AT ANY GIVEN MOMENT WOULDN'T WORK.
THAT'S WHY ARCHIE RAN HIS EXPERIMENT IN A VERY LIMITED AND *PREDICTABLE* ENVIRONMENT. I'M SURE HE'S PLANNED OTHER THINGS FOR THE *GRAND FINALE*.
THE PEOPLE WILL SPREAD *LEGENDS* ABOUT THE POWER OF ARCHIE, AND THE SONG WILL MAKE IT BELIEVABLE. HISTORY IS MADE OF INFORMATION -- SO IS THE SONG.
AND INFORMATION CHANGES *REALITY*. NOTHING NEW THERE.
SO BASICALLY, *AVOID* FRANK SINATRA.

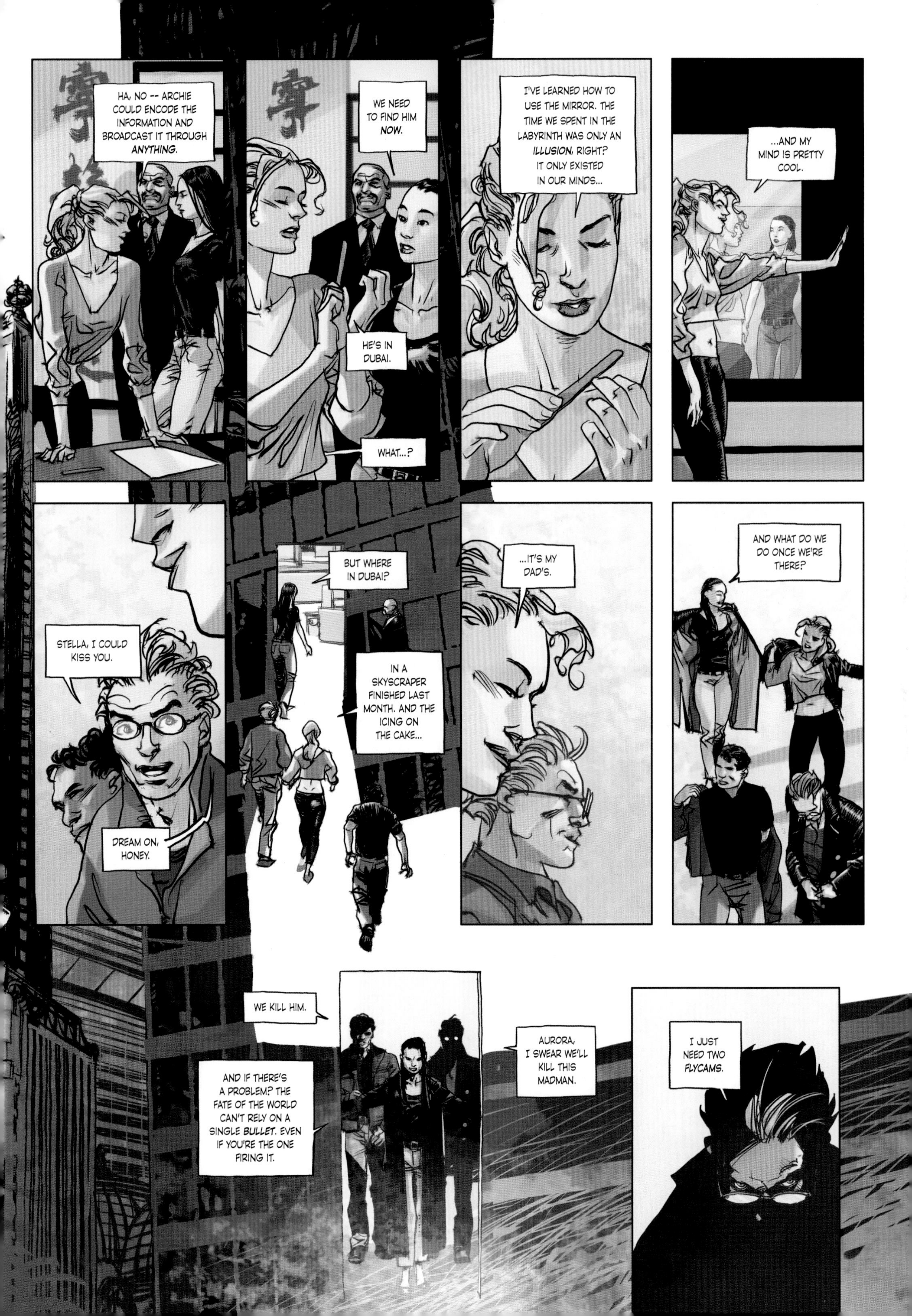

HA, NO -- ARCHIE COULD ENCODE THE INFORMATION AND BROADCAST IT THROUGH *ANYTHING*.
WE NEED TO FIND HIM *NOW*.
HE'S IN DUBAI.
WHAT...?
I'VE LEARNED HOW TO USE THE MIRROR. THE TIME WE SPENT IN THE LABYRINTH WAS ONLY AN *ILLUSION*, RIGHT? IT ONLY EXISTED IN OUR MINDS...
...AND MY MIND IS PRETTY COOL.
STELLA, I COULD KISS YOU.
DREAM ON, HONEY.
BUT WHERE IN DUBAI?
IN A SKYSCRAPER FINISHED LAST MONTH. AND THE ICING ON THE CAKE...
...IT'S MY DAD'S.
AND WHAT DO WE DO ONCE WE'RE THERE?
WE KILL HIM.
AND IF THERE'S A PROBLEM? THE FATE OF THE WORLD CAN'T RELY ON A SINGLE *BULLET*. EVEN IF YOU'RE THE ONE FIRING IT.
AURORA, I SWEAR WE'LL KILL THIS MADMAN.
I JUST NEED TWO *FLYCAMS*.

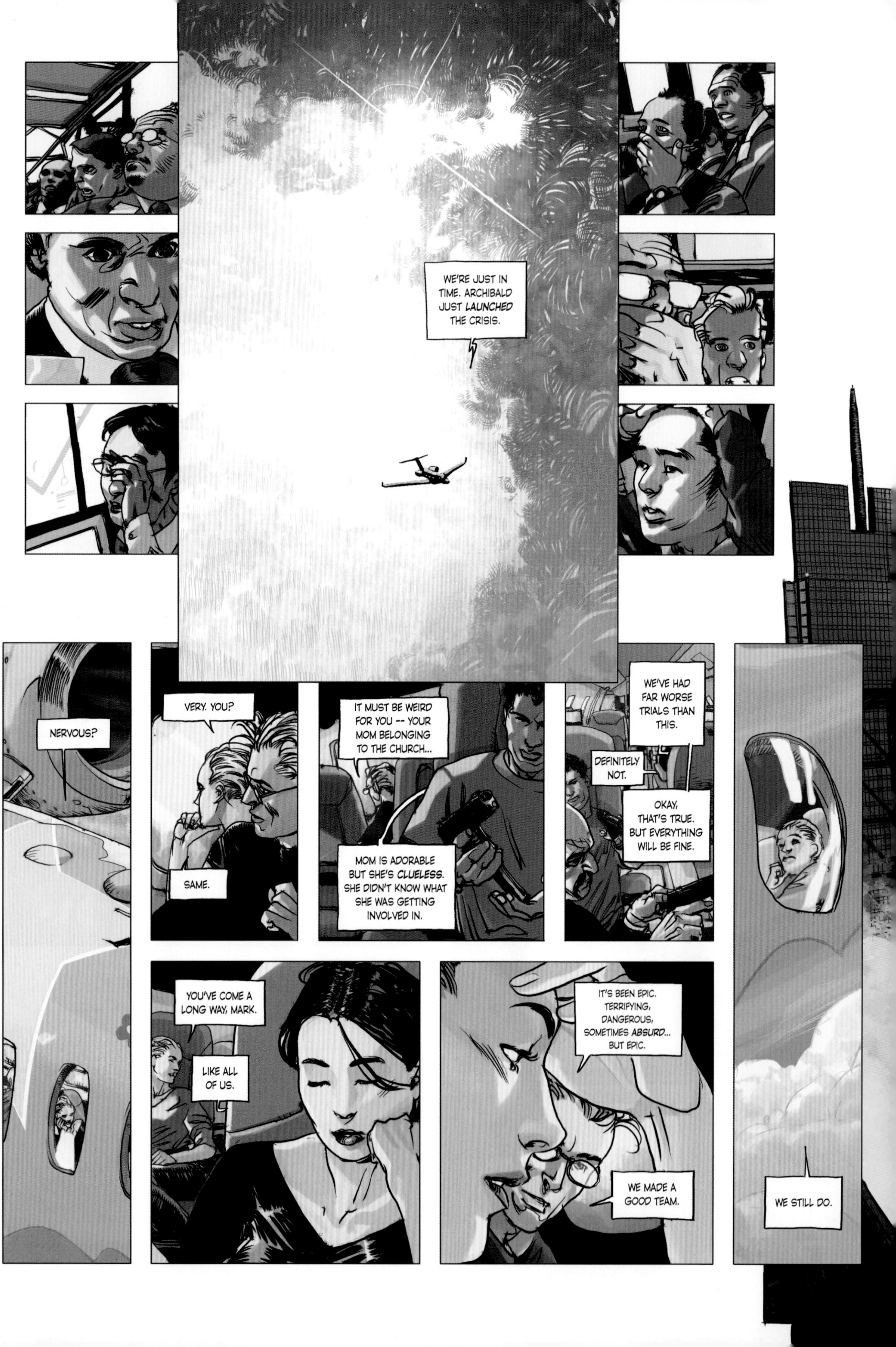
WE'RE JUST IN TIME. ARCHIBALD JUST *LAUNCHED* THE CRISIS.
NERVOUS?
VERY. YOU?
SAME.
IT MUST BE WEIRD FOR YOU -- YOUR MOM BELONGING TO THE CHURCH...
MOM IS ADORABLE BUT SHE'S *CLUELESS*. SHE DIDN'T KNOW WHAT SHE WAS GETTING INVOLVED IN.
WE'VE HAD FAR WORSE TRIALS THAN THIS.
DEFINITELY NOT.
OKAY, THAT'S TRUE. BUT EVERYTHING WILL BE FINE.
YOU'VE COME A LONG WAY, MARK.
LIKE ALL OF US.
IT'S BEEN EPIC. TERRIFYING, DANGEROUS, SOMETIMES *ABSURD*... BUT EPIC.
WE MADE A GOOD TEAM.
WE STILL DO.

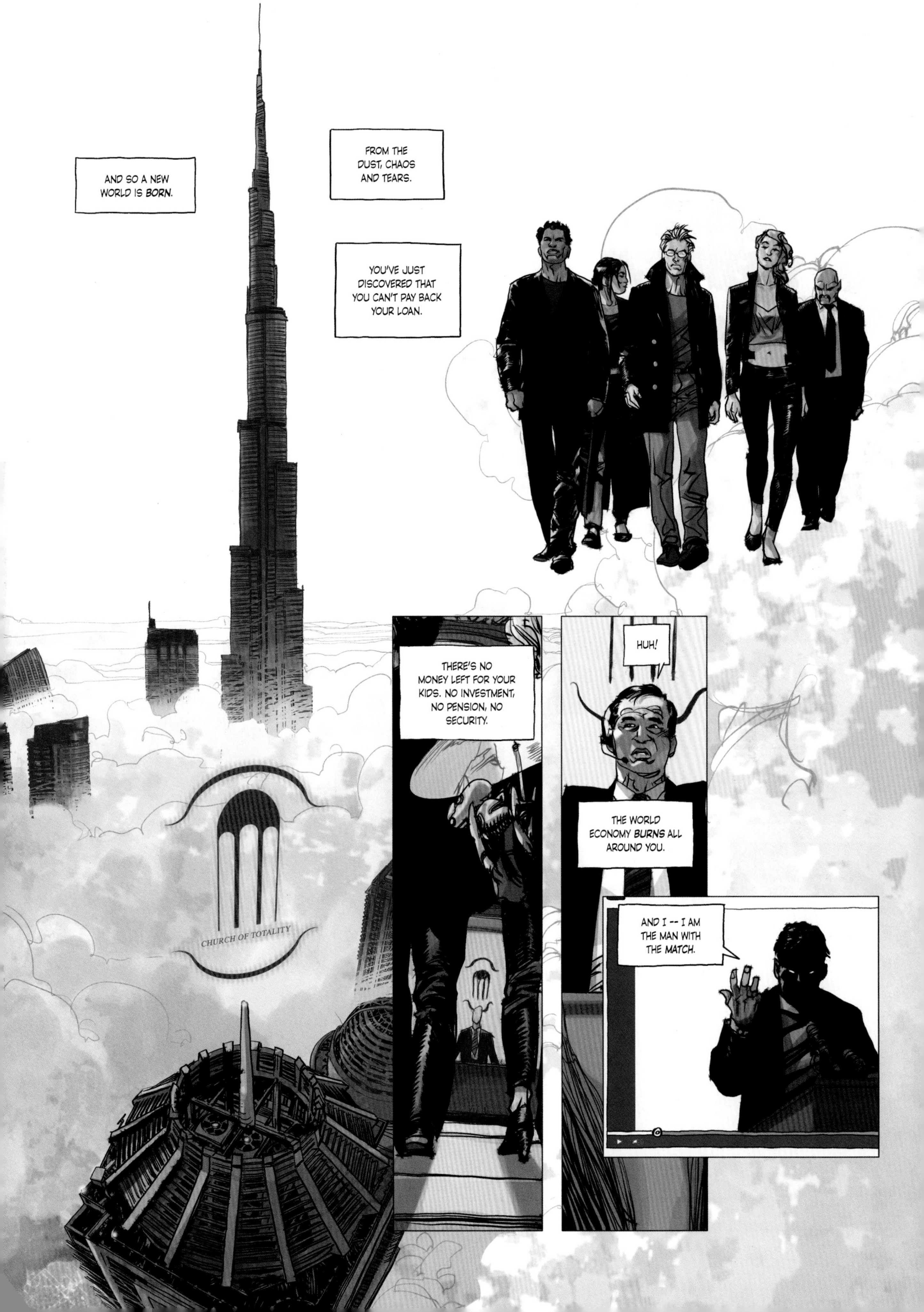
AND SO A NEW WORLD IS BORN.
FROM THE DUST, CHAOS AND TEARS.
YOU'VE JUST DISCOVERED THAT YOU CAN'T PAY BACK YOUR LOAN.
CHURCH OF TOTALITY
THERE'S NO MONEY LEFT FOR YOUR KIDS. NO INVESTMENT, NO PENSION, NO SECURITY.
HUH!
THE WORLD ECONOMY BURNS ALL AROUND YOU.
AND I -- I AM THE MAN WITH THE MATCH.

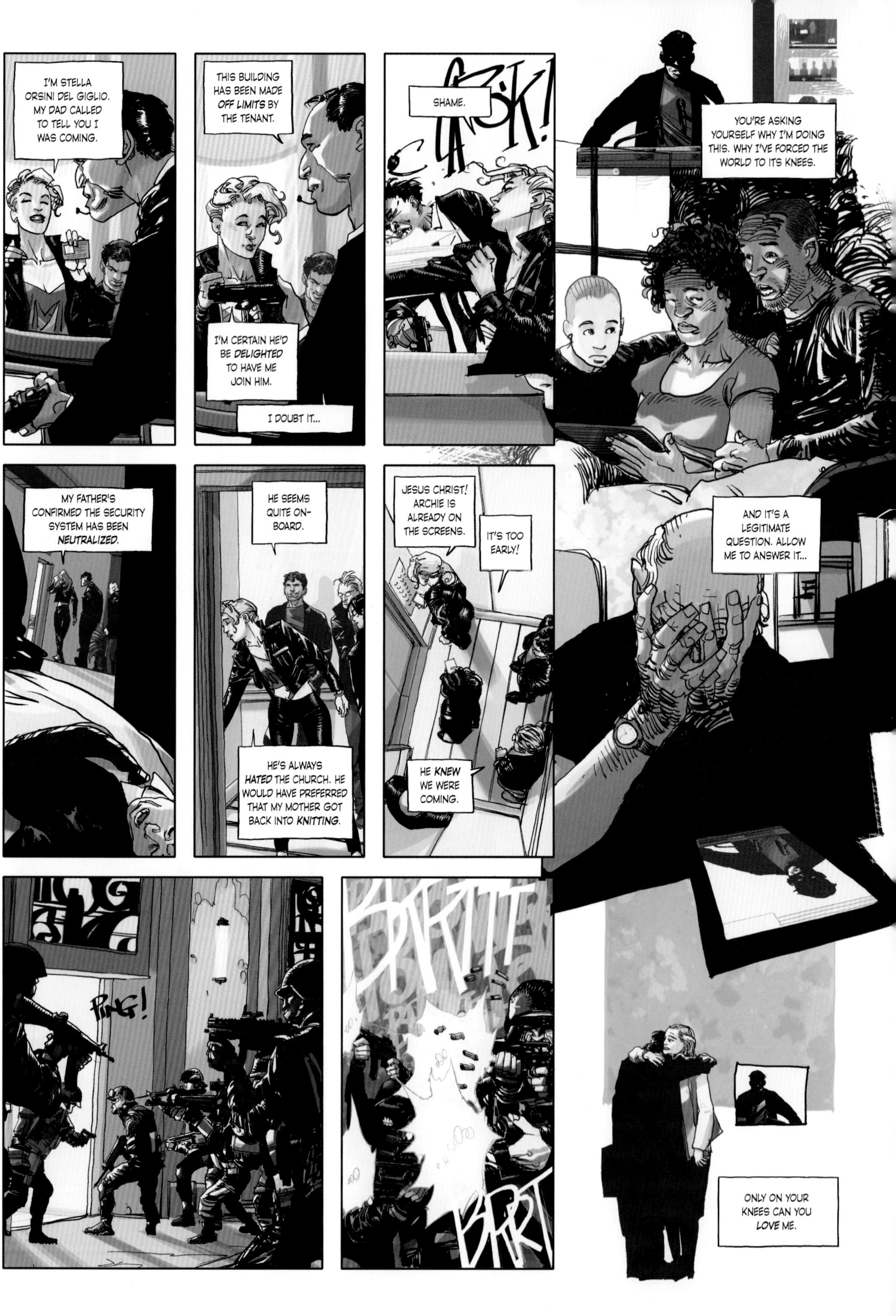
I'M STELLA ORSINI DEL GIGLIO. MY DAD CALLED TO TELL YOU I WAS COMING.
THIS BUILDING HAS BEEN MADE OFF LIMITS BY THE TENANT.
I'M CERTAIN HE'D BE DELIGHTED TO HAVE ME JOIN HIM.
I DOUBT IT...
SHAME.
YOU'RE ASKING YOURSELF WHY I'M DOING THIS. WHY I'VE FORCED THE WORLD TO ITS KNEES.
MY FATHER'S CONFIRMED THE SECURITY SYSTEM HAS BEEN NEUTRALIZED.
HE SEEMS QUITE ON-BOARD.
HE'S ALWAYS HATED THE CHURCH. HE WOULD HAVE PREFERRED THAT MY MOTHER GOT BACK INTO KNITTING.
JESUS CHRIST! ARCHIE IS ALREADY ON THE SCREENS.
IT'S TOO EARLY!
HE KNEW WE WERE COMING.
AND IT'S A LEGITIMATE QUESTION. ALLOW ME TO ANSWER IT...
PING!
BRRT
ONLY ON YOUR KNEES CAN YOU LOVE ME.

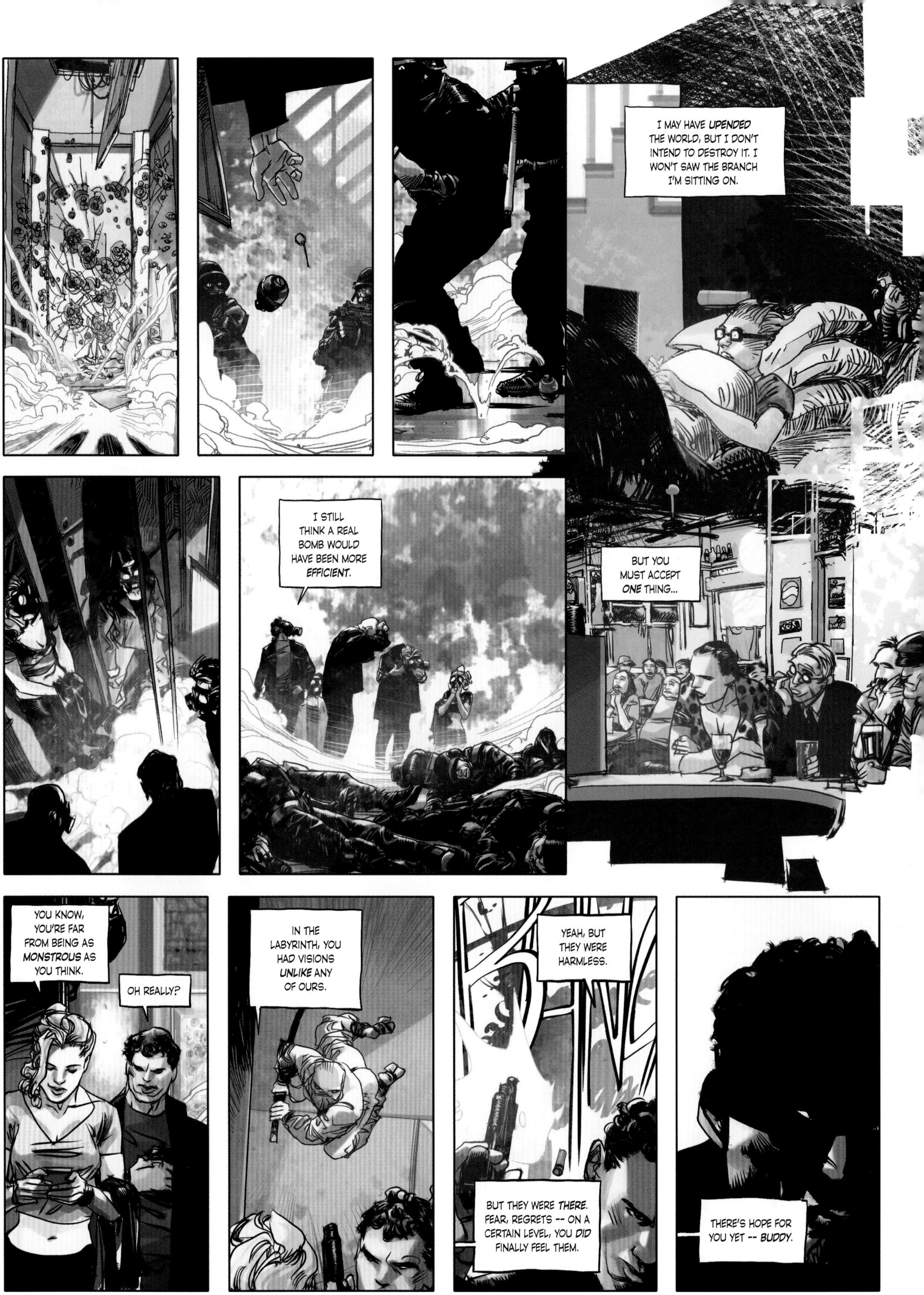

I MAY HAVE UPENDED THE WORLD, BUT I DON'T INTEND TO DESTROY IT. I WON'T SAW THE BRANCH I'M SITTING ON.
I STILL THINK A REAL BOMB WOULD HAVE BEEN MORE EFFICIENT.
BUT YOU MUST ACCEPT ONE THING...
YOU KNOW, YOU'RE FAR FROM BEING AS MONSTROUS AS YOU THINK.
OH REALLY?
IN THE LABYRINTH, YOU HAD VISIONS UNLIKE ANY OF OURS.
YEAH, BUT THEY WERE HARMLESS.
BUT THEY WERE THERE. FEAR, REGRETS -- ON A CERTAIN LEVEL, YOU DID FINALLY FEEL THEM.
THERE'S HOPE FOR YOU YET -- BUDDY.

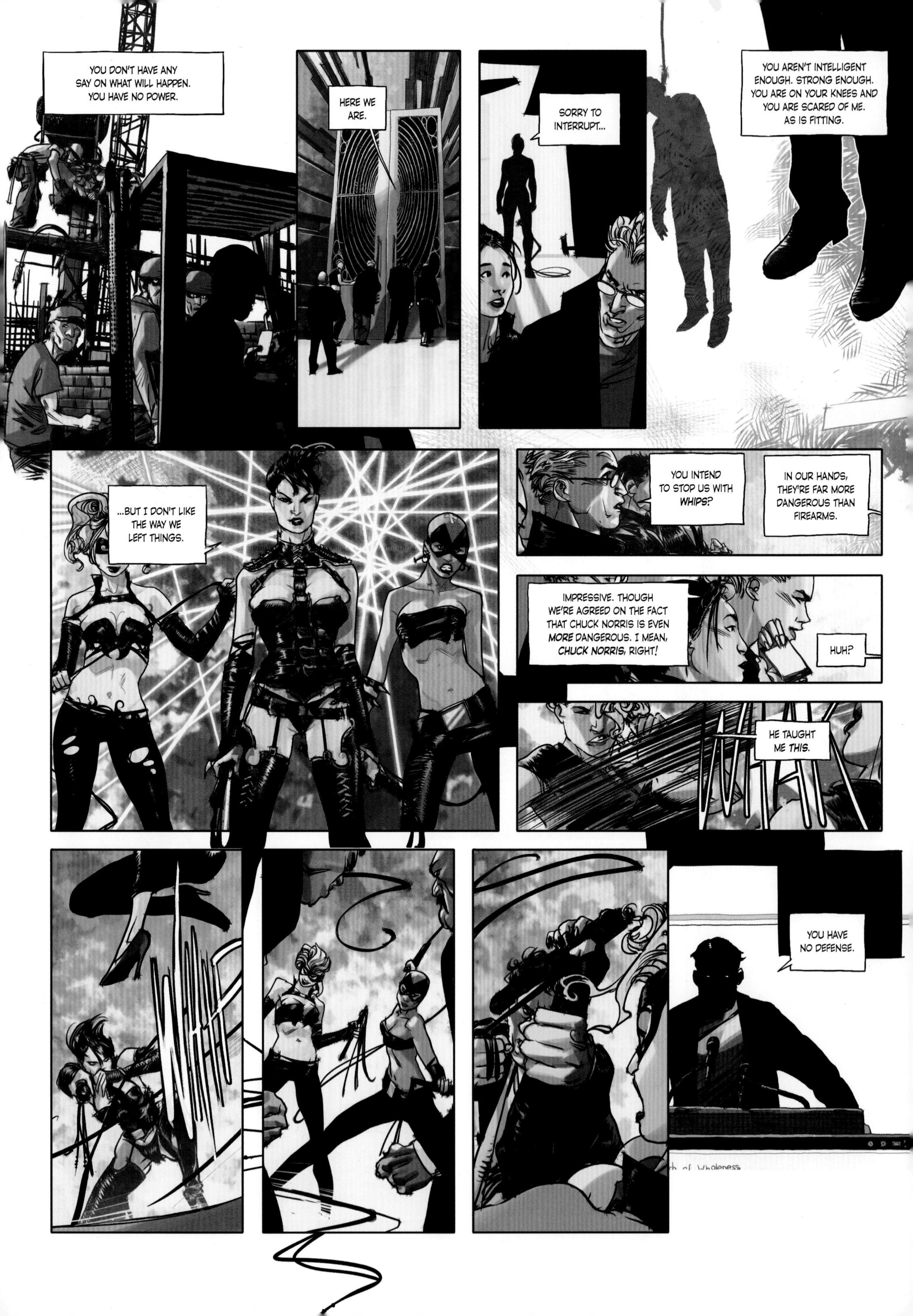
YOU DON'T HAVE ANY SAY ON WHAT WILL HAPPEN. YOU HAVE NO POWER.
HERE WE ARE.
SORRY TO INTERRUPT...
YOU AREN'T INTELLIGENT ENOUGH. STRONG ENOUGH. YOU ARE ON YOUR KNEES AND YOU ARE SCARED OF ME. AS IS FITTING.
...BUT I DON'T LIKE THE WAY WE LEFT THINGS.
YOU INTEND TO STOP US WITH *WHIPS*?
IN OUR HANDS, THEY'RE FAR MORE DANGEROUS THAN FIREARMS.
IMPRESSIVE. THOUGH WE'RE AGREED ON THE FACT THAT CHUCK NORRIS IS EVEN *MORE* DANGEROUS. I MEAN, *CHUCK NORRIS*, RIGHT!
HUH?
HE TAUGHT ME *THIS*.
YOU HAVE NO DEFENSE.

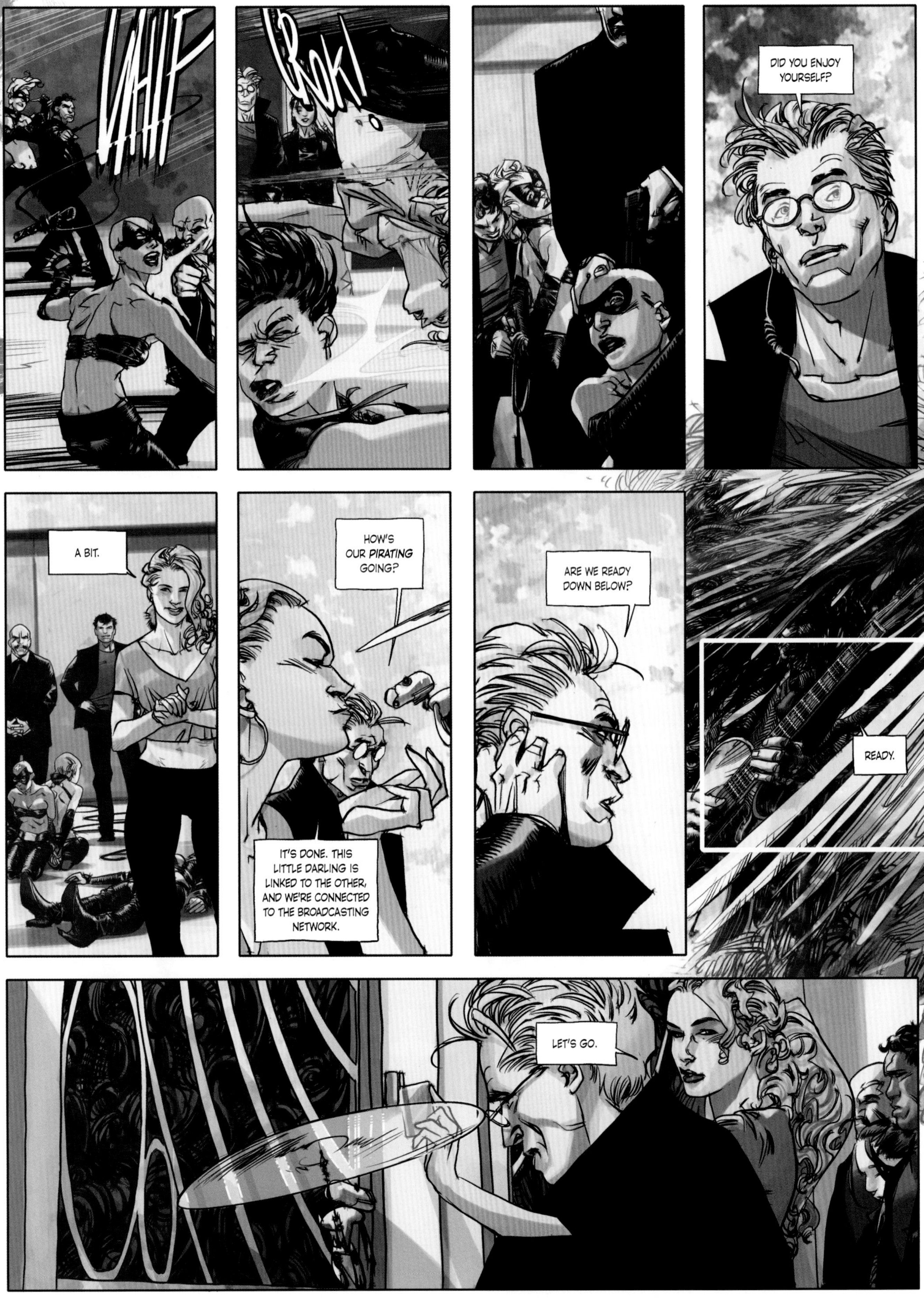

VHIF
CROK!
DID YOU ENJOY YOURSELF?
A BIT.
HOW'S OUR *PIRATING* GOING?
IT'S DONE. THIS LITTLE DARLING IS LINKED TO THE OTHER, AND WE'RE CONNECTED TO THE BROADCASTING NETWORK.
ARE WE READY DOWN BELOW?
READY.
LET'S GO.

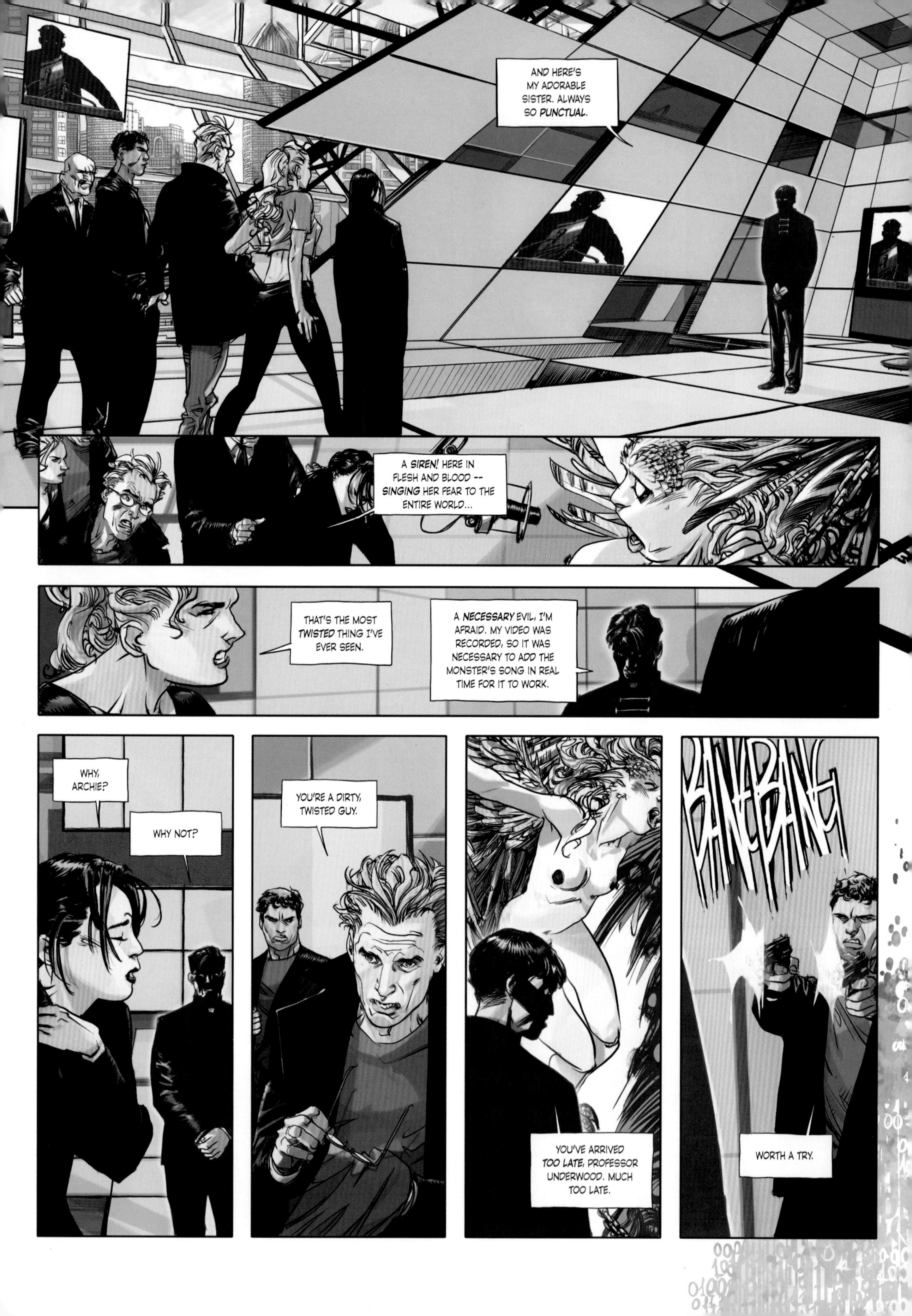
AND HERE'S MY ADORABLE SISTER. ALWAYS SO *PUNCTUAL*.
A *SIREN!* HERE IN FLESH AND BLOOD -- *SINGING* HER FEAR TO THE ENTIRE WORLD...
THAT'S THE MOST *TWISTED* THING I'VE EVER SEEN.
A *NECESSARY* EVIL, I'M AFRAID. MY VIDEO WAS RECORDED, SO IT WAS NECESSARY TO ADD THE MONSTER'S SONG IN REAL TIME FOR IT TO WORK.
WHY, ARCHIE?
WHY NOT?
YOU'RE A DIRTY, TWISTED GUY.
YOU'VE ARRIVED *TOO LATE*, PROFESSOR UNDERWOOD. MUCH TOO LATE.
BANG BANG
WORTH A TRY.

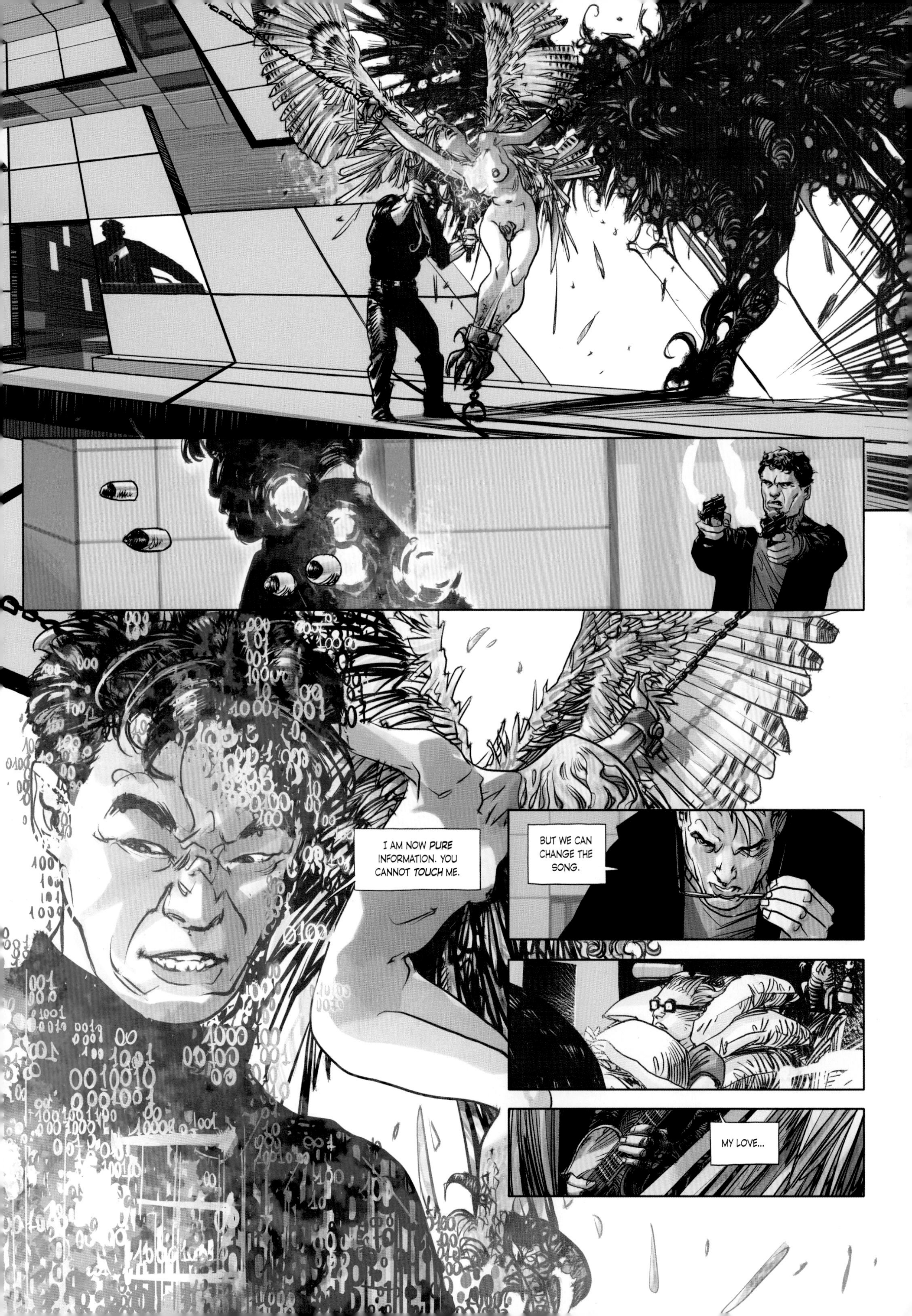
I AM NOW PURE INFORMATION. YOU CANNOT TOUCH ME.
BUT WE CAN CHANGE THE SONG.
MY LOVE...

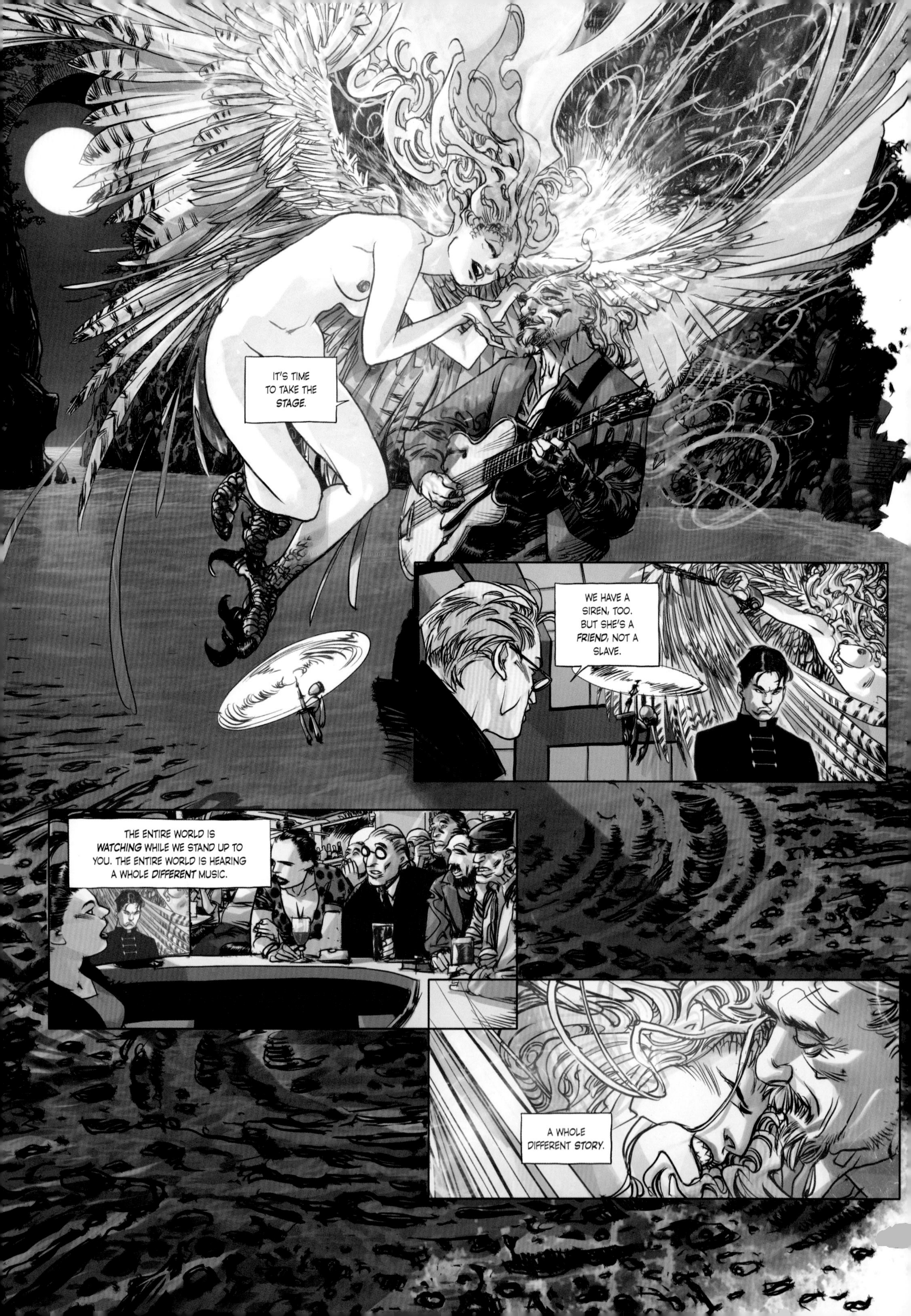
IT'S TIME TO TAKE THE STAGE.
WE HAVE A SIREN, TOO. BUT SHE'S A FRIEND, NOT A SLAVE.
THE ENTIRE WORLD IS WATCHING WHILE WE STAND UP TO YOU. THE ENTIRE WORLD IS HEARING A WHOLE DIFFERENT MUSIC.
A WHOLE DIFFERENT STORY.

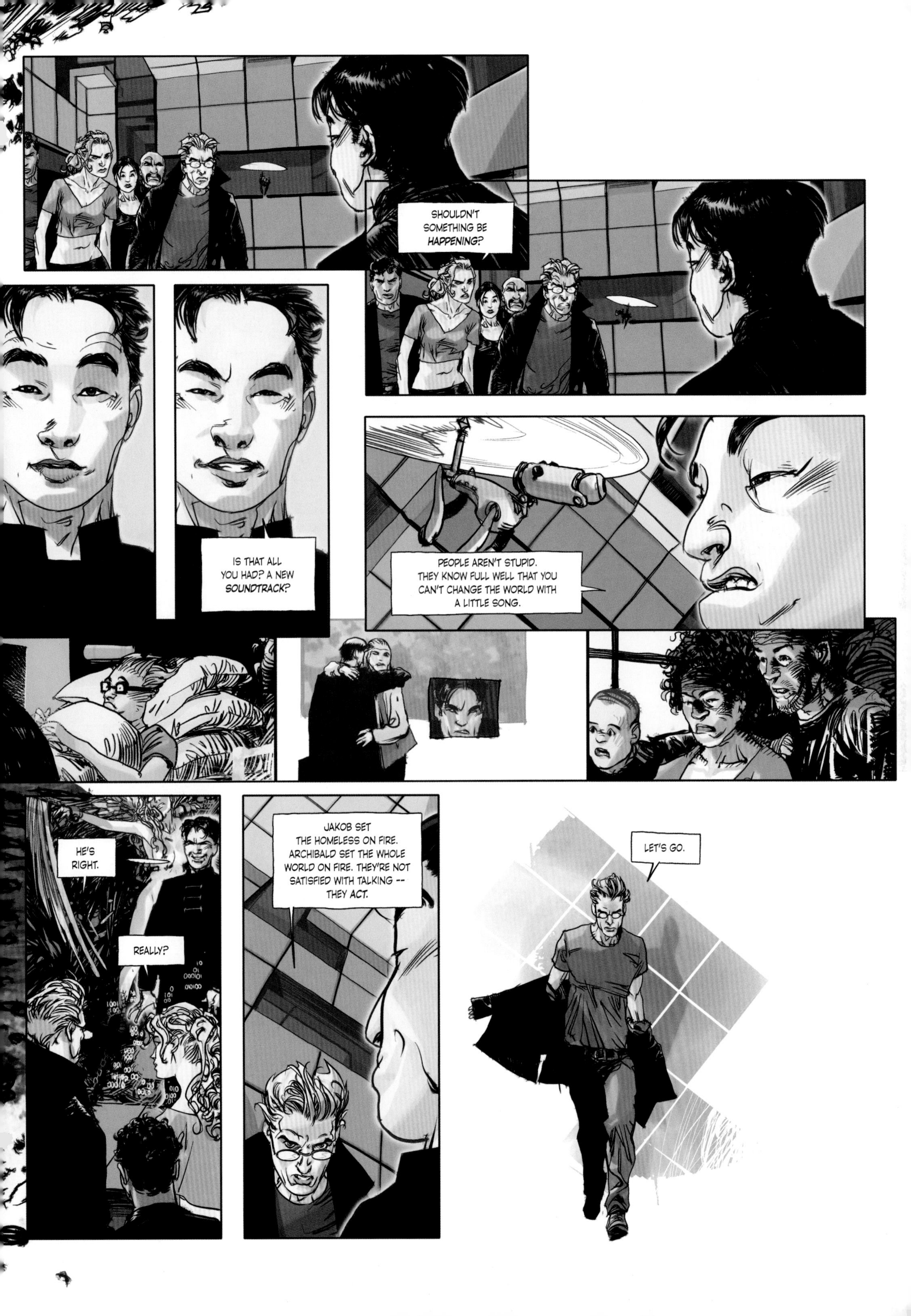
SHOULDN'T SOMETHING BE HAPPENING?
IS THAT ALL YOU HAD? A NEW SOUNDTRACK?
PEOPLE AREN'T STUPID. THEY KNOW FULL WELL THAT YOU CAN'T CHANGE THE WORLD WITH A LITTLE SONG.
HE'S RIGHT.
REALLY?
JAKOB SET THE HOMELESS ON FIRE. ARCHIBALD SET THE WHOLE WORLD ON FIRE. THEY'RE NOT SATISFIED WITH TALKING -- THEY ACT.
LET'S GO.

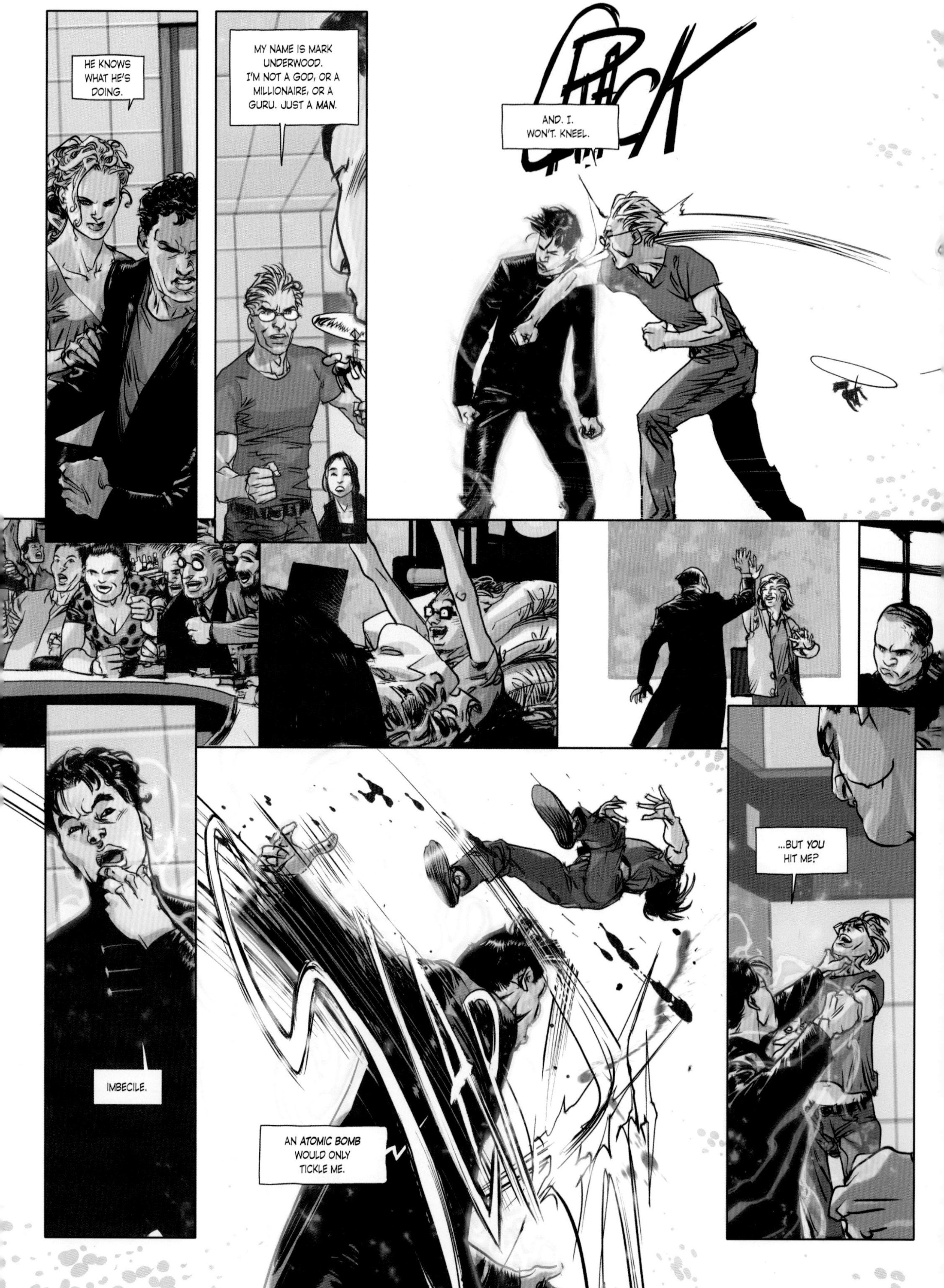
HE KNOWS WHAT HE'S DOING.
MY NAME IS MARK UNDERWOOD. I'M NOT A GOD, OR A MILLIONAIRE, OR A GURU. JUST A *MAN*.
AND. I. WON'T. KNEEL.
IMBECILE.
AN *ATOMIC BOMB* WOULD ONLY TICKLE ME.
...BUT YOU HIT ME?

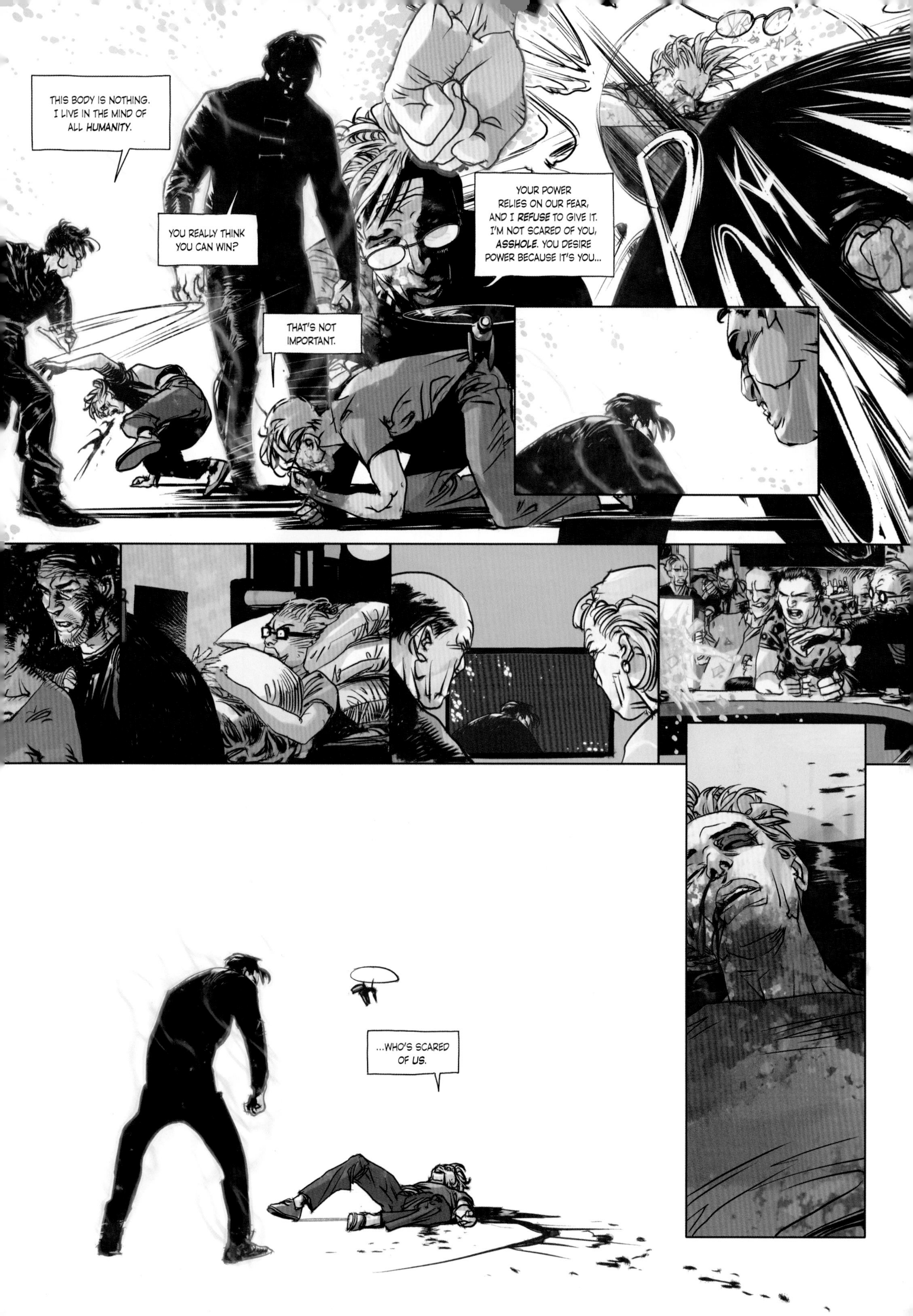
THIS BODY IS NOTHING. I LIVE IN THE MIND OF ALL HUMANITY.
YOU REALLY THINK YOU CAN WIN?
THAT'S NOT IMPORTANT.
YOUR POWER RELIES ON OUR FEAR, AND I REFUSE TO GIVE IT. I'M NOT SCARED OF YOU, ASSHOLE. YOU DESIRE POWER BECAUSE IT'S YOU...
...WHO'S SCARED OF US.

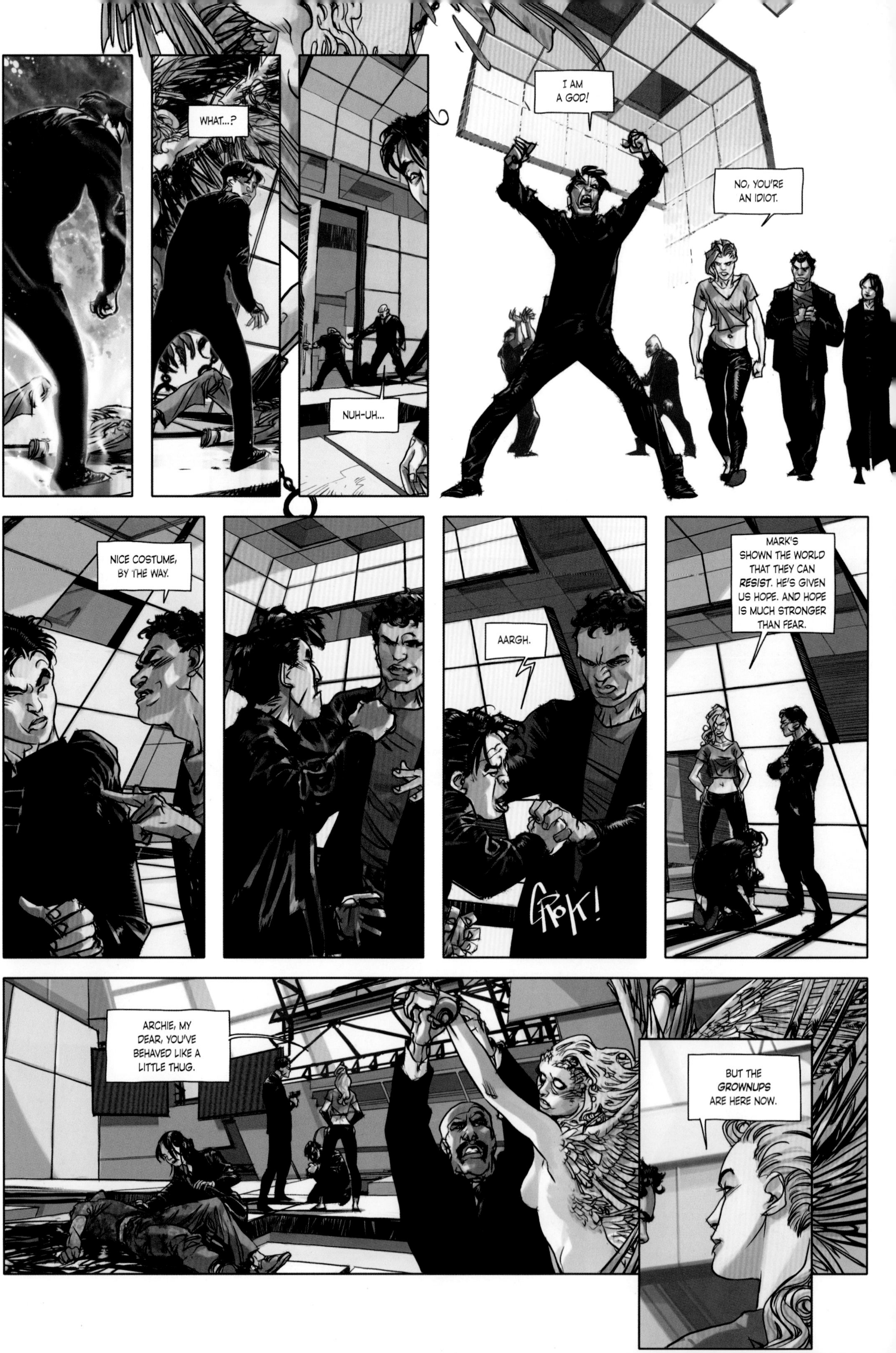
WHAT...?
NUH-UH...
I AM A GOD!
NO, YOU'RE AN IDIOT.
NICE COSTUME, BY THE WAY.
AARGH.
CROK!
MARK'S SHOWN THE WORLD THAT THEY CAN RESIST. HE'S GIVEN US HOPE. AND HOPE IS MUCH STRONGER THAN FEAR.
ARCHIE, MY DEAR, YOU'VE BEHAVED LIKE A LITTLE THUG.
BUT THE GROWNUPS ARE HERE NOW.

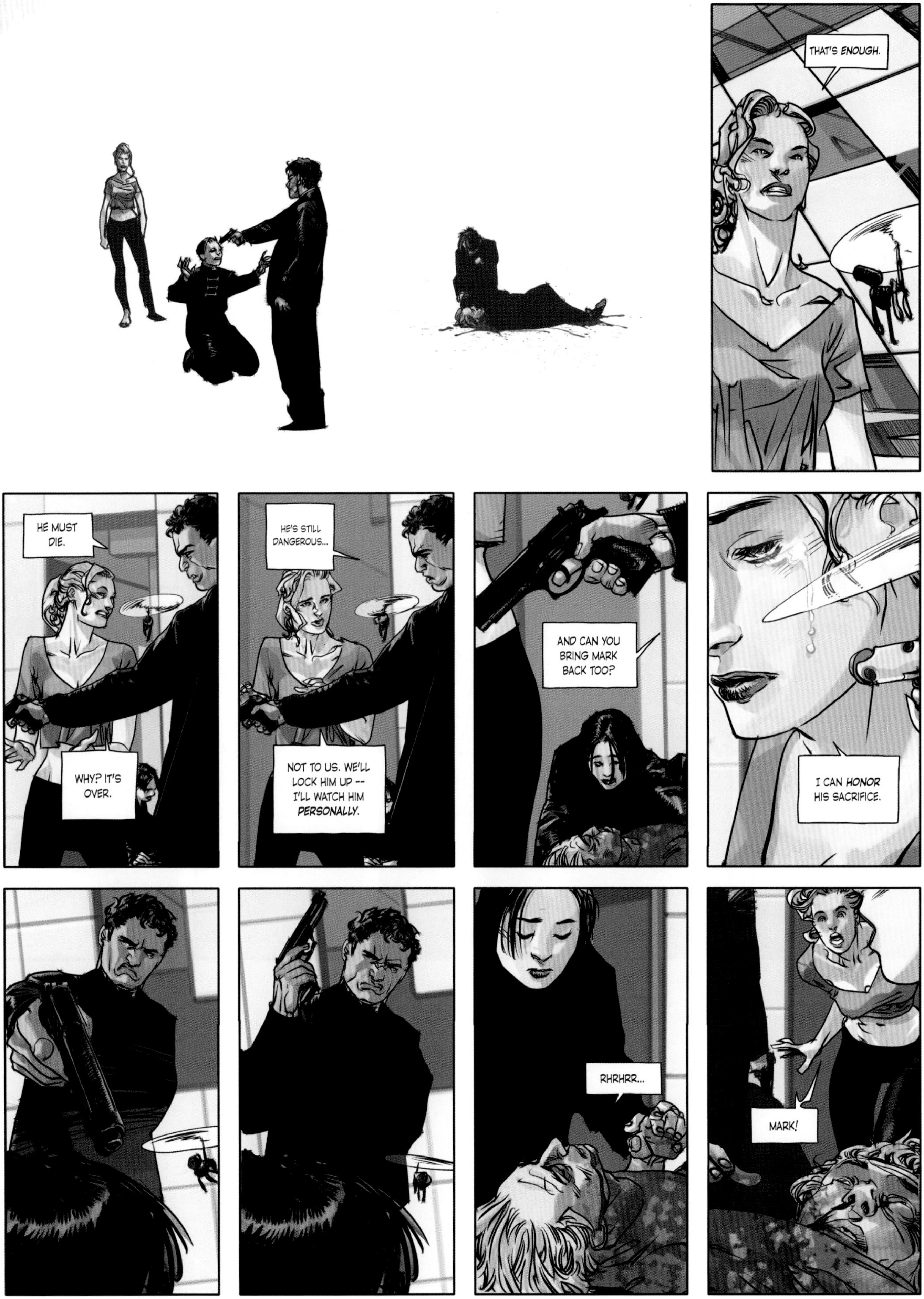
THAT'S ENOUGH.
HE MUST DIE.
WHY? IT'S OVER.
HE'S STILL DANGEROUS...
NOT TO US. WE'LL LOCK HIM UP -- I'LL WATCH HIM PERSONALLY.
AND CAN YOU BRING MARK BACK TOO?
I CAN HONOR HIS SACRIFICE.
RHRHRR...
MARK!

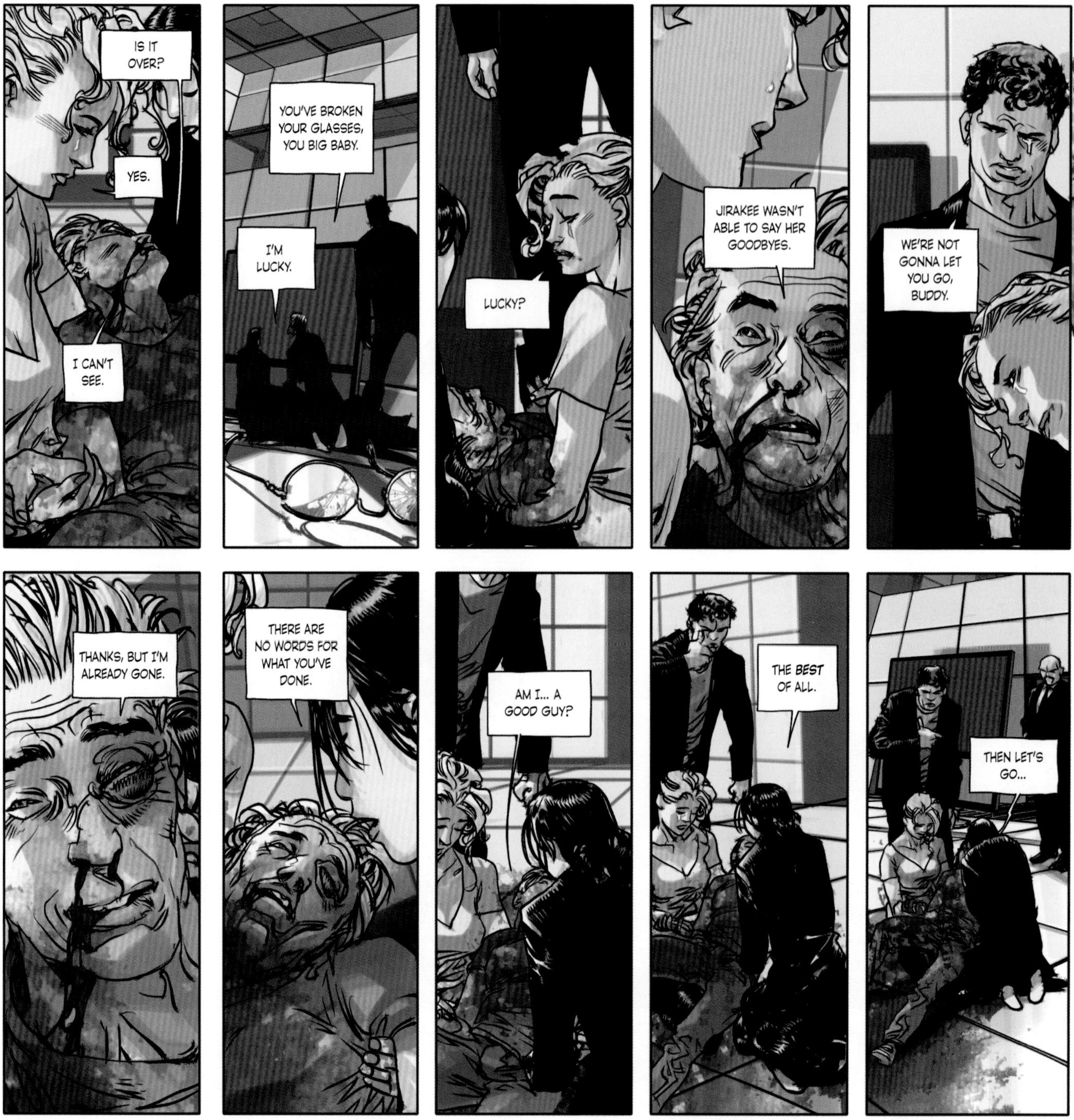
IS IT OVER?
YES.
I CAN'T SEE.
YOU'VE BROKEN YOUR GLASSES, YOU BIG BABY.
I'M LUCKY.
LUCKY?
JIRAKEE WASN'T ABLE TO SAY HER GOODBYES.
WE'RE NOT GONNA LET YOU GO, BUDDY.
THANKS, BUT I'M ALREADY GONE.
THERE ARE NO WORDS FOR WHAT YOU'VE DONE.
AM I... A GOOD GUY?
THE BEST OF ALL.
THEN LET'S GO...

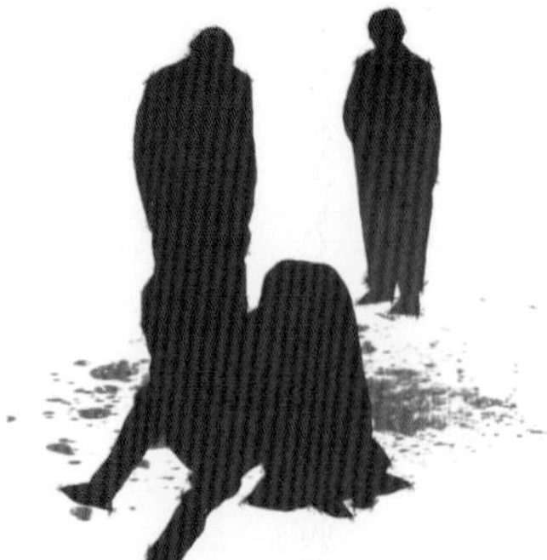

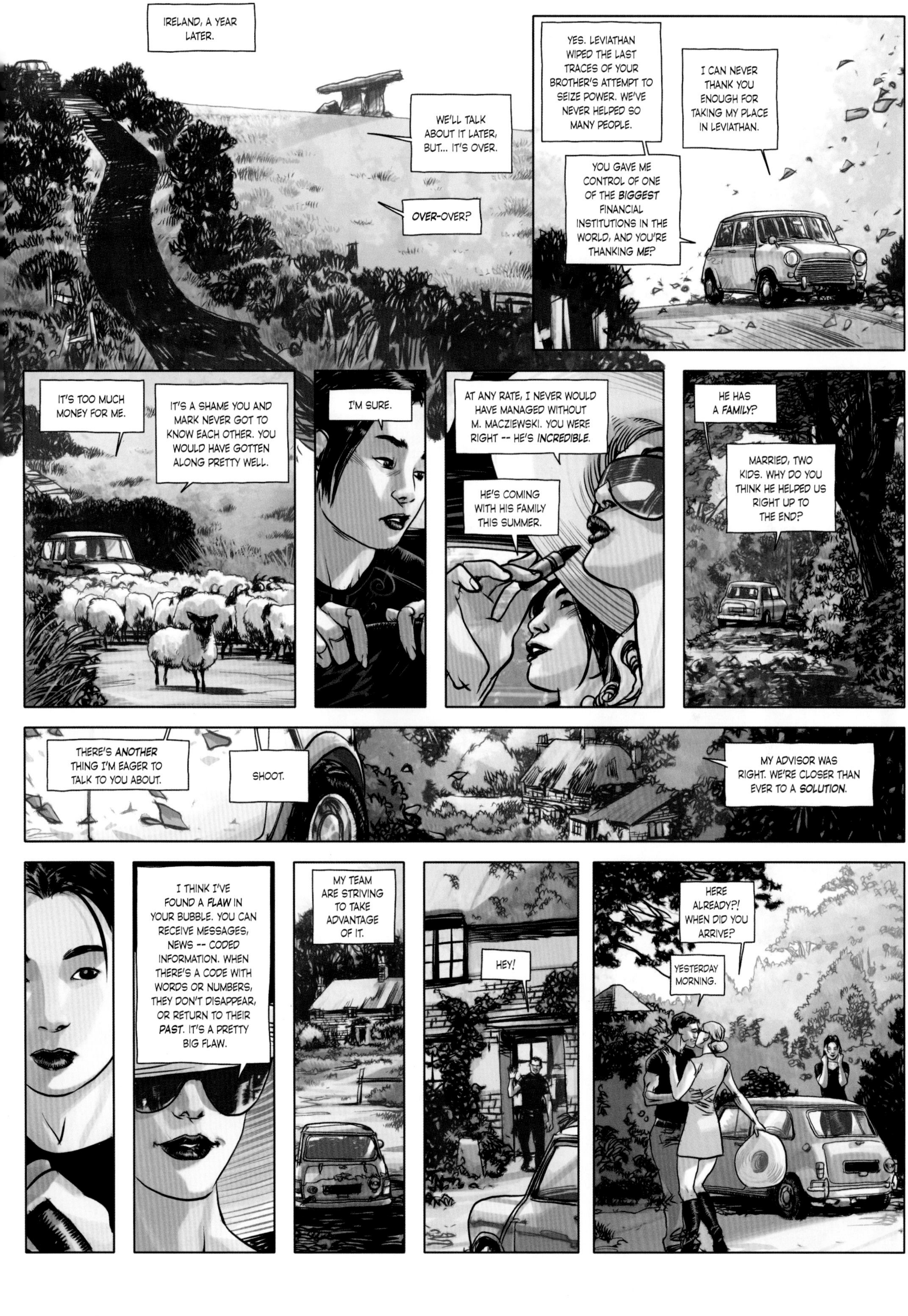
IRELAND, A YEAR LATER.
WE'LL TALK ABOUT IT LATER, BUT... IT'S OVER.
OVER-OVER?
YES. LEVIATHAN WIPED THE LAST TRACES OF YOUR BROTHER'S ATTEMPT TO SEIZE POWER. WE'VE NEVER HELPED SO MANY PEOPLE.
I CAN NEVER THANK YOU ENOUGH FOR TAKING MY PLACE IN LEVIATHAN.
YOU GAVE ME CONTROL OF ONE OF THE BIGGEST FINANCIAL INSTITUTIONS IN THE WORLD, AND YOU'RE THANKING ME?
IT'S TOO MUCH MONEY FOR ME.
IT'S A SHAME YOU AND MARK NEVER GOT TO KNOW EACH OTHER. YOU WOULD HAVE GOTTEN ALONG PRETTY WELL.
I'M SURE.
AT ANY RATE, I NEVER WOULD HAVE MANAGED WITHOUT M. MACZIEWSKI. YOU WERE RIGHT -- HE'S INCREDIBLE.
HE'S COMING WITH HIS FAMILY THIS SUMMER.
HE HAS A FAMILY?
MARRIED, TWO KIDS. WHY DO YOU THINK HE HELPED US RIGHT UP TO THE END?
THERE'S ANOTHER THING I'M EAGER TO TALK TO YOU ABOUT.
SHOOT.
MY ADVISOR WAS RIGHT. WE'RE CLOSER THAN EVER TO A SOLUTION.
I THINK I'VE FOUND A FLAW IN YOUR BUBBLE. YOU CAN RECEIVE MESSAGES, NEWS -- CODED INFORMATION. WHEN THERE'S A CODE WITH WORDS OR NUMBERS, THEY DON'T DISAPPEAR, OR RETURN TO THEIR PAST. IT'S A PRETTY BIG FLAW.
MY TEAM ARE STRIVING TO TAKE ADVANTAGE OF IT.
HEY!
HERE ALREADY?! WHEN DID YOU ARRIVE?
YESTERDAY MORNING.

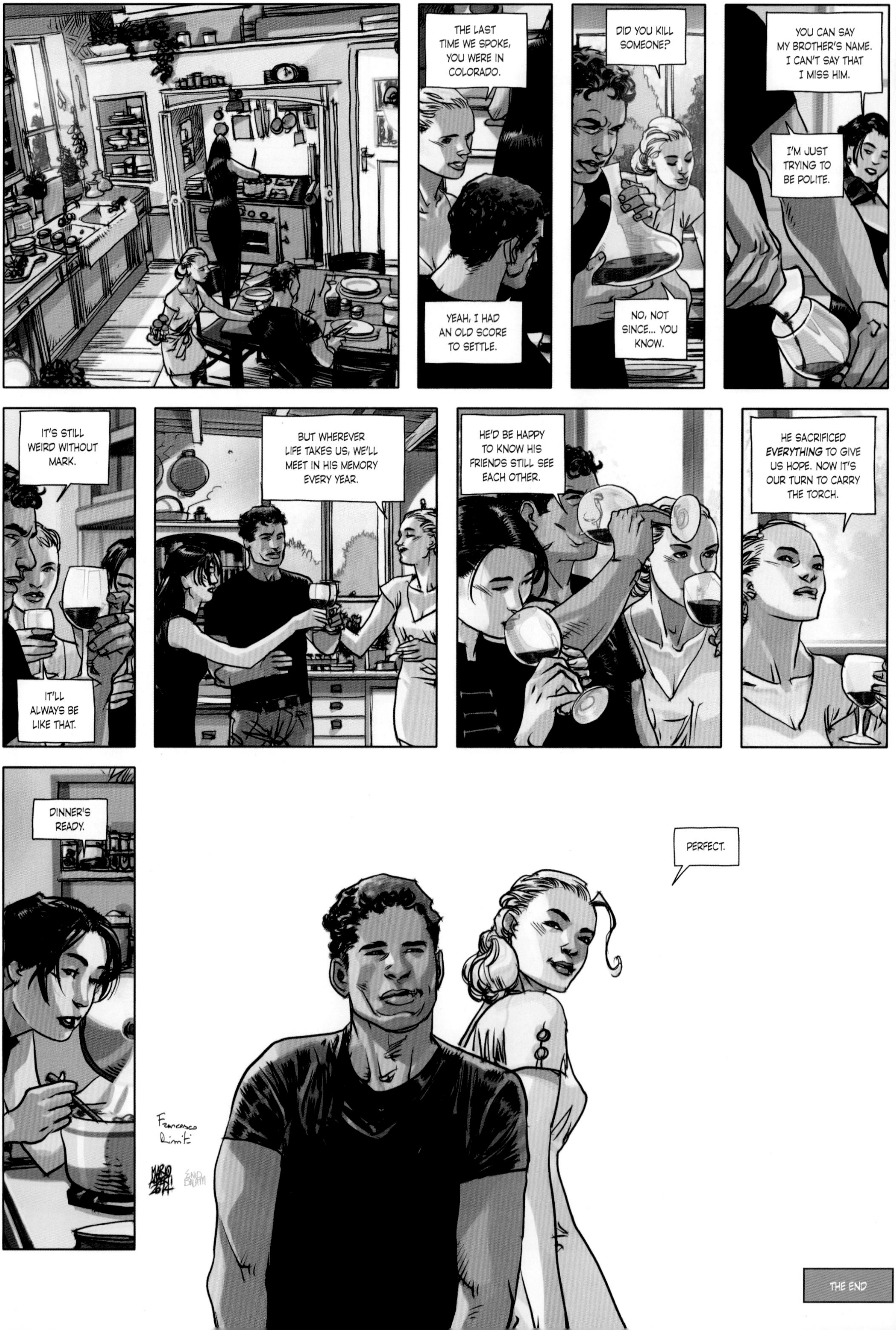
THE LAST TIME WE SPOKE, YOU WERE IN COLORADO.
YEAH, I HAD AN OLD SCORE TO SETTLE.
DID YOU KILL SOMEONE?
NO, NOT SINCE... YOU KNOW.
YOU CAN SAY MY BROTHER'S NAME. I CAN'T SAY THAT I MISS HIM.
I'M JUST TRYING TO BE POLITE.
IT'S STILL WEIRD WITHOUT MARK.
IT'LL ALWAYS BE LIKE THAT.
BUT WHEREVER LIFE TAKES US, WE'LL MEET IN HIS MEMORY EVERY YEAR.
HE'D BE HAPPY TO KNOW HIS FRIENDS STILL SEE EACH OTHER.
HE SACRIFICED *EVERYTHING* TO GIVE US HOPE. NOW IT'S OUR TURN TO CARRY THE TORCH.
DINNER'S READY.
PERFECT.
THE END

STATIX PRESS

ALSO AVAILABLE

TITAN COMICS AND STATIX PRESS

2021: LOST CHILDREN

ALISIK: FALL

ATAR GULL

ATLAS & AXIS

THE BEAUTIFUL DEATH

CENTURY'S END

CROMWELL STONE

THE CHIMERA BRIGADE - BOOK 1

THE CHIMERA BRIGADE - BOOK 2

THE CHIMERA BRIGADE - BOOK 3

THE CHRONICLES OF LEGION - BOOK 1: RISE OF THE VAMPIRES

THE CHRONICLES OF LEGION - BOOK 2: THE THREE LIVES OF DRACULA

THE DEATH OF STALIN

DEATH TO THE TSAR

DOCTOR RADAR

EMMA G. WILDFORD

EXTERMINATOR 17

FACTORY

HERCULES: WRATH OF THE HEAVENS

KHAAL

KNIGHTS OF HELIOPOLIS

KONUNGAR: WAR OF CROWNS

LITTLE VICTORIES

THE 6 VOYAGES OF LONE SLOANE

LONE SLOANE: CHAOS

LONE SLOANE: DELIRIUS

LONE SLOANE: DELIRIUS 2

LONE SLOANE: GAIL

LONE SLOANE: SALAMMBÔ

MANCHETTE'S FATALE

MASKED: RISE OF THE ROCKET

MCCAY

MONIKA - BOOK 1: MASKED BALL

MONIKA - BOOK 2: VANILLA DOLLS

MONSTER

THE NIGHT

THE NIKOPOL TRILOGY

NORMAN - VOLUME 1

NORMAN - VOLUME 2: TEACHER'S PET

NORMAN - VOLUME 3: THE VENGEANCE OF GRACE

NORMAN: THE FIRST SLASH

OSCAR MARTIN'S SOLO: THE SURVIVORS OF CHAOS VOL 1

OSCAR MARTIN'S SOLO: THE SURVIVORS OF CHAOS VOL 2

PACIFIC

THE PRAGUE COUP

THE QUEST FOR THE TIME BIRD

THE RAGE - BOOK 1: ZOMBIE GENERATION

THE RAGE - BOOK 2: KILL OR CURE

RAVINA THE WITCH?

ROYAL BLOOD

SAMURAI: THE ISLE WITH NO NAME

SAMURAI: BROTHERS IN ARMS

THE SEASON OF THE SNAKE

SHOWMAN KILLER - BOOK 1: HEARTLESS HERO

SHOWMAN KILLER - BOOK 2: THE GOLDEN CHILD

SHOWMAN KILLER - BOOK 3: THE INVISIBLE WOMAN

SKY DOLL: SPACESHIP

SKY DOLL: DECADE

SKY DOLL: SUDRA

ULTIMATE SKY DOLL

SNOWPIERCER: THE ESCAPE

SNOWPIERCER: THE EXPLORERS

SNOWPIERCER: TERMINUS

SNOWPIERCER THE PREQUEL PART 1: EXTINCTION

SNOWPIERCER THE PREQUEL PART 2: APOCALYPSE

THE THIRD TESTAMENT - BOOK 1: THE LION AWAKES

THE THIRD TESTAMENT - BOOK 2: THE ANGEL'S FACE

THE THIRD TESTAMENT - BOOK 3: THE MIGHT OF THE OX

THE THIRD TESTAMENT - BOOK 4: THE DAY OF THE RAVEN

TYLER CROSS: BLACK ROCK

TYLER CROSS: ANGOLA

UNDER: SCOURGE OF THE SEWER

UNIVERSAL WAR ONE

VOID

WKA

WORLD WAR X

THE WRATH OF FANTOMAS

YRAGAËL / URM THE MAD

COVERS GALLERY

#1 COVER A:
BUTCH GUICE & TOM ZIUKO

#2 COVER A:
MARCO TURINI

#3 COVER A:
HARVEY TOLIBAO & KEVIN TOLIBAO

#4 COVER A:
MARIA LLOVET

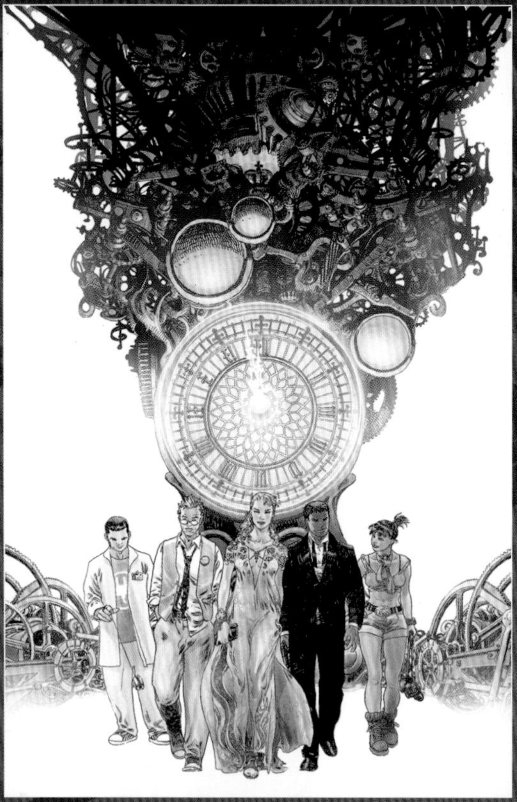

#1 COVER B:
MARIO ALBERTI

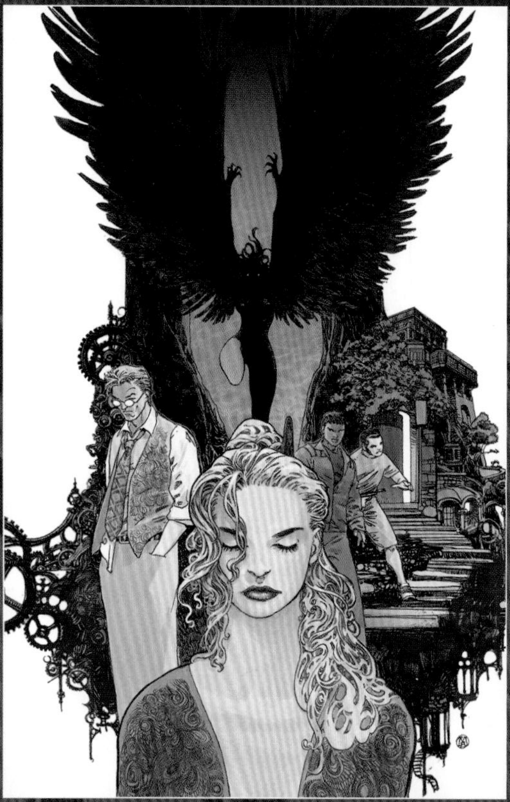

#2 COVER B:
MARIO ALBERTI

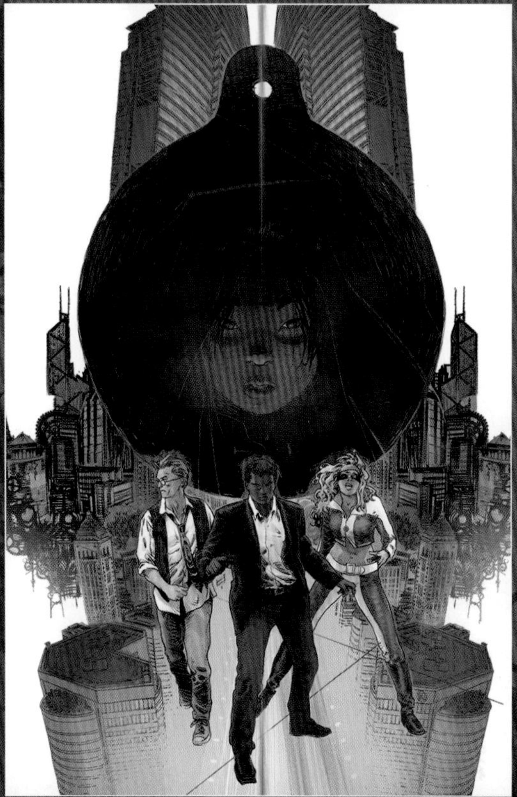

#3 COVER B:
MARIO ALBERTI

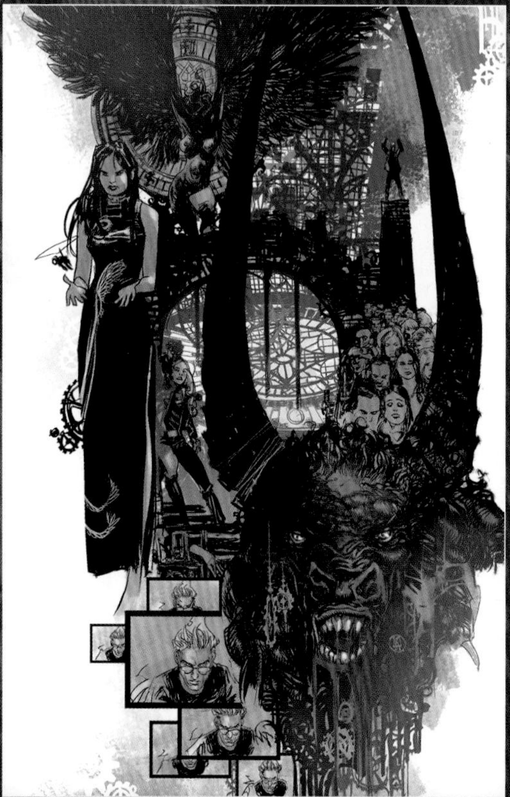

#4 COVER B:
MARIO ALBERTI

STATIX PRESS

COLLECTED EDITIONS
FROM TITAN COMICS AND STATIX PRESS

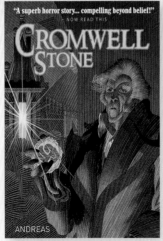

CROMWELL STONE

DOCTOR RADAR

UNDER: SCOURGE OF THE SEWER

THE BEAUTIFUL DEATH

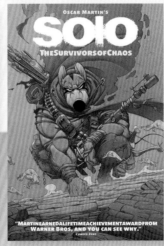

OSCAR MARTIN'S SOLO

ULTIMATE SKY DOLL

2021

HERCULES: WRATH OF THE HEAVENS

FACTORY

FOR MORE INFORMATION VISIT:
TITAN-COMICS.COM

BILAL LIBRARY

BILAL CHRISTIN
CENTURY'S END
THE BLACK ORDER BRIGADE
THE HUNTING PARTY

CENTURY'S END
9781782766810

ENKI BILAL
THE NIKOPOL TRILOGY

THE NIKOPOL TRILOGY
9781782763536

BILAL - DIONNET - BARANKO
EXTERMINATOR 17

EXTERMINATOR 17
9781785867330

ENKI BILAL
MONSTER

MONSTER
9781785868733

ENKI BILAL - PIERRE CHRISTIN
LEGENDS OF TODAY

LEGENDS OF TODAY
9781785868740

DRUILLET LIBRARY

DRUILLET
THE 6 VOYAGES OF
LONE SLOANE

6 VOYAGES OF LONE SLOANE
9781782761051

LOB DRUILLET
LONE SLOANE
DELIRIUS

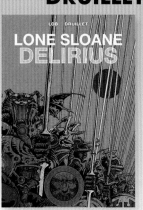

LONE SLOANE: DELIRIUS
9781782761068

DRUILLET
LONE SLOANE
GAIL

LONE SLOANE: GAIL
9781785864209

DRUILLET | DEMUTH
YRAGAËL
URM THE MAD

YRAGAEL & URM THE MAD
9781785864216

GUSTAVE FLAUBERT | PHILIPPE DRUILLET
LONE SLOANE
SALAMMBÔ

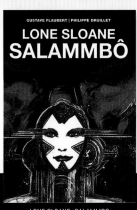

LONE SLOANE: SALAMMBO
9781785866647

DRUILLET
THE NIGHT

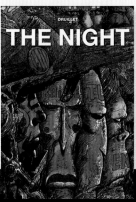

THE NIGHT
9781785866661

DRUILLET
LONE SLOANE
CHAOS

LONE SLOANE: CHAOS
9781787731646

BIOS

FRANCESCO DIMITRI

Francesco Dimitri is an Italian writer, author of fantasy and essay novels. His novels are urban fantasy, sometimes with weird, steampunk or horror themes, often dealing with magic, ufology, anthropology and pop culture.

After living in his native Manduria and then Rome, he moved to London permanently. Among Italian fantasy writers, he was one of the first to set his stories in an Italian city (in this case Rome).

MARIO ALBERTI

Mario Alberti graduated in Economics with a thesis on distribution in the comics market. He began working as a professional illustrator and writer in 1990 with *Holly Connick*, a short story published in the magazine Fumo di China.

In 1993, Alberti joined Sergio Bonelli Editore, working on the series *Nathan Never*, for which he won the Albertarelli prize in 1994. After that he worked on the series *Legs Weaver*, and in 1999 debuted as a script-writer with *L'immortale*.

In 2000, Alberti teamed up with Luca Enoch to co-write *Morgana*, published in France in 2002 by Les Humanoides Associes – the first issue was also released in the US. In 2004, he collaborated with writer Kurt Busiek to create the series *Redhand*.

Alberti has also illustrated some covers for Federico Memola's series *Jonathan Steele*, and most recently collaborated on covers for *Aquaman*, *Wonder Woman*, *Doctor Fate* and *Shadowpact*.

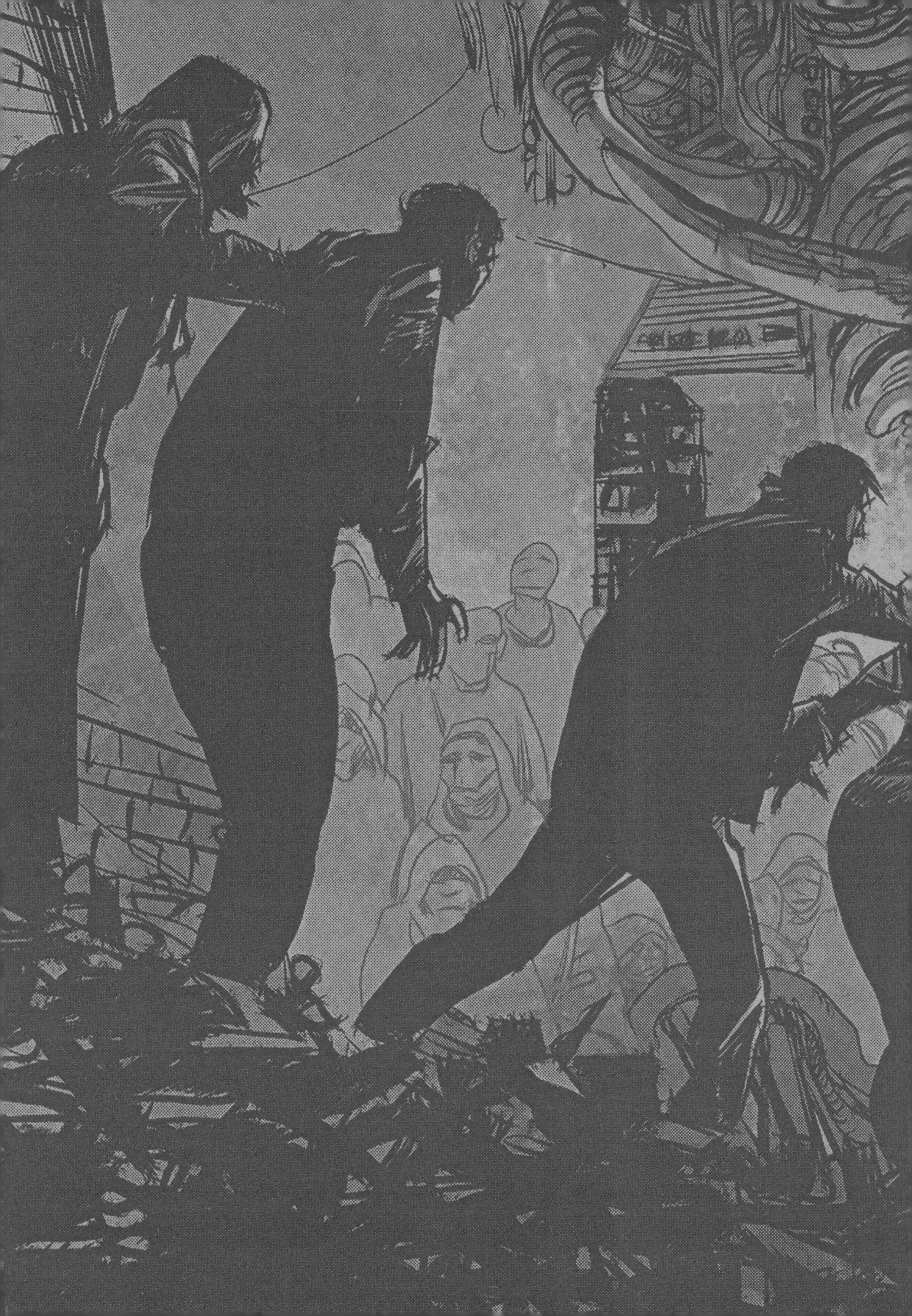